Gulzar Sa'ab

Hazaar Rahen Mud Ke Dekheen...

Gulzar Sa'ab

Hazaar Rahen Mud Ke Dekheen...

Yatindra Mishra

Translated from the Hindi Original by

Sathya Saran

Hardcover first Edition : 2025

vaniprakashan.com

VANI PRAKASHAN GROUP

Head Office

4695, 21-A, Daryaganj, New Delhi-110 002, India
Phone : +91 11 23273167, 23275710

Registered Bookstores and Offices
Ashok Rajpath, Patna-800 004, Bihar
Coffee House Campus, Mahatma Gandhi Marg, Allahabad-211 001, Uttar Pradesh
Mahatma Gandhi International Hindi University, Wardha-442 001, Maharashtra

sales@vaniprakashan.in
vaniprakashan@gmail.com

Gulzar Saab : Hazaar Rahen Mud Ke Dekheen...
by Yatindra Mishra
English translation and translator's note by Sathya Saran

ISBN : 978-93-7112-468-3
Cinema/Biography/Non-Fiction

Price : ₹ 2000

Printed at City Press, Delhi-110 095

Logo of Vani Prakashan from the brush of Maqbool Fida Hussain

For respected Amma and Papa,

Shrimati Jyotsna Mishra and Shri Bimlendra Mohan Pratap Mishra

Whenever they are pleased by my writing

That is the moment my creativity reaches its pinnacle

Contents

I cannot trust what the eyes say
No receipt or reckoning
Nor certainty even
The eyes will deceive

نینوں کی بات پہ مجھ کو بھروسہ نہیں ہے نا
لکھت ہے نہ پرچہ رسید، نہ گماں ہے
نیناں ٹھگ لیں گے —

INTRODUCTION

The Light of a Candle

It was like a beautiful dream, being in the company of the poet, storyteller, dialogue-writer and lyricist whom the world knows as Gulzar. This book, which began more than two decades ago in 2003, is a reflection of the admiration I have for his persona and his work.

How clearly I remember, even today, my first meeting with Gulzar-sahab! Along with some brilliant writers who wrote in different Indian languages, I was visiting New York for a celebration organised by the Sahitya Akademi, New Delhi, and the Bharatiya Vidya Bhavan. There, for the first time, I had the opportunity of meeting an individual wrapped in the transparent simplicity of white, whose songs had hypnotised me even in my youth. And the story of a master poet's entry into my life began.

I remember it well. We had all been accommodated at the Lexington Hotel on Seventh Avenue. One morning, there was a knock on my door. Vishwanath Sachdev, the writer and journalist who was sharing my room, opened the door. Gulzar-sahab was standing outside. Addressing both of us he said, 'I've been standing for such a long time outside your room, like an empty milk bottle. Come, let's go for a morning walk.' His simple, witty statement diluted some of my awestruck hesitation. That very first meeting laid the foundation for a relationship that would stretch well into the future.

Over the past twenty years, I have met Gulzar-sahab so often, in so many places, and remembering the many occasions gives me joy. In the process, I have travelled innumerable times with him, shared the dais with him at literary festivals, and had long discussions on a myriad subjects. Listening to him at his office in Boskiyana, or across the dining table, I have collected numerous memories I can dip into. They inspire me to pursue my own work with courage and commitment.

It was during such meetings that the long conversations with Gulzar-sahab began and I started to record them on tape. Over twenty years of meeting intermittently, he would share the insights that I preserved in my mind, notebook and tape-recorder.

When we began the conversations, I was unaware of the fact that I was associating with someone who, in the past fifty-five years, has done such superlative work in the realms of art and literature. His poetic mind is not unlike the satchel of an astrologer in which the lessons of life and understanding, art and creativity, ideologies and adjustment have been collected. For me, the challenge lay in knowing how to understand and interpret his seemingly simple conversations. It was like entering the life of a person and trying to gather up his creativity. However, much of it scattered spontaneously and try as I might, I could not contain it within my grasp.

Writing about a life dedicated to art that has drawn for itself the parameters of accountability, responsibility and discipline is not at all easy. If you try to comprehend what you perceive as Gulzar, he assumes a different role in the blink of an eye and disappears from view. Try to explore his poetic side and he will present himself as a storyteller! If you attempt to understand the delicacy of his lyrics, the committed filmmaker with relevant films to his credit shows up. And apart from all this, at times a dialogue-writer wraps himself in the many layers that make up his life's apparel, or then a poet appears, armed with imagery that can bring back childhood, who makes of his poem a ball and beguiles us to play with it.

The crux of the matter is that whatever I had hoped to collect by leafing through the pages of Gulzar-sahab's life, by parsing his poems and his film lyrics and catching the reflection of society in the films he has directed, is documented here for readers.

I make no claim that this is the ultimate portrait of Gulzar, nor has the thought occurred to me that whatever has been presented in this book is enough to portray his persona in its totality. I would like to state with humility that everyone has his own version of Gulzar, which is as complete for them as the affection they receive from him.

This book is the point of view of a young writer who is looking at an individual even as he jostles with imagination and questions in his mind. An individual who has thrown up many questions. Who, on his own way to helping others, has written songs, poems, stories and plays at different times and has opened up paths through his films.

Even after the writing of this book is done, new ways of understanding and presenting Gulzar still remain unexplored. It is the quality of a superlative writer and human being that, however hard one tries to record him for posterity, the writer finds himself at a loss for words and the picture remains incomplete.

This book has been made possible with the cooperation and permission of Gulzar-sahab and I owe him a debt of gratitude. Along with interpretations of his work are recorded the milestones in his journey from childhood to filmmaker to his evolution as an enlightened and experienced poet.

One section of this book is a conversation with Gulzar-sahab. In this, I have kept his responses in his own words so that the reader can enjoy them with ease.

Over this journey, I have been lucky enough to meet many kindred spirits who together create the extensive community of Gulzar fans. Towards them all I express love and respect. The blessings of my parents, respected Jyotsna Mishra and Bimalendra Mohan Pratap Mishra, have supported my creative efforts; to them I offer my salutations. I am also grateful to my entire family, especially my aunt, Aparna Mishra, for the love, guidance and support which has brightened my life as a writer.

This book now belongs to all of Gulzar's fans. The entire credit goes to Gulzar-sahab, who invested his trust in me and made a gift of many years of his life to me.

-Yatindra Mishra

24 October, 2023

Acknowledgements

I express heartfelt gratitude to those friends and learned people whose advice helped polish this book. I wish to thank those lovers of art and literature, accomplished practitioners all, without whose help this book would not have been possible.

Among those friends who have been offering suggestions from the beginning, reading the manuscript to strengthen it by checking facts and incidents are dear friend Pavan Jha, who has compiled all of Gulzar-sahab's work into a veritable treasure-house; writer and theatre person Salim Arif-bhai; Yunus Khan-bhai, who possesses an encyclopedic knowledge of film music; story-writer and reporter Narendra Saini; and story-writer Anulata Raj Nair. Thanks are due to renowned filmmakers Prakash Jha and Vishal Bhardwaj, and the actor Yashpal Sharma—my discussions about Gulzar-sahab with them allowed me to present this book in the form that it finally took. The two eminent personalities whose conversations with me over the years of writing yielded many rare memories are unfortunately no longer amongst us. With all due respect, I offer my heartfelt tribute to the great playback singers Lata Mangeshkar-ji and Bhupinder.

Sincere thanks are due to all of my friends whose help and suggestions always inspire me to create something new, and better. All of them, in some way or the other, read portions of the book to offer necessary feedback and amendments. Some friends made available rare material, copies of old film periodicals and magazines, as well as interviews given by Gulzar over the course of his journey in the film world. I am indebted to all of them. Among these friends are: Suresh Wadkar, Prasoon Joshi, Irshad Kamil, Shantanu Moitra, Gopi Gajwani, Anant Vijay, Sathya Saran, Lubna Salim, Piyush Daiya, Namita Gokhale, Sanjeev Paliwal, Iqbal Rizvi, Madhu B. Joshi, Sukrita Paul Kumar, Mohit Kataria, Manav Prakash and Indrajeet Singh. Malini Awasthi, Shekhar Sen, Sunanda Sharma and Ajit Sarathi are among the music scholars and artistes who have provided me special help in understanding the classical aspects of the music in Gulzar's songs as well as its western contexts.

I am grateful to the organizations that made available the documents which threw light on the history and progression of Hindi cinema, particularly in the context of Gulzar-sahab. Among these are National Film Archive of India (Pune), Vividh Bharati (Mumbai), Nehru Memorial Museum and Library (Teen Murti Bhawan, New Delhi), Akashvani Archives (New Delhi), Arushi India (Bhopal) and Sa Re Ga Ma Archive-HMV (Kolkata).

Special thanks are due to friend Shuaib Shahid for making the Urdu portions of the book available for Gulzar-sahab to read. I thank Gulzar-sahab's secretary Farhana from the bottom of my heart who, by translating this book from Hindi to Urdu and from Urdu to Hindi, has been a harmonious bridge between Gulzar-sahab and I. Over the last two decades, her company has always been a source of courage.

My sisters have always wholeheartedly supported my work. The most heartfelt of thanks will not be enough to convey my gratitude to my younger sister Shubhangi. He collaborative contribution to the writing, reading and editing of Gulzar Sa'ab over the years is unparalleled. Special thanks are due to my sister Manjari too, whose insights made useful ameliorations in the book time and again. I thank Ashwani Shukla, Ajay Pathak and friends Rohit Sharma and Ashutosh Shukla for their contributions to strengthening the text. I have taken most of the photographs and handwritten documents used to embellish this book from Vivek Ranade, Nirav Ghate, and the private collection of respected Gulzar-sahab. Most of the song booklets and film-posters are from my own collection and from friend Sumant Batra and his not-for-profit Cinemaazi.

My gratitude to friend Arun Maheshwari and his daughter Aditi Maheshwari-Goyal, who have always been steadfastly confident in my writing.

My thanks and my respects to all.

—Yatindra Mishra

न जाने कौन-सी मिट्टी थी
नज़र में धूल, जिगर में लिए ग़ुबार चले...

Grateful thanks are also due to the scriptures, saints and nirgun poets, the wise people, filmmakers, musicians and scholars of music, thinkers and achievers in many different fields whom I have taken recourse to during the writing of this creative work that delineates Gulzar-sahab's life and his journey in cinema:

Guru Granth Sahib, Kabir, Meerabai, Bulleh Shah, Amir Khusro, Rani Roopmati, Mir Taqi Mir, Ibn-e-Insha, Shakespeare, John Keats, Anton Chekhov, Alexander Pushkin, Robert Frost, Narayan Prasad 'Betaab', Khalil Gibran, Pablo Neruda, Faiz Ahmed Faiz, Octavio Paz, Kazi Nazrul Islam, John Berger, Franz Kafka, Rabindranath Tagore, Rainer Maria Rilke, Ismat Chughtai, Lata Mangeshkar, Kuldip Nayyar, Shailendra, Sahir Ludhianvi, Iqbal, Ali Sardar Jafri, Shankar Shesh, Samaresh Basu, Amrita Pritam, Pandit Ravishankar, Meena Kumari, Raj Kumar Moitra, Mary Oliver, Shamsher Bahadur Singh, Nagarjun, Martin Freeman, Mark Gatiss, Akira Kurosawa, Ingmar Bergman, Erich Segal, Sukhdev, Begum Akhtar, Joginder Paul, Kunwar Narain, Kedarnath Singh, Mahashweta Devi, Sonal Mansingh, Bob Dylan, Paul Willemen, Ashish Rajadhyaksha, Kamleshwar, Ameen Sayani, Nasreen Munni Kabir, Pandit Satyasheel Deshpande, Gopi Gajwani, Rita Ganguly, Naseeruddin Shah, Sathya Saran, Salim Arif, Pavan Jha, Saba Mahmood Bashir, Sunayana Kachroo, Pavan K. Varma, Maithili Rao, Yashwant Vyas, Aniruddha Bhattacharjee, Balaji Vitthal, Kausar Munir, Saibal Chatterjee, Vishal Bhardwaj and Meghna Gulzar.

Translator's Note

My Hindi teacher in school would be delighted. My mother too. When Gulzar-sahab and Yatindra Mishra placed Yatindra's book in my hands and bade me translate it, it led me to reading my first complete book in Hindi. Quite a start, considering the size of the tome, and the immensity of its subject.

Other books had been placed before me, through my school years, but most were abandoned after the first few pages. Reading in English was so much quicker, and then there was so much to read ready at hand.

As I slowly wended my way through the book that held fourteen years of research between its covers, I realised the enormity of the task before me. Through a shifting text that had passages from Gulzar's poems and lyrics as well as quotes from other poets and writers blended with the author's own literary prose, Yatindra had created a kaleidoscope that showed glimpses of Gulzar's creative genius in all its variety. Through it all, he was trying to create a composite picture of the man and his work.

That is what this book offered me; a deeper, clearer understanding of a multi-faceted mind that works on a fine balance between literature and popularity, without any compromise on art, in whichever genre he chooses to express himself.

It is the same balance I hope to have achieved in this translation. In keeping the cadences of the original Hindi writing, and the mood and rhythm of the poetry excerpts intact even as I shape the prose to reach out to readers of this book with the same impact that the author achieved.

So, welcome to Gulzar's splendorous world as seen through the prism of Yatindra Mishra's lens; as he analyses, evaluates, explains and interviews his subject.

I owe a debt of gratitude to both Gulzar-sahab and Yatindra for their faith in me to take this journey into the unknown; and to Arun-ji and Aditi of Vani Prakashan for their patience through the months of waiting for me to complete the book. Of course, I must mention how delightful it was to work with a conscientious and well-informed editor like Anurag Basnet, who made editing feel like a prance through the park.

To you, dear reader, I offer this book with a hope and a prayer that you will enjoy reading it as much as I enjoyed working on it. And it will leave you, as it left me, enriched by the voyage through Gulzar's world.

—Sathya Saran

Fourteen years it took me to reach Ayodhya

Yatindra Mishra, the prince of Ayodhya, interviewed me.

I don't really know what I said to him.

All the magic sprang from his questions,

And not from my answers.

It is Yatindra's special quality that

He could mine the earth of my consciousness so deeply.

It occurred to me that should we strike oil,

We would achieve something.

Yet it is possible that all we found was dry dust,

Or a well full of water.

The final decision about this rests with Arun Maheshwari,

Or you, dear reader, after you read this book.

If Yatindra has managed to find a few diamonds or pearls,

It is his generosity that he is sharing them with all of you!

—Gulzar

چودہ برس لگے مجھے ایودھیا پہنچنے میں۔

ایودھیا کے راج کنور 'پشپیندر مشرا' میرا انٹرویو لے رہے تھے۔

پتہ نہیں کیا کیا کہا میں نے، اُن الجھنوں میں۔

لیکن ساری عمر کی پشپیندر کے سوالوں کے لیے میرے جوابوں

کی نہیں — پشپیندر مشرا کی تھی یہ لگن کہ وہ میری زمین کو اپنی

گہرائی تک کھود جائے۔

مجھے لگتا تھا شاید کبھی نکل آئے تو کچھ حاصل ہو

لیکن ہو سکتا ہے صرف مٹی ہی نکلے یا پانی کا کنواں نکلے۔

اس کا فیصلہ اب اردو کے قاری کریں گے یا آپ!

یہ کتاب پڑھ کر!

کچھ یاد رہے اگر پشپیندر ہم عمر ہوتے ہیں،

تو اُن کی فراخدلی ہے کہ وہ آپ سب کے ساتھ

بانٹ رہے ہیں۔

گلزار

Gulzar Sa'ab

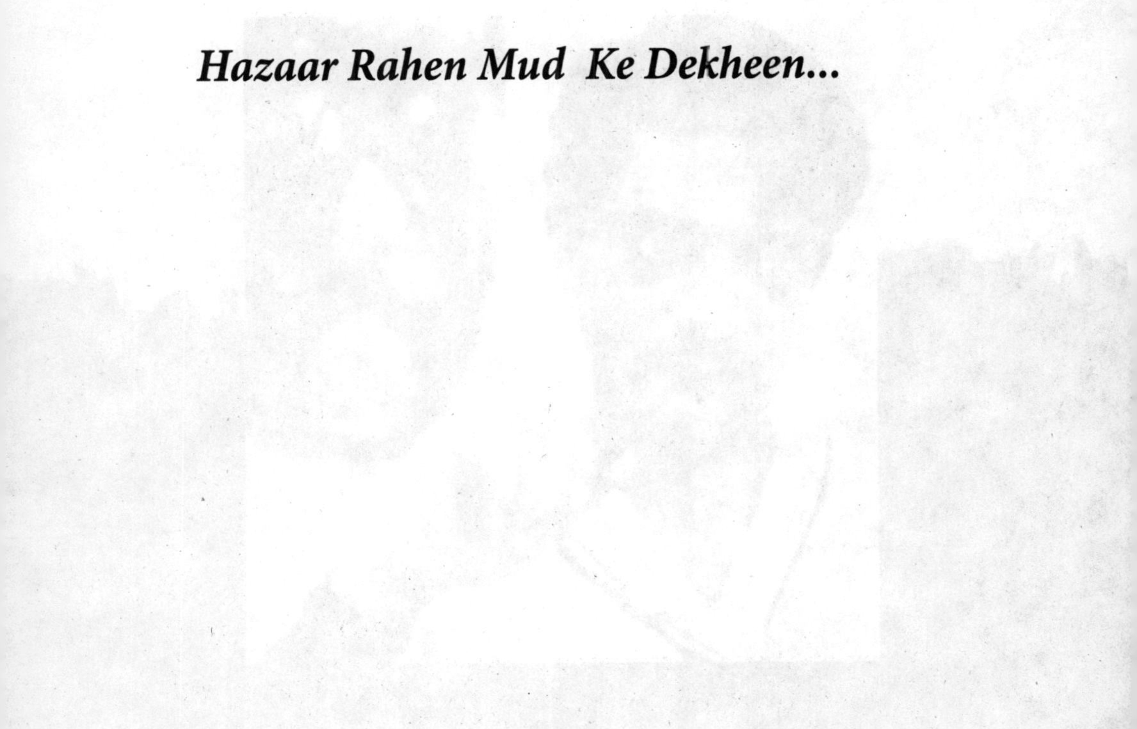

Hazaar Rahen Mud Ke Dekheen...

The disgrace that after death dogged me
It was better if I had drowned at sea

With no procession funerary
Or even a grave to mark me

—Mirza Ghalib

That which is past, is yesterday
It wasn't a lifetime, but a single night
Should we find again, but one end of the night...

1.

He's a voice, Gulzar! A dervish wrapped in white simplicity emerging from the mist, shining in the winter sunlight. To him his nights and days of leisure are but moments divided into songs and poems which reveal the soul of a multi-talented artist.

Countless are the letters of romanticism he has written but, instead of being dispatched to any address, they lie waiting in his notebook. Using the silken thread of emotions, he sews the binding of his book of everlasting hope. Often, on approaching the light twinkling in the distant dusk, one realises that the flame of that lantern is the ink that fills his pen.

A nomad in spirit, he will walk holding a poem by the hand for a distance, only to suddenly wander into the landscape of a story. Even as he pens lyrics for films he will imperceptibly shift to writing dialogues and no one can discern the moment of change. He sources the screenplays for films from the world of poetry and picks stories from literature to make them into films.

An enticing voice, trying to read the mirror of time, a poem that holds in it the seed of a prayer. Come, let us delve into the chapters of the life of one such scholar, let us turn some pages and listen to some conversations. Let us view our times through the eyes of a poet who creates for both literature and cinema.

> *Don't drop the curtain yet, the saga continues*
> *Don't drop the curtain, wait!*
> *The spirit is still smouldering with sorrow,*
> *and pain throbs in the heart*
> *Feeling has now come alive...*

2.

This story is a few years old. Inaugurating a literary festival, Gulzar presented the story of his poetry:

> When a vessel is placed on the stove, and when steam gathers, even the lid placed on top starts vibrating. At such times, I write inside the steam. The steam shapes my writing, my poems. Imagine that there are vessels of many languages. All have placed life on the stove, and they are on the boil, and these languages are doing a lot of things. So many vessels that have been put on boil...all of them have placed life on the stove. Unpeeled desires have been placed inside, their stems have not been broken, leavened dreams rise like steam yet every vessel is bubbling over. These intellectuals, so many of them, have joined to churn the sea and extract the nectar but nothing stays inside a shattered vessel...

Gulzar's use of this unique metaphor to explain his poetry is not to be praised as merely a poetic expression. He has raised a valid point and given the example of a poem cooking in steam. The writings of a poet like Gulzar are created by the heat of the steam created by water and fire. The heat of the verses can singe the fingers of those who, without understanding, reach out to touch them.

The poet is saying that the form of the steam that he is shaping his poems from is a stove on which countless vessels symbolising many languages have been placed. Not only do these languages benefit from the philosophies of life, life itself has been put on the same stove and is cooking in the flame of the poems. Many human emotions create unique creations in the vessel of life that stands cooking on the stove.

What Gulzar refers to as the bubbling of vessels is actually the sound that gives meaning to his own existence, which translates into new forms of poetic expression.

He speaks about learned people because he himself comes from the same lineage and works on his poems sitting in the same classroom in which, ages ago, his mentor Mirza Ghalib studied. Ghalib, Mir Taqi Mir, Zauq, Sauda and Nazir belong to the same tradition of using the vessels of their words to constantly seek new ways of composing and expression. They are the ones who have churned the ocean with their creative works and by distilling languages and dialects have created everlasting poetic masterpieces. This verse of Ghalib has been tempered and shaped on the flame of life:

Neither am I the joy that melody creates
Nor the string that creates music,
I am the discordant voice of my own ruin.

3.

Gulzar remembers his childhood well. The childhood that he spent across the border; the lanes of Dina in Jhelum district—now in Pakistan—which link his existence to that soil; he remembers it all. How the darling 'Punni' of mother Sujan Kaur and father Makhan Singh Kalra would, on receiving one anna from his grandfather, Bhag Singh, and two annas from his grandmother, immerse himself in his play. Bhag Singh was a resident of the neighbouring village that lay between Dina and Jhelum. Kurla, his paternal grandfather, Sardar Nihal Singh's village, was about a mile away.

Sampoorna Singh's childhood, as it traversed the towns of Kurla, Kala and Dina, experienced its best days, and a multitude of impressions and voices were imprinting themselves on his understanding. He remembers that in the localities nearby lived singers who would sing the Heer, traditional Punjabi folk songs of sadness and parting, as well as those who sang the Gurbani. Even as a child he had been accustomed to listening to the Japji Sahib which appears at the beginning of the *Guru Granth Sahib*, the holy scripture of the Sikhs, and Gurbani paath, and was enamoured by it. When the raagi, the priests, would sing the *Guru Granth Sahib* aarti in the traditional Raag Dhanashree, and play the instruments, his mind would respond with a strange exhilaration. The chorus line of the aarti, which is repeated after every antara, would fill his mind with the scents of spring:

O destroyer of the cycle of birth and death,
How amazing is the aarti that Nature performs

Even today Gulzar-sahab says with utmost respect that the Sampoorna Singh who listened to all these sounds learnt his Punjabi and Gurmukhi from them.

Dina was a commercial city. Actually, it was like a large town. Agents, wholesale merchants and cloth salesmen would all travel to Kala, his maternal grandfather's town, to sell their goods. Thus, Kala and Dina were two towns where business prospered.

In those days, World War II was raging. Trains with compartments reserved for the military would stop at Dina Station. This was between the years 1942 and 1945, and countless guiltless towns experienced some aspect or the other of the gloomy shadow that the World War had cast over them.

Today, when the ninety-year-old Gulzar looks back at Sampoorna Singh standing at Dina Station, his mind sickens at the memory. He was eight when he left Dina and moved to Delhi. When the poet remembers that time today, the wounds of World War II seem to pierce the edge of his consciousness with some unseen weapon. Those moments, though lost in time, remain trapped in his memory.

The child left behind in Dina, the poet who grew up to adulthood in Delhi, the persona who, sitting in Bombay, thinks back on the village haunts, his grandparents, Dina and Jhelum, sees nothing changed. Only the date is different, and almost seventy-five years lie in-between. Dina presents itself in much the same manner in the poem, 'Zero Line'.

But there was a quiet road that can still be seen
That road used to lead to Dina

A very small camp it was, at some time
And a station of small dimensions
Not all trains would stop there
But those were days of 'lam'
And those with carriages for the army would stop
Seeing the smoke from the engine, I would come running to the station
My father would return in it, with purchases for the shop.

But Punni's memories do not end here. They have been so closely integrated into his life that one cannot separate or keep aside the stories of Sardar Makhan Singh Kalra's family. Memories and childhood, the climate and the soil, the Shabad Kirtan and the Gurbani—how can they be separated from his subconscious? Dina too is no longer just a part of his memories but a vital component in the shaping of his ideas and daily life. The bazaars and streets of Dina, and the lessons imbibed there, form an indelible part of his creative work.

The poem of Dina continues:

A bazaar
And a 'tahliyon' road too
That's still there
A school where, sitting on a rough rug,
I'd write on a slate
That lane too...
One end of which would open into the fields

Touched the walls on which
I would write with coal in Urdu...

Gulzar's poetic mind still lives fragmented in so many ways in the streets and corners of Dina.

He was eighty before he could go to Dina again, to revisit the memory of his home, his maternal and paternal grandfathers. To listen to the chink of his grandmother's two annas. To imbibe his mother, Sujan Kaur, deeper into his breath and being. And yes, for one other thing! To look at that station in Dina, which now has two tracks. The train still pulls in here but, sadly, childhood does not alight from it. After seventy years, it is as if Gulzar is standing in Dina, hoping to gather everything into his grasp and, hidden in the mist of memories, Punni stands watching the soldiers of World War II alighting from the train.

Seventy years it has taken me
To return to Dina and understand myself
Long I have run in the wastelands of time
Long drawn out this game of hide and seek

Memories haunt him, but time has started fading them. Even as they turn golden, the memories and dreams of childhood are turning hollow. Only Baba Farid and Bulleh Shah and the songs sung on the ektara are saved. In Bulleh Shah's words he finds the notes for introspection:

Now that the soulmates of my neighbourhood
have departed forever,
O Divine One, tell me what I should do

His father, whom Gulzar addresses as Abbu, he sees standing at the station, but the heaviness in his heart about the time spent in Dina stays. It's like everything emerges from the casket of memories and, immediately slipping from his hands, spills on to the hem of his clothes and slowly disappears from sight. Confusion spreads in his mind and surrounds him.

An image long stuck in my mind, of a station
Of smoke from an engine unmoving in the breeze
Has now started fading
That was my father, standing at the door of the carriage...

4.

He has listened intensively to Baba Farid and Bulleh Shah in his childhood: 'Ranjha jogida ban aya', 'Jis tan lagiya ishq kamaal', 'Ki bedard ke sang yari', these and who knows how many such other compositions. The mystical songs that the group of singers would sing as they passed by would imbue his life with a unique flavour. He remembers too the early-morning sound of curds being churned with a wooden churner in a metal pot. His step-mother, Vidyavati, would put him to the task of churning curds. He would quaff the half-churned curds with butter floating in whey from a large metal tumbler every single day. He would churn the curds with such vigour that the sounds that emerged from the tug-of-war between the churner and the curds entered his subconscious to live there for a long time. Also a part of it are the memories of his other mothers who came after his own mother passed away. However, he could never be at ease with them. It is also true that no effort was made from the other side to knit new strands into the tenuous threads of the relationship.

Though Gulzar came away from Dina, the habit of listening to the Gurbani remained with him even in Delhi. Here too the singers of Heer would come to sing on days of celebration. He listened to singers of the calibre of Asha Singh Mastana. His own relative, Darshan Singh 'Awara', was a renowned Punjabi poet who participated in the poetry sessions organised there. Thus did the young Sampoorna Singh come under the sway of both music and poetry.

Gulzar cannot pinpoint when the rich Punjabi folk music of Dina rooted itself in the ethos of Delhi. But even when he lived in Roshanara Bagh, his young mind was charmed by it. There was another new and interesting aspect to the memories of his childhood. He enjoyed listening to Alha Gayan, ballads from the Bundelkhand region about the heroic deeds of the brothers Alha and Udal. Gulzar can recite stanzas of Alha as if he has scooped them up from his young mind:

Alha and Udal fought so well
That none could withstand them

He remembers that his elder brother Jasmer Singh had a friend, Dhruv, who would sing 'Vaishnav jan to tene kahiye je pida parayi jaane re' (A true Vaishnav is one who understands the woes of others as his own), Gandhi-ji's favourite bhajan, very beautifully. He regards Dhruv as an interesting influence who layered his mind with the colours of the bhajan's meaning. In school, he would listen to the two prayers that were read daily. One, Allama Iqbal's 'Lab pe aati hai dua banke tamanna meri' (My longing comes to my lips as prayer) and the other, 'Teri shaan jalla jalalahu' (Your glory is immense).

All of this painted his mind in colours that faded as he moved from boyhood into adolescence. Since then, till now, the young man Sampoorna Singh hidden inside Gulzar has been wanting to seek, sift and gather all that was inadvertently lost along the way. An effort, not always successful, to collect all these memories into a haversack. An effort in which the poet has lost much, the thought of which drives him crazy and fills him with a pain that seeps into his veins.

The agony of losing himself in this seeping pain, of having nothing left to remember, is evident in various poems from which a clear portrait of Gulzar emerges.

There, that very day, I threw my childhood away
But often in the deserts that lie silent across the border,
I have seen 'bhameeri' still dancing
A top still spinning!

('Bhameeri')

~

Just one round it takes, the chalk placed on the wheel of life
One circuit of the wheel is enough to grind it all down...
The rosaries of day and night are starting to break
Just one strong share remains, of age perhaps!
I'm returning to 'Dina' where the chalk started from.
('Ek Hi Chakkar Leta Hai')

~

But this is possible only in dreams
Political hurdles confront my going there
The homeland is still the same, but it's no longer my country
To go there, from the countless offices of two governments
I must wear stamps, to prove my dreams are real.
('Agar Aisa Bhi Ho Sakta Hai')

5.

Many are the pictures from the past collected in Gulzar's house. Just as old clothes and quilts are carefully stored away in big trunks to face a change in weather, Gulzar too has who knows how many cherished ledgers of memories stacked within himself.

He seldom talks about issues connected to life if relatives and family members are involved. He hesitates to speak openly about the Partition, not because he wishes to hide his past but because those memories are like wounds on his body that have grown scabs. They might bleed if he picks at them.

When Gulzar was a callow boy of ten or twelve, ready for school, the family arrangement was such that he had to sleep in the storeroom of the shop, away from the house. There was no electricity in the storeroom, only a dim lantern to light up his nights. Often the dark, the heat and humidity would conspire to keep him awake, and some source of support was needed to help the young man get through the night. Indeed, he had found an unbeatable solution to help pass the darkest night lit only by stars.

He enjoyed reading and there was a library next door. A refugee from Pakistan was running it and books could be loaned for a few paise. Gulzar would borrow a few books from him; mostly crime thrillers and spy stories. For four annas the refugee would give out books for a week. Gulzar says that he was so addicted to reading that every night he would read through a book and return it to fetch a new one. Once the library-owner even shouted at him, 'How many books should I give you for four annas?' Then, as a thought occurred to him, he pulled out a heavy book from another cupboard and handed it to him saying, 'Here, read this.'

That book, handed out thoughtlessly, became an amazing story. He had given Gulzar Gurudev Rabindranath Tagore's *The Gardener*, translated into Urdu, to read. Lifting the book in his hands, the young Gulzar realised that this was different from the books he usually read and a book of such weight would take him more days than usual. The man, just to be rid of having to hand out a new book every day, had packed the boy off with a tome!

This book would forever change his taste in books. It touched his mind in such a way that a new world bedecked with a new spectrum of dreams opened up before him. A new dawn beckoned, and Gulzar found his mind drenched by the emotion-laden rain that Gurudev's poems showered on him. In Gulzar's words:

> I fell in love with it. My style of reading books changed and even in my choice of books, I could now discern a shift. I remember even today the poem 'Mali' that presented itself on opening the book. This collection appealed to me so much that even as I borrowed other books and returned them, I would keep this book with me, week after week. This went on for so long that the man who was lending the books to me forgot about it!

The Gardener helped light new hopes for Gulzar despite the darkness of the storeroom. Even as life went on, memories of *The Gardener* continued to play a role. Years later, still under the book's spell, Gulzar would present an exceptional version of the book in translation as *Baghbaan*. Every page of the translated text seemed to hold something of the boy who, for the first time, had received the book with eager hands.

It is relevant to read a sample of the translation that reflects the deep influence Gurudev's poems had on the mind of the boy who sat reading the book in the small store room:

Neither does fear affect you
Nor do attractions bind you
Neither is there any desire
Neither slander, nor weeping
No home either
Nor bed awaits you
You have but a pair of wings
And a sky
No route can be discerned
In this dawn-smeared sky
O bird, listen my friend,
Never fold your wings!

('Panchi')

6.

Gulzar has retained many tough and tragic memories of the Partition of India and Pakistan. He remembers every moment of those events which left such scars on his psyche that he often sits up with a start from sleep and, sometimes, even sleep seems fearsome in the dead of the night. But if you dig deep, all he will say is, 'We would hear that in these places in Delhi: Sabzi Mandi, Sadar Bazaar and Paharganj, there was a lot of rioting during that time.'

He relates an incident which shook him to the core, a scene he has not been able to forget. The incident that took place in his school and concerned a Muslim student. Like all other days, the students of M. B. Middle School, Roshanara Bagh, were reciting their morning prayers. Gulzar was among them. A sardar, whose name he remembers as Samandar Singh, had tied a Muslim boy up with rope and was leading him away. People were watching through the windows of their homes, but no one stepped out. Someone called out, 'Where are you taking him?' The man replied, 'I will leave him in Pakistan.' No one said anything in response but their faces were marked with horror. When the sardar returned to Roshanara Bagh, he was holding a bloody sword in his hand. Gulzar recollects this incident like a lingering trauma. With deep pain and some guilt, he says, 'I have not forgotten his face till today. He was fair, there were pockmarks on his face and he was Muslim. I still remember this incident. No one cried. Even if someone had cried, I do not remember it. There was confusion all around, I remember the panic still. How the panic filled everybody's senses, I remember that still. That incident of panic and the face of panic, I remember both.'

Gulzar becomes sorrowful when he narrates these stories. To him this incident seems to be the most tragic truth of the Partition where he himself was present as a witness to a rioter bringing shame to humanity.

Of the effect the rioting in Roshanara Bagh and the other areas had on his young mind, he says, 'I was aware of the fact that India was being divided. It was being broken into two separate countries, but how many people were being killed on both sides of the border in the process? What was the need for this? What is happening here and for what? I have not found answers to these questions.'

It is true that not just Gulzar, but peace-loving citizens on both sides are still not able to fathom the reason behind the bloodshed and massacres. When we traverse through Gulzar's stories, this question presents itself even more urgently. His stories, 'Raavi Paar', 'LOC', 'Over', 'Jamun Ke Ped', 'Hilsa',

'Tumbe' and 'Khauf' are the collected memories of those times that he has placed on paper.

The moans from the agony of those times come alive in his writing. Take these two lines from his story titled, 'Over':

> What a wonderous thing our border is. When we read the papers, it feels as if a line of fire has been stretched out and a river of blood is flowing.

The stories gain a new relevance when he writes:

> Some stories erupted like boils. Given to us by circumstance, surroundings and society. Sometimes I would recite a poem and spit out blood; at others, I would write a story and bandage the wound. But be it a poem or a story, no brevity is possible. It is a sigh, a shriek and a prayer too. Never the cure for human suffering. It only documents the pain of humanity so that it remains in evidence for future generations.

Only someone who has suffered can know how much pain these carefully detailed documents can give. Someone who has survived those horrors and travels through these stories would have the same experience; like applying a bandage on a wound. Thinking of these bandages makes one think not only of Gulzar, but other writers too: Saadat Hasan Manto, Krishan Chander, Rajendra Singh Bedi, Ismat Chughtai, Intezar Husain, Qazi Abdul Sattar and Krishna Sobti come to mind.

7.

'A mirasi has taken birth in our house.' He would hear such statements as a boy, when the family became aware that he had started writing poems and stories, and enjoyed shayari. His father Makhan Singh used to say, 'Svane umriya jama karta rehta hai,' meaning he reads biographies and collects stories and magazines.

Everyone in the family would worry that he would turn out like Darshan Singh 'Awara'—'awara' is wanderer, or vagabond—though 'Awara' was a renowned Punjabi poet. But at such times, his father would find comfort when Gulzar's poems were sometimes published in a newspaper or an Urdu magazine. If something was published in the Sunday edition of *Pratap*, a renowned newspaper of that time, he would carry it around in his hand the entire day. His eyes would shine with the joy of seeing his son's name in print.

Gulzar's later achievements remained singularly his own. Neither his father nor his mother were present to witness them. He could see the fatherly love glistening in his photograph, but not the satisfaction that comes into a father's eyes on seeing his son's success. Sardar Makhan Singh Kalra's share of joy remained contained in seeing the Sunday Edition carrying his son's name. Remembering the joy that suffused his face at this small achievement fills Gulzar with regret that his father could not witness the height of his success.

8.

The period in which Gulzar's poetry was searching for its expression of language and ideas was peopled by progressive poets. Most new or young poets and writers of the time were influenced heavily by the poetry of Ali Sardar Jafri. The PWA (Progressive Writers' Association) used to hold its meetings at the Red Flag Hall in Khetvadi near Girgaum in Bombay, now Mumbai.

Poets and scholars would gather there and questions would fly: Who has written what? Who is writing something new? What comments have been passed on the latest doings of the government? All these matters would be explained and understood in minute detail.

This was a time when the Pakistani poets Faiz Ahmed Faiz and Ahmed Faraz cast long shadows over Indian poetry. It was the time of Sahir Ludhianvi and Jan Nisar Akhtar. The presence of Allama Darpan also had its effect on society. Allama-sahab was the editor of the Urdu paper *The Inquilab* and his cordial relations with the youth, especially those who remained connected to their culture, was praiseworthy.

Gulzar-sahab remembers, 'We would mostly sit in the *Inquilab* office and recite poems to one another, and unfettered discussions would follow.'

It so happened that Faiz-sahab was in Bombay to attend a mushaira, a poetry soiree. Every young poet was restlessly thinking up ways to recite his poems to Faiz-sahab. When he came to know about this through Allama Darpan, he asked, 'Where shall I listen to them?' At this, Allama Darpan took him to the *Inquilab* office. A rug was spread out in the empty space underneath the stairs and a baithak was organised. Only Faiz-sahab was offered a chair to sit on. What a wonderful mehfil it was. Faiz-sahab listened intently and with interest to the new voices, giving generously of his time.

This was very significant for those young poets who were starting their journey and who may not, at that time, have been serious about crafting their verses but nonetheless nurtured in their secret hearts the desire to recite their poems to Faiz-sahab. This event created in Gulzar the conviction that being a poet was a matter of great esteem. Later, when Gulzar became famous and started touring overseas, he met Faiz-sahab first in Moscow and then in Tashkent. This was how Gulzar was introduced to a poet of great sincerity and warmth. Faiz was a believer in the idea that the garden should always be in bloom, which could be possible only if new ideas were welcomed.

Filling the flowers with colour the spring breeze passes
Do come now so the garden continues to flourish.

9.

He has no memory of his mother's face. Whenever the conversation turns to his mother, Sujan Kaur, Gulzar turns serious, as if he has started living his past in the present. His mother's absence brings an emptiness to his life. For a mother to leave such a person so early in his childhood that no shred of memory remains for her son to grasp and hold saddens him to such an extent that Gulzar cannot escape from it even after trying. He wants to emerge from it, and steps out, but again delves into himself in the very same search.

This delving into the self, the descent into the deep well of feelings, troubles him. But all he says is, 'I was so young that I don't remember my mother's face.' He searches for his mother in his songs, complains in his poems and holds conversations with her. Somewhat like the poet Iqbal questioning God in his long poem 'Shikwa' (Complaint). It's another matter, though, that Iqbal subsequently answered on behalf of God and wrote 'Jawab-e-Shikhwa' (A Reply to the Complaint). The crux of Gulzar's complaint to his mother also holds the thought that perhaps she saw the face of God and thus abandoned him and went away.

The poem goes thus:

Ma
How will I recognise you; whom I have never seen
In my own face I look for you with eyes keen

They say my eyes are like my mother's
Though brimming with liquid, their thirst can be seen

My ears are pierced, perhaps from birth
Did you have your own pierced after pledging a troth

The gap in my front teeth, must be in yours too
And the same circle must show on your sole too

Wonder what your hurry was, that you gave birth and chose to flee
Did you see God himself that you had to leave me

I try to match, that by coincidence that I will find my lookalike

Without you the world at times seems a stranger
How will I recognise you; whom I have never seen
In my own face I look for you with eyes keen.

Reading this poem heavy with questions, it is not easy to decide whether it is his depression that is weightier or the love for his mother. Is he plumbing the depths of the void or is it love that has bubbled up despite his pain and permeates the words? By writing the poem, Gulzar ensures that he keeps the memory of his mother safe and achieves a catharsis. Wherever she is, beyond the seven skies, Sujan Kaur must be sending blessings to her son. Gulzar believes that when monsoon comes, his mother's love comes to him dissolved in the rain. One can see the comfort he gets from this thought in his portrayal of the mother in his films. When Dina Pathak sings a lullaby to her son in *Kitaab*, it seems as if his mother is lulling Punni to sleep. This is clear because the expression that comes into that lullaby could not have been possible without the director having experienced the emotion:

I have no one to accompany me
No cloak to shield me
Loved ones lost, dreams lost
Divest me of desires
Hari, the day is done, evening has come
Help me across the night...

10.

Three poems written by Gulzar stand apart from the other poems by him on the Partition. They focus in a different way on the relationships that exist on either side of the border, in words and concepts presented with simplicity.

'Humwatan' (Fellow Countryman) is for Ahmed Faraz. The second poem, 'Aankhon Ko Visa Nahi Lagta' (Eyes Don't Need a Visa) expresses a desire to hear Mehdi Hasan singing his ghazals, and the third is 'Zindan Nama', in which there is a reference to Faiz Ahmed Faiz. All three poems on their part give us a unique and interesting understanding of the Partition, as they look at it through the lens of a shared culture.

Right from the start, Gulzar has been expert at writing portraits in which he draws out a character's qualities in words with the same detailing a painter uses to create portraits. In the three poems dedicated to the three personalities living across the border, Gulzar abandons his familiar style and, focusing on how their presence affects the climate, tradition and music of that country, brings out the bonds they forge between India and Pakistan to make a deeply significant statement.

The poet's dilemma in 'Zindan Nama' is how to persuade his peer poet who lives across the border, that he should somehow get the pulse of time, which has stopped beating due to the tension between the two countries, to start beating again. Gulzar creates magic in the last five lines of this small ten-line poem:

Traversing the lanes of Lahore one night,
Scaling the high reaches of the jail wall, the moon
Jumped with such commando-like stealth into the cell
That there was no sound
The guards remained unaware.
It's said that it went to meet Faiz
To tell him, 'Write a poem,
The pulse of Time has stopped beating
Recite something
So that the pulse may throb again.'

In the same way, the poem 'Humwatan', written for Ahmed Faraz, using other references, links India and Pakistan to the same portion of the Earth. Gulzar writes—

Every single day have I prostrated on your soil
Every night have I kissed your skies

As my moon and stars are even today the same
Which you look at as you lie on your terrace.

The pain with which the poet expresses his yearning for the lost mementos that were left behind in his birthplace is evident in the poem. In fact, it is possible to say that the poem, using Ahmed Faraz as an excuse, places Gulzar in the same surroundings and lets him roam there freely. The poem ends with an emotion that will bring tears to the eyes. The poem achieves significance thus, and through the emotions of the two poets, conveys some advice to both nations. The last lines of the poem must be read in this light:

Your country is dear to you, that I know
I am also in love with it, believe me
Just one difference, if you can understand it
That you remain in it, and I belonged to it.

'Humwatan' reminds us of the poem 'Berlin Ki Tooti Deewar Ko Dekhkar' (Upon Seeing the Shattered Berlin Wall) by the renowned Hindi poet Kedarnath Singh, in which he has mentioned Ahmed Faraz with great reverence and respect.

This, then is a small hotel
Where we, some Hind-Pak writers
Have stayed for some days
And regardless of what our passports say
Here, each of us,
Is a bit of Hind, and a bit of Pak...

It's a land he's familiar with, on which Gulzar has based his 'Humwatan'. Kedarnath-ji, while gazing upon the ruins of the Berlin Wall, uses the pretext of Ahmed Faraz's ghazal to look beyond the window of the hotel room where a mad woman is tearing through Faraz's ghazal as she roams round and round the place. Something exists that is embedded like a nail in the woman's soul. Some meaningful lines at the end of the poem shed some light that India and Pakistan, by messing each other up, fragmented, and are lost in the subcontinent. The lines read:

I see that in the middle of the ghazal
Ahmed Fazal is forgetting some thought
Between the last couplet and this
A strange silence
Has occupied the hall…

So many years have passed
In this subcontinent rich with songs
I am still waiting for that one forgotten thought.

Such poignant lines prove the relationship of thought between the two poems, 'Humwatan' and 'Berlin Ki Tooti Deewar Ko Dekhkar', as both speak in a tone that gives authenticity to the corresponding sufferings of both India and Pakistan.

Similarly, Gulzar's popular poem 'Eyes Don't Need a Visa', using the metaphor of dreams as a device to ease the pain, sets forth everything that an ordinary person suffers: the pain lodged in his chest which he cannot share with anyone. When Gulzar says, 'With eyes shut, I often cross the border,' you can understand the pain of someone who is separated from the soil of his birthplace. Empathising with the meaning of the lines, it is inevitable that the poem's thought grows on the reader, which holds the hope that the poet will see in his dreams the flowers that he had pressed between the pages of the books he left behind.

Anything that accrues from the flashes of emotion and ideas of human beings often gets transformed in poems of grief into something bigger. When Gulzar refers to Ahmed Faraz or Faiz Ahmed Faiz, poets on both sides of the border illuminate each others' gardens with the light that spills forth from their pens. It becomes difficult then to find any difference in the thoughts and writings of India's Gulzar and Pakistan's Ahmed Faraz. Only then will the understanding come that the meadows of the two countries may have been divided, but which of the countries could gain a singular hold on the citizens of either?

It is at this point that Gulzar's poem becomes meaningful and enlightening:

Eyes don't require a visa
Dreams have no borders
With eyes closed, I cross the border every day
To meet Mehdi Hassan.

I've learnt his voice has suffered hurt
And facing him, the ghazal sits
With lips a-trembling
When he says,
'The flowers have dried inside the books'
Friend 'Faraz' has also left now, perhaps to meet only in dreams.
Through shut eyes, I often cross the border.

Eyes don't require a visa
Dreams have no borders.

11.

Gulzar often remembers his stint with Bimal Roy Productions whenever he thinks of his younger days. The recollections are so vivid and beautiful that on hearing him recount them, one wonders if such a time truly existed in Indian cinema. That life behind the scenes, during a shoot, could be so unclouded and free. A group of four assistants worked with Bimal-da, and they got on famously together. They were Debu Sen, Raghunath Jhalani, Mukul Dutt and Gulzar. This group of four would not only get scolded by Bimal Roy, and receive advice, but thanks to his fatherly, affectionate nature, also enjoy the feeling of being part of a family.

It can be said that these four might not have received as many scoldings from their own fathers as the rebukes that the father-like Bimal-da rained on them even as he was shaping them.

The story is that Bimal Roy was a man fully immersed in cinema. The world of cinema and the shining celluloid sheets were to him his food and water, sleep, family and life. The four assistants, disregarding his strict demeanour, had given him a nickname. They would refer to him as 'married-print' behind his back; like students in a class bestow a nickname on a strict teacher and, by calling him that among themselves, feel like they have won a battle.

Similarly, with Bimal-da too, without his being aware of it, the entire production house knew that thanks to these four, that the strict director was also called 'married-print'. The common joke in the unit was that Bimal Roy was actually married to films. In cinema, a married print is the term used for the positive print that is made when the visual and sound negatives are fused into one.

The four assistants, buoyed by their sense of humour, would spend days and nights on the sets with Bimal-da. Each of them wanted to do his best in following Bimal-da's instructions. Those days, they worked double shifts. The first shift would last from 7 a.m. to 2 p.m., and the second from 2 p.m. to 10 p.m. One can imagine how many hours the assistants of a director would put in when the director himself toiled ceaselessly for fifteen hours a day.

12.

There is an interesting incident that connects Gulzar to K. Asif, the creator of the magnificent film *Mughal-e-Azam*. This harks back to those days when the offices of K. Asif and Bimal Roy were situated in Mohan Studios. The room in which the tailor Maqsood-mia used to make the costumes for the actors was also in the same compound. Attached to the room, just outside, was a telephone booth which everyone used. Often, there would be a long line of those waiting their turn to use the phone.

One day, Gulzar was talking to his friend, Sukhbir, on the phone. It was a friendly chat and Gulzar was quite immersed in the conversation. When he turned, he noticed that K. Asif was standing outside, waiting patiently his turn at the phone. Alarmed by the fact that K. Asif might have been waiting a long time, Gulzar told his friend in Punjabi, 'I will talk to you later, now put down the phone,' and hung up.

Asif-sahab placed a hand on Gulzar's shoulder and said, 'Mian, you spoke exactly like a Punjabi. Where did you learn the language?' Gulzar promptly replied, 'Because I am a Punjabi.' K. Asif responded in Punjabi, 'I thought you were a Bengali, everyone in the studio too knows you as a Bengali.' Gulzar says that even after this, K. Asif was not completely convinced that he was Punjabi and not Bengali!

13.

In the early days of his struggle in Bombay, he lived in a rented room in Char Bangla, a suburb of the metropolis. During this time, he found a job as a car mechanic in a garage owned by Sudershan Bakshi. The garage was situated on Bellasis Road, near Alexandra Cinema in the Bombay Central area. Gulzar was deployed to mix paint in the exact colour that matched the colour of the car that needed a patch-up painting after an accident. He had the knack of mixing colours to create new shades. He had also worked out how to mix the right shades without wasting any paint.

Gulzar gets absorbed in recounting how he enjoyed the fact that once a damaged car had been mended, he would help paint it in such a way that there would be no sign of the damage, even to the most searching eye. He says, 'I applied myself with complete dedication and care to the job. I don't remember a single instance where I was casual in my attitude to work, or that any car owner came back with a complaint.'

He also says that close to Vichare Motors there was a Sarvi Hotel where, in those days, he could get two 'pav' buns, two kababs and a bunch of mint leaves for four annas. Enough for a satisfying meal.

Gulzar-sahab adds excitedly, 'You won't believe me, but I still miss that taste. The joy of taking time off from work to relish that kabab and pav still lives within me.'

Today, as I write about his work in Vichare Motors, I must add my story of Gulzar's love for colours that at one point he was immersed in creating a number of paintings on canvas, which exist even today in some form or the other. The colours that gave him joy as he painted cars have now moved to the canvas and easel in Boskiyana, his Bandra home.

14.

In his fourth decade, Gulzar wanted to learn the sitar. He loved to wake up and practise every morning. His daughter, Meghna, must have been just seven when she watched her father performing riyaz, his practice. This gentle, loveable picture of Gulzar must certainly form part of her childhood memories. Besides this, Gulzar enjoys tennis. Once, when I asked him about tennis he said, 'I write songs only sometimes but I play tennis every day.' His many friends who play tennis with him as also old friends who have partnered him in badminton are bound to him in friendship and he loves them more than the world of cinema. Among these are Dr. Kishan Morwani, Umesh Pachigar and Dr. Husain Tailor.

His most engaging discussions on poetry have been with Ahmed Nadeem Kasmi, Pakistan's renowned poet and editor, whom he affectionately calls Baba. A poem he has written on Baba bears witness to his immeasurable love. A stanza:

There stands a tree under whose dense shade
When the sun filters through

In that little space on the ground
It scatters words like coins
Thousands of which lie strewn around.
Round, square, shining, weighty coins
Who knows what the sunlight writes
As she rests in the dappled shade.
I have stood in this shade,
Many a time, over the years
And filled my pockets with these coins
Then often with loneliness by my side
I have listened for hours to their music.
I would read the faces that emerged
One would tell a story at times, another a nazm.

So committed is he to his friendships that he has written a poem for each of his friends. It is as if he wishes to bind the friendships with words. Showing off one's love is a stereotype in Urdu poetry, and Gulzar has countered this by bringing friends into the domain of love. Pancham, or Jagjit Singh, Amrita Pritam or Vishal Bhardwaj, he calls out to all of them. The lines written for Amrita Pritam are like a love-tipped arrow that pierces the soul:

When I come by your nazm, I am struck with fear
As if I am stepping into a wet landscape...painted by Imroze
Images spring out from your nazm
Colours drip off your brush.
He, on his blank canvas writes a nazm
You, on your pages, paint a poem.

Going beyond, he does not hesitate to express the love in his heart for a writer like me. Once when my sister Manjari and I had visited him in Bombay, he had presented me with the English translation of one of his books of poems, after writing something in it in Urdu. Then reading it out to my sister, he started laughing because he knew she had studied Urdu. Both of them were having a good laugh because what he had written for me was beyond my comprehension. When we left

Boskiyana, my sister told me, Gulzar-sahab has written for you, 'For dear Yatindra, who does not know Urdu.' Cheerful and affectionate towards his friends, Gulzar is a superb host too. If you are close to him and he comes to know that you are in Mumbai, it is unthinkable that you will eat your breakfast anywhere else. Not only will he personally treat you to a lavish spread of dishes, but he himself will not eat anything till you reach his place. Often, I have been amiss in reaching his house late, only to find that he has bravely waited without eating or drinking till I showed up. On such occasions friends from his inner circle, Ashok Bindal and Atul Tiwari, are often also present.

Many aspects of his personal life are such that elaborating on them will be like paraphrasing poems from a poetry book. Like making sure that the sash of his daughter's uniform is tied every day in an artistic way, thus adding a beautiful touch to an everyday chore. Or like when he pulls the leg of a waiter when he brings a small spoon along with the sweet dish, asking him jokingly, 'How can I eat kheer with this spoon, son? It's meant for drinking gripe water.' Or when posing for a photograph with a fan, he instructs, 'Don't look towards the camera, look at me.'

Such are the countless stories that dot the landscape of Gulzar's personal world. He is a school for all of us because we discover that at every stage of his life, he has embarked on learning something new. From learning the sitar to translating the writings of poets of different languages, he keeps expanding his art. A senior poet who is so contemporary that he receives fresh images from the Hubble telescope on his iPad every day! Which is possibly why, in 'Pluto', Gulzar is able to say:

There are countless other planets in the universe
Let's look to find some other master of our life
There must be yet another god somewhere...

15.

The grammar of Gulzar's poetry is unique. He transforms the tradition of Urdu into Hindustani and presents it. From the simplicity of Kabir to the refinement of Ghalib, one can find both in Gulzar's imagery. Seers and sages have ploughed their thoughts into the soil from where his poems originate.

His poetry is friends with the moon. A later chapter elaborates on the image we get in his poems and songs resulting from his affinity for the moon. It's worth seeing how he washes the grey meanings of words used in poetry with the waters of the rivers and makes them sparkle. This is the reason that the Ravi at times, and the Chenab at others, flow from his pen. It's another matter that his poetry is also friendly with the cities, where often the car horns that sound from the thoroughfares can shatter the deepest sleep. Even as he sinks deep into his many worlds, he also moves ahead in life in contemporary ways. Keeping in step with his poetry implies marching along with his modern thoughts but keeping alive the legacy of the past. That is quintessential Gulzar; though wrought out of the clay of tradition, his vision includes progressive thought. Even as he explores the potential of new ideas, he will engage in kite battles on the terrace.

The journey of his poetics is such that his poems repeatedly search through his being and he tries to capture poetry in all possible variations of form. If we express this using Neruda's poetic style, then Gulzar's poetry never leaves his hem, clinging regardless of age. Even as he grows older, Gulzar's poetic expression too extends itself to keep pace.

16.

Gulzar's story, 'Satranga'. Some stories have their own history that come into existence due to some ideological debate. As a youth Gulzar would attend gatherings of progressive writers where his seniors would often engage in heated discussions on a variety of issues, Gulzar too would enter such discussions seeking answers to complex questions that he was not confident of understanding at his age. Once just such a gathering of the PWA was in progress, attended by many senior writers, including Balraj Sahni. The topic of discussion was, 'The role of writers in society'. Many were of the opinion that the farmer, the labourer and others of the working class would play the most important role in structuring a progressive state. Gulzar was not quite in agreement with this thought. However, he had no counterpoint to offer. He was new to the group, so he would try to reconcile the issues with his existence.

Gulzar wondered if they were all collected there for something immaterial but he did not put forth his thoughts at the meeting. He wanted a solution to the dissonance between his beliefs and those of his seniors. This was the circumstance that urged the writing of 'Satranga', a story that referenced the non-vital existence of the arts against the importance of work. He read out the story in the next meeting of the PWA. 'Satranga' was a response made in defence or as a parallel line of thought to counter the reference made regarding artists.

The village where Khairu, Najjo, Mamdu, Heera and movie actors weave the story of 'Satranga', has Khairu singing 'Ghutan-tung, Ghutan-tung' as he strives to makes tassels, paint the bullocks' horns, tie bells around their necks, and etch pictures in different places. This makes the story remarkable from the point of view of art too.

Here, music is a metaphor hidden in the efforts that the labourer does not comprehend but which an artist, by pointing out, makes into a comprehensive example of incomparable art. Poignantly written, the purpose of this story was to segment the difference between art and labour, which Gulzar does, creating an argument of his own in the group of progressive writers. Reading 'Satranga' brings to mind the many other stories like 'Seema', 'Michaelangelo', 'Narangi' and 'Saanjh' that identify the combination of poet and writer in Gulzar's psyche.

17.

Gulzar is an artiste with a philosophical bent of mind. We can see this very clearly in his film songs. Even in films with commonplace themes, he writes songs for his characters that, through their inner meanings, are rooted in literature. He spontaneously creates moments which convey a philosophical joy. In other words, Gulzar has emerged as a lyricist who puts forward weighty concepts in a simple way, yet packs a philosophical message of some kind in them.

For example in the film *Gharonda*, this philosophical concept is shown very beautifully.

The heart is an empty vessel
And the night a blind well
In these deserted, dark eyes
Smoke wells up instead of tears

There is no reason to live
I seek an excuse to die
I, alone in the city

(*Gharonda*)

In these lines are encapsulated the conflicts of loneliness and displacement that Gulzar faced in his childhood and youth. By describing a city which cannot accept people as they are and scratches at their failures to deepen the wound, Gulzar invests meaning into the emptiness of days and the silences of the night.

It's another matter that this 'emptiness' that Gulzar mentions always comes like the evening, instead of the night. He has cast the evening, the time between day and night, in a manner suited to the poet's temperament and has always said that the evening is that special period that makes its own space between old and new memories, between ties and detachment and in the interval between words and poetry. He explains this in a film song:

I found the dawn, the night and noontime too
But I chose the evening, no I am not sad
It's just a quiet that has come upon me
Somewhere my breath has stilled, no, I'm not sad

(*Sannata*)

Using emptiness as a concept, Gulzar adds additional layers to his film lyrics, which proves that he is a poet who does not just mirror the character's mood. This is no mean achievement for a lyricist who, even in his commercial work, manages to find a way to save a corner for his poetic conscience. In this song from *Maachis*, the evening's desolation must be seen in the same context:

Haunt not my memory, cause not my blood to weep
He lived in my eyes, but rising
Went who knows where...
The lamps of the evening had not even opened their eyes
The night left us blind
Do not torment me anymore, haunt not my memory

(*Maachis*)

Trapping the emptiness differently, he interprets it to contain and express sorrow, separation, depression and pain which, as evening approaches, suddenly find expression. When choosing a metaphor to describe loneliness, Gulzar always thinks that it should bring with it the silken perception of an evening approaching quietly.

Empty-handed the evening has come
Empty-handed she will return

The night's inkiness
Will someone not erase it

If not erased today then she
Will go back tomorrow too
Empty-handed the evening has come

(*Ijazat*)

The evening is present beyond the realm of his film songs, and even in his poems and trivenis (succinct three-line compositions). We can state that Gulzar the lyricist and Gulzar the poet think and walk together on the same path. These lines from his book *Kuch Aur Nazme* (Some More Poems) describes the beauty of the eventide:

Blurred and lazy, the evening
And time too was stale when it came to the city
Silence stood wrapped around every bough
And clung to every wall

It is not necessary to add that this emptiness and silence also hold within them the deceit and fear of being left behind, which the poet experiences constantly. Reading the various versions of metaphors of the evening that Gulzar uses to describe loneliness brings to mind many other writers, some of whom are his contemporaries.

When the matchless Hindi poet Shamsher Bahadur Singh says of the shadow of the evening: 'Ek peeli shaam/ Patjhar ka zaraa atkaa hua patta' (A yellow evening/ An autumn leaf still left on the bough), this conceit is similar to Gulzar's thought. And if we go to the masters, then Mir Taqi Mir has: 'Shaam hi se bujhaa sa rehta hai/ Dil hai goya chiraag muflis ka' (Come evening, it extinguishes/ This heart, like a beggar's lamp) or Faiz Ahmed Faiz for whom the evening arrives to share all kinds of loneliness, silence and pain. The colour of Faiz-sahab's evening is somewhat like this: 'Ab kabhi shaam bujhegi na andhera hoga/ Ab kabhi raat dhalegi na saveraa hoga' (Now, never will the evening fade, nor darkness fall/ Never will the night pass nor morning come). And this mood is also worth examining: Shaam-e-firaaq ab naa pooch aai aur aa ke tal gayi/ Dil tha ke phir bahal gaya, jaan thi ke phir sambhal gayi' (Ask not about the evening of separation, it arrived and ended of itself / The heart consoled itself, life got back on keel).

Gulzar's depiction of the evening in his films, even as it walks in step with the legacy of Mir, Faiz and Shamsher, takes on a new form. When Gulzar writes songs, especially film songs, he presents the same situation in different lights; experiences that we understand in the present context. Having seen life up close, the poet often invests the character he is creating with some of the pain. Though it is not any less meaningful to see the positive side of his poetic self which, despite the deceitful world, believes in being affectionate and cordial. Without this, we would not be able to glean from his films and poetry the moments that teach us life's lessons. In the songs of *Sadma* and *Thodi Si Bewafai* we can glimpse the positivity that comes from the poet's own experiences that always looks at life with hope. Perhaps going through these lines will lift our spirits:

Apart today, with no fear of the morrow.
Life is not that short

Those who pass judgment have nothing to lose
They who bear the pain do so with grit
Who will seek the answer to suffering...
People just ask questions
Apart today, with no fear of the morrow.

(*Thodi Si Bewafai*)

~

Come life, embrace me
I too have embraced
Every one of your sorrows...haven't I?

It was a small shadow, cast upon my eyes
With two droplets, I filled my heart
O life, I have found the shore.

(*Sadma*)

There are countless songs in which Gulzar reaches out to embrace life. In innumerable songs, his creative expression shows ways of coming to terms with life when it seems to be put out of joint, and of bringing it back on track, in a manner that lifts it to the level of literature. One cannot separate the poem from the poet, or the thought from the experience of life. As is evident in this poem:

Come, let's recite a poem again

Yet again embrace a sorrow and inflame our eyes
Yet again lance an aching nerve
Or, turning to look back on a forgotten path
Call out to some namesake
Let's recite a poem...

18.

In the hallowed ground of Hindi film lyricists, Gulzar inarguably holds a high position. His unusual entry into the field happened at a time when a long line of talented lyricists like Sahir Ludhianvi, Majrooh Sultanpuri, Shakeel Badayuni, Kaifi Azmi, Jan Nisar Akhtar, Hasrat Jaipuri and Raja Mehdi Ali Khan ruled the roost. Poets who were partial to the Hindi language included Pt. Narendra Sharma, Shailendra, Prem Dhawan and Yogesh Mazbooti. Apart from all of them, the Punjabi-speaking Anand Bakshi also gained fame during this time. He claimed his place in Hindi lyric-writing in the 1970s and his track record in writing songs is matched only by Laxmikant Pyarelal.

Among these names, Gulzar has his own presence as a respected poet, whose role as an Urdu poet blends with his persona as a writer of Hindustani lyrics. Cleaving his way through life, he makes his own way to balance Hindi and Urdu and take his place as a writer of songs in Hindustani. Hindi, Urdu and Punjabi words percolate through his work in much the same way as the common man juggles languages while speaking. This is his strength, and the route that set Gulzar zooming on the musical highway.

Gulzar has always been adept at delicately weaving beautiful words, laden with meaning, into his poems. He is alert to the fact that his writing must not remain confined to a gathering of poets, a mehfil, but must delight the common man.

In writing the pain-laden song for *Masoom*, he has translated a thought he has often expressed: 'One day he came face to face with life. Life asked him, "What is pain? Why does pain exist? Where? Even this no one knows. What is loneliness; with so many people around, why are you lonely?" Life looked me in the face and said, "I am your twin. Do not be angry with me."' Such monologues mark his relationship with his songs, and one understands the emotional link a creator has with his creation.

I am not angry with you, Life
I am exasperated
Your innocent questions
Make me anxious

I am not angry with you, Life,
I am exasperated

To live life, I never thought
I would have to cope with pain
If I smile, I will need to
Pay off the debt of that smile
Whenever I smile, I feel
As if a debt is placed on my lips

I am not angry with you, Life,
I am exasperated

(*Masoom*)

Perhaps Gulzar is the only film lyricist who, in almost every alternate composition considering the character, situation and background, creates an argument for himself. Check the LPs launched by various music companies of their selection of favourites, or the opinions on Vividh Bharati or even the interview with broadcaster Ameen Sayani for Binaca *Geetmala* and there is enough evidence of the fact that he wrote the poem first and the music directors composed the music for it later. This is unusual and throws light on the calibre of the song writer. As an example, listen to his commentary in his record *Fursat Ke Raat Din* and you will realise that the poet is articulating his thoughts. And this is true not only of Gulzar's writing but can be found in the work of any capable songwriter in any era; be it Sahir Ludhianvi or Majrooh Sultanpuri, Indeevar or Anand Bakshi.

In Gulzar's words:

> A song is a portrait of a mood, a situation. Plant some fitting words, draw the line of a song along it, and the song starts breathing. Comes to life. That is the brief life of a song, just for that moment...*haan*! Some songs live for years. Songs do not age, they grow no wrinkles on their faces, they continue to flourish, to keep going on... the age of the listener changes, then they say, 'Yes, when the peak of that mountain is shrouded in cloud, then a voice resounds.'

Explaining the forging of a poem in poetic words, Gulzar does love the songs he writes, but he can sometimes detach himself from them too. When he says, 'songs do not age', one of the subtexts is also that poets will keep appearing and composing as the ages change but the poems will remain fresh and relevant. Even after the poet is gone, each word will glow with life. Ali Sardar Jafri has said this in his own way:

> *Tread respectfully, this is Ghalib's territory*
> *Tread respectfully, here is Mir's mausoleum*

Gulzar's lyrics lean towards the liberal and the humanist. He gives them a form and substance that is always fresh, even though the reader who experiences them ages. To an extent this is the responsibility of the arts to contemplate the possibility that even when the poet himself is gone, his art becomes timeless. Just as Gulzar endows the poems of the moment with the gift of agelessness, this is also true of poems in languages from across the world. Though, in his case, even the songs that are by definition songs written for films can also be seen as timeless creations.

The emotions and poetry that Gulzar has gathered for us in connection with film songs can be experienced through the character who is dealing with life's problems. In the long list of his compositions, we can find such songs that will continue to be relevant beyond the present.

19.

Gulzar's first film as a director was *Mere Apne* (1971). With this film, he brought to the fore those aspects of filmmaking experiences that he had shared with Bimal Roy and Hrishikesh Mukherjee over a period of time. His very first film as an independent director was a clear sign of how, emerging from the learnings, he was ready to put forth his ideas and thoughts.

Mere Apne was based on Tapan Sinha's National Award-winning Bengali film *Apan Jan*. An interesting story connected with *Apan Jan* is that producer N. C. Sippy wanted to buy rights to remake the film in Hindi. He was aware that the rights were in Gulzar's keeping, which N. C. Sippy hoped to get for some well-known director to direct for his banner. Tapan Sinha, desirous of a Hindi version of his film, had got Gulzar to work on the screenplay. Later, it transpired that Tapan Sinha changed his mind on the remake in Hindi, but the script remained with Gulzar, who approached N. C. Sippy and told him with great self-confidence, 'I want to direct this.'

Gulzar-sahab says that when N. C. Sippy came over to his place to listen to his narration, he told him something with such emphatic confidence that Sippy was convinced enough to make *Mere Apne* happen.

Gulzar said, 'Tapan Sinha has made a Hindi film in Bangla, using a dream sequence, dance and songs. I want to make a Bangla film in Hindi, but with a straightforward narrative, and no romantic angle.'

These were the words of a young songwriter who had written only screenplays and dialogues and the financing and making of whose first film was yet to be finalised. This was the training of the Bimal Roy 'school' expressing itself, and the confidence of a poet steeped in poetry that advocated social reform, and the self-esteem of a writer who had successful film scripts to his name. N. C. Sippy agreed, and work on the planning for *Mere Apn*e began.

Gulzar used the medium of film in *Mere Apne* to reflect the image of the social and political condition of the time.

The seventies had spread anger and desperation among the youth, as there were not enough jobs for all. Graduates with a B.A. degree to their name were unable to find even low-paying jobs, and political parties had infiltrated colleges to create followers who would, end up eventually as offenders of the law. To depict this condition of discontent and desperation, the scenario of *Mere Apne* was shifted from Calcutta to Allahabad in Uttar Pradesh.

The film operates at three levels. Gulzar knits three strands to create his story. First, he uses Anandi Devi or Nani-ma, a widow, as the narrator or, in dramatic terms, as the sutradhar, a role essayed with much empathy by Meena Kumari. Her role portrays a woman steeped in humanity and love who tries to apply the salve of maternal love in the lives of strife-ridden, warring youths. Anandi Devi portrays a woman who knows the harsh truth of life and that life cannot be lived without accepting it. Despite this, she lives in hope and tries to sidestep the challenges and humiliations that come her way. In one of the most gut-wrenching portions of the film, actor Ramesh Deo takes her to the city with the intention of making her a house-help, having given her the false assurance that he is distantly related to her. Later, Anandi Devi realises the duplicity and Ramesh Deo and his wife Sumita Sanyal throw her out of the house. The dialogue that Meena speaks lingers in memory. 'So, are mothers too sold on the market now?' she asks.

The second strand is that of the youth who are good-hearted and work for one another with team spirit, but are aimless and lost. Society feels they are of no use, though that is not the case. From keeping their neighbourhood safe to helping the poor and hungry, and dealing with their friends with empathy despite their joblessness, they behave like good human beings. Gulzar gives these young men a song of sarcasm that focuses on the state of society and the politics of that time:

We are tiptop
Everything is A-okay
We have a BA, we have an MA
What for, we say
There are no jobs to be had
But with your blessings
Everything is A-okay

The youth have divided themselves into two groups. One is led by the kind and honest Shyam (played by Vinod Khanna) and the other by the somewhat cunning and crooked Chenu (played by Shatrughan Sinha). Their friendship, enmity and the diverse ways in which they become pawns of political parties who exploit them, is depicted in detail. When Gulzar was making this film, he would not have imagined that what he thought was relevant to the times fifty years ago would still be half a century later.

The third strand is made up of a collage of small scenes that have no direct bearing on the story, but supplement the main theme, adding strength to its development. Hark back to the scene when, as the angry students are breaking up the furniture in the university campus, one of the group starts playing, 'Saare jahaan se achcha Hindustan hamara' (Our Hindustan is the best in all of the world). When Shyam's gang beats up Asrani, who belongs to Chenu's gang, Meena Kumari takes him to her house, where two orphans have given her shelter, to tend to him. When he starts back after being bandaged, Anandi Devi says, 'Beta, don't put your feet on the ground, give them rest so they can heal quickly.' Hearing this, the awakening of sympathy in the wicked man's heart in the way he turns to look with a measure of love at Meena Kumari is a unique picturisation of the return of humanity to a lost soul.

Throughout the film, flashbacks are used whenever Anandi Devi thinks of her husband Niranjan (played by Deven Verma). His quiet entries and the episodes where he is seen interacting with his wife are filmed so that they symbolise a cool, soothing breeze in Anandi Devi's strife-torn life. This adds a contemporary feel to *Mere Apne*.

Meena Kumari's role remains the most pivotal one in the film. Weighed down by grief, she leaves her lonely but quiet life in the village to move to the city, where her deception begins. She is unable to comprehend why life in the city lacks warmth and humanity and does not allow bonds to form between people. Anandi Devi's biggest sorrow is that there is not one person in the city whom she can call her own. The sorrow she feels about this is what Gulzar alludes to in the title and he imbues the character with the qualities of piety, empathy and maternal love, and no negative traits. She meets every situation with neutrality and this results in her being hit by a bullet fired during a fight between Shyam and Chenu. Meena Kumari's loneliness in *Mere Apne* is akin to Ingmar Bergman's hero in *Wild Strawberries*, who is cursed to always be lonely. In a dream sequence in Bergman's film, the hero asks the judge about his punishment. The judge responds,

'Your loneliness is your punishment.' In a different scenario, Meena Kumari is suffering from the same condition and, instead of a dream sequence, a flashback allows her to imagine the happiness of her past moments of companionship with her husband, Niranjan.

If the plot adds a touch of melodrama to the ending, a closer examination shows that to close the infighting that divides those of the new generation one from the other, and to bring them back from where they have strayed, the intervention of a respected elder from the older generation has always been necessary. Whether it is in connection with the changing of ideas or with social or political change, Nani-ma tries to erase the animosity between Shyam and Chenu. She is fond of Shyam, but is not against Chenu. The film tries to put forward the idea that the language of hate and anger does not differentiate between right and wrong. Meena Kumari's character is a metaphor for the inability of even accountable people to solve the negative issues that hound the political and social aspects of a society. In this context, Gulzar successfully presents a possible political solution in *Mere Apne*.

One of the highlights of the film is Salil Chowdhury's music. He used his genius to create four exceptional songs in an experimental style. Though the music disc of the film has four songs, only two of them have been filmed, 'Haalchaal theek thak hai' (We are tiptop) and 'Koi hota jisko apna' (I wish there was someone I could call my own) both sung by Kishore Kumar; whereas 'Roz akeli aye, roz akeli jaye/ Chand katora leke bhikaran raat' (The night arrives alone every day and leaves alone / Carrying the moon like a begging bowl) by Lata Mangeshkar and the song in Manna Dey's voice, 'Ganga ki bhari godh mein/ Ganga ke raahi chale re' (Wayfarers of the Ganga traverse her fecund lap) are also on the disc.

'Roz akeli aye', which is based on Nazrul geet, songs created by the cult poet Kazi Nazrul Islam, and sung to the tune of the Bangla original 'Meghla nishi bhore/ Mon je kemon kore' (It's clouded over night and day/ What shall the heart do) by Lata Mangeshkar, is a wonderful adaptation. It is regrettable that despite all his efforts, Gulzar could not shoot the song with Meena-ji. Her health was failing at that time and the film had to be completed without further delay. He did not want to use the song, expressed so beautifully, as a background number either. By the time the film was in its last stages, Meena Kumari was too sick to return to the sets. Finally, Gulzar did use a brief version of the song in the film. Meena Kumari passed away in 1972, a few months after the release of *Mere Apne*.

'Koi hota jisko apna', sung by Kishore Kumar for Vinod Khanna, is a rare gift to the film from Salil Chowdhury. The song highlights a new aspect of Gulzar's skilful penmanship. Two songs sung by Kishore Kumar which had been written by him, and were released before *Mere Apne*, come to mind in this context. These were the timeless numbers, 'Hawaon pe likh do, hawaon ke naam/ Hum anjaan pardesiyon ka salaam' (Write upon the breeze/ Greetings from us wayfarers) (*Do Dooni Chaar*, 1968) and 'Woh shaam kuch ajeeb thi/ Yeh shaam bhi ajeeb hai' (That was a strange evening/ This evening is strange too) (*Khamoshi*, 1969).

'Haalchaal theek thak hai', is a sarcastic comment on the times, but must also be viewed as a mirror of Gulzar's sentiment. Moving away from the very popular romantic songs he had written so far, the social issues that Gulzar portrayed in *Mere Apne* remain as tangled and real today. In some ways, the song is even more relevant now. The 5 November 2017 issue of *Brunch* carried the fact that in an interview with lyricist Kausar Minar, Gulzar had said, 'My songs are neither angry nor bitter, because I am not filled with bitterness myself. I am also full of hope, as an artist should be, not just for his own future, nor for his children's future, but for the entire world.' This statement gives us a deeper insight into the song.

More than fifty years have passed since *Mere Apne* was released. Across villages, towns and cities, students are involved in politics, as both national and local parties, including state-level parties, have staked claims. The resultant turmoil is evident everywhere. Even today, qualified youth have no means of earning a livelihood as jobs are scarce. Added to this are the layoffs happening across the world, especially of those working in the digital space. A new form of conflict, suppression and anger is evident among a large portion of today's youth. *Mere Apne*'s message and the societal questions it poses resonate louder today. Even today there are countless Shyams and Chenus around us who have become pawns in the hands of power brokers. It's another matter that the angry young men are now armed with modern weapons that have replaced the hockey sticks, knives and country-made bombs.

Viewing *Mere Apne* from all aspects and comparing it with our present, the fact emerges that Gulzar is in all ways a filmmaker portraying hope. His films raise questions and evoke dreams of inclusive ways of solving them. If he were not a poet and filmmaker leaning on hope, he would never have created a character like Anandi Devi. He emphatically feels that there should be someone whom one can call one's own:

Someone who would share my sorrow,
Someone who would be a friend
If only there was someone, someone my own,
I could call him my own, my friends
There would be some comfort, someone who was mine
If not nearby, then at least afar, someone who was mine...

20.

The softly flowing river face shrouded in evening mists
Eyes burning in the mistiness of a tawny visage
The spiral of smoke from the endlessly burning cigarette
The faraway voice heavy with sleep.

Shadowed below unknown thoughts that flew above
A face that seemed etched out of molten wax
The sound of every new dream transforms him
Making it seem he would neither sleep, nor wake, nor speak
A silent flowing river shrouded in evening mists.

('Bimal Roy: A Portrait')

A point worth noting about the nature of the poet in Gulzar is that he, at some point or the other, has created portraits of whosoever he might have worked with in the worlds of cinema and literature and learnt something from. In fact, this extended to anyone who impressed him. It is as if he wishes to cage in the relationship he has with that person by creating a portrait that defines it.

In the process of creating these bonds, he has, almost without being aware of it, instinctively delved into each of their lives.

Gulzar-sahab once explained in detail his special reason for the portraits he creates of friends and mentors. I had wondered whether, like cartoonists who pick subjects from the society around them to draw in their unique style, he too crafted his portrait poems for a similar purpose.

In response, Gulzar-sahab explained succinctly, 'No, it's not like that. I had a connection with painting and would visit art exhibitions. I did have a leaning towards painting, and would often sit down with a brush to paint. It is a beautiful experience, playing with colours. It's quite a different sensibility when you pick up colours with a brush and apply them on canvas. It's very beautiful...it's not necessary to paint a portrait or figure. It's a way to express the love felt for the brush and colours and to broaden one's sensibilities in a spontaneous way.

'As you are aware, I worked in a motor garage before working for Bimal-da. My job there was to mix colours and apply them to accident-scarred vehicles so that the faults could not be seen. The experience thus gave me an understanding of this art form. Which is why I started writing landscape poems. I wrote some sketches too, in which you get the feel of sketches drawn by a pencil. I also made sketches that were more like portraits, and named them as such. You can write a portrait only when you know the person intimately. When a painter paints a portrait of someone on canvas, it is not necessary for him to create a perfect likeness. Neither is it necessary that the complete personality of the person be captured on canvas. It is quite enough to show an impression through with a few strokes. What the painter says as a comment through his brush and paint is more important, and the reason why people go to art galleries to see the works of great painters. A faithful facsimile of the face is also unnecessary; that can be seen in a photograph. A painting should reveal some aspect of the personality that no one has seen. Or even if someone has, he has not expressed it in this manner. Just as it is possible in painting to make a comment through a portrait, the same possibility exists in poetry. As an example, I will say that I wrote the portrait of Bimal-da exactly as I saw him.'

This logical explanation adds greater value to these poems. These are not just tributes to Gulzar-sahab's contemporaries and elders, but a conceptual design that includes the ability to see a person close to him reflected through a comment, an idea. Which is why giants like Mirza Ghalib, Rabindranath Tagore, Jibanananda Das, Ahmed Nadeem Kasmi, Gopichand Narang, and film personalities like Bimal Roy, Salil Chowdhury, Rahul Dev Burman, Basu Bhattacharya, Sanjeev Kumar, Naseeruddin Shah, Meghna Gulzar, and painter Jatin Das, when seen through the eyes of a portrait creator like Gulzar, show up in a new understanding. The poem dedicated to the memory of his inseparable friend, the ghazal singer Jagjit Singh, is also an expansion of his own view of the singer. Besides the portrait, Gulzar has also written a 'Marsiya', an elegy, for him:

A strange chill had arrived
And settled like a lump of ice in his heart
He would set alight a kangri of ghazals and warm himself

When he returned after lighting his son's pyre
He skipped stones across the water's surface
Watched them like horses run

Trembling at times with the cold
He would shroud himself in sunlight

I heard that when the snow fell yesterday on the mountains
He opened his window and went to warm himself
On the fire of a burning pyre.

('Marsiya')

The respect Gulzar has for all the subjects of his poems is evident as one reads through them, as is the warmth of the relationship each had with him.

If you are a follower of Gulzar's work, you will understand the hope that shines through the portraits. Despite this, to get closer to his feelings, it is necessary to know the background to each poem. Tagore's portrait, for example, should be viewed through these lines that show Gulzar's own relationship with Rabindranath Tagore, which resulted from his passage through the poet's literary work. The poem is about a person he could never meet. In fact, he meets him through this poem, and the poem is a testament to the relationship between the two poets,

With a chunk of gur tied on his head, a rustic
Was crossing a vast maidan, long and wide
Hearing the fragrance of the gur,
A canopy of bees hummed over his head
The sun rose higher and in the growing heat
The gur started to melt.

The simple villager was astonished
Drops of gur were running down his face
And he was licking them.

I'm a villager too,

Who placed the sweet gur of Tagore's poems
On my head?

'Tagore'

As it was with Tagore, so it is with Mirza Ghalib. Fans of Gulzar are aware of the depth of his relationship with Ghalib. He adopts Ghalib as a teacher without ever having met him. Much like the thread that bound Nizamuddin Auliya and Amir Khusro. Much like the intimate bond that links a disciple of classical music to his guru. This bond between the skilled professional artiste and his student creates an innate harmony. Gulzar has linked himself to Mirza Ghalib, in just the same way, following the tenets of the guru-shishya tradition. This needs to be kept in mind while reading the poem 'Portrait of Ghalib', which I am presenting in full:

The lanes of Ballimaran that like 'tedious arguments' run
Odes on quails by people standing at the firewood shop,
Mouths full of paan, wah wah
Curtains of tattered jute hang from some doorways
The sound of a goat bleating
And the gloomy shadows of the evening mists
Move so closely embracing the walls as if
'Badi Bi' of Chudiwalan, with dimmed sight
Is groping her way to find the door.
From this gloomy and dark 'Gali Qasim'
Lamps send out trails of light
A page opens in the Koran of the intellect
And the address of Asadullah Ghalib's home is revealed!

Ghalib's world, in all its multi-coloured detail, complete with emotions and the pulsating stories of his life, is reflected in this poem.

Jibanananda Das too enters Gulzar's world through the same prism of respect. To live in that world permanently as a friend of the poet. A few lines of the poem 'Mone Podh! Jibananda Das' may be read to understand the warmth and beauty of this relationship:

I was half asleep when he called out.
Perhaps he had jumped down from a moving tram, and...
his feet splashed into the waters of a lake
Spreading both his wings the swan left the lake and
Flew away with a 'shain shain' of its wings
Shedding the 'shunali' fragrance
The eagle to its nest has returned...

In his unique poetic style, Gulzar presents us with poems that celebrate his links with literature, through his links with Mirza Ghalib, Rabindranath Tagore and Jibanananda Das. His method of delineating their portraits brings to mind the definition given by Octavio Paz who has said, 'Every reader is a poet, and every poem is another poem.' Similarly, as he sketches the three poets through his poem, Gulzar uses his pen like a reader who expresses his feelings with the capability of a poet.

We can also view the poems Gulzar has written on those whom he shared a long stretch of his personal and creative life. Bimal Roy, Salil Chowdhury, Basu Bhattacharya, R. D. Burman, Sanjeev Kumar, Naseeruddin Shah and Jagjit Singh are relevant here.

The poem on Salil Chowdhury is Gulzar's expression of gratitude for Salil-da:

The trembling surface of a pond
The roar of a storm held in check by a thread
Spring into sound at the slightest touch

Let not the speed of a flight entangled with itself
Fall behind in fear of itself
The speed of a flight defeated by itself

(Salil Chowdhury)

If we read the poems written about Bimal-da and Salil Chowdhury, we can see how, through a hint, comment or some impression of the subject's personality, Gulzar presents the person to us:

The softly flowing river face shrouded in the evening mists
Eyes burning in the mistiness of a tawny visage
The spiral of smoke from the endlessly burning cigarette
The faraway voice heavy with sleep…

Reading these opening lines one can recollect the last days of Gulzar's connection with Bimal-da, when Bimal-da was working on the screenplay of his ambitious feature film, *Amrit Kumbh Ki Khoj* (In Search of the Divine Kumbh) with Gulzar. The film was based on a novel by Samaresh Basu. Bimal-da would write notes connected to the screenplay every day. This was at a time when, riddled with cancer, Bimal Roy was facing his last days. Addicted to smoking, he had, all through his life, smoked incessantly and surreptitiously. When Gulzar talks about the soft voice soaked in sleep, it reflects the unspoken companionship between master and pupil. The portrait that emerges is pure verisimilitude.

The perspectives of viewing art that British art critic, John Berger, talks about in his renowned book, *Ways of Seeing*, are vindicated by Gulzar in the very unique way he writes his portraits, landscapes and sketches. Berger writes, 'Seeing comes before words…The way we see things is affected by what we know or what we believe.'

Gulzar too does the same through his experience, making the most of the opportunities to study people closely. He uses this to capture the personae in his portraits. In one way he has created a new definition for these pictures, which needs to be viewed from the point of one artist looking at another.

As an example, one should read the a few lines of the portrait of Naseeruddin Shah which, drawing from the words and gestures exchanged between an actor and his director, creates an image that comes alive:

A performer am I
Yet not just an actor
But one who must live
Many lifetimes in one life.

My persona changes, each day on set
My circumstances change.
My looks change too, to match story and spectacle
My habits I change, and then,
I cannot rid myself of the stains my garbs leave on my skin...

The poem written about Ahmed Nadeem Kasmi, Pakistan's famous poet, and Gulzar's dear friend should also be mentioned here, as it celebrates the bond between the two men. Only someone who has discussed Kasmi-sahab with him can understand the respect Gulzar holds for him. In any meeting that a reference to Ahmed Nadeem Kasmi would come up, Gulzar-sahab's face would light up. He has written a portrait as well as an elegy on Kasmi. Notice how in the portrait, he pays his respect to Kasmi-sahab as he assumes new forms in a changing landscape:

When the lamp burns out
A slight smoke rises
When the diminished sun sets
Long after sunset
The sky of steel glows with its light
When leaves break away
They float for a distance.

Why then, as you were leaving
Did you not turn and look back even once
You just held your breath and
Wrapped in soil, you went to sleep

Even today, as he stands in the garden of words holding a fresh sheaf of new poems, ghazals and stories, he uses all the colours he ekes out of the verdant surroundings to continue his journey as a writer.

Sometimes he feels it necessary to etch a 'Self Portrait'. Perhaps so that it is documented and can come in handy when needed. Here are the opening lines:

On the mirror, every day, I record
My face and all its distinguishing features

So that I make no mistake in recognising it
When I return.
Yet, something or the other changes
On each succeeding day.

21.

The literature that Gulzar has been writing about his birth place, Dina, (now in Pakistan) contains documentation that were added incidentally. Though he might never have considered it to be a part of history, his writing is fast being identified and remembered as such.

By writing a memoir-like story on the well-known journalist, Kuldip Nayyar, titled 'Kuldip Nayyar and Pir Sahab', he has lit up the literary world. Though it presents the story of India intimately, starting from Independence to the first quarter of the 21st century, Nayyar, in his own autobiography *Beyond the Lines* does not portray himself in this manner. Gulzar writes about Nayyar-sahab as if he is creating a character to embed into his realistic film.

For many years, Gulzar has been visiting the Wagah border on 14th August, the eve of Independence Day. He, along with his friends, raise slogans to celebrate Indo-Pak friendship, and when the hour of midnight strikes, they light torches to welcome India's Independence Day. Innumerable people gather at this demonstration, but the important fact is that Gulzar depicts a scene through which he shows what can be considered a testimony to the friendly connections between India and Pakistan.

In the heart of this short story nestles the memory of Pir-sahab which is attached to Nayyar-sahab's house. One winter day, Nayyar-sahab had come to offer a traditional chadar at the tomb of Nizamuddin Auliya, which he carried back with him to Sialkot. The memory of Pir-sahab might gladden your heart through the end of the story, but the barb that continuously grates against the heart is perhaps what Gulzar experiences, which is his reason for writing this story.

Through the medium of Kuldip Nayyar this is what Gulzar thinks is important to say:

> If a road runs straight like this, and neither gate, nor hurdle come in the way, nor anyone stop to question why, or check passports, and I travel around Pakistan and return, will I be looting that country? There is no dearth of looters in this country, nor in that! Why do they need to come from outside?

But he does not end there. Gulzar says the following lines too, through Nayyar: 'Finally, that is my country too! A big part of me lies there...'

It is this that takes Gulzar and Kuldip Nayyar to the Wagah border, to see whether the road could continue in this manner, and both of them could go to Sialkot and Dina. It would be like going home and returning.

22.

The poet Amrita Pritam wrote an opinion piece after reading Gulzar's poem in the January 1994 issue of *Dharmyug* magazine. According to Amrita Pritam:

> 'In putting his thought into words, Gulzar has maintained the dignity of a silence that can be felt but not expressed. That kind of silence that despite finding a script cannot utter words. Gulzar is a very adorable poet. I am presenting one of his poems:
>
> *The cold wind blew all night*
> *All night I warmed my hands at the fireplace*
> *I broke up some dry branches of the past*
> *You tore up some leaves of moments gone by*
> *I pulled out some dried poems from my pockets*
> *You too opened some withered letters with your hands...*

She elaborates on the poem and adds:

> Passing by these words, I can feel the trembling of a smouldering relationship; to the extent that the eyes move to that part of the paper that is blank, and one feels a trembling has spread over that blank space...Gulzar has recognised the strong point of the relationship wrapped in years, and has borne the weight of it too, which for, who knows how many years, has sat heavy in his heart...I can say that what Gulzar has written in this condition today, sheltering the pain of his condition in his heart and filling his veins with its blood, is a document that is created by weaving minute idea-threads together.'

Even now, it is reassuring to know that nothing has changed in almost a decade and a half, when a renowned Punjabi poet felt a sympathetic trembling and wrote openly about it. For Gulzar, his poems have never walked the route taken by his successful contemporaries. Despite being active in the medium of cinema and writing songs for films, the poet in him, while writing for himself, has kept a constant distance from the romanticism of film music. You will never see him following a trend that prevails in film music while writing his poems. Though often, at various times, he does bring in issues that concern society and which trouble him. But the question is whether, while crafting songs of romantic love, this poet has ever turned his back on contemporary problems.

The answer is simple. Never has the poet ever turned away from his most important role of questioning. It can be said, reading what Amrita Pritam has said further on in her critique, that Gulzar has always, with poetic protocol, used his poetry to highlight bitter truths. So many of his poems are proclamations to make one conscious of the prevailing times. Examples include, 'Speaker', 'Parinde Hain Ya Parcham' (Are These Birds or Flags), 'Kabaddi', 'Muhafiz' (Protector), 'Bahut Se Masle Le Kar Gaya Tha' (I Had Gone with Many Complaints), 'Jalsa' (Celebration), 'Ek Manzar' (A Spectacle).

Poems that are interventions in society that a poet places before the world.

It's surprising that Amrita Pritam, who was partial to the romantic content of Gulzar's poems, while gauging the poems revolving around social themes, has also tried to subtly grasp his societal concerns.

Her view on the poem, 'That poet, he would remain silent/ He would ramble meaninglessly…' is worth reading. 'Whosoever has discovered the result of annihilation of self will find it very difficult to hold on to those tough moments when the threads of a relationship are being torn asunder.'

If we weigh Gulzar's more recent work with his older creations, we will find that he has written a moving, sympathetic poem on the 'Ghar Wapsi' (The Return Home) of labourers, who had to return to their villages due to the Covid outbreak: 'They will go die there/ Where life is…' which he posted on many digital media.

The agitation he feels as he looks at the events that take place in society and the world beyond is evident in his poetry. Amrita Pritam has termed it the capacity to 'shelter the pain of the times in his heart'. Often he even includes his favourite poetic motif, the moon, in his perception of society; changing the very nature of the moon in the process.

The imagery of the moon in the poem below sheds further light on Amrita Pritam's statement about Gulzar:

> When the moon, up in the sky, sees what weighs down the breast of the earth, he hides himself in a dirty bale of clouds; and when he stretches out a hand from the bundle, his hand holds a shining sword…Why was the moon hiding in the bundle of dirty clouds?
>
> Wanderers in the blood-soaked night, falling over each other
> Had cried, 'Light, Light!'
> Looking in the sky's direction
> The moon had stretched out a hand from the bale
> And shown them a shining sword!

23.

Let us turn our attention to some interesting aspects of the film, *Parichay* (1972). Gulzar weaves the interaction between the characters into the intricate fabric of the story with empathy. Thus, no judgement of right or wrong is passed on any of the film's characters.

The essence of the film is compassion. Though he has a compassionate mind, Rai Sahab (played by Pran) does not let anyone see it. His son, Nilesh Rai (played by Sanjeev Kumar), is also full of compassion in his pursuit of his passion for art, which Rai Sahab refuses to see. Even at the screenplay level, there are some signs that point to the tension in the dramatic scenes. To integrate these scenes into the plot, Gulzar used the 1965 film, *The Sound of Music*, and Rajkumar Maitra's Bangla story, 'Rangeen Uttariyo' as a base.

There's an interesting story about this too. Rakhee had read the story in the Bangla paper, *Ulto Rath* and, impressed by the story, had shown it to Gulzar saying it could make a good film. Jeetendra, the actor, was keen to act in a film directed by Gulzar and had asked to see a few story plots so he could choose one. Gulzar thus narrated quite a few stories, including the one by Maitra, that Rakhee had shown him. However, Jeetendra found none of the stories to his liking and requested a new selection. A few days later, Jeetendra met Gulzar again and excitedly narrated to him the very same story that Rakhee had recommended, and which Gulzar had already narrated to him. Jeetendra could see the potential of the story and he told Gulzar, 'I like this story, Rakhee narrated it to me.' To which Gulzar replied, 'I have already told you this story and you rejected it.' Jeetendra responded, 'Then you must learn from Rakhee how to narrate a story.' That was how the story for *Parichay* was finally chosen.

It's also interesting to note that the film leans more towards Rajkumar Maitra's story than towards *The Sound of*

Music. Parichay also does not include any aspects of World War II that feature prominently in *The Sound of Music*. Gulzar translates the crux of the story into an Indian context. The conflicts between three generations is shown sympathetically in *Parichay*, and filmed with a subtlety that allows the depiction of the many shades of emotion that are experienced by the hero, Ravi (played by Jeetendra).

Ravi comes from the city to the village at the behest of his maternal uncle (played by A. K. Hangal). Here he is appointed as a tutor to Rai Sahab's four children and given the task of teaching them manners and culture. Thus, in the course of the film, as he tutors the four children and interacts with their elder sister, Rama (played by Jaya Bhaduri), he finds himself being drawn into an emotional bond with them.

The principal idea behind *Parichay* suggests the soul connections between people, giving significance to the thought that every embittered relationship will, in due course of time, not only mend but also assume a degree of sweetness. At this stage, the misunderstandings between the three generations are also erased.

A certain respect is created among them, and the very thing that Rai Bahadur wanted: that his grand-children not misunderstand him, is slowly achieved. Rai Sahab's statement is an indication of his mental angst, 'If love were a medicine that could be mixed with water and given, I would do that too. But the problem is that there is no tablet for love that I can give to these children.'

Ravi's response: 'The comfort and ease you call love, Rai Sahab, is not love. It is just that kind of comfort which any patient can get at any hospital. You have given these children what a nurse provides, not a parent's love. You are giving them the basic medicine they require, but not love, given freely, which only a mother and father give.'

The dynamics of the film revolves around the reconciliation of the points of view between these two characters. The love and understanding that Ravi refers to as necessary for the children is the leitmotif of *The Sound of Music*. Ravi's statement is similar to what Maria (played by Julie Andrews) says when she tells the Captain (played by Christopher Plummer), ' Oh please Captain! Love them, love them all!'

Gulzar writes the song 'Saare ke saare ga ma ko lekar gaate chale,' in which he takes the children out into the open spaces inspired by the classic song in *The Sound of Music*, 'Do re mi…' where Maria takes the children to a verdant field and sings the captivating song based on the seven musical notes. Gulzar, when he reaches the note 'pa', or pancham, makes a respectful gesture towards his close friend R. D. Burman who was also known as Pancham.

Thus, in the song's antara, the notes flow thus: ga for gun gun ga ga ga; ma for madhyam ma ma ma, pa for a pujari…. Even as he sings, he asks Rama, 'Do you know what we are singing?' And Rama replies, 'How would I not know! You are teaching them the seven notes.' 'And so, where had we reached?' Ravi asks, to which Rama replies, 'Up till Pancham.' Thinking of his friend, Gulzar uses a cinematic technique which we refer to as the Easter Egg.

Among the many notable things in *Parichay* is the duet by Lata and Bhupinder Singh, which won Lata her first National Award. R. D. Burman creates the song in the classical raag Yaman Kalyan and infuses it with tenderness. The song sung by Kishore Kumar, 'Musafir hoon yaaron/ Na ghar hai, na thikana' (I am a wayfarer/ Neither home have I, nor destination) for the same film is a good example of Kishore Kumar's carefree singing style. The song, 'Mitva bole meethe bain' (My beloved speaks sweetly), sung by Bhupinder for Sanjeev Kumar who plays a supporting role in the film is a simple, expressive composition.

The comic element in the film is well essayed by A. K. Hangal, Leela Mishra and Asrani. Narayan's (played by Asrani) habit of hiding his mouth at every excuse tickles the funny bone. Laughter is forbidden in Rai Sahib's bungalow, and servants who laugh suffer a cut in their salary. Narayan is helpless as, every month, he loses ten to fifteen rupees for laughing. I personally believe that of all his films, *Parichay* is Jeetendra's best. Even before taking on this film, Pran had achieved the status of legend, which this film reaffirms. His essaying of the role of the disciplinarian grandfather is so nuanced, it is like a masterclass in acting. Gulzar also got from Jaya Bhaduri a performance worthy of her talent, made all the more effective by her artful underplaying.

In his successful adaptation and Indianisation of *The Sound of Music*, Gulzar has set forth the maxim that love conquers all. And music brings together and heals broken hearts. The statement that comes through Ravi, 'How can a closed fist ever entrap a fragrance?' is realised through the sixteen reels of the film.

24.

It's worth examining the many interesting milestones in R. D. Burman's career. The mingled threads of subtlety and complexity in his work; his prowess in creating tunes based on classical music that he would adapt to appeal to modern tastes. Then his ability to mine the music imbibed from his father, S. D. Burman, an unparalleled musician himself, and to take it down completely untrodden paths—these are the hallmarks of this music director's genius. R. D. Burman was a revolutionary musician who started new trends.

The influence of Western music, mingling subtly with that of Hindustani classical music, is evident in almost all his film music compositions. It is interesting to note that R. D. Burman absorbed the impressions of Western music from his childhood among the South Calcutta elite. The eminent royal Deb Burman family he belonged to was a part of this society too. The famous record shop on Calcutta's Rashbehari Avenue, called Melody, was instrumental in first acquainting Pancham with this music. Later, Kersi Lord, the principal instrumentalist in his team of musicians, who was also a dear friend, cemented this knowledge. Lord was a masterful accordion player and drummer, and a vital part of many ensembles.

Lord acquainted Pancham with the music of Latin America, Europe, Cuba, as well as jazz through the medium of long-playing records. Thus the West-obsessed mindset changed, thanks to the influence of friends who had an affinity for and knowledge of the music of other spheres. This helped Rahul Dev Burman create a modern version of music that was his very own.

To understand R. D. Burman's music, it is necessary to first understand those opinions that shaped his thought as a musician and also helped him in finding his direction. For example, as a youth, he took lessons in tabla from the noted tabla exponent Brijen Biswas. The fact that he continued to learn the tabla on and off throughout his life adds an interesting facet to his journey as a musician. At the age of fifty, he learnt the intricacies of the tabla from Pandit Samanta Prasad, 'Gudai Maharaj', in Bombay. Besides this, he lived in Calcutta to learn the sarod from Ali Akbar Khan. But the practice sessions during which Ali Akbar and Ravi Shankar worked on their duets interested him even more than the lessons. R. D. Burman has admitted that listening to these great artistes practising their duets gave him access to new ideas about music.

As important a factor in setting him apart as a musician was the way in which R. D. Burman assembled his orchestra, with talented artistes with new ideas and modern concepts. At any time, his team would have eighty to ninety artistes. It's worth mulling over the craftsmanship that instrumentalists like Manohari Singh, Kersi Lord, Jayaram Acharya, Brijen

Biswas, Kishore Desai, Tony Vaz and Louis Banks, each a master in his field, added to the music that was being created as they worked together under R. D. Burman's baton.

And then there was the lasting alliance with a poet like Gulzar which, in turn, resulted in some incomparable songs. The chemistry between R. D. Burman and Gulzar was much like what existed between Naushad and Shakeel Badayuni, Roshan and Sahir Ludhianvi, Shankar Jaikishen and Shailendra, and Laxmikant Pyarelal and Anand Bakshi.

There are many popular stories centred around the friendship between Pancham and Gulzar, which most fans of cinema must already know. Like how they would roam the city all night by car, and how while playing a rhythm on the dashboard, the complete tune of 'Musafir hoon yaaron' was created. Or when, during the recording of 'Iss mod se jaatein hain' (From this crossroads), RD asked, 'Gulu, where is this nasheman?' He thought nasheman was a place till Gulzar, laughing, explained, 'Nasheman means nest.'

There are other similar anecdotes, among which the one about the song, 'Aapki aankhon mein kuch mehke hue se raaz hain' (Your eyes are aglow with fragrant secrets), from *Ghar* is rather enjoyable. As it happened, a stanza in the song had the line, 'Aap ki badmashiyon ke yeh naye andaaz hain' (Oh, and these are your new ways of mischief) and R. D. Burman was anxious about what Lata Didi's reaction would be when he gave her this line to sing. The word, 'badmashiyon'—which could be interpreted as naughtiness or mischief—was grating on him, with the thought that Lata-didi, finding the word objectionable, might refuse to sing it. Pancham had in fact requested Gulzar to change the line.

Later, when Lata Mangeshkar sang the duet, she told Pancham and Gulzar, 'That is the very line that makes this song unique.' Even today, if you listen to the song on You Tube, you will hear her laughing as she sings the word, 'badmashiyon', which heightens the expressiveness of the line.

Gulzar's story about Pancham in the *Filmfare* column, 'Geet Gaata Chal', explains the style of Pancham's music composition:

> Very rarely did I and Pancham sit down to compose a song. He was very creative, very impulsive and very reckless. He would compose tunes while sitting or walking hither and thither. Most of the tunes from this time were created while driving.
>
> If a tune entered Pancham's head, he could not keep it to himself. Once it so happened that we were driving in our own cars, in the same direction, when we got stuck in a traffic jam. Pancham thought up a tune at that point. I don't know how, but a car was stuck between our two cars. Pancham asked the driver of that car to lower his window because he wanted to talk to me. Then he started telling me about a tune. He explained the metre of the song and how he planned to compose it. The condition of the man in the car in the middle must have been worth watching, as he struggled to understand what was happening. This was Pancham's typical style, and the extent to which he was involved in his music.

Elsewhere, in other chapters, the songs that were created from the partnership between Gulzar and Pancham are discussed, sometimes at length, at others as opinions shared. What is being done here is to shine a light on their bonding, friendship and their musical partnership. And to understand the regard they held each other in.

A statement Gulzar made about Pancham referring to their friendship comes from close to his heart: 'I can say that most of my songs play about like children in Pancham's house…'

R. D. Burman's statement about Gulzar is as loaded with meaning, 'Sometimes when I am working on a composition, your face presents itself before me. Then it becomes necessary for me to keep that song aside. I tell myself, "This song will feature only in his picture, no one else can take it."'

25.

With the story, screenplay and dialogues of *Guddi* (1971), Gulzar reached a new level. A collection of Gulzar's short stories, *Chouras Raat*, published in 1963, included a story called 'Guddi' which Hrishikesh Mukherjee had chosen as the theme for his film. The name of the title character in the original story was changed from Guddo to Guddi. The darling of the family, Kusum, fondly called Guddi (played by Jaya Bhaduri), is crazy about the evergreen Hindi film hero, Dharmendra. This is that stage of involvement that adolescent boys and girls often pass through as they search for a film idol to fix their romantic aspirations on.

If the film is to be explained in one line, it is about the attempt to deconstruct the attraction a young girl feels towards a film star. The most important point that comes up is that even as the distraction of films takes one away from reality, seeing the reality of a film being made dulls the dream that the mind has imagined. To depict this simply, Gulzar has infused humour into his dialogues.

He balances the portrayal of Jaya Bhaduri as Guddi, a girl lost in daydreams, with the intelligent character of Professor Gupta played by Utpal Dutt. In the interactions between these two characters, we can see the film's significance as it highlights the difference between illusion and reality. In the *Encyclopaedia of Indian Cinema*, compiled by Ashish Rajadhyaksha and Paul Willemen, the authors write, 'The film's tentative critique of stardom involved drawing a comparison between contemporary screen idols and gods.'

The film has many memorable scenes. Among them, that of Kundan (played by Asrani) stealing money from home and running away to try his luck in films; of Naveen (played by Samit Banj) who is sincerely in love with Guddi but remains tormented by the fact that Guddi does not take him or her own life seriously. Professor Gupta's way of seeing and evaluating films through a psychological lens is another important scene.

All these scenes use circumstantial humour as a tool for Gulzar to write witty dialogues. This scene filmed on Utpal Dutt gives us an example: Professor Gupta asks his friend, whose novel has been made into a film, 'Deshpande! Your novel has been filmed, has it not?' The reply the writer friend gives is indicative of the humour that infuses the entire film. 'Yes, my friend! Till they made a film of it, the story was mine. But don't ask me about the way the film destroyed my story. The hero disguises himself in ten different beards to romance his heroine; the comedian climbs on to his father's back to play "horsy horsy"! I can't begin to tell you the ways they destroyed it, mutilated it…They make the hero and heroine run around the tree in such circles that you cannot make out who is chasing whom. And then, even if the heroine is lame, they will make her dance, at least in a dream sequence. And let me share another hilarious bit: the hero chases the villain in the climax, sometimes in a car, sometimes on a horse, sometimes on foot…When he finally hits him, phew! You will wonder why did I not die before suffering this!'

This scene is a sarcastic reference to the fact that filmmakers do not respect literature. When they choose a literary work to film, they toe the line of ensuring popularity and commerce and kill the very soul of the story. Gulzar must have enjoyed writing this scene, as being both writer and filmmaker, he could delineate this humorously.

The film's most sensitive scene is the one where, under the pretext of showing a film's shooting, the real life of the artistes is shown. Like the fact that Pran, who has been the eternal villain in films, is in real life a true gentleman, being embedded in the narrative as a small scene.

During the shooting of the film, Dharmendra compliments Pran on the watch he is wearing. Pran takes off his watch with a smile and offers it to the actor. Guddi thinks that the actor should not accept anything from the villain as he is a bad man. Dharmendra responds to this by telling Guddi that what is shown in cinema has little relationship with real life. And that Pran is a very kind-hearted person who takes on negative roles only in films. The ability to understand good and evil comes from real-life experiences, cinema has no role to play.

The screenplay of *Guddi* minutely explains the distance between illusion and reality by balancing the inner and outer lives in the world of films. Gulzar has always been alert about bringing balance to the relationship between society and cinema.

The understanding of this is seen as becoming more effective when the questions raised by life are addressed with sarcasm, humour and with no moralising.

Khubsoorat, a film in the same vein as *Guddi*, written by Gulzar in 1980, comes to mind in this context, in which compromise is shown as a way to solve problems. Just as *Guddi* explains the difference between reality and daydreams, *Khubsoorat*, in a different way, draws the line between discipline and enjoyment. *Guddi* tries to convey a lesson through its characters. The film tells us that life exists in all its variety beyond the world of films. *Khubsoorat* takes the example of *Guddi* forward and infuses ethics inside the four walls of a household. If you view *Guddi* and *Khubsoorat* as a unit, the advice contained in these two films could present itself as a solution to many societal issues.

26.

An interesting story about the film *Guddi* is worth retelling. The film was released in January 1971. Coincidentally, at that time, Gulzar, Hrishikesh Mukherjee, the film's director, and N. C. Sippy, the producer, happened to be together in Delhi. The three of them wanted to watch the film 'first day, first show' only to gauge the reaction of the audience. Gulzar says, 'We went to Delhi's Delight Cinema to watch the film.'

When the film reached its ending, Vani Jairam was singing a bhajan by Meerabai: 'Hari bin kaise jiyun?' (How do I live without Hari?) filmed on Jaya Bhaduri. The moment the bhajan started, the audience started hooting and laughing. The three were terrified as this was the film's climax. Immediately, Hrishi-da, along with Sippy-sahab, went out of the hall and called up Ajit Banerjee, who was the film's art director. He advised Ajit-da that he should put up a set immediately in his house, and that he would return that very night from Delhi and re-shoot the scene the next morning. Hrishi-da had understood instantly: the film was sure to flop.

Gulzar recounts that the next day, on reaching Bombay, Hrishi-da removed the bhajan and shot the popular song from *Madhumati*, 'Aaja re pardesi' (You who has gone away, come back) with Jaya Bhaduri. 'Till today I have not understood what was in Hrishi-da's mind regarding this song, and why he chose it for the ending. Then the issue arose that the scene had been reshot, but reels of the film had been sent to cinema halls across the country. The question was how could the new negative be sent to all the halls and the end reels substituted to show the new version.

'N. C. Sippy-sahab was a very balanced and understanding producer. He had complete trust in his directors. Besides, he was also Hrishi-da's business partner. He managed to get the change done during the interval within a few days. Thus, the ending of *Guddi* was changed and the song from *Madhumati* kept the film from sinking.'

Gulzar-sahab laughs as he recounts that Lata Mangeshkar entered *Guddi* in this way, with the picturisation of her classic composition on the heroine. He does not fail to add that this is something one must learn from the masters. What was it that Hrishikesh Mukherjee understood about how the film could be saved? It was beyond understanding why a perfectly good song, composed well, did not fit into the ending. In the same way, how did adding an old song to the climax, which had not only been part of a very famous film but had attained great popularity in its own right, make such a big difference? Gulzar has not been able to fathom this strategy of Hrishikesh Mukherjee.

27.

At one point in time Gulzar was so impressed by Satyajit Ray that he nursed a dream of working with him. Thanks to his continued interactions with learned writers in the Indian People's Theatre Association (IPTA), his understanding of realism deepened, moving him away from romanticism. The dilemmas and conflicts of the common man's life were the themes that fired his romantic poems.

Besides, he had been an assistant to Bimal Roy, a contemporary of Satyajit Ray, and their respective films, *Do Bigha Zameen* and *Pather Panchali* had been crafted from the same mine of thought. *Do Bigha Zameen* was released in 1953 and fast on its heels came *Pather Panchali* a year later, bringing with it a new way of thinking. Perhaps the appeal of Ray lay in the eagerness to learn what he felt remained incomplete despite his long tutelage under Bimal Roy. Working with Ray on his films could fulfil that need. His desire came close to being realised when Ray planned to remake his children's film, *Goopi Gyne Bagha Byne* in Hindi. He had entrusted Gulzar with the task of writing the screenplay and dialogues for the Hindi version.

It is indeed a wonderful coincidence that Ray, despite being a veteran filmmaker, enjoyed making cartoons and films for children and, on his part, Gulzar too had been writing stories to educate and entertain children right from the start of his career. Thus, there was no surprise in Ray choosing

Gulzar to work on the remake of *Goopi Gyne Bagha Byne.*

In Gulzar's words: 'I had always nurtured a desire to work with Ray-sahab. He had written a script for the film *Goopi Gyne Bagha Byne* based on his elder brother Upendra Kishore Ray's story in Bangla. I was re-making it in Hindi.'

But for reasons still unknown, Ray changed his mind about the remake even though Gulzar had written the songs for the film which were a part of the script. The songs were embedded into the screenplay as a cohesive unit, as the film was being made as a musical. But Ray had lost the will to continue with the remake and a project that was underway was obliterated. Gulzar remembers this episode with pride over the offer made by Ray, and despondency over the project's closure leaving his dream broken and unfulfilled.

Though he engaged himself in making his own films, Gulzar continued to keep a sharp eye on Ray's work. This period is considered the height of his successful stint as a director, with *Koshish* following *Parichay* in 1972, and *Khushboo*, *Aandhi* and *Mausam* creating a trail from 1974 to 1976.

Around the same time, Satyajit Ray decided to make a Hindi film based on Premchand's *Shatranj Ke Khiladi.* On learning about this, Gulzar repaired post-haste to Ray. He was anxious to work with a filmmaker who, like Bimal Roy, would add to his learnings about the craft. But Ray apologetically told him, 'Forgive me, I have already promised someone else.' Gulzar felt he had lost his chance once again!

His dream of working with Ray remained unfulfilled, and he let the screenplay of the abandoned remake sink into oblivion. A memory which was dredged up during the telling of this story, not without its shade of regret.

Nonetheless, both filmmakers continued to work in their own styles to enrich cinema. 1977 saw *Shatranj Ke Khiladi* being released at almost the same time as Gulzar's *Kitaab* and *Kinara.*

It's a matter of interest that even though Ray himself decided to remake his much-loved film *Goopi Gyne Bagha Byne* in Hindi, the idea had occurred to another filmmaker long before Ray's decision. Just a few years after the Bangla film's release, Raj Kapoor, impressed by the film, had thought of remaking it in his own style. He felt it could be a great film in Hindi. All arrangements and preparations connected with the project were readied, but when Raj Kapoor approached Ray offering to buy the rights to make his version, Ray refused. Thus the Hindi version remained an aborted idea as neither the 'Showman' of Hindi cinema nor Ray got around to making the film.

28.

Gulzar's friendships too come with a unique flavour. It is wonderful to realise that the man can do anything for friendship. And that includes some hilarious things that, in the light of his stature today, seem incredible, yet reveal the humane aspects of his nature. Like writing love letters for his friend, Mukul Dutt, in the days when he was working for Bimal Roy. Mukul Dutt was in love with Chand Usmani, a yesteryears heroine. The funny twist to this story is that when Gulzar would have finished writing the letter and would want to read through it for corrections, Mukul Dutt would say to him, 'Just write it, don't read it.' Gulzar says in jest that he had to be like a 'Ganesh' writing the *Mahabharata* without stopping to cross the 't's and dot the 'i's when he wrote letters to feed the flame of Mukul Dutt's love affair.

Similarly, he spontaneously gave up his deep-rooted habit of eating paan on Sanjeev Kumar's request. This happened while *Parichay* was being shot.

The shooting of the song, 'Beeti na bitai raina, birha ki jaai raina' (It's impossible to get through this night, this night of separation) was underway. In the antara of the song sung by Lata Mangeshkar, when Jaya Bhaduri, overwhelmed by emotion, stops singing at 'chand ki…' Sanjeev Kumar joins in effortlessly to complete the stanza. In Bhupinder's voice he continues to sing '…bindi wali, bindi wali ratiyan.'

Gulzar says that Sanjeev Kumar slipped into the scene so seamlessly and performed so convincingly that his heart was filled with admiration. Expressing his joy, he told Sanjeev Kumar affectionately, ' Hari-bhai [Sanjeev Kumar's real name] what a shot you have given! Tell me what can I do for you in return?' As was his habit, Sanjeev Kumar replied with his usual seriousness, 'Yaar, give up eating paan.' And from that moment the betel leaf and the habit exited Gulzar's life!

Another popular story related to friendship is about the time when music director S. D. Burman, during the making of *Bandini*, had a falling out with the film's lyricist Shailendra. Shailendra and Gulzar used to meet often at the Bombay Youth Choir, where they were regular members. Actor-singer's Kishore Kumar's first wife, Ruma Devi was the conductor of the choir. A friendship soon developed between the two like-minded young men, which was further strengthened by their common love of poetry. Shailendra, after the episode with Dada Burman, persuaded Gulzar to join the *Bandini* team and complete writing the songs for the film. Gulzar has time and again repeated the fact that he had never wanted to be a songwriter for films. He conveyed his reluctance to Shailendra. But finally, on Shailendra's repeated persuasions, Gulzar went to Bimal Roy's set and, in collaboration with Burman-da, wrote his first film song, 'Mora gora ang laile/ Mohe shaam rang dai de' (Take away my fair skin, Lord/ Colour me in your deep blue).

S. D. Burman and Bimal Roy liked the song so much that it was promptly recorded in Lata Mangeshkar's voice. By then, the discord between Shailendra and Dada Burman had melted away. Shailendra returned to the film to write the remaining songs, as Dada Burman was somewhat unsure about working with a callow songwriter. Shailendra was upset by the fact that the friend he had persuaded to join the *Bandini* team was now being rejected due to S. D. Burman's attitude towards him. Bimal Roy too found it unpalatable that S. D. Burman, independent of the director, was taking decisions on his own, as it suited his moods. Gulzar was aware of all this. What he said to Shailendra immediately erased the poet's misgivings. 'This is your chair,' Gulzar told Shailendra. 'I was just looking after it for you. Now that you are here, take charge of it.'

Gulzar is also unique in the way he confers dignity on anyone he meets in the course of daily life. A story from the making of the film *Aandhi* is worth telling. As it happened, Gulzar completed the script of the film, which he had been working on at a stretch, holed up in Delhi's Akbar Hotel. JK, a bearer employed by the hotel, was tending to his every need through the long hours. So impressed was Gulzar by his dedication to his job that he promised the boy that he would name the hero of his film after him. And indeed, Sanjeev Kumar was named JK in *Aandhi*.

There are countless stories that give us an insight into Gulzar's inner self. He has placed his relationships and friendships at a precious level. This is what makes him a poet who can convey the warmth of a relationship through his writings. The love he carries for the people whose company he keeps, his sense of belonging and ability to give of himself make him a very special person. All through his life, if he realised that a friend was telling him something, he would accept it respectfully, without argument or discourse. Perhaps this is why Gulzar's songs, more than any other poet's writings, celebrate human dignity, to help us keep our faith in life.

This song from *Griha Pravesh* (1979) seems to be an extension of his nature:

Life, not made of flowers
But should, like flowers, always be scented

When a flower blooms somewhere
No sound reaches us, yet
The news of its fragrance floats past
May the fragrance linger...

29.

Noted astronomer and scientist Galileo Galilei, though innocent, was branded guilty by the Roman Catholic church. The anger rose from Galileo's attempt to add to Copernicus' finding that the Earth rode around the sun. It was indeed considered very dangerous to take a stand against Catholicism in those times, and the lines between science and religion were clearly drawn. For his crime against religion, Galileo was sentenced to life imprisonment, and forced to spend his life in house arrest. He was also ordered to stop supporting such ideas and put an end to his scientific research.

Gulzar often found himself disturbed by the injustice of the sentence given to Galileo, and the behaviour of the Church. He was saddened by the fact that society had not treated such a brilliant scientist and astronomer well. It is easy to understand that Gulzar keeps himself well informed about the events in the world of science. Just as the moon is a vital part of his poetry, he finds joy in rifling through the pages of scientific history and progress. He has always been eager to know the secret of creation.

Time and again, Gulzar would find himself disturbed by the injustice meted out to Galileo, despite the fact that it had all happened in the sixteenth century. One day he spoke about this to his friend, the writer Bhushan Banmali. Then it was decided that Gulzar should write to the Pope and request him: 'Please allow Galileo to be forgiven as he has committed no crime. Instead he has shown the world an important scientific truth.'

With great sincerity, Gulzar wrote the letter and dispatched it to the Pope, adding in the letter that science had indeed proved that the earth revolved around the sun and not the other way around. Galileo had earned his pardon and the Church needed to pardon him and ask for his forgiveness.

Gulzar recalls that it must have been in 1970 that he wrote the letter and sent it by air mail to the Pope. It was as if he felt he owed the astronomer a debt that he was keen to pay off. A strange thing indeed that a poet should try to bring justice and right a wrong done to a scientist almost three centuries ago and write a letter that was almost an affidavit stating his innocence. This was just an ethical expedition to ensure justice to a man who had lived and died centuries ago!

The brightest fallout of this exercise was that three hundred and fifty years later, in 1992, the Church finally admitted that Galileo was right and the Pope granted him an official pardon. For Gulzar it was a red-letter day, because the wrong that had spurred him into action forty years earlier had finally been officially corrected.

30.

Among the many films that he has written the dialogues for, *Anand* (1971) holds its own as a special film which reflected a different type of creative thought through its screenplay, dialogues and songs. Most of Hrishikesh Mukherjee's films have followed family-oriented themes, with humour as a vital element. But *Anand* and *Mili* (1975) are two films of a different kind that raise the sensitivities of the audience with respect to disease and infirmity through questions of life and death.

Gulzar was an important part of this film, as he was playing the dual roles of dialogue-writer and lyricist. He has written two of the four songs in the film. The other two were written by Yogesh Gaur, commonly credited simply as Yogesh.

Cancer remains a deadly illness that still defies treatment in most cases. To theme an entire film like *Anand* around cancer was a new thought fifty years ago, especially in commercial cinema. We can place this film somewhere between commercial and parallel cinema, in which the protagonist, Anand Sehgal (played by Rajesh Khanna) is shown, without excessive melodrama, to be suffering from the last stages of cancer. He has just six months left to live, which he wants to spend like a normal, healthy person. The irony is that the man who is nearing his end with each passing day wants to spend each day like a healthy being, while medical science, despite trying desperately, watches him dying.

Gulzar lifts the emotional situation of the film to a universal level by the effectiveness of his dialogues. It is a challenge for any dialogue-writer to add incidents of compassion in such a measure that it soaks the film in emotion. Despite this, the natural way the complex issue is handled ensures it places no emotional burden on the viewer's mind.

It is made clear from the first frame that the film's hero has been given the poetic licence to celebrate his impending demise. His friend, the cancer specialist Dr Bhaskar Banerjee (played by Amitabh Bachchan), is frustrated and tormented by the fact that he is helpless, with no way of treating Anand Sehgal. The film has tragic overtones for cancer sufferers, whose hope for life can be dashed by the smallest downturn. The film focuses on the thought that if the end of life is within sight, then living it to the hilt is the best option. Rajesh Khanna's dialogue with Dr. Bhaskar is related to this thought: 'Death is just a moment, Babu Moshai. The hundreds of thousands of moments that I am going to live through in the six months ahead, what about them, Babu Moshai? Life is meant to be grand, not long…'

Gulzar has never been of the thought that a character should be pathetic throughout his existence in the film.

Every single person connected to the structure of the film has ensured that *Anand* flows smoothly, keeping in mind the mental dignity of a dying man; whether it was Hrishikesh Mukherjee directing the film, or Yogesh writing two songs and giving Anand Sehgal lines like, 'Zindagi kaisi hai paheli, hai…' (Oh, life! Such a conundrum…)

Gulzar shows a new aspect of his skill in *Anand* when he highlights the positive approach of the hero towards his friends, Dr. Prakash Kulkarni (played by Ramesh Deo) and his wife Suman Kulkarni (played by Seema Deo) when, at their request, he sings these lines on their anniversary:

Small, insignificant things, linger for long in memory
Not forgotten, is a small memory, long past
For many births have I watched these paths, waiting for you
I have chosen seven-coloured dreams, just for you
Dreams, musical dreams…

Anand must be watched for its heart-touching subject, its meaningful songs and especially for its dialogues. Even in its poignant moments, Gulzar's dexterous turn of phrase helps ease the tension. In the interactions between Rajesh Khanna and Amitabh Bachchan the poetic touches are evidence of a poet at work on the dialogues. A few examples clearly demonstrate this:

> 'Babu Moshai, as long as I am alive, I am not dead. When I die, then, damn it, there is no me…'
>
> 'Sadness is not beautiful, Babu Moshai!'
>
> 'Babu Moshai, I can face my death but I cannot watch your frightened countenance.'

Using such lines, Gulzar dilutes the tension of the film, which lifts the film into the realm of art. A poem is read out in this film, 'Death, you are a poem…I have been promised a poem…' Written in 1971, this poem was included in an amended form in his collection, titled 'Kuch Aur Nazme' (Some More Nazms). Here, he changed the word 'kavita' to 'nazm'.

I have been promised a poem, I will get it
When pain falls asleep in the failing heartbeat
Pale-faced, the moon has climbed the sky
The day is still afloat, the night nears the shore
Neither dark, not light, this is neither night nor day
When the body ends and the spirit takes breath
I have been promised a poem, I will get it...

Anand is a poem caught between emotion and destiny, and the poem recited by Anand Sehgal 'We are all puppets on the stage,' reminds us of Shakespeare's lines,

All the world's a stage
And all the men and women merely players:
They have their exits and entrances;
And one man in his time plays many parts.

Notwithstanding the lamentations of the puppets on stage, the film stands on the foundation of faith and belief in life. The line that affirms that life must be grand, not long, gives a positive fillip to every downcast and wretchedly sick soul who has decided to give up hope.

To remain healthy and happy by colouring the lives of others in rainbow hues is the message that Hrishikesh Mukherjee has managed to inspire his team with and which everyone in the film, from actors to singers and composers to technicians and Gulzar himself has tried to follow.

31.

The practice of writing couplets and poems with the moon as a subject has prevailed in Urdu poetry through the ages. However, the usage changes significantly by the time the practice filters into Hindi poetry. Gulzar, standing as he does at the confluence of the two languages, creates a new lexicon around the subject in Hindustani. The moon thus becomes his friend, and the most dependable part of his poetry. Never, even in his childhood, was the moon a kindly uncle like it was for other children. Instead, as a sympathiser and confidant, his relationship with the moon seems to echo that which features in the songs sung by Bob Dylan. A relationship that holds friendship, love, sorrow and almost every shade of emotion that one can experience in life.

For Gulzar, the moon symbolises a relationship wherein he can engage it in conversation, visit it or have it drop in at his place, and to whom he can bare his heart. If we understand it from the point of view of the famous poet Ibn-e-Insha, the moon attains a status that states not just the end of poetic compositions in its absence, but a change in the very meaning of life.

Insha says:

Those nights left along with the moon
Those conversations too
How then to dream of happiness
When the sun of sorrow is overhead.

The moon appears in Gulzar's courtyard bearing this conceit of Ibn-e-Insha to share the joys and sorrow, days and nights of his life with him. In this friendship, the point to note is that Gulzar consults the moon on every issue. To the extent that the moon struts and swaggers above his head.

Having emerged readily from the sky
The moon is now going straight to my head

One more example from among his trivenis is worth examining:

Night brings the stars in the moon boat
They are all sold out before morning comes

The night does such good business these days!

Examine a random sheaf of poems and film songs written by Gulzar and you will find the moon shining through in every second poem. It plays a role: that of a motif. The moon in

Gulzar's poems is a changeable character, different at every encounter. In a way the moon is his best loved character, whom he depends on more than on himself. We can almost believe then that the moon holds a place in his poetry superior to all other creations of Nature. Yet, Nature is evident in abundance in Gulzar's work. The sun, stars, mountains, rain, autumn, night and day, evening, snow, sand, mist and fog, wind, the leaves and flowers, trees and branches—anything can feature in his poetry. But the moon alone has the ability to add meaning and depth to his expressions.

Regard his ghazals, or poems, songs or even the small but meaningful trivenis, his enduring link with the moon is obvious.

A few selected phrases from the cornucopia of his work should amply illustrate this.

> *'Again, today, the smoke rises from the forehead of the moon.'*
>
> *'It kisses the moon's forehead.'*
>
> *'He fell from the moon and died.'*
>
> *'A bit of the moon is hanging in the remnants of the night.'*
>
> *'Wearing a golden face, the moon reached the sky.'*
>
> *'The moon was just about to ripen and fall.'*
>
> *'Each day the moon has risen to hang up the night on the sky.'*
>
> *'Why is the moon hiding inside that dirty bundle of clouds?'*
>
> *'Arrest the moon if it comes out.'*
>
> *'Should the moon prick your finger, it will draw blood.'*
>
> *'There were a lot of people on the moon-boat last night.'*
>
> *'The moon-like bride mother gave me as a blessing.'*
>
> *'Come, let us sail across the lake with the moon as a boat.'*
>
> *'Using a rolling-pin, the night regularly shapes a flat moon.'*

In a non-film album of songs titled *Sunset Point* that was released two decades earlier, Gulzar likens the height of the moon to that of a mountaintop from where one could assay a bungee jump for the joy of it. Which implies that wherever the moon may be, in whatever form, Gulzar can reach out and make it his own. It's quite another matter to ponder over what the moon must be thinking on finding itself cast into so many situations and roles.

Here is a song from *Sunset Point* that bears scrutiny:

Come, let us dive down and see
Jump off from a moon or two...
Spend the night sailing
In eyes like seafaring vessels
Let us spread out sleep
On the lake's waters
Come, let us dive
Come let us dive down and see
Jump off from a moon or two...

Almost an obsession for him, this love of the moon finds new expressions in his songwriting for films too. The moon as subject becomes a cause for celebration, as Gulzar's unique thought process presents it to his audience:

'Some moon-carriages did roll past, but no one dismounted from them' (Lekin)

'Pushing aside the clouds/ Secretly the moon peeps out' (Bandini)

'Daily she comes alone, daily returns alone

The beggar-night, holding the moon as her bowl' (Mere Apne)

'The moon dotted forehead of the night/ The night wearing a bindi...' (Parichay)

'If you say so, the moon will not set tonight/ Hold back the night...' (Aandhi)

'A hundred and sixteen nights of moonlight/ And the mole on your shoulder' (Ijazat)

'Across the blue river, a wet moon blossomed...' (Libaas)

'O mother moon of mine/ Your moonlight burns my body...' (Rudaali)

'Without you, the golden moon is only gilt/blowing a false yellow dust...' (Guru)

'I've swallowed the moon, oh dear/Inside me a fire burns' (Omkara)

'If you come to mind, I will sway calling your name

When evening comes, I will reach up and kiss the moon...' (Soorma)

Going beyond these examples, there are countless other songs in which Gulzar's obsession with the moon makes him narrate a variety of stories about it, giving it different personalities and tasks.

While forging familial, romantic, or emotional relationships with the moon, Gulzar the poet is sanguine about the fact that he has a life-long companion with whose help he can sprinkle moonbeams and starlight over his songs and poems. We can call his penchant for creating motivational and fictional compositions a part of his unique poetic legacy. Which is why any metaphor created around the moon's presence is for Gulzar a celebration of life, bestowing the ability to bear sorrow and troubles with equanimity.

In the film *Sitara*, this pain comes across as comfort:

Many moons have I lit up and extinguished
Long have I craved for some sleep to come to me.

In many other film songs too, thanks to this practice, the possibility of changing the contexts of words to create a mood is created due to which all the other images also fit seamlessly. As the completely different image of the moon in this song from the film *Devta* creates:

I have stolen the moon and brought it along
Come let us sit behind the church
No one will see or recognise us
Let us sit under the tree

The romance in this imagery is taken further in the film *Kitaab*, where it translates into the meditative aspect of love: 'Dhanno ki aankhon mein/ Hai raat ka surma aur chand ka chumma' (The eyes of Dhanno hold/ The kohl of the night and the kiss of the moon.)

In delicate moments, Gulzar can portray the moon as a character in its own right. Perhaps the best example of this comes from his self-directed film, *Lekin*:

Your eyes that have feasted on others
Give you away
Like the moon always brightens
Shrouded nights

At the same time, in another song, the presence of the moon can become the other face of life's coin. The 1999 film *Jahan Tum Le Chalo* has one such example:

It dropped like the moon
I found it lying by the wayside
It rang out like a shriek
It slipped out of my pocket
This half-rupee of a life
This life...

I am convinced Gulzar-sahab has made the moon the milestone of his poetic journey. Which is probably why he says in one of the songs from the film *Bunty Aur Babli*:

Passing by the moon, the road continues
A little further on it, lies our destination.

Gulzar gives the moon the same respect that his poet mentors have showed for the full moon. Yet, Gulzar still feels, despite his closeness to the moon, that he has not been able to portray it as beautifully as his friend and song-writer Shailendra imagined seventy years ago:

Turn your face away for a moment
O moon, I will show my love for him
Tell him a thousand things...

(*Awaara*, 1951)

Like Ibn-e-Insha, he is a traveller walking the moon's pathways, for whom there cannot be any other image of love, even though Shailendra, in his own fashion, also steeps the imagery of the moon in romance. Ibn-e-Insha also says with characteristic delicacy:

Yesternight the moon was full
And all the talk was about you
Some said this is the moon
Others that it was your face fair

32.

Sanjeev Kumar. Gulzar's beloved 'Hari-bhai'! One of his favourite actors. A vital part of six films made by Gulzar: *Parichay*, *Koshish*, *Aandhi*, *Mausam*, *Namkeen* and *Angoor*. And an actor in three films for which Gulzar wrote the screenplay; among them H. S. Rawail's *Sunghursh* in which he played Dwaraka Prasad, Hrishikesh Mukherji's *Arjun Pandit* in which he was Arjun, and Basu Bhattacharya's *Griha Pravesh*, in the role of Amar. The chemistry between Gulzar and Sanjeev Kumar was somewhat like that between Bimal Roy and Dilip Kumar—an alliance that created *Madhumati*, *Devdas* and *Yahudi*.

The relationship with Sanjeev Kumar harks back to the 1950s, when both were connected with the Indian National Theatre. Gulzar would write plays and Sanjeev Kumar was a stage actor. They would often meet at Bhulabhai Auditorium, where Sanjeev Kumar would be rehearsing for some new play. Sanjeev Kumar was a pupil of P. D. Shenoy, who taught acting at the Filmalaya School of Acting and went on to become a director.

Gulzar remembers an incident about Sanjeev Kumar that he cherishes. He must have been about twenty-two or twenty-three years old, when Gulzar watched him performing in

All My Sons, a three-act play written by Arthur Miller. He was playing an elderly man and Leela Chitnis was playing his wife. The play's best compliment came from Prithviraj Kapoor who asked, gesturing at Sanjeev Kumar, 'Who was that old man?' Commenting on this, Gulzar says, 'As far as my connection with him is concerned, Sanjeev Kumar was born old and he has worked in films that were much ahead of his time. I have always believed that there have been two big supports in my creative journey. First R. D. Burman and second, Sanjeev Kumar.'

In keeping with Gulzar's statement, Sanjeev Kumar has indeed played either an old man or a mature one in most of his films. Whether it be *Parichay*, *Koshish* or *Mausam*; in each, Sanjeev Kumar is portrayed as a senior citizen. To the extent that even in *Aandhi*, he plays a middle-aged hotel manager, JK, whose politician-wife, Aarti (played by Suchitra Sen) is also elderly.

In *Arjun Pandit* his persona is that of a directionless hero whom the disciplined and principled Ashok Kumar, who belongs to the same village, tries to change. And so this character who is creating havoc in the rural environment transforms into a reformed Arjun Pandit.

In every character and role that Gulzar wrote for him, Sanjeev Kumar is burdened by one responsibility or another. Whether he is the father is *Parichay* trying to give his daughter and other children a way to live with dignity, or the elderly deaf-mute of *Koshish* who has to bring up his child in a way that he grows up to be a good human being. Or yet again the helpless father in *Mausam* who sets out in search of his lost daughter, and who has to struggle against many odds because the daughter who has grown up in a brothel looks upon him as yet another client.

Gulzar thus bound Sanjeev Kumar in the roles of such exemplary character that made viewers believe that only someone like Sanjeev Kumar could handle such responsibilities in life too. Gulzar believed Sanjeev Kumar was the actor he could most depend upon for his ability to translate his cinematic vision and bring it to life on the screen.

Both would make time for their friendship. Each respected the other's talent and depended on it. Both knew the important aspects to be kept in mind while working in a film, what qualities identify one as a performer or artiste, and both had learnt this from effort and experience. And they continuously tried to fulfil all the requirements of their art with each other's support. To understand this, one needs only to watch their films from *Parichay* to *Namkeen*. *Koshish* and *Mausam* show Sanjeev Kumar's hold on emotional acting. *Arjun Pandit* and *Aandhi* showcase the assimilation of dialogue with the character, *Angoor* his comic timing, and *Parichay* his command of facial gestures.

And whether it is 'Dil dhoondta hai phir wahi fursat ke raat din' (The heart seeks those days and nights of leisure) or 'Tere bina zindagi se koi shikwa to nahin' (I am bereft of you, yet I bear no grievance with life), the twosome of Sanjeev Kumar and Gulzar excel in every project they partnered in.

33.

Gulzar and Bhushan Banmali wrote the screenplay of *Mausam* (1975) based on Kamleshwar's novel, *Aagami Ateet* (The Past That Is to Come). It is said that the novel was in turn influenced by A. J. Cronin's *The Judas Tree*. *Mausam*, influenced by both books, is a touching story, in which Dr Atmaram Gill (played by Sanjeev Kumar), who has lost his beloved, Chanda (played by Sharmila Tagore), reaches the same place in Darjeeling twenty years later, only to learn that his beloved had gone mad pining for him and died eight months ago. She has left behind a daughter, but the villagers know nothing of her or her whereabouts. Even as he grapples with the dilemma of looking for her, he comes to know that his daughter, Kajli, who is a spitting image of her mother, has landed up in a brothel and, under the protection of Gangu Rani (played by Dina Pathak) become a sex worker.

Mausam takes shape from this point. Dr Amarnath Gill wants to take his daughter with him and give her back her respectability. He wishes to then adopt the daughter of his dead lover as a way of atonement for the fact that he did not keep his promise of marrying Chanda.

A deep feeling of regret permeates the film from the start, deepening as the story progresses. Gulzar uses his signature style in developing the film, using his much favoured flashbacks to join the past with the present. As the elderly doctor, Dr Gill recollects his past as he struggles to come to terms with his present situation. He has lost his beloved, but he does find her daughter. The plot of the film revolves around the search for Chanda, and in the process also reveals Kajli to the audience. The director makes it very clear that though it is an enjoyable love story, the film tells a touching tale.

In the film, the relationship between Dr Gill and Kajli is also one of love, but a love touched with parental affection, as the hero and heroine are actually shown linked as father and daughter.

Mausam starts with tension, moves toward creating compassion and ends on an emotional note. Despite this, a song from the film looks at the entire plot through the lens of leisure, presenting an unusual angle. 'Dil dhoondta hai phir wahi fursat ke raat din', shown early in the film, is filmed again as a love duet between Dr Gill and Chanda to a slightly altered tune. It shows us how the love story between the two must have developed in the days of leisure when Dr Gill, as a young man, repaired to Darjeeling from Calcutta to study for his medical examinations.

Mausam takes stock of the changing climate of life. Viewing the film as a metaphor, we see Chanda's life experiencing a brief, verdant spring of happy thoughts that slowly turn into the leaf fall of autumn's sombre mood, in which she spends most of her life. Dr. Gill's life too is crafted on a similar note. But the rainy season he looks forward to brings such a downpour of troubles and the misery of times past that it sweeps away all his hopes and promises in a flood. And Kalji never experiences spring in her life. The reality of life in a brothel makes her experience harsh, wintery nights with icy winds buffeting her into misery. Gulzar presents each of his characters in the film with a season that, instead of giving them joy, creates an upheaval.

To an extent the film has an element of melodrama, as it is engraved with scenes of life's miseries. Even as Dr Amarnath Gill makes a move to give Kajli a respectable and fulfilling life, what she tells him tears through his heart. Kajli says, 'Sitting among the naked, I do not feel naked anymore. I only feel ashamed when I sit among people. My nakedness starts to show.' This is a sorrow that shows no sign of exiting from Kajli's life. When the doctor tells her that she should live a better life, she replies in torment, 'Are we ever allowed to remain good and decent? No child is born a prostitute, we end up meeting those who make us prostitutes.'

Gulzar deals with the complex theme of *Mausam* in a systematic way. He is aware that he is putting forth a serious point of view before his viewers: that even a woman living in a house of ill repute should be given the right to turn respectable and lead a normal life. He ensures that the film does not remain a tear-jerker that is viewed and forgotten, and endeavours to protect each frame of the film from being simply voyeuristic. He puts forward the vital point of his film in a simple way, and slowly pushes it to where it becomes obvious to the viewer. *Mausam* thus leaves a definite impression. When the doctor brings Kajli home, the gyrating brothel-style dance that she executes for him only highlights her artlessness and innocence. The song, 'Mere ishq me laakhon latke/ Balam zara hatke' (Make way, my darling/ Thousands hang on in hope of my love) sung by Asha Bhosle, shows us Gulzar's intention of showing his character's naivete intentions.

There are countless moments in the film that bear testimony to the director's poetic vision. Like the artless scenes of the love between Dr. Amarnath and Chanda, early in the film, where she is trying to get the doctor to return her father's cane. Or when her lover gifts her a necklace which Chanda, taking it to be made of ivory, asks its cost. Such scenes give the film a delicacy of sentiment.

Kajli's dialogues that echo her mother's way of expression are a way of linking the past to the present, which function is also given to the songs of the film, making them unique. Towards the end of the film, when Kajli, who has returned to the brothel, weeps, another inmate asks her, 'What is the matter?' The dialogue at this point lifts the film to a new level, bringing to light the issues that women had to struggle helplessly against almost half a century ago.

It is worth listening to Kajli's response to Champa, 'It's nothing…I had lost my way, Champa. There is still a woman living within me. I had thought she died long ago, but she is alive…'

It is a matter of amazement that a woman living in the worst possible situation can still nurture a desire for life. That such a woman is alive in spirit and wishes to continue living is significant indeed. Gulzar propounds such ideas, conveying a positive message through the film. The song composed by Madan Mohan in his unique style and sung by Lata Mangeshkar expresses this emotion succinctly, and encapsulates the motif of *Mausam*. Lata Mangeshkar's articulation of this through the modulations of tone as she sings the song beggars any comment. The following lines can be examined in this context:

My faltering steps stop, and start again

> *I leave your door with peace, yet restless of heart*
> *Before the break of day, often I would wake from sleep*
> *The span of a night, this life, that I have passed through*
>
> *I have been carrying the weight of your favours in my heart*
> *See, I leave now having placed my debts at your feet*

Dr Amarnath's endeavour of giving Kajli's life a worthwhile direction, as a way of atoning for his abandonment of Chanda, gives his own life worth. At the end of the film Kajli addresses him like a daughter would and says, 'It is you, isn't it, who made my mother wait for twenty years? You were the reason my mother went mad, for whom her life was destroyed. It's all your fault! My mother will never forgive you, never ever.'

To which Sanjeev Kumar replies, 'Yes, my daughter! Chanda will never forgive me. But my Kajli can forgive me. I know I am guilty, a sinner; which is why I keep returning to you, to ask for atonement, my daughter! Forgive me, my daughter! Will you come with me? Neither of has anything to look back upon. Come with me.'

This scene acts like a catharsis, bringing tears to the eyes. At the end of the film, after this dialogue, Kajli leaves with Dr. Amarnath for a better life. The climax that includes scenic views of flowers dancing in the breeze, conveying to the viewer that the weather has once again turned beautiful, leaves a lasting impression on the mind.

Mausam has been critiqued by reviewers as a serious film, a classic. This film won Gulzar the National Award for Best Direction in 1976. Sharmila Tagore won the Golden Lotus for Best Actress. That same year, *Mausam* also won the National Award for Second Best Feature Film. *Filmfare* judged *Mausam* as the Best Picture of the Year and awarded Gulzar the Best Director Award. In a 2014 survey conducted by *Filmfare* to rank the 100 most outstanding films, *Mausam* was placed 48th. Writing about the film, the magazine said:

> *Mausam* is an example of a story that has been narrated in a sympathetic and mature manner. The way it has

handled characters and issues makes it an important and noteworthy film.

It is also worth mentioning that Madan Mohan, the film's music director, passed away on 14 July, 1975. The film was dedicated to him at the time of its release.

34.

Gulzar finds himself beguiled by local dialects. They could be dialects derived from Hindi, which get their inspiration from Poorvi, Avadhi or the tongues spoken in the western regions, or the Bangla spoken in the eastern belt or the dialects of Punjab. In the maxims contained in the stories, phrases and idioms contained in folk songs, he finds an important component to enrich his own language. It is as if he understands well that our dialects create the foundation of our language, and the introduction of the stories, poems and songs into the language adds eloquence to its flow. To quote Kabir in this context, language is 'constantly flowing water'. Perhaps this is why while writing his songs, Gulzar places such importance in finding the appropriate words from his selection of dialects.

Whether he is writing words to fit into a tune, or creating a song using the metre created by the writing, in each case, words from many other dialects that bring with them intimations of a way of life join in to add their colour. At such times, some unexpected words culled from the treasure house of his memory that are added in to keep the metre intact, suggest changed meanings. Blended into Hindustani, they assume a new form of expression.

Many memories of childhood, of shabad-kirtans heard, or plays seen in his locality are all a part of Gulzar's journey into dialects. While writing a song for Vishal Bhardwaj's film *Omkara*, he adapts the traditional warrior ballad of Alha Udal from the Bundelkhand region that he often heard in his youth, giving the rhythm and the wording a new twist. He writes the song keeping in mind that the original is read or sung at a high pitch and has a unique rhythm:

Dham Dham Dhadam
Lo! the biggest warrior of them all
Omkara, hey Omkara
Eyes swift as wasps,
The hiss of a snake with a forked tongue
Omkara, hey Omkara
Whose sword strikes the head with the sound of lightning
Omkara, hey Omkara

Much in the same style as *Omkara* are many other songs that we can pick from the abundance in his diary, where other languages enrich his own expression, giving it a seductive flavour. It must be noted, though, that Gulzar favours Punjabi and Bengali when incorporating words from other languages. One is from his birthplace, while he developed an affection for the other because he came into contact with veteran Bengali artistes early in his career.

It's interesting to see how he chooses folk elements from different languages to create new imagery. I will first discuss the Punjabi language, which is in a way his return to his roots through the medium of language. A song from the film *Sitara* goes, 'Thodi si zameen, thoda aasman/ Tinkon ka bas ek aashiyan' (A little bit of earth, a little sky/ A refuge made with mere twigs). The last stanza of the song goes thus:

When the night is spent, how will we spend the day
We will chase the crows from the bajra fields
Our sons grow up tall like bajra stalks
One shelter, built of mere twigs...

The imagery of sons growing up tall like bajra stalks has been borrowed from a Punjabi folk song in which the line goes, 'Dhiya kyon jamiya ni mai/ Kanka lamiya ni mai' (O mother, why have you birthed daughters/ That grow so quickly like wheat). Though in the original the reference is to a mother and daughter, the imagery he borrows from the Punjabi song transforms itself when he uses it in Hindi in *Sitara*.

Many such examples of stanzas rich with the fragrance of the Punjabi ethos can be found, which are kept intact even as Gulzar weaves them into his songs in Hindustani. Even though he could have easily translated the line and added it, which would still have kept its meaning, he maintains his affiliation with other languages by incorporating them into his writing. Possibly because he is trying, by deftly seasoning his lyrics with the flavours of his language, to extend the song into being truly Indian and resonate with the Hindi-speaking belt that stretches across Uttar Pradesh, Bihar, Rajasthan and Madhya Pradesh.

The song 'Chappa-chappa charkha chale' (Chappa-chappa runs the spinning wheel) from *Maachis* is another example that presents itself. In the very second stanza of the song, the phrase, 'Auni-pauni yaariyan teri, bouni-bouni beriyan tale' brings in the flavour of Punjabi. The song 'Banjar hai sab banjar hai/ Mera yaar mila de saaiyan' (Fallow, all is fallow/ Take me to my love, Lord) from *Saathiya* also uses the same device. In fact, the song uses more Punjabi words in other stanzas. Gulzar's use of this device of blending two languages seamlessly in his songs is pure artistry.

There are countless such examples of an interjection of Punjabi words or even lines in the middle of a stanza, which include songs in *Paheli*, *Bunty Aur Babli* and *Satya* with its refrain of 'O munda mera' and 'O kudi meri' throughout the song 'Sapne me milti hai' (I meet her in my dreams). 'Munda' and 'kudi' in Punjabi are, respectively, boy and girl. In *Slumdog Millionaire*, in which in the very first line of 'Jai Ho', the word 'jinde', meaning alive, which is used to describe the sky adds a different slant to the song.

The song, 'Beedi jalaile jigar se piya' in *Omkara* has a line

'Ja padosi ke chulhe se aag layi le' which translates as 'Go get some embers from the neighbour's fireplace.' This phrase was oft used as an idiom in Punjab, from a time when coal was used for cooking. The line implied that the oven must be already alight in the neighbour's kitchen, go and get some fire to light our hearth. The use of such phrases is not just Gulzar's way of using his memories lyrically, but also to refresh the memories of traditions from his younger days and give them a new interpretation and relevance. Thus giving characters in films, songs that combine the contemporary idiom with traditional elements.

While discussing Gulzar-sahab's use of his mother tongue, Punjabi, in Hindi film lyrics, it is also necessary to take a look at how film music has changed in the past two decades. One dominant trend seems to be the fact that every second film deems it necessary to include a Punjabi song. Even lyricists not conversant with Punjabi are faced with the demand that some of their writing must have the twang of Punjab. The film scene itself has changed to include stories that focus attention on NRIs who hail from Punjab. Even from the angle of rhythm and percussion, songs with Punjabi lyrics work well as dance numbers and translate into hits.

Thus we see a new trend that while Gulzar used only a word, a phrase or a line in Punjabi to flavour his lyrics, today entire songs are written in the language with not a single Hindi word in them.

In this context, we also see a long list of newer songs by Gulzar that over the past twenty years have toed this trend. Songs in films like *Pinjar* (2003), *Jhoom Barabar Jhoom* (2007), *Raavan* (2010), *Veer* (2010), *Jab Tak Hai Jaan* (2012), *Kill Dil* (2014) and *Soorma* (2018) lean heavily towards Punjabi with Hindi lines sparkling in between, adding their own lustre.

Of all the songs that were relevant in the films mentioned above, a song from *Jab Tak Hain Jaan* merits examination as it stands apart as a special example of the language used in films of this period. Also because the song is a Heer, which is a much-loved musical form used in Hindi film music, despite it being quite rarely used. The writing or reciting of a Heer follows a particular traditional style, and is mostly centred on themes of separation and sorrow. It's worth looking at the intent behind the writing of this 'Heer':

Do not call me Heer, O friends, I've become Sahibaan
I hope he comes on a horse and takes me away,
I wish some prince comes for me and takes me away

I am like him, he is like me only
He smiles like it is morning,
And if he closes his eyes, it is cold and dark

Just as with Punjabi, there are an ample number of examples of the use of the Bengali language in Gulzar's songs. Understanding the influence of Rabindra Sangeet, Nazrul Geet, puja geet, the bhajan tradition of Bengal, Bhatiali and the Baul tradition opens up grounds for a discussion. In fact it has often happened that while writing a song that borrowed from these traditions, the music director himself decided that the tune as well as the lyrics must follow the metre of Bangla poetry. Similarly, it has often transpired that captivated by some song or tune, he would write his lyrics keeping intact the background and mood of the original.

Many of Gulzar's songs have been influenced by Nazrul Geet, penned by the revolutionary poet Kazi Nazrul Islam. The song, 'Roz akeli aye/ Roz bichari jaaye/ Chand ka katora liye bhikaran raat' from the film *Mere Apne* (1971) is based on a song by Nazrul, 'Meghla nishi bhore'. Salil Chowdhury too based his tune mirroring the original, thus giving Hindi film music an off-beat tune that was rendered by Lata Mangeshkar.

Another song comes to mind, one that is considered one of the most loved compositions of Nazrul Geet. This has been rendered repeatedly in their individual styles in Bangla by renowned Bangla music directors and singers: among them,

S. D. Burman, Manna Dey, Manvendra Mukhopadhyay and Akhil Bandhu Ghosh. Gulzar had written this song for his incomplete film, *Devdas* and Lata Mangeshkar had sung R. D. Burman's composition with utmost sensitivity. The original Nazrul song goes thus:

Kuhu kuhu kuhu kuhu
Koyaliya koyaliya
Kuhrila mahua bole, mahua bole

Gulzar, keeping the 'mukhda' or opening stanza of the song intact, added his words to transform it into a song composed following the lines of a classical thumri or dadra of Uttar Pradesh.

Kuhu kuhu
The koel calls
Near the mango tree
Sweeter than sugar
Is my lover's call
Glowing in my heart
Like the mahua in the forest
The koel calls out in the garden
Kuhu kuhu

R. D. Burman too kept the tune of the song as close to the original song as was possible. In the Bangla song, the words 'Mahua bole' appear thrice in the third stanza. In the *Devdas* song too, Lata Mangeshkar sings 'Mahua bole' thrice in the third stanza. Though it is obvious that the entire imagery of the song is borrowed from Nazrul Geet, the colouring given to it is eastern in nature, as Gulzar adds words from other languages into his lyrics.

Countless such examples are evident in Gulzar's writing that show how he fruitfully reaped the two rich fields of languages and folk music. One such is a song in Rajan Tarafdar's film, *Ganga* which goes, 'Aamaay dubaili re/ Aamaay bhashaili re' (You are drowning me/ You are setting me adrift). Gulzar based the first song of his career on the tune of this song to write:

Where do you come from, O Ganga,
Where do you go
Light and shadow dance upon your waters...

(*Kabuliwala*)

In the film *Kitaab*, too, he wrote a sweet lullaby based on Rabindra Sangeet, which R. D. Burman set to music. Veteran singer Rajkumari has sung the song with such attention to the words that they create layers of meaning and evoke a sense of calm. The use of Kal and Kul in this Rabindra Sangeet-inspired song has been sieved out from a poem by Tagore. Gulzar's lines are:

Hari, the day is spent, it's evening,
Help me cross the night
My time is done, help me get across

I have no one to accompany me
No cloak to shield me
My loved ones are lost
My dreams are gone
Divest me of desire

It is also worthwhile to seriously examine how Gulzar picks up the opening lines from old bandishes—melodic compositions in Hindustani classical music—of the masters, Sufi compositions and phrases from poets and traditional folk music and completes them by adding the rest of the song in his signature style. By absorbing the concepts from traditional metres and converting them into a part of a new composition, he is able to give his film music a different hue. We can see many versions of this as examples. Like his creating two different versions in his film, *Lekin*, of the traditional Rajasthani song sung in Raag Mand: 'Kesariya baalam, aao ji, padhaaro maro des' (Come, my beautiful love, welcome to my land). In the opening stanza, 'Kesariya baalam' is used as in the original, but in the remaining two places the entire bandish changes, transformed by the adeptness of Gulzar's unique style. An example of both bandishes is given below:

My beautiful beloved
People call me the mad one
Neither am I alive, nor am I dead
Separation is my malaise
People call me the mad one

And next:

My beautiful beloved
Our eyes, they met…our eyes
Our eyes, they met.

I have now steeped
Every limb of my body in your colours
My body, my mind have become golden…
The night is moonlit, come now, my love…

Hridaynath Mangeshkar who scored the music for the song sung by Lata Mangeshkar used the original folk raag, Mand, for the composition. Composed in the dadra rhythm, the song uses traditional instruments from the region like the sarangi, the tabla, ghungroo and the ravanahatha, an ancient bow and string instrument. This song that features twice in *Lekin* uses two different emotions to evoke completely different moods, using the same base line.

Just such a situation presented itself to Gulzar when, in *Gulami*, music directors Laxmikant Pyarelal created a tune based on the immensely popular couplet composed by Amir Khusro, and Gulzar had to write the rest of the lyrics. The lines were from those poems of Amir Khusro that were written in a mixture of Persian and Hindi, with one line in Persian and one in Avadhi. An example:

Do not overlook my misery
By fluttering your eyes and weaving tales
My patience has over-brimmed, O sweetheart
Why do you not take me to your bosom

According to Gulzar, the producers of the film were not in favour of using such difficult Persian words. But Laxmikant-ji was keen on retaining at least the first line from Khusro's poem (Zehaal-e-miskeen makun taghaful/ Duraye naina banaye batiyan). The lyricist did just that; taking the thread from Amir Khusro, he wove the entire song, thus bringing the blended lines of Persian and Hindi into Hindi film songs.

Don't view my heart with enmity
The poor heart is wounded by separation
The thudding heartbeat that can be heard
Is it your heart, or is it mine?

Gulzar also presses the bandishes of traditional dadras and thumris into use in his songs. He takes the famous lines of the Begum Akhtar song, 'Humri atariya pe aa ja re saawariya/ Dekha dekhi tanik hoi jaye' (Come up to my terrace, my beloved/ Let us gaze at each other) sung by the doyenne of the ghazal in the dadra style and grafts it into the film *Dedh Ishqiya* (2014). What makes the grafting interesting is that except for the first lines, the rest of the song is completely Gulzar's own. Yet, not for a moment does the song lose its link with classical music or suffer in comparison with the original compositions by the masters of yore.

Also worth keeping in mind is the fact that the song does not start with the lines of the original dadra; six lines in the form of a chorus precede the line, and the seventh line is 'Humri atariya pe aa ja re saawariya/ Dekha dekhi tanik hoi jaye' taken from the song, which comes in accompanied beautifully with the rhythm of the tabla. Gulzar's bandish must be read from the very first line till the first stanza with this fact in mind. The chorus starts thus:

Dressed and decorated she sits
His being on her breath
Where has the stranger gone
She lit lamps

But the moth did not come to the flame

Who is my rival, who has entranced him…
Come up to my terrace, my beloved
Let us gaze at each other

From the doorway, peeping
My lover looks on
He throws money on others, my lover does but,
Swears on my life about his love for me
Come let me feed you a paan with kimami
So that your red lips grow redder still

This song, based on folk music, sayings and the poems of those dialects prepares one to understand the imagery Gulzar uses. The long list of his songs is evidence of the lyricist's ability to assimilate the lexicon of many languages into Hindustani and create lyrics that are all his very own.

Just as in Punjabi and Bangla, we can find some melodious and poetic creations that are sweetened by the influence of Rajasthan's dialects and folk music. We can see evidence of this in films like *Dhola Maru* (1983), *Paheli* (2005), *Mirzya* (2016) and *Pataakha* (2018). Some of the songs he has written for Rakeysh Omprakash Mehra's film *Mirzya* demonstrate the adaptation of Rajasthani dialects. Incidentally Gulzar has also written the screenplay and dialogues for the film. Among the songs, 'Aave re hitchki', 'Kaaga re kaaga', 'Aree dola/ Aasman pe ude chakora' and 'Doli re doli chali' are examples.

Oh beloved,
The chakora flies in the sky
Flies the chakora, the chakora flies

Look the chakora flies in the sky
Goes to grab the moon, it goes, it goes
When his love meets the moon's sharp edge
Both his wings he cuts, cuts, cuts…

The wick burns in its own flame
On that the moth
Clinging close, burns

Just as with Rajasthani, he uses the dialects and phrases of Uttar Pradesh in songs when an event, nautanki or wedding scene demands it in the flow of the story. It is worthwhile (to examine some examples of his use of the Avadhi dialect of western Uttar Pradesh here: Like the excellent song in *Mausam* which goes, 'Mere ishq me laakhon latke/ Balam zara hatke' (Make way, my darling/Thousands hang on in hope of my love) and in *Naram Garam* he wrote the song, 'Kaisan saadee rachaye ho dekhi humari bahinia/ Arre mehendi se hatheliyon pe likhiyo kahaniya' (Look how my sister celebrates her wedding/ With mehendi writing stories on her palms). The song for the film *Aashirwad* which goes 'Jhir jhir barse saawani ankhiyan/ Sanwariya ghar aa, sanwariya ghar aa' (My eyes pour like the monsoon rain/ Come home, my beloved, come home...' Every one of these and many other songs use the phrases common to the eastern regions of Uttar Pradesh.

One must also keep in mind that there are songs that use the khari-boli tongue spoken in Meerut, Hapur, Bijnor, Saharanpur and Muzaffarnagar. The pure Hindi spoken in these eastern towns is evident in Gulzar's writing in *Omkara*. One can find this in the two songs, 'Naina thag lenge' (The eyes shall betray) and 'Lakad jal ke koyla hoye jai' (Wood burns to become coal). The former gives us the scent of the dialects of eastern UP:

Do not believe what the eyes say
The eyes will deceive you
Do not listen to what the eyes say
The eyes will deceive you...

Eyes, as the night moves on
Will take you to heaven
Sowing dreams of the monsoon ragas
Will promise happiness

No way of trusting the language of the eyes
Nothing written or read out, no receipt or ledger
Everything only in the air...

Finding inspiration in language goes back deep into Gulzar's past. We know that he not only listened to Sufi singers and nirgunis in his youth, but also read extensively of their works. Of these, the name of Baba Bulleh Shah comes immediately to mind. A name which is associated with the fragrant soil of Punjab. A seer known for pitting himself against hypocrisy, a simple man who tried to breach the ill feelings between Hindus and Muslims, Baba Bulleh Shah was a singer of humanitarian themes. His songs and teachings won him the acceptance of the entire country, and his writings have made him an acknowledged poet in Punjabi, Urdu and Hindi. Gulzar's relationship with him goes back to his childhood, when he felt kinship with the writings of this Sufi seer. These famous lines of Bulleh Shah:

Your love makes me dance thaiya thaiya

Your love makes me dance madly
Like from a cup of poison have I drunk
Come my healer, or I will surely die
Your love makes me dance thaiya thaiya

Keeping the rhythm of this verse intact, taking the words 'thaiya thaiya' as a base and adding 'chaiya chaiya', he created a rhyming couplet. Thus creating an everlasting song in the Sufi tradition for Mani Ratnam's film *Dil Se* that owes its provenance to Bulleh Shah. I am presenting here the antara of the song as well as the chorus-like opening lines. It is important to note here that Gulzar, often using free verse in his songs, creates a rhythm by linking the antara stanzas to a repetitive chorus-like set of lines in the opening stanza. In this song too, the refrain occurs repeatedly and creates a lyrical mood. It is much like Bulleh Shah used the line 'Your dance makes me dance madly,' repeatedly like a refrain. The altered form of that refrain comes across in dialect:

She's my melody, my holy verse,
My love who walks like soft dew drops
Paradise under her feet lies

Sometimes on the branches
Sometimes on leaf after leaf
I search for a sign of her, in the wind...

That friend who is like a fragrance
Whose speech is sweet like Urdu
My evening and night, my universe
That friend of mine, my love,
Come walk in the shade...
Head shaded by love, come walk in the shade
Come walk in the shade...

35.

Reading Gulzar's lyrics brings to attention the fact that the wordplay and central themes of his film songs are also present in his non-film poems, though they hold no connection with the characters in the films he writes for.

The song, 'Aanewala pal, jaanewala hai' (This moment that was to come, is now passing) from the film *Golmaal* for example, bears a strong link to the poem 'Aadmi bulbula hai' (Man is but an ephemeral bubble). Both songs are expressions, in different ways, of the same thought. It becomes an interesting insight to examine how a poem resembles a film song, and how the expression of a film song can be glimpsed in a poem. One imagines the poet to be like the craftsman who, after cutting strips of silken cloth, uses the pieces to create garments of varying styles. The Hindi poet Kunwar Narain refers to something similar in his diary:

> A poet creates dreams—dreams of love, beautiful dreams, everlasting dreams—but all for the sake of others. Himself, he is like the pitiful craftsman who is denied the dreams he has wrought.

Keeping this in mind, let us read both the poems written by Gulzar. The lines of 'Aadmi bulbula hai' go thus:

Man is but a bubble
And it's on the water's surface
That he breaks; he drowns
Then, rising again to the surface, he flows again
Man is but a bubble.

The song from *Golmaal* in this context departs somewhat from this main idea when the last stanza is examined, where the changing and transient nature of life's moments are described:

Once, from Time
A moment fell away
A story remained
The moment, nowhere to be seen
It made you laugh
It made you cry
This moment that was to come, is now passing

Reading the poems and ghazals of Gulzar that bear a similarity to film songs could well be an interesting exercise, if we can study them divested of their references. We could then more easily glimpse the nature of the poet which remains hidden while reading songs crafted for films.

But examining two writings with a similar theme from the different spheres of his work and grasping their meaning does give us the chance to glimpse the mind of a poet, song-writer and storyteller, and find the three aspects of his creative persona blending into one.

These similarities in creative output help combine the poet with the lyricist, as a couple of examples will show. The poem 'Alaav' with reference to the song from the film *Dil Se* and in the same way, the poem, 'Chandghar' which is linked to the song from *Maya Memsahab* are two excellent examples:

All night, the cold wind blew
All night we warmed ourselves by the bonfire
All night whatever we found growing on our bodies

We cut away and cast into the fire
All night we blew the flames to life
And fuelled two bodies to keep burning.

('Alaav')

And the song that echoes this poem:

My heart burns, my soul is aflame
The smoke clouds the eyes
All night the smoke rises
He looks at my body, his gaze pierces my mind
My lips should be sealed by his soft lips
Instead I keep counting the times I toss restless in bed
What can I do, whom can I tell
How I passed the night...

(*Dil Se*)

How many years since we lit a hope
Ages have passed since a candle was lit

('Chandghar')

...and the song that connects with it in thought:

Light up some dreams by my bedside
Allow me to sleep just a little

(*Maya Memsaab*)

The echoing of thoughts in Gulzar's film songs and poems is only natural. Because while writing a song, the poet in him draws from the same inspiration that fired his poems at an earlier stage. It is possible too that while writing a song, some thought takes hold that lingers in his mind and will not be shaken off. At such times, it becomes necessary for him to look at it from different perspectives and find ways to express it through his poems.

It's thus easily said that the poet and the lyricist are seen walking hand in hand into the distance. Even after the sun has set, even as the lantern's glow grows red and dim, they continue walking towards the horizon.

36.

Asha Bhosle. This renowned playback singer's place in Gulzar's life as a director shines with a special luminosity. Look at Asha Bhosle's playback songs for films directed by Gulzar, where she is given songs that give her singing a new persona, apart from the style she developed singing for Omkar Prasad Nayyar. Of course, along with Gulzar and Asha Bhosle, R. D. Burman too had a prominent role in crafting these songs. Both the Mangeshkar sisters have sung some unforgettable songs for R. D. Burman in Gulzar's films. While Lata-ji, with her melodious exposition of emotions in her unparalleled voice holds her place as supremo, Asha-ji too displays a playfulness and maturity in singing for Gulzar's films.

There was a phase in Asha Bhosle's musical journey when her collaboration with R. D. Burman was heading to its peak, and her stint with O. P. Nayyar had almost come to an end. Of the few songs for O. P. Nayyar that she sang at the time, the songs, 'Kitna haseen hai yeh sama…' (How beautiful it is today) for *Humsaaya* (1968) and 'Aao huzoor tumko sitaron me le chaloon' (Come, my lord, let me take you to the stars) for *Kismet* (1968) remain memorable. As do the songs 'Akeli hoon main, piya aa…' (I am all alone, come my love) for *Sambandh* (1969) and 'Chain se hum ko kabhi, aap ne jeene na diya' (You never let me live in peace) from *Pran Jaye Par Vachan Na Jaye* (1973).

Even before she became part of Gulzar's films, R. D. Burman had successfully created some exquisite songs for Asha Bhosle. The early Asha-Pancham collaboration can well be said to span the years between 1971 to 1975. By then, many compositions had given a new impetus to Asha Bhosle's career. Among them, 'Daiya yeh main kahan aa phasi' (Oh dear! What a pickle I'm in) from *Caravan* (1971), 'Dum maaro dum, mit jaaye gham' (Go on, smoke up, all your sorrows will be wiped out) from *Hare Rama Hare Krishna*

(1971), 'Logon, na maro jse, yahi to mera dildaar hai' (Do not beat him, people, he's my love) from *Anamika* (1973), 'Chura liya hai tum ne jo dil ko' (Now that you've stolen my heart…) *Yaadon Ki Baraat* (1973), 'Sona roopa laayo re' from *Joshila* (1973) and 'Sapna mera toot gaya' (My dreams are shattered) from *Khel Khel Mein* (1975).

These unforgettable songs were being viewed as indeed establishing a new identity for Asha Bhosle, but by then her niche had been fixed as a singer of cabaret songs and item numbers.

When she began singing songs written by Gulzar and composed by Pancham, and later, with the regular partnership of Asha Bhosle and Pancham for Gulzar's films proved to be the emergence of a new impetus to her role as a playback singer. Much of this was also due to the poetic turn the songs she sung took, thanks to the lyricism of Gulzar's writing, which added a new range to Asha Bhosle's repertoire.

It is worth studying this new turn in Gulzar's journey in film music. It holds many examples of Asha Bhosle's emergence as not just a singer of up-tempo dance numbers, but as a singer of songs steeped in emotion and meaning. At the time the Asha-Pancham partnership was creating waves in films under various banners such as *Hare Rama Hare Krishna*, *Caravan*, *Anamika*, *Mere Jeevan Saathi*, *Yaadon Ki Baraat* and *Khel Khel Mein*. Gulzar's *Khushboo* sparkled with songs like 'Bechaara dil kya kare' (What will this poor heart do). They brought into focus the power of the new partnership that was wrought by Gulzar's poems adding their weight to Pancham's tunes sung by Asha Bhosle. The freshness and coquettish nuances she brought into the songs for *Khushboo* had not been evident even in her cabaret numbers:

She will go home
Climbing into her doli
With mehendi-decorated hands

And kajal-lined eyes
The bride will die of happiness...

Yet another song from *Khushboo* in Asha-ji's voice, through its music and words presents itself as a song free from any influences of the past. The song: 'Bechara dil kya kare/ Saawan jale, bhadon jale) (What will this poor heart do/ With envy it burns night and day)

Asha Bhosle's expression of her new range of voice and technique expanded to become increasingly poetic. By bringing the poetic imagery to life, and accentuating the play of words, she increased the 'shelf-life' of the songs, making them perennial favourites. This song from *Namkeen* is one such:

Come again, O clouds
With pearls I shall embed your wings
Fill my pond before you leave
Near the pond's edge I will be waiting
I place you under oath of my lord, Kali Kamli Wala
Come again, O clouds

Asha Bhosle's songs through the latter part of the 1970s hold special significance because during this phase she had started singing serious-themed songs for other banners too. We can safely say that what R. D. Burman accomplished in bringing out new nuances in Asha Bhosle's voice in his songs for Gulzar's films, was much akin to what Shankar-Jaikishan for the R. K. banner and C. Ramchandra for Filmistan had done for Lata Mangeshkar's growth as an artiste.

Intimations of the freshness and maturity that is evidenced in Asha's singing for *Khushboo* can be seen even in the 1974 film, *Doosri Sita* where the threesome came together to create this song:

Wherever I find you
There I will find both my worlds
Both my worlds exist there
Where I find you...

In *Angoor* (1981), his own directorial venture, Gulzar, in a simple manner shows us the personality of the actress through a picturisation of a song that, besides highlighting Deepti Naval's attractiveness, also focuses on her musical abilities. Asha Bhosle's singing of the song at a high pitch and R. D. Burman's ability to include extremely melodious interludes give the song a modern freshness and zest. Some other aspects of the very unique trends started in film music by the coming together of this threesome also merit discussion. Reading through these lines of the song from *Angoor* will refresh memories of this happy collaboration:

Day after day, on every branch
The love-crazed bee
Writes something and goes
To the flowers
Some messages he writes
The love-crazed bee.

Following this, the music created by the team of Asha, Pancham and Gulzar for *Namkeen* (1982), *Ijazat* (1987) and the non-film album, *Dil Padosi Hai* (1987) set Asha Bhosle on a new and exciting direction in her musical career. The genius of each sparkles so brightly in each of the four songs of *Ijazat* that music connoisseurs and critics have opined that the trio has created poetry in celluloid. Reading extracts from the four songs shows us the results of this tri-cornered creative friendship:

Some things of mine
Are lying with you
Some rain-soaked days too
And the night, wrapped in my letter
Snuff out the night
Return to me my belongings...

~

Drop by drop I receive
Let me live in these moments
Life flows, let it flow

Thirsty am I, let me remain so...

You spread out the sky
My bare feet tread the earth
Having you, I still seek you
Perhaps this is the beauty of life
Let it on desire flow
Thirsty am I, let me remain so...

~

From a short story
From the falling of rain
The entire valley is full
I don't know why, my heart is full
I don't know why, my eyes brim over...

~

Empty-handed the evening has come
Empty-handed she will return
If no one comes even today
She will return empty

Empty-handed the evening has come

~

Indeed, with *Ijazat*, Asha Bhosle reached a new point in her career with Gulzar's penmanship and direction of the songs adding to the fresh approach she had found to her singing, starting from *Khushboo* in 1975. The decade between 1975 and 1987, when *Ijazat* was made, helped her shape her voice and expression very differently from what it had been during her association with O. P. Nayyar.

Even in the films for other production houses where the three worked together, the output stands apart. Songs like 'Man bahak raha hai baar baar shaam se' (Since evening my heart has been running amok) for *Ratnadeep* (1979), 'Aap aaye garibkhane me/ Aag si lag gayi zamane me' (You came to my humble abode/ A conflagration of envy swept the world) for *Sitara* (1980), 'Piya baanwari' (Mad lover) in *Khubsoorat* (1980), 'Mera chehra me chupa hai/ Meri maa ka chehra' (In my face/ Hides my mother's visage) in *Naram Garam*

(1981) and the song for *Musafir* in 1984, 'Saawan saanwari akhiyan choom ke/ Phir jaye' (The rain kisses my eyes are a few examples of countless such songs that explore different themes and emotions that are yet unexplored by critics who write on cinema music.

The music of *Jeeva* which was released in the 1980s reflects the same qualities. It is impossible to determine whether the music is better than the lyrics or vice versa, or whether it is the singer, Asha Bhosle, along with Amit Kumar who are the real stars of the songs. The song that lingers in memory is one whose words can be read as a love poem even today:

Every day, I have a dream
All night the kohl smoulders
Like a lamp of longing

Ever since I have touched the sugar of your name
To my lips
A sweet sorrow remains
And a sweet loneliness
Every day, I have a dream

A song from *Sitara* also merits mention as a composition that highlights the perfect synergy among the three main players. The benchmark created by this song by them is not easily reached by others. Any discussion, be it about Asha-ji's talent as a playback singer, or about the perfect fit of a song's words to a film situation, or the uniqueness of the composition of the tune and the interludes, is incomplete if this song from *Sitara* is not added in the list. I have often felt that this composition is perfect, for there is nothing out of place or jarring in it. Just reading a few lines takes us to a zone from which we are reluctant to emerge:

These are but shadows,
The world is made up of reflections
And loneliness even in the midst of crowds
These are shadows, this is the world...

There are no shores to shelter upon

No riversides to save the drowning
Here only the infamous shine brightly
These are but shadows...

Gulzar narrated the writing of this song with some measure of emotion. According to him, 'This song was written for an actress because she was playing the role of a film actress in a film. That day, she was tired out by the lights during the night shooting. She was feeling that everything was temporary and unreal. To the extent that even her life seemed to be on loan to her. To be frank, I kept thinking of Meena-ji [Meena Kumari] while writing this song. She would often recite a couplet:

The fear of being lost, throbs incessantly
Is life but an ornament borrowed from a neighbour

Smiling, Gulzar recounts that despite his repeated questioning, she would not share the poet's name and despite searching for it, it eluded him too.

One needs to consider how he navigates the countless evenings of introspection before pitching the song he has written to the other artistes working on it for the film. The composer and the playback singer have to work towards reaching the same level. While listening to Asha Bhosle singing this song with a blend of pathos and playfulness, few movie buffs would know that the emotions of a tragedienne lurk somewhere in the consciousness of the poet.

There are countless stories surrounding the creation of the non-film album, *Dil Padosi Hai* launched by HMV. Even today, the album can fill us with nostalgia for the time when the three creative artistes were working closely together. The album has many experimental forays. Though made almost thirty-three or thirty-four years ago, the disc retains its freshness. Created with the idea of being quite different from film music, the disc remains a testimony to the collaborative genius the three could attain in their work together. Asha Bhosle also sings each song with a new expression:

It was the night of Christmas
Things weren't in your control
Or in mine

The moon was above the trees
And I was in the church
You touched my lips while I was in prayer
How can I forget that moment of my swooning

This song is just one example of how poetry has been used in this album to create diverse scenes. Similarly, Pancham gives the song, 'Juthe tere nain/ Soutan ki chhabi choo ke aaye/ Soutan sang bitaai rain' (Your eyes are impure/ They have touched the image of that other one/ With her they've spent the night) a classical bent and sets it in the challenging eight-beat rhythm. The composition of yet another number reflects the use of folk music blended with western elements:

Boatman, O boatman
Ramaiyya boatman
I have to cross the Moini River
A yogi has arrived on that side
A yogi said to be enlightened
I have to go to the other side, Ramaiyya
Boatman, O boatman...

Other songs in the album mirror the warmth of the relationship that linked Gulzar, Asha Bhosle and Pancham. Some lines reflect this:

Let me go, let go
Of the quarrels, the complaints
The promises of fidelity
That which has gone, let go of it

There will be some pain
Some sorrow too
And loneliness
A blunting of emotion

Though these songs are evidence of Asha Bhosle's interesting second chapter as a background singer in Hindi films, Asha

Bhosle never failed to jokingly rebuke Gulzar, whom she addressed as a brother, that though Pancham and he did give her some wonderful songs, they reserved the best songs of a film for her elder sister, Lata Mangeshkar. Gulzar would be somewhat astonished by this statement. Whenever I approached this subject with reference to Lata-ji and Asha-ji, Gulzar would smile and say, 'It was not my job to tell Pancham of my preference for a voice for a song. Whenever Pancham made a tune, he was clear in his mind whether Lata Didi would sing it or Asha-ji. I have never interfered in this for any song, as that is the prerogative of the music director. Even if it was my own film, my job was to write a song to fit a given situation. Though there was a lot of banter between us. If Pancham would tell me that he would give Lata Didi a certain song, I would laughingly tell him, watch out for Asha.'

Continuing on the theme, Gulzar-sahab says that he once told Asha-ji, 'Both of you are superlative singers, and it is my good fortune that both of you have sung so beautifully for my films. I want to share this about my work that I have pledged two films to highlight the respect I hold for Lata-ji and Asha-ji. Thus *Ijazat* is completely Asha-ji's film, and in the same way, *Libaas* is dedicated totally to Lata-didi's genius.'

Gulzar gets emotional as he recounts this. He cherishes the films he has made not from the viewpoint of his poetry, screenplay or direction, but by holding both playback singers as the main stakeholders.

This is significant; the addition of the two unparalleled voices gives meaning to the relationship between Gulzar and R. D. Burman. Of course, it is the individual listeners' choice whether they like listening to 'Mera kuch samaan' from *Ijazat* along with 'Seeli hawa choo gayi' (The stale breeze caressed me) in *Libaas*; or whether, while listening to 'Ab ke na saawan barse' (The rains do not come) from *Kinara* they sway to 'Saawan saawari akhiyan choom ke' (The rains kissed those dark eyes) from *Musafir*.

37.

Gulzar wrote the screenplay and the two songs, 'Ek akela sheher main' (I, alone in the city) and 'Do deewane sheher main' (Two in the city, madly in love) for the film *Gharonda* produced and directed by Bhimsain. Gulzar and Bhushan Banmali wrote the dialogues together. Naqsh Lalpuri wrote a song too, the lyrics of which started with 'Tumhe ho na ho, mujhko to, itna yakeen hai' (You may or may not be, but of this I am certain).

Bhimsain had illustrated and designed many of the children's books that Gulzar wrote. He was keen that Gulzar should direct his film, but Gulzar persuaded him to direct it himself as it was his first film.

Gharonda was by all counts a successful film, with Gulzar's deft adaptation of Shankar Shesh's story. The songs were also very popular. The film featured three main characters and Gulzar gave the film's hero the right to be a weaker person compared to his beloved. In the film, the heroine abandons her lover to marry an older man, but the hero does not fault her for it, or hold her guilty. Thus, in a way this is a feminist film where the heroine's right to take an independent decision is recognised. When, just before the film's climax, the husband (played by Shriram Lagoo) learns that his wife (played by Zarina Wahab) is in love with Sandeep (played by Amol Palekar), he does not exert his husbandly right to interfere. These are some aspects which mark the film as a significant one.

The heroine, Zarina Wahab, goes with her businessman husband to his village, where the dialogue Gulzar writes for them reveals the crux of the film. Chaya tells her husband, Mody, 'How good it feels to be in the village. There is no tension, no rushing about. There seems to be so much time. In the city, one runs after time and the days elude us.'

Mody says in reply, 'Here we are grounded, linked to the

earth. In the city our feet hardly touch the ground. Everyone is climbing upwards using the other person's shoulders. Someone has his feet on my shoulders, and someone else is climbing, placing his feet on his shoulders.'

Gharonda tries to compare human relationships psychologically where a young man, frustrated by the heartless selfishness of the city, is forced to curse it as:

These roads that stretch longer than a lifetime
I have not seen them reaching their destination
They just keep running about
I have never seen them stop

In this stranger-like city
I search for someone familiar
I, alone in this city...

Through the medium of this song, we understand the frustration and the feeling of defeat felt by the youth as he starts leaving the city. In this state of mind, he tells the heroine at the end of the film, 'Chhaya, this city, which has broken me...I am leaving it. All my roads that led to you are now broken off from you and I do not know where they will take me.' The film does not offer any opinion; rather it gives every character space to be understood in their own right. By doing this, Gulzar is able to portray the tension and struggle that a city imposes on the middle class, by not just squashing their dreams but also forcing them to take decisions that may seem intellectually sound, but mask the mental agony behind it.

The screenplay clearly delineates how the heroine leaves her beloved quite suddenly and adjusts to marriage with an older man; an act that proves how carefully the screenplay has been handled. To adapt such a bold subject into a film in the late seventies was risky indeed. Bhimsain's effort while directing this low-budget film to creatively ensure that each character is viewed as a real and complete human being is evident. It is clear that the subject of this film, made four decades ago, is still relevant today, and is a trailblazer in championing the right of a woman to take decisions independently and live by them, even if they are tough ones. Though the film does not beat the drum for 'feminism', it is a good subject for those interested in gender studies in the fact that the hero, despite all his merits, is rejected by the heroine.

When, at the end of the film, the hero Amol Palekar is leaving the city, the supporting hero, Shriram Lagoo tells him, 'When you would leave the office, I would imagine that you were ready to take on life. I felt you would be able to fight it out. But you started the battle wrongly. You adopted a shortcut, which is why you lost even before the battle began.' The hero's response to this gives the message of the film an enlightened interpretation. Palekar's response is, 'This time I will start the fight properly, right here...Life is not just shadows, there is reality too somewhere. And that which is real is not shadowy.'

Gulzar also gives the hero the chance to use his logic to reject the heroine, for the real meaning of life goes beyond just finding love. The film shows up in sharp contrast the fact that the heroine and hero leave each other for different reasons; she for her self-preservation, he for his own reasons. At the point where the film ends, there is hope about the hero starting a new life as from the background, a fragment of song says, 'Make your path your destination.'

Thus the story of *Gharonda* is psychologically unravelled by three main characters. Bhupinder's sad rendition of the song, 'Ek akela iss sheher main' continues to haunt the viewer.

38.

Focus on the collaborations between Gulzar and R. D. Burman often result in sidelining the partnership that was also forged between Gulzar and Salil Chowdhury. Despite this, the fact remains that while writing for Salil-da, Gulzar created lyrics that were not only distinctive but, through experimental forays, created a new niche in Hindi film music. The first song written by Gulzar was 'Mora gora ang laile' for Bimal Roy's *Bandini* (1963). It is quite a different matter that *Kabuliwala* was released first, in 1961, which is why the song, 'Ganga aaye kahan se' (Where do you come from, O Ganga) is said to be the first of his long list of songs that would follow. When Gulzar started making *Mere Apne* (1971), the producer of the film, N. C. Sippy had already signed Salil Chowdhury as music director. Respecting this, Gulzar partnered with Salil-da with the same commitment that he showed while working with his friend, Pancham. In fact, going further, Gulzar credits Salil-da for introducing him to western music and western symphonies. Besides *Mere Apne*, Gulzar and Salil Chowdhury have worked together on just five songs in four films. Leaving aside the one from *Kabuliwala*, the songs include one for *Prem Patra* (1962), two songs for *Anand* (1970) and one for *Anokha Daan* (1972). The remarkable fact is that these five songs and the songs of *Mere Apne* bear testimony not just to a superlative collaboration, but are still heard today. Besides this, the Bangla film *Lal Pathor* (1964) also has a song by Gulzar in it. But we will discuss that interesting story later.

Some aspects of Salil Chowdhury's offbeat tunes for Gulzar's lyrics merit examination. He is the sole composer who, along with Occidental music, also gathered the music of Assam, Bengal and Kumaon into his compositions. He could pick up a stick and create a rhythm with it, or simultaneously adapt a traditional classical instrument for a folk tune. In the same way he would use some unusual, little known instruments to craft classical songs that did not demand classical knowledge from listeners. His mind was always actively creating different rhythms, movements and symphonies.

Also significant is the fact that in his youth, he joined IPTA, the Indian People's Theatre Association, where he came into contact with Balraj Sahni, Sahir Ludhianvi, Majrooh Sultanpuri, Avtar Kishan (A. K.) Hangal and Gulzar. The influence of IPTA can be seen in his early compositions where we see shades of 'Gan-sangeet', IPTA's easy-to-understand motivational songs written for the common man. Perhaps it was this stint with IPTA that inspired him to create ensemble songs for films and outside of film music that would establish him as the innovator of choirs in Indian music. Part of Salil Chowdhury's fame rests on the incomparable songs he got the Bombay Youth Choir to sing under his baton; with Mukesh, Lata Mangeshkar, Manna De and Ruma Ganguly among the singers. Later, he created a similar team with the Calcutta Youth Choir.

Contrasting strands form part of Salil Chowdhury's music. On the one hand we see his neo-real, communist thought active, while on the other the emotional overtones in the traditional tunes of Assam and Bengal are evident. Thus we see Salil Chowdhury's creations balanced at the meeting point between communist thought and artistic creativity, where romance meets ideology, to create a new musical idiom. Perhaps this is what allows Salil Chowdhury's art to be seen as different because it stays away from the groove that many others follow. Many singers, both male and female, often find this causes difficulties in their rendition of his songs. They find so many complexities in this musician's compositions, and so many usages of musical devices, that to understand and absorb them quickly takes some effort.

Many music critics have slotted Salil Chowdhury as a musician who created revolutionary music with folk overtones for the IPTA plays. In this mould, he presents himself as a musician who has assimilated all the musical streams from other countries. It is interesting to note too that his music shows influences from the symphonies of Beethoven, Mozart, Chopin and Hans Izler, which then get embedded in his tunes as chords that bear similarity to western orchestration.

Elements of contemporary Latin American music, the marching songs of Russia that reflect communist thought, and the echoes of the folk music of many countries including that of Afghanistan also find themselves transformed as Indian musical compositions. In no way can we call these influences stolen; instead, he has used his knowledge of music to adapt and transform them. For the same reason, Salil Chowdhury's orchestra is also considered a balanced arrangement of eastern and western tunes. Just as we find the sitar, tabla, flute and dholak representing Indian instruments in his orchestra; the violin, cello, oboe, clarinet, saxophone, guitar and the bongo also form a vital component.

In each of the songs in the rather small filmography for which Salil Chowdhury and Gulzar worked together, the lyrics are set in a new, different arrangement of music. For example, the two songs of *Anand*, Lata Mangeshkar's 'Na jiya laage na/ Tere bina mera kahin jiya lagae na' (Without you, my heart is no longer interested in anything), and Mukesh's 'Maine tere liye hi saat rang ke sapne chune' (I have chosen dreams in the seven colours, just for you) are very different from each other.

Raag Malgoonji is created when the komal gandhaar (minor third) present in Raag Bageshri is blended into the shuddh gandhar (major third) of Raag Rageshri. Lata Mangeshkar deftly navigates this raag as she sings 'Na jiya laage na'. Gulzar's imagery in one of the stanzas opens up a new vista for listeners:

Where did I forget to live, I don't remember
Where I found you, there breath returned to me
Life, without you, alas I cannot enjoy
My heart is restless...

Mukesh is not left behind either in this film. Salil-da weaves an absolutely new pattern of orchestration in this song where, blending original western symphonic tunes with some extraordinary music, he creates interludes that impress themselves on the listener's mind. The modulation of Mukesh's voice in the last lines of each of the antaras is worth noting, after which the line leads back to the rhythm of the opening line. All three stanzas, namely: 'Janam janam se aakhen bichhayi tere liye in raahon main' (Over many lives have I have paused on the pathways of life, hoping for a glimpse of you); 'Kabhi kabhi to awaaz dekar mujhko jagaya khwabon ne' (At times my dreams called out to me, and jerked me awake) and 'Tere bina bhi, tere liye hi, diye jalaae raahon mein' (Without you, for you, I lit lamps by the wayside) showcase the skilful weaving of the lyrics with the sweetness of the music.

All the songs of Bimal Roy's *Prem Patra* were penned by Rajendra Krishan. Only one song, 'Saawan ki raaton mein aisa bhi hota hai' (This happens too on rainy nights), delineating the revelation of love, was written by Gulzar. The song from the film *Anokha Daan*, which followed a year after *Anand*, for which Gulzar wrote, 'Madhbhari yeh hawaein/ Paas aaye, naam lekar mujhko yeh bulaye (These intoxicating breezes/ They call me by name) is similar.

This was a significant creation, both from the point of view of lyrics and composition. It is amazing how Lata-ji brought an added layer of softness to her voice while singing for Salil Chowdhury and Roshan-sahab. Some of it was because of the way the tune was structured, and some of it because both music directors preferred to understate the loudness of the voice. If Lata Mangeshkar had sung the same song for either Shankar-Jaikishan or Laxmikant-Pyarelal, the orchestration would have been completely different to match the signatures of the duos. But the likelihood is that this could have been possible only at a high pitch. Salil Chowdhury comes across as a great musician who delicately presented some songs that were recorded only in a soft manner.

Gulzar had written a song 'Ruke ruke se kadam, ruk ke baar baar chale' (Hesitant my feet, stopped and walked) for the Bangla film *Lal Pathor* which Salil-da had recorded in

Mubarak Begum's voice. Written as a 'mujra', a fast number, the song was later adapted by Gulzar for *Mausam* (1976), where he used the opening lines to craft a new poem. Lata Mangeshkar, under Madan Mohan's direction, has sung the song completely differently from the *Lal Pathor* number, and the lyrics of both songs are different. The Bangla song has the words, 'Mud ke baar baar chale' (They keep changing directions) which in *Mausam* Gulzar changed to 'Ruk ke baar baar chale' (They pause, and start again). Let us read a stanza of the Bangla song, which Salil-da composed using traditional instruments like the sarangi, tabla and harmonium:

Hesitant my feet, stopped and walked
Restless I was, but am leaving your home with peace
The sun came many times without the dawn
In waiting, I spent this night too...

Salil Chowdhury created some off-beat tunes even for Gulzar's first film *Mere Apne*. But as these have already been discussed earlier, we shall not go into that here. Though it is interesting to note that Gulzar, for his maiden production, decided to work with a music director who could, even while remaining mainstream, not bend to the demands of popularity. Interestingly, when Lata Mangeshkar later offered Gulzar the chance of directing a film of his choice in which she could sing the kind of songs she had sung earlier, she gave the example of *Madhumati* for which Salil Chowdhury had composed music.

39.

Hrishikesh Mukherjee's *Aashirwad* (1968) is an important film in many ways. Music and poetry join to build the structure of the film. Gulzar proved himself a superlative dialogue-writer and songwriter. He holds this film in high esteem. Whenever it is discussed, he speaks with near reverence about the story, the screenplay and the film itself. He emphasises the fact that Ashok Kumar's presence in this film lifted it to the status of cult cinema. As Jogi Thakur, Ashok Kumar plays an ethical man who, despite belonging to a high caste and the upper class, prefers to live with the poor and downtrodden Dalits as their guide and leader. He learns to play the dhol from a Dalit (played by Harindranath Chattopadhyay). A poet by temperament, he lives a parallel life in a poetic world, preferring to stay far removed from the violent, discriminatory world outside. The film revolves around the poignant relationship between Jogi Thakur and his daughter Neena (played by Sumita Sanyal).

As I watched *Aashirwad*, it was clear to me why this film is so close to Gulzar's heart. In the way the film delineates the relationship between father and daughter through poetry, which is revealed in an unusual way through the screenplay and dialogues. Even at an early age the daughter is aware that the task that her father is engrossed in is related to the writing of poetry. Whenever Jogi Thakur, after a disagreement with his wife, Veena, who is addressed as Rani Ma, leaves the house in the middle of the night, it is his daughter who runs after him to hand over a shawl and his satchel of books. Rani Ma is a heartless member of the landlord class who can never get on with her principled and fair-minded husband. One of the unique aspects of the film is the fact that the father writes poems for his daughter. The poignancy of these poems cannot but tug at the heartstrings...

Once, there was childhood
A small, infant childhood
In childhood, there was a father
A good-true father there was
And the bond between them was beautiful
Once, there was a childhood...

The parallel narrative wrought out of Gulzar's poems make *Aashirwad* a significant film. Harindranath Chattopadhyay 's songs, 'Railgadi' and 'Naav chali, nani ki naav chali' (The ship has set sail, Granny's ship has set sail) are his artistic contributions to the film. Jogi Thakur reads poetry to escape life's sorrows. In this, the poetry, read from jail, rising from depression is a delicate aspect of Gulzar's writing, which he has been polishing since 1968. The continuous practice of decorating the field of poetry with his poems is akin to the sadhana of a disciple of music who strives to achieve perfection in articulating the first note, sa. This poem, read by Ashok Kumar in a sorrowful state of mind is worth re-reading:

With the same single note
With the same steady rhythm
Look how, since the morning
The sorrowing rain has been falling
Showers flying like muslin scarves
All of nature is dripping
The entire universe is oozing
Every reclining branch soaking wet
See how they are as if weighed down
In tired, weary bodies
With small, slow breaths
The hot frankincense is burning...

After this scene, the camera goes straight to the room of Jogi Thakur's now grown-up daughter. For her, the rain does not convey sadness but, under a different circumstance, becomes a reason for joy. Lata Mangeshkar sings this song, composed by Vasant Desai, immensely melodiously on behalf of Neena's ringing voice,

Jhir jhir my eyes rain incessantly
Beloved, come home
With you come the colours of spring
Without you everything is barren

It's worthwhile studying the contrast created by the juxtaposition of the two scenes. Gulzar makes this possible because he has written the lyrics for both and can make Jogi

Thakur's sad rainwater turn into silken drops for his daughter. Gulzar finds this film special also because much of it is rooted in native Indian elements. When Jogi Thakur goes for the first time to listen to music, he listens to a Lavani song, a genre popular in Maharashtra. Similarly, while learning to play the dhol from Baiju Dholakia, he engages in friendly contests with his teacher in the recitation of the words of the rhythm and the playing of the instrument. While showing children the bioscope images, the actor recreates scenes which reflect the innocence of a childhood.

Throughout the film, Gulzar sprinkles ancient wisdom on the film's dialogues. Take this bit spoken by Ashok Kumar, 'Yes, yes, fall! Fall again at my feet! This is why people stamp you down...get up!' Pointing to his heart he says, 'Can you not fall here?' In the same way he says, showing indifference to material wealth, 'Money corrupts everyone, brother Mohan. Otherwise no one is intrinsically bad.' And indeed, only Gulzar could have written the exchange of salutations between the jailor and the newly released prisoner. His poetry explores socio-political philosophies in the film. As when the jailor says, 'We keep the guilty in jail so that they can free themselves from all the familiar ties outside and live with themselves. Look at themselves. And understand and evaluate the good and the bad that lives within them.'

Aashirwad discusses the role of poetry and music, honesty and respect, truth and trust throughout the film. Which in turn seems to demand great sacrifices, if the needle should shift from its point where life can be led truthfully. Ashok Kumar's realistic acting, Harindranath Chattopadhyay's amazing dexterity on the dhol, and Baby Sarika's portrayal of the innocence of the young Neena not only touch the heart, but also evoke poignant emotions.

Using poetry, music, the percussion of the dhol, Lavani and traditional bandishes like 'zingapur takur-takur' gives the film a lyrical base, a collage that reflects true India. This song by Manna Dey which creates a sense of peace as it takes the film towards its ending is an insight into what Hrishikesh Mukherjee and Gulzar were aiming to achieve. The lines keep resounding in the mind,

Life is measured, measured out by day and night
Short is the measure of the breath, long the road ahead...

Those aiming for the dawn, start out before dawn breaks
On these, life's roads
Longer than life, my friend, are these roads of life...

40.

Aandhi (1975) was in essence a love story. The background of politics which moves the story forward also adds tension to it. The theme of the film revolves around the love marriage between a lady politician, Aarti Devi (played by Suchitra Sen) and a hotel manager, JK (played by Sanjeev Kumar), and the subsequent movement of the conjugal relationship towards disintegration. An ambitious businessman father (Rehman) wishes to see his daughter who has just returned after studying law overseas, succeed as a politician. The only impediment in the path to her success as a political entity is the love marriage, which the father wishes to destroy.

Aandhi is inspired by noted writer Kamleshwar's Hindi novel, *Kali Aandhi*, which Gulzar changed in some measure. It is well known that when *Aandhi* was released, the Emergency had not been imposed on the country but when Emergency was declared on 26 June 1975, the film was banned from theatres. At the time of the banning, Gulzar and Sanjeev Kumar were attending the International Film festival in Moscow, for the screening of the film there. It had so transpired that *Filmfare* magazine had published an article on *Aandhi* with the headline, 'See Your Prime Minister on Screen' and the Congress Party leaders felt that the film depicted Indira Gandhi. This was also because of the way Suchitra Sen was portrayed. Her manner of walking with quick steps, descending the staircase holding a file in one hand, the slight white streak at the hairline, and the handloom saris she wore seemed to mimic Indira Gandhi's mannerisms and clothes.

Thus, though the film was indeed released pre-Emergency, thanks to the publication of the article, the film was banned in the thirtieth week of the Emergency. Soon after, the film was released in theatres with changes. Gulzar cut off a few scenes and filmed a new segment to be added to the film. In this new scene, Suchitra Sen is involved in a discussion with her father about entering politics and the advantages of doing so. A photo of Indira Gandhi is shown hanging on the wall behind them. Suchitra Sen, as Aarti Devi, looks at the photo and says, 'I hold her as my role model.' The addition of this scene quelled the tempest and *Aandhi* could be screened again.

In every interview he has given on *Aandhi*, Gulzar has maintained that he did not base Aarti Devi on Indira Gandhi, and that his film is basically a love story; which is indeed a fact. If you watch the film attentively, you will see how even from the very first scene till the last, *Aandhi*, through flashbacks merging into the present, through fragments of scenes, concentrates on drawing the thread of the relationship to show the chemistry between and the closeness of the couple. The individuality of husband and wife is brought out. We learn at two points in the film that Aarti Devi and JK have been living apart from each other for nine years yet the tender feelings that they nurture for each other continue to linger. Though Aarti Devi blossoms as a mature politician during this period, the pain of her broken home lies deep within her mind. The political setting of the film is superficial but effective in taking the story forward. The flashback scenes that depict the two playing golf, or meeting in the bookshop, or Aarti persuading her father to agree to the love marriage and the many instances through the film where we see the hero reading a poem to his wife highlight the theme of the love story. Gulzar gets the poem-reading hero to say beautifully, 'Every image has been ruined,' which testifies to Gulzar's own love for poetry. Thus, in Gulzar's film, he does not allow the mood or the emotion of the poem to be ruined, only the image is affected. Aarti Devi makes a statement, 'If you did not have poetry, you would just be very ordinary,' which is something that only a wife who is also a friend can say.

In fact, Gulzar draws out the mutual understanding between the couple beautifully. To Sanjeev Kumar's query, 'So you remember everything?' Suchitra Sen responds with, 'You too have not forgotten anything,' which is almost a line from a poem.

Even at the very beginning the dialogue between JK and Binda, his servant, (played by A. K. Hangal) establishes the mood of the film. Binda says, 'So much has changed, so much has broken in the space of these years,' and JK responds with, 'Do relationships break because of the passing of years?' At this, Binda says, 'The relationship with this home has broken after all.' Musing to himself, JK says, 'I have not yet understood where it is broken and where it remains intact.' From this we are made to understand that the distance between Aarti Devi and her husband is ideological. Some thread still links them, something keeps alive the love between them. If this were not so, on knowing that she is staying in the same hotel where the husband she left nine years ago is the manager, Aarti Devi would not go to meet him at his bungalow behind the hotel at night. Perhaps no actress except Suchitra Sen could have expressed this delicate but tumultuous relationship. The mutual understanding between Sanjeev Kumar and Suchitra Sen comes across in the film.

In *Gulzar's Aandhi: Insights into the Film*, written by Saba Mehmood Bashir, the author points out that the married life of JK and Aarti Devi was marked by the humour which characterised their relationship. To the extent that instead of telling her husband during breakfast that she is pregnant, Aarti informs him about it through a telegram, thus underlining the excitement and romance that marks their relationship. Bashir analyses *Aandhi* thus:

> At one level, Gulzar's *Aandhi* depicts the love possible between two stubborn, independent minded people. At another, it is a satirical commentary on the political scenario.

This is a perfect analysis, by which, through the prism of *Aandhi* we can talk about the state of society and politics of that time.

Much effort has been expended in ensuring that those aspects are filmed precisely, which we see evidence of even in the present political arena and in relation to the equations of election politics. The characters of the leader of the Opposition, Chandrasen (played by Om Shivpuri) and Aarti Devi's colleague, Lallu Lal (played by Om Prakash) show up the nature of politics. Gulzar successfully shows us the final result of the dilemmas, internal conflicts, and imaginary divisions that beset politics. As a metaphor, *Aandhi* stands for the stormy relationship that has existed between the public and society through the ages. Raising clouds of dust, sometimes political, sometimes religious and sometimes social in its wake.

There are many ways of assessing the film from the point of view of women's independence. Even the short dialogues between Sanjeev Kumar and Suchitra Sen are angled towards poetry. Aarti Devi's dialogues in various situations are also very effectively used. Some of these can be studied here on their own: 'Who keeps their house so clean?', 'Once I had come back home...you were not there...I had delayed too...', 'Truth cannot be won by speaking untruthfully'. 'I was entering politics to serve my country, not to run your shop, and if I'm leaving now, it is to set up my home.' These dialogues help establish Aarti Devi as a woman who is self-reliant, strong and far-sighted.

Sanjeev Kumar, in his perfectly played role as JK, says seriously, 'Your going is necessary, I understand. Whatever you have begun, complete it. I want to see you always successful...always.' The expression of the husband's desire to see his wife succeed gives her the confidence to progress. The strong path of love identifies the road on which the two characters who started on a slow moving path move ahead with fast moving feet. The meaningful exposition of feminism in this film reminds one in another context, of Satyajit Ray's *Mahanagar* where a woman wishing to devote her life to politics is denied the companionship and support of her husband who is a hotel manager.

Aandhi is a milestone of Gulzar's filmography which has been considered one of the most notable films of the 1970s. A film whose music resounds in memory even today. An artistic creation with music paving its way, in which the lyricist says:

In you, I find a reason for living
Life else was devoid of meaning
With you, the light has come back to my life

41.

From this crossroads diverge
Some paths that tread slowly
Some roads that hurry along

A lonesome path
Approaches from afar
Nears, veers all at once
And stops not, moves not
I sit by myself and think
Surely there is a way
That leads straight to you

Some songs that bedeck Gulzar's film journey have been sung by Lata Mangeshkar and Kishore Kumar in such a way that they shine like stars in the sky. The combination of Lata Mangeshkar and Kishore Kumar with Gulzar and R. D. Burman has resulted in songs as notable as those that the teaming of Gulzar and Pancham with Asha Bhosle gave us. The three unsurpassable love duets of *Aandhi* sung by Lata Mangeshkar and Kishore Kumar: 'Iss mod se jaate hain,' (From this crossroads diverge), 'Tum aa gaye ho, noor aa gaya hai' (With you, the light has come back to my life) and 'Tere bina zindagi.'

It is safe to say that the lyrics by Gulzar contributed to making them unforgettable, and that he played a significant role in the success of the second run of their partnership.

Perhaps the three love-duets of *Aandhi* can be said to be the most successful among the songs in films directed by Gulzar. Lata's high-pitched alaap which starts the song, 'Iss mod se jaate hain', has a hypnotic quality to it. R. D. Burman adds a *teevra madhyam* (sharp 'fa') to his composition to take it into Raag Yaman. Adding to the beauty of Lata Mangeshkar's voice are the instruments which include the sarod played by Zarin Daruwalla, the sitar by Jairam Acharya and the flute by Hariprasad Chaurasia. Kishore Kumar's measured cadences add the desired contrast to make the duet among R. D. Burman's best compositions.

The soft strains of Jairam Acharya's sitar in the prelude add a layer of sentiment to the heart-touching 'Tere bina zindagi se shikwa to nahin', shot against the backdrop of Kashmir's Shalimar Bagh and the Martand temple. Aniruddha Bhattacharya and Balaji Vittal who have written a biography of R. D. Burman share in it the interesting story that the song has strains borrowed from another RD composition, 'Jete dao amay deko na', in Raag Nand. And that R. D. Burman had composed the tune for a Bangla song to be sung during Durga puja, to the words, 'Jete jete pothe holi deri'. Gulzar used the tune to write 'Tere bina…'

'Tum aa gaye ho...' is composed in R. D. Burman's favourite minor scale. Through Gulzar's lyrics too contribute to the song's soft mood in which two people, drawn by love, try to come to an understanding. Gulzar delineates this very well in these lines:

I did not know
Where I started from
Or for where
Yet this much I knew
You would be there
Wherever the roads meet
Because your prayers were
Reaching me

Gulzar's statement about the songs of the film reflects his ideological stance, 'Song situations come in a natural way while writing the screenplay of a film. Generally, I prefer creating a song rather than avoiding it. I appreciate music and believe that songs are a necessary element to experience cinema completely. Which is why while writing a screenplay, if I feel a situation demands a song, I definitely write it in. I adopted the same method in *Aandhi*.'

In singing the duets of *Aandhi*, both playback singers have replicated the composer's style and sung in exactly the way he has composed the songs on a minor scale. The dialogue between the two that is carried on through 'Tere bina zindagi se koi shikwa to nahin' creates a subtext of suppressed passion that even the lyricist, music director or the singers themselves may never have thought was possible through a background song. In the lines spoken by Sanjeev Kumar to Suchitra Sen, he says, 'This moon that is up there, look at it at night. It does not appear by day.' Suchitra Sen says, 'It appears every day.' Sanjeev Kumar then says, 'But the amavasya comes in between. Normally, the dark phase of the moon lasts fifteen days, but this time it has lasted much longer.' And then the song flows on.

R. D. Burman has also orchestrated the prelude and interludes of the songs of *Aandhi* in a masterful manner. And in the same masterful way, the dialogues written by Gulzar that are interspersed in 'Tere bina...' create their own impact. Let us also at this point note some other songs that this combination of Lata Mangeshkar, Kishore Kumar, Gulzar and R. D. Burman have created that stand at the high point of melodic compositions. Among them, 'Aap ki aankon mein kuch mehke hue se raaz hain...' (In your eyes lie fragrant secrets) from *Ghar*, 'Hazaar rahen mud ke dekhi...' (On a thousand paths I turned around to look) from *Thodi Si Bewafai*, 'Chand chura laya hoon...' (I have stolen the moon for you...) and 'Gulmohar jo tumhara naam hota' (Had your name been Gulmohar) from *Devta*.

42.

I wonder what I kept thinking
That not a moment of the night passed
Not a single hour journeyed past
I wonder what thought kept it from passing

Kinara (1977) is a fine example of a sentimental film. If anyone from today's generation watches this film, it is possible they might find it slow-moving. Which is natural in this age of technical advances and special-effects photography in cinema. Yet, this film holds its own place in Gulzar's filmography. A creation that has been wrought delicately by weaving the threads of emotion, and whose message still holds relevance today.

The film revolves around the guilt suffered by the film's hero, Inder (played by Jeetendra), a man whose mistake ruins the life of the heroine, Aarti Sanyal (played by Hema Malini). Aarti, a dancer, is engaged to marry her fiancé, Chandan Arya (played by Dharmendra). But just five days before the wedding, he loses his life in an accident caused by Inder. This is a sorrow that will walk with Aarti through the rest of her life. The film starts tragically at a point where Aarti is beginning her dance performance and her fiancé and Inder, in their rush to reach 'Vidya Hall', are involved in an accident. As a result, Inder ruins Aarti's life, throwing it into despair. When Inder comes to know he has been responsible for Chandan's death, he is beset by guilt. He tries to atone for it by bringing some joy into Aarti's life, but another mishap occurs: Aarti slips and falls down the steps of the ruins of Bagh Bahadur's palace in Mandu. The fall results in damage to her retina, causing her to lose her eyesight. This time too, Inder is guilty of bringing tragedy into Aarti's life.

The entire story is about these two accidents which cause irreparable harm to a woman's life. A single man is responsible for this and yet he tries, though unsuccessfully, to share her sorrow and empathise with her.

Gulzar adapted a story written by Bhushan Banmali to create the screenplay and a psychoanalytic depiction of the complexities that surround the destinies of two people. At first glance this film seems to be about a woman's sufferings and her fight for survival, but reading between the lines of the film will show that it is about a man sincerely striving to atone for his mistakes. Interestingly, the filmmaker does not try to evoke sympathy for the heroine by creating a backstory for the dead man. Instead, he takes the story of a distressed woman and tries to strategise her rehabilitation and return to living again.

Shriram Lagoo plays an effective role in the film as a practical and clear-sighted person. He tells his nephew, Inder, the profound truth that an accident is just an accident. It was as easily possible that could have been you, he says, instead of Chandan who died. To help Jeetendra absolve himself of the guilt of having caused Aarti's fiance's death, he makes a suggestion. That he should try and forget that he wants to help

Aarti only to assuage his guilt. But if he had genuinely fallen in love with her, then 'putting aside the insults and humiliation, loathing and anger, go and tell her that you love her truly. Don't ever leave her side, even though she is in trouble and has become blind because of the accident. If you are able to do this, then I am by your side through thick and thin.'

This dialogue by Lagoo is the pivot of the film, around which many emotional themes revolve. You can thus view the film as a melodrama, or as the process of mending the hurt caused accidentally by one human being on another. Or yet again, the film could be the unravelling of varied situations in the various characters according to their ethical and psychological makeups. In the delineation of Aarti's character, the emotions are kept close to reality. It is difficult to think of any other film in which Hema Malini has expressed her emotions so eloquently through her eyes.

Similarly, many small devices are cleverly used to bring out the hero's sensibilities and throw light on his nature. He has made it his mission to fulfil faithfully whatever responsibilities Aarti may have expected from Chandan and to bring all her dreams to fruition. He immerses himself in the effort of rehabilitating Aarti.

Whether it is getting the book published, or ensuring she regains her confidence and self-reliance by reawakening her desire to dance again. If he has to change his name and present himself before Aarti, so be it. Aarti detests Inder but is comfortable around Prakash, the name he has assumed, and so he is seen as prepared to negate his name and identity too, to this end.

The publishing of Chandan's manuscript despite his death is another objective that runs parallel with the main story of the film. Aarti considers it her most precious dream, and Inder strives to make it come true. In fact, using the book written by Chandan as a metaphor, *Kinara* can be read like a visual book, a book resting on the pillars of music, dance, history and love.

Lata Mangeshkar has sung a poignant song in the film which is based on classical music. R. D. Burman has taken the tune of the song, 'Ab ke na saawan barse, abh ke baras toh barsegi akhiyaan' (The clouds will not bring rain this season, this year the eyes shall shed tears) from a tune his father S. D. Burman had composed for a Bangla song. The song was recorded in 1936 as part of a private record titled *Raag Based Bengali Songs* for the Hindustan Record Company. R. D. Burman, by adding modern elements to it, gave it a new life in Lata Mangeshkar's voice.

A song in Bhupinder's voice showcases Gulzar's artistry with words even as it affords relief from the pall of pain that permeates *Kinara*. The song: 'Ek hi khwab kai baar dekha hai maine/ Toone sari mein uras li hai meri chaabiya ghar ki' (I have dreamt the same dream many times/ That you have tied my house keys to the end of your sari). This song has been filmed very delicately to showcase the chemistry between Dharmendra and Hema Malini. Gulzar shares a fascinating story about this cameo role. When he mentioned to Hema Malini at one point that he wanted a star to play the role of Chandan in the film, Hema Malini asked him, 'Why don't you take my friend for it?' At that point neither did she take his name nor did Gulzar mention it, but it was clear to him who would be essaying the role.

Some of the most eloquent examples of Gulzar's dexterity as a director are the small flashback scenes filmed on Dharmendra and Hema Malini with a light touch of romance that lightens the seriousness of the storyline.

The following scene is an example: There is a palace called Ashrafi Mahal in Mandu, Madhya Pradesh, which is so named because the Emperor Jehangir is said to have placed a gold ashrafi coin on each step to entice his pregnant wife, Noorjahan, to climb up the stairs. In the film, Dharmendra and Hema Malini relive that moment from history in the present, donning the roles of Jehangir and Noorjahan. As

Aarti, pretending to be pregnant, climbs each step, Chandan places a 100 rupee note on it. By recreating this simple demonstration of a legendary love in this playfully romantic way, the director is able to show the purity and depth of the love between Chandan and Aarti. Indeed, if these small but significant flashbacks are removed from the film, it would be a dull art film burdened with more pain and grief than the viewer could deal with.

It is also significant to note that there are no romantic scenes, songs or dialogues between the main hero of the film and the heroine. Through the turmoil of their relationship, there is not a single moment when the viewer is led to believe that the relationship would lead to a resolution. The climax too only gives them a chance to understand each other's emotions, which allows two people to come closer to each other.

Any expectations of leaving the theatre carrying the fulfillment of seeing at least a frame where love is shown blossoming between Jeetendra and Hema Malini are belied by the film's ending, which stops at a point when both understand and decide to abide by each other. Only the two candles burning in front of the image of Mother Mary inside the church points to the need to offer thanks when dreams are realised. This very typical 'Gulzarish' imagery depicts the life situation of two characters standing on opposite banks of the river of life. It's an ending that leaves us dissatisfied. Try though we might to grasp the feeling of contentment or closure through the film's ending, it slips away like sand through the fingers.

Much of the film's success hinges on the fact that the director has conveyed a social message more through silences than through dialogue and emotional outbursts. R. D. Burman's music playing softly in the background adds its own poignancy. There is an amazing continuity in the way the scenes come full circle: when, at the beginning of the film, a bead breaks free from the ghungroos worn by the heroine, and at the end of the film, she shines with happiness on wearing the ghungroos the hero has presented to her. Presenting through it, very simply, the fact of her leaving behind the tribulations of the past and starting on a new path of life. This is perhaps *Kinara*'s greatest achievement.

This film is among those that translate Gulzar's idioms perfectly. At the time he was making this film, all the three actors, Dharmendra, Jeetendra and Hema Malini were already successful stars in commercial cinema, starring in box office hits. It is laudable that Gulzar, without bowing to the requirements of the box office, wrought his film to impart a purposeful message in a poetic manner.

A song from the film, written by Gulzar is worth noting here, as even beyond the storyline of the film, its lines hold inspiration for us as we navigate the ups and downs of life:

There's no one, anywhere
Why are you lost in thought

What happened was a dream
And in a dream it has passed
Dreams do not recur
Life is not a dream
There's no one, anywhere...

43.

Often, while searching for locations for his films, Gulzar has found himself in such beautiful parts of India that he has been beguiled by their beauty. Mandu is one such place with which he feels some ancient kinship. He says that on every trip he has made towards the north, he has always preferred to stop for the night at Mandu. The architectural evidence of the love between the king of Mandu, Baz Bahadur, and Rani Roopmati has always held a special fascination for him. The well-preserved ruins of structures that once bore witness to the love between the two fuel his poetic imagination.

Baz Bahadur and Rani Roopmati, besides being famed for the love they bore for each other, are also held in high esteem by serious practitioners of classical music. Baz Bahadur was not just a connoisseur of music, he was also a talented singer. Similarly, Roopmati was renowned for her sharp mind and her poetic and musical abilities. According to the *Muntakhab-ul Lubab*, an eighteenth-century 'selected records of the wise and the pure' written by the historian Muhammad Hashim 'Khafi Khan' and the *Siyar-ul-Mutakhkherin*, Sayyid Ghulam Husain Tabatabai's historical work, Roopmati was unparalleled as a singer. She could create delicate compositions in Hindi, ensuring that her name was featured beautifully as a part of each. We should stop to examine a bandish composed by Rani Roopmati here, because a love duet from Gulzar's film is set in the city built for her as proof of a king's love. The beautiful bandish goes thus:

Youth is a mean betrayer
All colours have faded into the dun dullness of age
Make even the black crow don a white visage

According to the *Tarikh-i Malwa*, Roopmati lies buried in Sarangpur. But the *Ma'athir-ul-umara*, a collection of biographies of nobles in the Mughal court written in the eighteenth century by Samsam-ud-Daula Shah Nawaz Khan, claims that both Baz Bahadur and Roopmati lie together in the middle of the vast lake of Ujjain. Some other experts opine that Roopmati's grave is in Mandu's Rewa Kund opposite the palace of her paramour.

One can quite understand the yearning of the poet who wished to capture the essence of this historic love and trap it in his poem. As if Mandu is a symbol of their love, and the song from *Kinara* could be seen to derive its source from their relationship. Gulzar did tell me that he was very clear in his mind about where the song he was writing would be shot. Mandu was where his heart was set on, to fan his own love of poetry and music where the lovers had expressed theirs. And the song he wrote for the location was:

My name may be lost, my face will change
But my voice is my identity, should you remember it...

The song which was then filmed at the location had Dharmendra, Hema Malini and Jeetendra articulating it. It remains one of the everlasting songs from among the poet's vast repertoire, notable for the contemporary interpretation it suggests of the love between Baz Bahadur and Roopmati. As if, using this song as a medium, the love story becomes universal, blending the past and the present through love poetry. The stanzas:

The tyrannies of time are no less beautiful
We are here today, nowhere tomorrow
If, beyond time, we meet somewhere
My voice is my identity, should you remember it...

This song sung by Lata Mangeshkar and Bhupinder is a part of film music history because it has a significance beyond Mandu and the love story between Baz Bahadur and Roopmati; a significance that even its writer did not dream of at the time he was writing or filming it. The song, after its role as a film song, gained a new dimension as a song that identifies Lata Mangeshkar, by poetically describing her individuality. If we view this song in connection with Lata-ji, it becomes such a poetic definition that it is impossible to view it in any other context. And the manner in which Lata Mangeshkar has sung it adds dignity to the way she seems to be defining herself. 'My voice is my identity...' has become, like a maxim, a line to describe Lata Mangeshkar.

44.

Made in 1968, *Sunghursh* was based on the Bangla novel *Layli Asmaner Ayna* by Mahasweta Devi. The novel, based in the early years of the 19th century, highlights the distortion of religion through *thugee* and ritualism by the pandaas of Benaras. A dark film in today's parlance, the film depicted the feud between two families of Brahmin priests and the resultant violence that devotees to the city were made to suffer. Gulzar wrote the dialogues for the film. Abrar Alvi had been working on the screenplay of the film in the beginning, but had left. The film credits Abrar Alvi too as screenplay and dialogue writer. *Sunghursh* stands apart from the rest of the films for which Gulzar has written the screenplay and dialogues. The significance is that the dialogues he wrote for *Sunghursh* are very different from those he wrote for the other films, and far removed from his own disposition as a writer.

It is remarkable that Gulzar was part of a contemporary, purely entertainment-based melodrama rich in scenes of killings, crime and revenge with loud music to match. When we look back and examine the dialogues Gulzar has written for films, the list includes *Anand*, *Bawarchi*, *Guddi*, *Namak Haram*, *Aashirwad*, *Griha Pravesh*, *Baseraa* and *Masoom*. Adding *Sunghursh* to this list makes one wonder why, even as he propagated the case for art films, he plied his pen in the service of a purely commercial film. Yet, watching *Sunghursh* today, it becomes evident that Gulzar maintained harmony and pertinence throughout as he worked on this melodramatic creation.

Especially keeping in mind that just a few years before this film was made, he had been working on the screenplay and dialogues of Bimal Roy's film. The script for Bimal Roy's dream project, *Amrit Kumbh Ki Khoj* had been written, on which Bimal Roy would constantly ask Gulzar to make changes and additions. Gulzar's poem 'Bimal-da' can be viewed in this context, where he portrays the agony of watching the senior man die lingeringly of cancer.

Gulzar seems to be present whenever any opportunity for meaningful expression presents itself. Which is why he considers writing screenplays for Hrishikesh Mukherjee and

Basu Bhattacharya an expansion of his capabilities as a writer. I believe that he took up *Sunghursh* as a challenge and to prove that he could bring dignity to writing even a purely entertainment film. Gulzar agreed readily to take up writing for S. H. Rawail's banner, which had some successful, good films to its credit. Rawail-sahab had earlier made *Shararat* (1959), *Mere Mehboob* (1963), *Mehboob ki Mehendi* (1971) and *Laila Majnu* (1976); laudable films which were also studded with songs that became very popular.

We are looking at the dialogues written for this film almost half a century later. How many layers of meaning can be given to dialogues written for a serious film that has mainly negative characters? It is worth examining how a multi-faceted writer does justice to his assignment with sincerity. *Sunghursh* shows us that had Gulzar continued to write screenplays or dialogues for commercial cinema, perhaps the decades ahead would have shown us some interesting and meaningful commercial films. When we consider the dialogues of *Aashirwad*, released a year after *Sunghursh*, we can understand Gulzar's amazing range.

Compare the dialogues of the vain, religious sinner and Kali-worshipper Bhavani Prasad (played by Jayant) with those spoken by the ethical father (played by Ashok Kumar) in *Aashirwad* and it will be clear that Gulzar entered the depths of the screenplay to grasp the persona of the characters and to do justice to each one's dialogues. No mean feat in a film filled choc-a-bloc with stars of the calibre of Dilip Kumar, Balraj Sahni, Sanjeev Kumar, Jayant, Sapru, Ulhas, along with Durga Khote, Sulochana and Vyjayanthimala, all of whom had strong personalities. Gulzar added colour to each of their dialogues to match their internal natures. The dialogues of *Sunghursh*, a period film that has achieved cult status today, stand on a pinnacle of achievement. Appropriate words that carry weight, taunts that sufficiently highlight the thirst for revenge, and harsh words that assault along with some lines in a philosophical mode on life and death, virtue and sin, and karmic justice help make the story line clear. Through his dialogues, Gulzar creates a contrast between two characters to reveal the underlying tensions and their contradictory images. He thus speeds up the pace of the story so the viewer can understand the 'sunghursh' or tensions existing between the two opposite poles of ideals and emotions.

Gulzar-sahab admits that he feels a connection with the writing of dialogues for *Sunghursh* mainly because he felt he was giving a cinematic shape to the grand canvas created by Mahashweta Devi in her novel. This was the reason he worked so hard on the project before submitting it to Rawail-sahab. As a viewer and author, my observation is that *Sunghursh* stands alone among his cinematic writings as a film that showcases his range which, even at the level of entertainment, can be elevated so it becomes both beautiful and simple.

45.

Hrishikesh Mukherjee's *Namak Haram*, which was released in 1973, is among the hallmarks of Gulzar's dexterity in screenplay and dialogue writing. This film was based on the play *Becket* (1959) by French playwright Jean Anouilh, which had been adapted as a film of the same name in 1964 by Peter Glenwis. *Namak Haram*, moving away from Hrishikesh Mukherjee's simple family themes, focuses on the lives of workers who are affiliated to trade unions. Gulzar successfully adapted the play to fit into an Indian ethos.

Raising questions about the needs and toils of blue collar workers, he placed the theme against the backdrop of the textile mills; a subject that had, a decade earlier, loomed like a cloud over the sixties. This was a new direction for Hrishikesh Mukherjee too, as the film seems to lean towards contemporary cinema. In 1976, he would make another film, *Arjun Pandit*, on a contemporary social theme which was based on the reformation of an illiterate village ruffian through understanding and education.

It is interesting to note that even while dealing with social themes of a contemporary nature, Hrishi-da does so with empathy and emotion. Though he is best evaluated through his social and family-themed films like *Anuradha* (1960), *Memdidi* (1961), *Chhaya* (1961), *Sanjh Aur Savera* (1964), *Anupama* (1966), *Aashirwad* (1968), *Satyakam* (1969), *Chaitali* (1975), *Guddi* (1971), *Gol Maal* (1979), *Kotwal Saab* (1977), *Naram Garam* (1981), *Khubsoorat* (1980), *Bemisal* (1982), *Rang Birangi* (1983) and *Kissi Se Na Kehna* (1983).

We can thus understand that Gulzar is writing his screenplay and dialogues for the film to highlight the tensions and opposing viewpoints of mill-workers and mill-owners. We must keep in mind the fact that Gulzar had been part of a progressive group of writers, and attended their meetings regularly in his younger years, where views of a progressive and even revolutionary nature were freely exchanged. It was thus natural that he would present a new and thought-provoking concept of the nation through his dialogues in a simple and balanced way.

The film is based on the close friendship between Vicky (played by Amitabh Bachchan) and Somu (played by Rajesh Khanna), which is tested sorely by the tension caused between the haves and have-nots. Gulzar gives Rajesh Khanna, who plays the spokesperson for the mill-workers, dialogues that are rich in philosophy. This dialogue spoken by Rajesh Khanna anchors the film's theme: 'Whether it is hunger or thirst or money, the poor share it all, the idea of yours or mine does not exist.' Countless such dialogues highlight the class conflict between the rich and the poor in the film. The character of Alam (played by Raza Murad) is presented as a metaphor for the deprived masses. Exhausted by incessant battles with the rulers, he has taken to drink. And strangely enough, his disposition is that of a poet who comments with bitterness on society.

This is a masterstroke by the writer, who keeps the character as a symbol through which to present and analyse progressive ideas. He has tasted few of life's joys yet, as he dies, he bequeaths his 'estate' of kites and strings to children to give them joy, though it be momentary. A poignant scene in the film is when he hands over the verses of resistance that he has written to Rajesh Khanna, sanguine in the knowledge that he will now take forward the fight against want and pain. There is little need to mention that flashes of Saadat Hasan Manto and the revolutionary Majaz Lakhnawi can be seen behind the melancholy, the anger against society, the wayward poetic disposition and the fondness for alcohol that Gulzar depicts.

The screenplay simplifies a serious concept. Simi Grewal, as Manisha, plays the rich daughter of a business tycoon. Her character has been created to show that despite being brought up wanting for nothing, she holds progressive ideas. She believes in socialism and is in love, though unrequited, with Vicky. The irony of her relationship with Vicky is in the fact that he is immersed in feudalism, and represents that section of society that has no concern for or understanding of the needs and sorrows of the working class. Despite this, she guides him at every point. And at the end of the film, he is compassionate and sincere in his friendship when, after Somu is eventually murdered, he takes his father's guilt upon himself and goes to jail for it.

Through the dialogues in *Namak Haram*, Gulzar tries to show how equality and happiness can be brought into society. With this end in mind, he has wrought the character of the trade union leader, Bipin Lal (played by A. K. Hangal) as someone who is fair and honest and always sticks to his principles. Dialogues between Hangal and Rajesh Khanna point to ways to lessen the gap between capitalists and working class labourers.

One could say that *Namak Haram* is like a textbook for the way it delineates the conspiracies, ambitions and greed of the capitalists and their relationship with the common man. Gulzar ensures that the screenplay is neither too emotional nor didactic. The film is singular in the way it shows the adjustments between two friends in the face of circumstances in a pragmatic manner. One must also mention those scenes that have dialogues between the wealthy Seth Damodar Maharaj (played by Om Shivpuri) and his son Vikram Maharaj, or Vicky. The gap in temperaments, practicality and values; the resulting dissonance, the deceit as well as the ethics have all been evaluated thoroughly.

Hrishikesh Mukherjee has also filmed this screenplay with the same fervour shown by Gulzar while writing it. Fifty years after its release, this film still holds relevance for which Gulzar deserves credit. The Indian adaptation of *Becket*, like the original, continues to live.

46.

Gulzar's dialogues in Ramesh Talwar's *Baseraa* are notable. He also wrote the songs for the film. Based on the Marathi novel by Leela Phansalkar, the film showcases the loving relationship and happy home shared by Neema (played by Rekha) and her professionally qualified husband, Balraj (played by Shashi Kapoor). Balraj's first wife Sharda (played by Rakhee) has gone into a coma after an accident fourteen years ago. Despondent over the fact that Sharda might never emerge from her coma, Balraj marries her younger sister, Neema, to help bring up his son Sagar (played by Raj Kiran). Neema too later gives birth to a son, Babu (played by Master Vikas).

The film erupts in melodrama when, fourteen years later, Balraj's first wife emerges from her coma and returns home, to her baseraa. Shashi Kapoor, Rekha and the entire family hide the fact of Balraj's second marriage from Rakhee. Whereas the home, which was once Rakhee's, is now Rekha's. So there is Rekha on the one hand, trying to hide her relationship and yet keep it alive, and Rakhee on the other, attempting to reclaim the position and love she used to enjoy in her earlier life, complete with her trust in her husband. Such is the quandary that takes the story forward.

Baseraa is the story of relationships changing under tension and conflict. Both the heroines of the film have built their homes for the same man. In the title song, Gulzar writes about two kinds of shelters for life, even as he depicts the endurance of those trying to build, save or sacrifice for the other. Which is why he writes the lines in two different ways: 'Jahan pe saweraa ho, baseraa wahin hai' (Wherever the morning dawns, there home is) and 'Jahan pe baseraa ho, saweraa wahin hai' (Wherever the home is, there the morning dawns). It is as if these two lines hold the complete emotional content and theme of the film.

Directors like Shakti Samanth, Pramod Chakravarti, J. Omprakash, Raj Khosla and Ramanand Sagar made clean social dramas in the 1970s and 1980s. There were other filmmakers too who made socially relevant films but on a smaller budget, starring fewer actors and shooting in ordinary, rather than exotic, locations and sets. Perhaps Hrishikesh Mukherjee can be counted as the biggest exponent of this kind of filmmaking. And Gulzar would himself join this list. I am looking at his presence as a director here. There are countless films that were commercial in nature and revolved around social themes. *Baseraa* is one film that cannot be classified as either an art film or commercial cinema.

Many such films exist, written by Gulzar and other gifted writers, that have intimations of being art. In the same year, 1981, Gulzar's *Namkeen*, Chetan Anand's *Kudrat*, Sai Paranjpye's *Chashme Buddoor*, Shashi Kapoor's *Kalyug*, Yash Chopra's *Silsila* and Hrishikesh Mukherjee's *Naram Garam* held the banner aloft for middle-of-the-road cinema. *Baseraa* can be counted among them.

As mentioned earlier, the film's dialogues are superlative in that each character has lines that express their emotions so well that they take you along with complete conviction. The film has no great visual appeal. The entire action is filmed inside a big house yet it never seems boring. This is because the development of the emotional story has given enough weight to the dialogues. And the minute knitting of relationships has been carefully done through their conversations, to keep the pace and tension taut throughout the film. Examining a scene can explain this.

Rekha comes to know that her elder sister, Rakhee, could return home at any time, and the doctor has advised that everything must be just as it was before she left it. Gulzar gives this scene its measure of seriousness with just a single dialogue. Sitting on her sofa, Rekha despairingly asks of her old servant, Ramu, 'How can I give her the world as it was fourteen years ago? In fourteen years, minds change, the colour of the eyes change, our years change. I can change the colour of the walls, the sheets on the bed, but how can I separate the fourteen years that are melded into the walls, the sheets? It is not in my power…Ramu!'

This outburst is evidence that Gulzar could infuse an ordinary film with the seriousness of an art film. *Baseraa* does not often feature in discussions on the films for which Gulzar has written dialogues, which is why it has been discussed here.

47.

Gulzar's *Kitaab* (1977) was a film ahead of its time. This film, based on celebrated Bangla litterateur Samaresh Basu's novel *Pathik*, leans towards the off-beat. This commercial film had music that, compatible with its story line, was experimental and unmatched.

With a child as the central character, Gulzar crafted a full-length feature film based on the child's psychological responses to his surroundings and events. This, at a time when only successful commercial films were considered mainstream cinema. Amitabh Bachchan's golden period in his persona as the angry young man was at its height. The super-hit films released the same year as *Kitaab* were *Amar Akbar Anthony*, *Chacha Bhatija*, *Dharam-Veer*, *Dream Girl*, *Dulhan Wahi Jo Piya Man Bhaaye*, *Hum Kisise Kum Naheen*. Though, along with Gulzar's own film *Kinara*, other productions like *Bhoomika* by Shyam Benegal, Bhimsain's *Gharonda*, Girish Karnad and B. V. Karanth's *Godhuli*, Basu Chatterjee's *Khatta Meetha* and *Swami* and Satyajit Ray's *Shatranj Ke Khiladi* held up the flag for films of another flavour.

Kitaab is among its director's own favourites. I believe it could be because the depiction of the film's protagonist, Babla (played by Master Raju) is in some way a reflection of Gulzar's own boyhood. The attempt to project the psychology of a child in the film raises many questions. It also adds a poetic expression to the entire film. The film revolves around the issue of whether we are able to raise our children with sensitivity, using many scenes to explore this thought, with small incidents delivering vital messages.

Master Raju is a child who approaches boyhood with many questions and a curiosity about life. But nobody has the time to address them or understand either his dreams or his anxieties. Having come from the village to live with his sister (played by Vidya Sinha) and brother-in-law (played by Uttam Kumar), he often feels a sense of isolation. His sister has no time for him and though the brother-in-law chats with the boy whenever he returns from work, he is unable to read what is in the boy's mind. Despite this, the energy and impetus of childhood is potent enough to lift the boy from his dilemmas and allow his mind to fly with the lightness of a butterfly. He is troubled by his school, the rebukes he receives from his masters, and his social inability to be truly friendly with his schoolmates.

Gulzar uses signals to explain life's philosophy. Thus, like the different pages of a book give us knowledge on various subjects, small and varied incidents and scenes depict the excitement that buffets the young boy's mind. Two examples can help understand how this is effected.

The first instance is when Babla and his classmate Pappu (played by Master Tito) go to a halwai, a maker of sweetmeats, who is making jalebis and ask him whether he would teach them how to make the sweet. He turns around and tells them, 'Son, first learn to eat. That is enough. You are boys from good families. What will you gain by becoming a halwai!'

Master Raju's response to this is startling. He asks, 'Why? Are halwais not from good families?'

To which the halwai replies, 'You will study and learn and become an officer, son. This work is for insignificant people like us.'

The second boy, Pappu then asks innocently, 'Are you an insignificant man?'

The second scene is when Babla and Pappu approach a madaari, a street magician, and request him to teach them magic tricks. Here too, the dialogue reveals a serious thought. Babla asks the madaari, 'Will you make us your sidekicks?'

He replies, 'Son, if I make you my sidekick, who will go to school?'

Babla gestures towards the man's son and says, 'But he does not go to school.'

At which, the man says with sadness, 'Son, this is his misfortune that he is struggling alongside his poor father. You are fortunate in that you attend school, your parents are educating you.'

The two scenes explore life's truths and espouse the thought that if most of the children of the poor could be educated, poverty and the gap between rich and poor could, to a large extent, well be erased.

At every point in the film, the advice repeatedly given to Babla is that going to school and studying are very important. That doing so makes life meaningful. The contradiction is in the fact that neither the school principal nor the master feel any obligation towards the all-round development of the children. They come to the school as a matter of routine, fulfil their duties and go home. The principal even says, 'Write everything down and send it to the parents.' The letter the master sends that points out a student's mistakes, as a way of completing his obligations, is an apt metaphor. A satirical song in the film has Gulzar saying:

Aa-aa, ee-ee, aa-aa, ee-ee
A letter has come from masterji
Out of the letter stepped a cat with elan
The cat takes tobacco with its paan
Dark glasses, yellow ears
Ears wear danglers, a lamp on the nose
And an incense stick in his hands.

In fact, this film is the cinematic version of the brilliant poem by the progressive Hindi poet, Nagarjun, in which he shows a true picture of the madrassas. In the Nehruvian era, when the desire for new ideas was fervent, and society seemed ready to fulfil its dreams, then the divergence that started in all sectors was seen most keenly in education. Teachers lost the sense of responsibility and the real thrust of education as a way towards social service was left behind. It was to express the anger he felt against such social changes that Nagarjun wrote his poem:

Mites eat away the beams
The master reads out the alphabet
The wall has cracks, the roof is broken
Lizards dance on the floor
Raining on the helpless students
Blows that fall minute by minute

The miserable master
Creates the moulds that will shape men

The tribe of lethargic masters continued to grow, incapable of befriending the straightforward mindsets of their pupils. The result was an unwanted distancing between teacher and pupil, by which schools started to feel like prisons.

Gulzar explores this fact carefully to write *Kitaab*, but keeps in mind that he brings no harm to the respect that education deserves. He creates the universe of the film through the eyes of children. The satire in Nagarjuna's poem seems to be a part of the original thought behind *Kitaab*. The capability with which Gulzar intervenes in Samaresh Basu's story also converts the screenplay into a semi-autobiographical narrative.

Just as in his childhood, Gulzar had to stay away from his father and spend the night in the godown, with the books from the library taking on the role of friends through his loneliness...these aspects can be seen reflected with seriousness in the film. The only difference is that while the young Gulzar consoled himself by reading books, Babla, in the film, writes about his misery to lighten his heart.

The wounds of the poet's past have found expression in the film without any trace of anger in them. These are but the poetically rendered portions from his life story which the film presents with the same emotions.

A unique character in the film is that of the blind beggar, a role played by Shriram Lagoo. Babla meets him at the railway station when he runs away from home. The beggar's dialogue gives the film a philosophical meaning when the beggar, trying to make the boy understand, says, 'I have seen that people do not pay a labourer as much money as they give as alms to a fakir. However bad their deeds are, they must keep their conscience safe.' The dialogue continues to its end when, despite knowing that Babla has missed his train, he asks, 'Which train have you missed? Do not sorrow over missing your train, my boy. You must not miss the station.

Even if you do not remember where you boarded, do not forget where you must alight…'

Kitaab is able to create such emotional moments that fill one's heart with ease. The song filmed to show the nature of the beggar has its own flavour:

My shadow does not walk with me
No piety, no good deeds
A life wasted

For me, the days are darkness
For me, the night does not bring the day

He who gives me light shows me the day
Only he is my fellow traveller

No piety, no good deeds

This song that presents life's truths with a sense of detachment also answers some of the questions that Gulzar puts forth in the film at every available opportunity through the character of Master Raju. He has a notebook with him in which he writes his innermost thoughts, often when he sits with his homework, or when late in the night his loneliness urges him to question the world outside. Some montages of dialogues in the film not only startle us, but also tickle our funny bone. These are conversations with the boy's brother-in-law, or his classmate, Pappu, and at the beginning of the film, with his mother (played by Dina Pathak). These dialogues help us understand a child's thought process through the medium of cinema. As when Master Raju asks Uttam Kumar, 'As a student of the sitar, what would Pandit Ravi Shankar gain by learning geography?' Or when he asks his friend in irritation, 'I wonder when we will grow up. Everyone needs grown-ups, but grown-ups don't need anybody. This world does not understand our problems.' In the same way, when he is scolded by his sister for reading *Devdas*, Uttam Kumar comes to his rescue saying, 'No one gets corrupted by reading Saratchandra.' These are moments which give rise to spontaneous laughter, but also deliver a message that sinks into the mind and lingers there.

Gulzar has created every scene of this film beautifully. When Babla gifts his Parker fountain pen to his friend Pappu, then Pappu gets a scolding from his father and Babla from his brother-in-law. Babla is dismayed by this and quietly writes in his notebook, 'Is this any kind of life, in which a friend cannot be gifted even a pen?' The director cleverly puts forth the premise that gifting and taking are also valued in monetary terms by mature adults. Such effective situations that continue in society almost unchanged more than four decades since the film's release make *Kitaab* a contemporary work.

There have been other films too which, like *Kitaab*, have a child as the focal point. Among them, *Boot Polish* (1954), *Ghar Ghar Ki Kahani* (1988), *Do Kaliyan* (1968) and *Nanha Farishta* (1969) come to mind. But these films, though based on children, were not entirely their stories. *Kitaab* is the first film that explores a child's mental makeup and presents it in a delicate and tactful way. Some films made after *Kitaab* that have delved creatively into the mind of children include Shekhar Kapur's *Masoom* (1983) Mahesh Bhatt's *Kaash* (1987), Vishal Bhardwaj's *Makdee* (2002), Nagesh Kukunoor's *Iqbal* (2005), Aamir Khan's *Taare Zameen Par* (2007) and Santosh Sivan's *Tahaan* (2008).

Two songs of *Kitaab* also deserve mention. 'Hari din to beeta shaam hui/ Raat paar kara de' (Hari, the day is done, evening has come/ Help me across the night…) and 'Dhanno ki aankhon mein raat ka soormaa/ Aur chand ka chumma' (The eyes of Dhanno hold the kohl of the night/ And the kiss of the moon). The former, a lullaby, has been sung by Rajkumari, a renowned playback singer of the fifties. For music lovers, this song with shades of Rabindra Sangeet created by R. D. Burman holds a different appeal. Maintaining the ambience required when lulling a child to sleep, Rajkumari has sung it in soft tones set in the middle octave. This song remains one of the notable ones from Rajkumari's second turn as a playback voice. The second song, 'Dhanno ki aankhon mein', is remembered as a classic example of the partnership between Gulzar and Pancham. Few songs in Hindi films have such frank romanticism as has been bestowed on this song by Pancham. If we examine some of the lines, then besides the simple rhyming of 'chand ka chumma' and 'raat ka soorma' there are lines of sheer poetry that impress themselves upon the mind.

Dhanno I've have seen you in my dreams
Seen you in the books of Laila and Heer...

The song has been filmed in a novel way too. A train rushes through stations in the early morning, a train draws into one late at night and some stations rush past, empty. The engine-driver continuously piles coal into the furnace causing the smoke to rise out of the engine's chimney. It seems as if a horseman is riding his horse through the sky, wrapped in a muffler of smoke. According to the story, the engine-driver is singing the song for his wife, who lives in a village near a station which the train rushes through. On the days the train is to pass through, the driver's wife comes from her village to the station to catch a glimpse of her husband.

I am sharing here some interesting aspects of this song's creation, told to me by Gulzar-sahab:

> 'Dhanno ke aankhon mein' is an ordinary song based on a simple tune. When Pancham first sang the tune to me, he did it in his bass voice. That very day I decided that Pancham should sing this song. I knew for certain that no one else could match the modulations he had brought into its rendition when he sang it to me. The question then arose on how we could introduce the sound of the train and its wheels into the song. RD had bought a synthesiser from abroad with which it was possible to create some unusual sounds, including the sound of a train. We decided then that we would use the synthesiser and use the sound of the

> train right at the start of the song. This way, it could also become the film's title song. This was just an experiment, but it succeeded.

Gulzar-sahab also shares a huge compliment given by a renowned actor. He says, 'When Shammi Kapoor saw this song, he complained to me, "Why did you not call me for this song? You should have told me about it." This is a big compliment for me. You will not believe it, but after watching this song, whenever we would meet at any event, he would always complain accusingly, you did not call me to sing this song on screen.'

The song is indeed as fascinating as the story about it. If Rajkumari's lullaby is sweet, this engine-driver's song holds it own place among the artistically composed songs of its time. The song, 'Mere saath chale na saaya' (No shadow walks with me) in Sapan Chakravarty's voice is also pleasant, in the presentation of a new voice. Interestingly, none of the four songs of *Kitaab* are sung by well-known playback artistes. Besides Rajkumari, Sapan Chakravarty, and R. D. Burman, the voices of Shivangi and Padmini Kolhapure can be heard as they sing the children's song, 'Masterji ki aa gayi chitti.'

Kitaab is the effort made to see an ordinary theme through an unusual lens, and present a child's emotions and mind set in a social context. It is an attempt to prevent the delicate thoughts and emotions of a child from being destroyed before its time. While setting forth many poignant thoughts through the film, the director steers clear of emotion and avoids contrived situations that often endanger its effectiveness. Just as Dina Pathak efficiently portrays the mother's role, Om Shivpuri, T. P. Jain and Keshto Mukherjee also fulfil their roles as the principal and teachers effectively. The tension between husband and wife is depicted in just a few scenes by Uttam Kumar and Vidya Sinha. Indrani Mukherji's role in the film needs special mention. As are the roles enacted by

Master Raju and Master Tito. Credit is due to the director for this. Besides which the tightness of the screenplay and the innocence of the children win our hearts.

48.

Do Dooni Chaar (1963) was Bimal Roy's remake of the Bangla comedy film *Bhranti Bilas* starring Uttam Kumar that was based on Ishwar Chandra Vidyasagar's novel of the same name. Both these films were inspired by Shakespeare's play *The Comedy of Errors*. It is also said that Ishwar Chandra Vidyasagar's novel too is based on *The Comedy of Errors*. In spite of these two films, Gulzar felt the need to present the theme in a contemporary context. When *Do Dooni Char* was being made, Bimal Roy was suffering from the last stages of cancer.

Bimal Roy's assistants and unit were burdened by a need to keep the banner alive in some way or the other, and the film was started with this end in mind. United Producers joined hands with the Bimal Roy team to keep the banner flying. Subodh Mukherji and Mohan Segal were part of this production house. It was necessary to show the duo whatever had been shot, which greatly constricted the creativity of Bimal Roy's young co-workers. This was also the reason for the film progressing slowly. Though weighed down by sorrow, work on *Do Dooni Chaar* continued, with Debu Sen directing the film and Gulzar writing the screenplay and dialogues. The film did get made, despite these conditions, but Gulzar had reservations about it. Perhaps that was the reason that he decided to make it again, and fourteen years after *Do Dooni Chaar*, he made *Angoor* (1982).

Gulzar made minor alterations to the screenplay of *Do Dooni Char*, using his signature style of expression, realising that the remake of a film made under his guru's banner could evoke criticism resulting from changing mores. By 1980, he had reached the tenth milestone of being a director, having made nine films for his own as well as other production houses. His films had found critical acclaim, even as they set the cash machines ringing at the box office. The important point with *Angoor* was that it would be his first foray into comedy. It is the only film in his career that has the screenplay, dialogues and songs all written in the same comic vein, and one can see the keenness of sometimes political, and more often, social satire in his writing.

There is an interesting story connected with the making of *Angoor*. Around the time Gulzar was toying with the idea of the film, Yash Johar approached him to direct a film. After listening intently to all aspects of the idea of *Do Dooni Chaar*, the producer exclaimed, 'This film will flop in just four days! People remake hit films, why are you bent on remaking a flop film!' Be that as it may, the collaboration with Yash Johar failed. However, Jay Singh, a businessman, showed interest in producing this film, when Gulzar later discussed the possibility of making the film with him. He had read the play in college and had loved it. With no hesitation, he agreed with Gulzar's idea of adapting Shakespeare's comedy as a screenplay. Thus, Gulzar's long held dream seemed closer to becoming a reality.

It is an acknowledged fact in film circles that Gulzar has never bowed to the demands of the market in his work. If he so desired, he could have made as many commercially successful films as he wished and stood at par with other contemporary commercially successful filmmakers. But standing apart from hit producer-directors like Shakti Samanth, Yash Chopra, J. Omprakash, Ramesh Sippy and Manmohan Desai, Gulzar blazed his own trail and found success on his own terms.

Noted Urdu writer Ismat Chughtai's writes in 'Baatein Gulzar Aur Unke Filmon Ki' (About Gulzar and His Films), an essay published in the October 1983 issue of *Dinman*:

> On watching the film one realises that okay, this one too is a lost cause. He will have to be included in the New Theatres list. One more addition to the camp of Bimal Roy, Hrishikesh Mukherjee and Satyajit Ray. Shyam Benegal, Basu Chatterji, Girish Karnad and Govind Nihalani had not blossomed by then....After every film of his, one fears it might be his last, because Gulzar has no interest in the box office. Many impressive directors have bowed before the box office. Like the films of Bimal Roy and Hrishikesh Mukherjee, Gulzar's films too may not be sweeping returns at the box office. The box office is an irritation, as it defeats the purpose of a film.

Indeed, despite pressure from established producers that he should make a hit film, Gulzar held his own. It was not that he shunned commercial success. But he was steadfast in his decision to engage himself with only those films which could be made according to his thought process and understanding. If such films succeeded, all the better. Looking at the films directed by him, we can see that they stand equidistant from both commercial and parallel cinema. The films carrying his unique signature stand at a point where success and art meet in equal measure.

Coming back to *Angoor*, we see it as the perfect adaptation of a play. Side-stepping Ishwar Chandra Vidyasagar's *Bhranti Bilas*, Gulzar takes his story directly from Shakespeare's *The Comedy of Errors*. As mentioned by him in interviews, he worked on this script in full measure, with none of the hurdles that had stood in his way while writing *Do Dooni Char*. *Angoor* also remained untouched by the kind of banal comedy that was becoming popular at the time. This is one of the successes of the film. Every frame of the film is infused with gentle humour. Witty dialogues, and scenes that hint at satire also give food for thought.

Sanjeev Kumar and Deven Verma are in double roles. Both are seen as master and servant; and while Sanjeev Kumar in both roles is called Ashok, Deven Verma is Bahadur in both roles.

One of the two Ashoks is fond of reading detective novels and therefore views all events around him with a detective's suspicious eyes. This Ashok meets a farmer in relation to his business; an exchange with the farmer's assistant, Mastana, follows, which is worth reading. Ashok tells Mastana, 'I never keep more than ten rupees in my pocket because it's very risky.' At this, Mastana replies, 'Huzoor, danger lurks everywhere. Keep it at home, that's dangerous; keep it in the bank, that's dangerous. Keep it at home and the thieves know of it, and in the bank, the government sees it.'

Angoor is replete with such humorous lines. As are the dialogues spoken by Yunus Parvez playing the role of Mansoor Miya, who is a jeweller in the film. Whenever he speaks in, which he does in chaste Urdu, the careful crafting of the dialogue and the exquisite comic timing are indeed exemplary, resulting in spontaneous laughter. When Ashok, the elder brother, tells him the cost of the necklace is rather high, his response is, 'The price of gold too, like the mood of wives, keeps rising.' The sharpness of the dialogues does not hurt; rather, it tickles.

Other scenes, like the two brothers and their servants getting accidentally exchanged, or the repeated entry of the taxi-driver in the story and his being looked upon with suspicion by the younger Ashok, the presence of Ganeshilal (played by T. P. Jain) and his insistence on getting paid by 11 a.m. are all embedded so effortlessly into the story that they create easy occasions for situational comedy. Gulzar's films are never loud, but follow the minimalist style learnt from Bimal Roy and Hrishikesh Mukherjee. In the clean entertainment that *Angoor* offers, it is much in the same bracket as films like *Bawarchi*, *Naram Garam*, *Chupke Chupke* and *Gol Maal*, all directed by Hrishikesh Mukherjee.

Sanjeev Kumar and Deven Verma, at the centre of the film, effortlessly create easy simple humour. Three main characters intersect the twin sets of Ashok and Bahadur: Sudha (played by Moushumi Chatterjee), Tanu (played by Deepti Naval) and Prema (played by Aruna Irani). Each shine in their roles. Moushumi's character has been etched wonderfully. She is a self-centred, easily upset woman who is suspicious of her husband. Each time she loses her temper and cries on screen, the audience bursts into laughter. Watching Moushumi in *Angoor*, one wonders why such a sensitive actress did not command better roles in more films. Deepti Naval, however, bagged good roles in films that followed *Angoor*, including *Rang Birangi* (1983), *Katha* (1982), *Chashme Buddoor* (1981), *Kamala* (1984) and *Ankahee* (1985). The interactions with her elder sister and brother-in-law in the course of the film where she tries to solve their misunderstandings have some interesting dialogues. Her rendition of the song, 'Roz roz dali dali, kya likhta jaaye bhanwara, bawara…' (What does the bumblebee write every day on the branches and on the leaves…) is natural and appealing.

Gulzar has given the entire film a comic air that makes it a pleasant experience. Right at the beginning, the acknowledgement of his debt to Shakespeare, giving the song by C. H. Atma, 'Preetam aan milo…' (Come meet me, my beloved…) in a comic avatar, the use of the James Bond theme as he depicts the suspicious nature of the younger Ashok and, at the ending of the film, the wink that Shakespeare shares from his portrait on the wall, are elements that make the film a unique comedy.

If Satyajit Ray had remade *Goopi Gyne Bagha Byne* into Hindi, perhaps Gulzar would have had yet another comedy in his quiver. But for now, *Angoor* remains the only one from the genre among his films.

49.

Some analysis of Gulzar's journey as screenplay and dialogue-writer is necessary. More often than not, we see that any discussion on his work centres around the films he has directed and the songs he has written for films. He has a vast estate of admirers who love his non-film poems. They enjoy travelling with him as he delineates the ups and downs of his life. As though through his work he is comforting them, or reaching out to heal the distressed. It can easily be said that in the past many years, Gulzar's name heads the list of communicators who help those seeking succour from gifted communicators, as he links with them through his healing words. While this has built his reputation, on the other hand it restricts the full flowering of his skills.

One wonders how he finds, even as he delves into so many genres, ways to fuel his creative endeavours with so much energy. Many of the films he has written display a new side to his abilities as a writer, when we study them closely and examine the story, screenplay and the dialogues written for them. These also need to be examined in connection with his literary relationships. An expert filmmaker, a story-writer who delves into life to write about life's many aspects and a poet who looks at his life through the prism of poetry... when these three personas of the same individual meet over a cup of tea, stories and screenplays about life and broken dreams come to light. The three personas decide that they will consult that face that they share under the name of 'Gulzar' and use their skills to narrate the stories of the middle class with simplicity. Gulzar, whose mind works simultaneously on all three levels, then writes screenplays that create hope for society, with the support of which one can find new ways of rising from despair.

Even when a man is feeling helpless, some hope should remain in him, as happens in *Griha Pravesh*. If life can maintain a balance between pleasure and duty, then life remains fresh and radiant, this was the message of *Khubsoorat*. No film shows us better than *Anand* how we can help lessen the pain of others. As youngsters living our dreams, we are so awestruck by the shining world of cinema that we cannot grasp the reality behind the pomp and show. Once we understand it, the attraction is lost. To help one understand the optical illusions created by cinema was the purpose behind the making of *Guddi.* While *Namak Haram* puts forward the cruel truth of relationships between the toiling industry-worker and the owners. And, to stress the importance of abiding by one's values and principles, however hard one may be tested is the message shared by *Aashirwad.*

Gulzar serves a winner with his screenplays and dialogues when they reveal a woman's psyche. Understanding the female character and her thought process intimately, then to etch it out perfectly without sloganeering is one of his innate strengths. He makes no fuss about it, nor does he glower at the man beside him and say, 'See! Through my stories, in how many different ways have I shown women living life with dignity.' Instead, his writer's persona walks silently and companionably with women. Perhaps his mother, Sujan Kaur, whom he lost in his childhood, comes to his mind. Or perhaps he is transferring the memory of his dear friend, Meena Kumari and her emotionality into the character of one of his creations. To identify the women as individuals in his screenplays, he adds nuances to their roles that portray the desire to live life despite the turmoils that beset them. The characters of Hema Malini in *Khushboo*, Rekha in *Ghar* and *Izajat*, Sharmila Tagore in *Griha Pravesh* and *Namkeen*, Zarina Wahab in *Sitara*, Rakhee in *Baseraa*, Shabana Azmi in *Masoom* and *Ek Pal*, Sridevi in *Sadma*, and Dimple Kapadia in *Rudaali* are testimony to this. It is amazing how well he is able to etch the feminine mind while writing for each of these films. He peers into their deepest desires with detachment and portrays even those women who flit briefly through a film as complete characters. Waheeda Rehman in *Namkeen*, Dina Pathak in *Kitaab*, Leela Mishra in *Kinara* and Rakhee in *Rudaali* bear out this fact. They are vital to the story, and omitting the roles they played would mar the story completely. All the female characters in his films remain unbowed by tribulations, banish hopelessness and despair successfully and, when they smile, their inner dignity can be seen blossoming.

Steering clear of melodrama, and emotionalism, keeping relationships as the medium to depict life, and watching with detachment the knitting of relationships between his characters, Gulzar creates an alternate world in his films. To read these screenplays anew, and connect with them intimately, is important to be able to analyse Gulzar thoroughly as a screenplay writer. We can, in this connection, also mention screenplay writers like Wajahat Mirza, Kamal Amrohi, K. A. Abbas, Nabendu Ghosh, Rajinder Singh Bedi, Abrar Alvi, Akhtar-ul-Iman, Vijay Anand, Sachin Bhowmik, Shama Zaidi, Rahi Masoom Raza, Javed Siddiqui, Salim Khan, Javed Akhtar, Sagar Sarhadi and Kamlesh Pandey.

50.

Centred on the lives of the aurally challenged, *Koshish* (1972) carries the message of how one can live an ideal life even under adverse circumstances. A story of the love and mutual understanding shared by Haricharan Mathur (played by Sanjeev Kumar) and Aarti Mathur (played by Jaya Bhaduri), the film deals with the issues that arise from their being deaf and dumb not just with poignancy but also in a way that we can comprehend how the lower middle class deals with its struggles with society and yet seeks out the small joys that gleam like gems in their lives. As with all his films, Gulzar keeps his empathy on high, through which he fuels his characters' spirit of survival. The film also has a character named Narayan, played by Om Shivpuri, who can speak and hear, but is blind. Gulzar beautifully shows how smoothly they navigate the course of their friendship despite their handicaps.

Some of the scenes in the film emphasise the director's hold on the medium as he creates scenes that, without the use of dialogue, still communicate their import clearly to audiences. Perhaps the most beautiful of such scenes is the one when Haricharan and Aarti, after their wedding, in their private moments express their love for each other and share their dreams of living together as a couple. The amazement that Sanjeev Kumar expresses when he hears his heartbeat is eloquently captured. Gulzar communicates through this scene that emotion can be expressed even without words. Hariharan and Aarti understand each other easily without words, and the audience too is able to understand the scene with the same ease and experience the couple's sense of contentment.

An unusual scene in *Koshish* shows the couple at the seaside, where they chat with Narayan. When Hariharan and Aarti feel uplifted watching the sunset, Narayan shares their joy. When Narayan asks them if the sun is setting, they are amazed, wondering how he could be aware of it. Gulzar's dialogue at this point is eloquent in itself. Narayan says, 'I cannot see, but I can smell the light.' Thus dialogue indicates to society that those who have all their faculties intact can learn valuable ways of improving the texture of their lives from those who are less blessed.

Yet another dialogue, delivered by Aarti's teacher, Seema Deo, delivers a rebuke to society. Seema Deo says, 'We start with a benediction: Children, you are blessed that you will hear no evil, speak no evil.' This masterfully worded line is a comment on our degenerating society. *Koshish* is like an emotional poem in which the dialogues are expressed through the silent emotions of its protagonists. No one who has seen this film can remain unmoved by the way Sanjeev Kumar and Jaya Bhaduri have played their roles. With ease, Gulzar has transformed a small story into a film with a significant message.

Koshish was inspired by the Japanese film, *Happiness of Us Alone*, written and directed by Zenzo Matsuyama.

Interestingly, the Japanese film had touched Raj Kapoor too, who had wanted to adapt it. Khwaja Ahmed Abbas was to write the screenplay.

Koshish won the National Award for Best Screenplay. It also won the Golden Lotus for Best Actor for Sanjeev Kumar.

The film's message comes strongly at the end of the film. Sanjeev Kumar finds an aurally challenged bride for his son, Amit. The climax of the film makes it clear that the effort should continue. The director wishes to convey that able-bodied people should marry a physically challenged person to give them a chance to live a normal life as a partner.

51.

Gulzar's astonishing use of language in film songs, ghazals and contemporary poetry shows us how he incessantly works on blending the rhythm of words and tune to create harmony. Rather than embellishing the poetic aspects of a tune, he prefers to use language with a simple idiom so that it can easily resonate with the listener. Through enunciation, words, sounds that are sometimes complex, sometimes easy, sometimes absurd, and at times used very differently, he lifts his songs to the level of literary writing. The nuances of sounds have always influenced him. We must keep in mind the strong impact of the music of Bengal, Tagore's philosophical poetry, and the fact that he has continued the tradition of writing excellent poetry in Urdu. Besides this is his love for all things that Nature offers as gifts. Together, they keep his creative forces afloat, while cementing his affiliation with sound. If this were not so, we would not be able to experience such an artistic blending of repetitive words with the movement of tunes.

I present here some songs which are unique in the way they combine poetic sensibilities with repeated words. 'Roz-roz dali-dali, kya likh jaye…'(*Angoor*), 'Chappa-chappa charkha chale,'(*Maachis*), 'Mahi re, mahi mahi re' (*Fiza*), 'Maiya-maiya gulabi tare chunle sare chun'(*Guru*), 'Dil hoom-hoom kare', (*Rudaali*), 'Chhalka-chhalka re kalas ka pani' (*Saathiya*), 'Katra katra milti hai, katra-katra jeene do' (*Izajat*). These echoing word combinations are part of Gulzar's unique poetic signature.

Often this repetitive quality, moving from the opening verse, is also used in the stanza without affecting the beauty of the composition; rather it enhances and adds emphasis to the meaning. In the song from *Khushboo*, 'Do nainon mein aansoo bhare hain', the lines that come in the stanza, 'doobi-doobi aankhon mein sapnon ke saaye', the repetition is effective in drawing a picture. There are many such examples where Gulzar uses the words more than once as a part of his craft. In 'Piya baawari' from *Khubsoorat*, the repetitive words, 'daar-daar' and 'kale-kale' at the start of both antaras add beauty to the tune. Such blending of words and tune creates unforgettable music.

When asked about his use of similar words used in tandem he replies, 'That is my style.' He keeps experimenting, and when he feels a repetition fits well with the tune at any point, adds it in. This is yet another 'Gulzariyat', that comes to the fore through the medium of words.

52.

'A Song Travels' is an essay written by Gulzar in which he traces the journey of songs in Hindi films, and discusses their nature and the changes in the period between 1903 to 1960. The essay which is a part of Britannica's *Encyclopedia of Hindi Cinema* was written keeping in mind intellectual lyricists and the songs they wrote. Gulzar makes some important inclusions in the essay. He discusses the leading songwriters of the early years of film music in connection with the trends of the time. Among them are Munshi Aarzoo Lucknowi, Dina Nath Madhok, Pandit Pradeep, Kedar Sharma, Qamar Jalalabadi, Tanvir Naqvi, Pandit Bhushan, Nakhshab Jarchavi, Gopal Singh Nepali, Rajinder Krishan, Nazim Panipati, Shevan Rizvi, Prem Dhawan and many others. Gulzar explores and analyses the creative inputs of these poets against the setting of the social, political pressures of popular culture, thus preparing the readers to delve into their minds.

Gulzar assesses sixty years of film music with arguments to support his viewpoint. One of observations he makes is:

> Hindi film music went through some changes in the 1940s. Earlier, dialects like Bhojpuri, Awadhi and Purvi were mostly used, in comparison with khari-boli Hindi. The songs written in khari-boli Hindi became a part of songs that were later written in modern Urdu and Hindi. This metamorphosis of the language started in about 1945 and continued till well after Independence. The effect of this was that film songs and screenplays slowly moved towards the use of urbanised Hindi and Urdu, a trend that became very noticeable in the majority of films made after 1945.

Gulzar traces the changes in the use of language in screenplay and music, the evolving vocabulary of songwriters in a historical context in 'A Song Travels'. He himself used not just words from other languages, but through his journey as a writer for films has also used Hindustani extensively in his writing. Thus joining that stream of language that was brought into cinema by Pandit Pradeep, Kedar Sharma, Arzoo Lakhnavi and Wali Sahab. In a way, he created a bridge at the point where Urdu and Hindi met to launch his own trajectory as a writer. Almost every significant songwriter in Urdu and Hindi, both from earlier as well as contemporary times, have found themselves using the simplified Hindustani as a means of speech.

Using 'A Song Travels' as reference, if we examine

Gulzar's own journey, we can hear the echoes of past traditions throughout his work.

53.

There was once a strip of wood
On that a horse stood
A hammer flailed on its tail
The horse ran, tail held up like a sail

The horse had no grace
It reached a marketplace
In the marketplace was plenty of snow
The snow made a cold wind blow

(*Masoom*)

Many personal and homely experiences too feature as an intrinsic part of Gulzar's poetry. This is considered one of his most prolific genres. Of course, here we are looking at this genre through the universe of children and their emotions.

As far as my knowledge goes, most earlier film songs related to children, or written for them, do not go beyond being emotional or beautiful to link directly with children. Even if children are present in such songs, they seem to be portrayed as puppets who, directed by adults, show their childlike qualities only to entertain us. Gulzar breaks this mould in one fell swoop. He writes the songs from a childlike mindset and films them with all the uneven but realistic childish imperfections. We thus get a means to view that aspect of childhood that cinema has not deliberated upon before: whether you look at the childlike friendships of *Masoom* or the appearance of Chachi in *Chachi 420*. Whether it is the song sequences of *Makdee* or *Kitaab*, they are all centred around how children view the world around them.

I believe the 'horse song' quoted above reaches a summit in portraying children's minds. Only two other songs can be counted as being on par with it. One is 'Nani teri morni ko mor le gaye' (Granny, the peacocks took away your peahen) written by Shailendra for a 1960 film, also titled *Masoom*, and the other is the song 'Dadi amma dadi amma maan ja' (Granny dear, granny dear, listen to me) from the film *Gharana* (1961) written by Shakeel Badayuni. In connection with his song in *Masoom*, Gulzar has said about R. D. Burman, 'I can say that most of my songs blossom like children in Pancham's house.' This is a statement of the respect he held his contemporary musician in and a measure of the childlike joy and ease that he experienced when working on songs with Pancham. Much like the naturalness that is evident when two children play together. Of course, the music for both *Masoom* and *Kitaab* was given by R. D. Burman.

Besides 'Lakdi ki kaati' (There was once a strip of wood), the song, 'O papad wale panga na le' (Don't you mess with me, you papad-seller) from *Makdee*, and 'Chupdi-chupdi chachi' from *Chachi 420* as well as 'Masterji ki aayi chitthi' (A letter has come from Masterji) from *Kitaab*, can be mentioned among the songs for children. Though Gulzar's song, written for a series that ran on Doordarshan is also remarkable enough to set us humming:

Across the forest there is talk and song
A flower wearing knickers has just been born

And:

The boat bobs upon the water
The water goes hither thither

Gulzar has also been writing songs for children who are differently abled. He articulates the immeasurable possibilities of the children of Arushi, a not-for-profit from Bhopal, giving wings to their dreams. He has produced literature for children to help hone their skills and expression.

He has also created a unique alphabet in Devnagari to entertain children. Referring to this he says, 'It can become necessary to learn a language at any age. Just as one can fall in love at any age.' I present here two poems from the book *Mirrors of the Heart* that help children learn two letters of the alphabet:

Remember my friend, Mona?
Used to play mehendi-mehendi with me?
She's run away with Mohsin. (For the devanagari letter 'ma')

From jungle to jungle the word has spread
Call the rain jaldi se
The jugnu's tail is on fire...(For the letter 'ja')

Gulzar's love for and sense of belonging where children are concerned reminds one of the lines by Khalil Gibran in his book *Mirrors of the Soul.* The seer says, 'Keep me away from that knowledge that does not weep, from that scene that does not laugh, and keep me away from the greatness that does not bow its head before children.'

54.

He has had the opportunity to write many of the first films made by well-known producer-directors of their time. It has been noted as part of Gulzar's journey in films that most of such first films that he has written screenplay, dialogues and songs for have been successful, and owe some of that success to his craft. The friendship and camaraderie that binds two creative people together can give rise to great art.

It is possible to list most of these first-time successes. Ramesh Sippy's *Andaz* (1971), for example, had Gulzar's dialogues for the screenplay written by Salim-Javed and Sachin Bhowmik. The screenplay and songs for Meraj's film, *Palkon Ki Chhaon Mein* (1977), screenplay, dialogues and songs for Bhimsain's off-beat *Gharonda* (1978), *Ek Pal* (1978) by Kalpana Lajmi for which he wrote the screenplay, dialogues and songs, as he did too for Prakash Jha's *Hip Hip Hurray*

(1984). He also wrote the screenplay, dialogues and songs for Shekhar Kapur's *Masoom*, which was based on Erich Segal's novel *Man, Woman and Child* in 1982. He wrote the screenplay for Ramesh Sharma's *New Delhi Times* (1986) and dialogues and songs for Shaad Ali's *Saathiya* (2002) and songs for Meghna Gulzar's *Filhaal* (2002) and *Chupke Se* (2004) by Sona Urvashi.

Gulzar remembers Shekhar Kapur asking him if he had read Eric Segal's novel in the early discussions on the writing of *Masoom*. He was keen to know if, after hearing the story, Gulzar would want to read the book. Gulzar only said this in reply, 'You have narrated the story to me, that's enough. Let it remain with me, let me absorb it. If, after I write it, you feel something is missing or you wish to change it somewhat, I will surely read the novel.'

Surprised, Kapur exclaimed, 'Will you work only on the story line that I narrated and not read the novel!'

In those days, Gulzar's favourite haunt for writing screenplays was the West End Hotel in Bangalore. He roughly sketched out the storyline and, reaching the West End Hotel, worked steadily for days at a stretch till the screenplay of *Masoom* was ready. That was how a debut director's first film, now being recognised as a classic, was written.

Gulzar also remembers that while writing the script, the lines of the song, 'Tujhse naaraaz nahin zindagi/ Hairan hoon main' ('I'm not angry with you, Life/ I'm only confused) presented themselves to him. When this idea was shared with Shekhar Kapur, it was agreed that they would be the opening lines of a song that encapsulated the theme of the film. Afterwards, the song was completed on his return to Bombay over many sittings with his friend, Pancham, and recorded as two solos in the voices of Lata Mangeshkar and a new singer, Anup Ghoshal.

Gulzar laughs. 'I was a bit foxed by Anup's voice because his Bengali accent made it difficult for him to sing some words correctly. Especially the phrase “hairan hoon main”, which he would sing as “hoiran hoon main”. When I would point out his mistake, Pancham would glare at me and say, “He’s saying it correctly.” I would vexedly reply, “He is a Bengali, you are a Bengali, how can either of you know the correct Hindi pronunciation?” Though the fact is that Anup really worked hard on the song. Even today I feel that there was a rawness in his voice; it was not perfect, and maybe that is why the song came across as sincere and heartfelt, and touched the listener’s heart.’

Gulzar has countless stories related to the screenplays and songs he has written and I eagerly took every opportunity to listen to them. Each time the window of his mind was pushed open by some moment in a song’s creation, the memories would flow like a stream. All of which I was trying to record. To adapt Amrita Pritam’s words, I am engaged in documenting Gulzar’s ‘ilm ke dastavez’—the record of his knowledge and experience.

Like the songs on *Masoom*, the emotions the film evokes also crowd the memory,

In two little pools they float
And talk
Though there may be no one listening
Some words written and some spoken
A small cloud
A little rain
And a tale...
Of two eyes, a tale...

(*Masoom*)

55.

Gulzar, besides writing poems on love and romance, also writes on issues concerning society. These concerns are deeply embedded into his psyche and have had political implications too. His filmography clearly shows us that every time he sees the common man buffeted by social, political or religious storms, he makes the issue the theme of a film. His very first film, *Mere Apne*, centred on the helplessness of the jobless youth. Gulzar portrays their hopelessness, aimlessness and the anger they harbour against society through the medium of his film. Even as he was writing romantic songs at the time of making his first film, the theme he chose for it was contemporary and urgent. In sharp contrast to the songs he was writing for *Khamoshi* (1969), 'Hum ne dekhi hai' (We have seen) and *Aashirwad*'s 'Jhir jhir barse', his tone in *Mere Apne* becomes satirical. Presenting a realistic picture of the social milieu of the time he writes this song:

We are tiptop
Everything is A-okay
We have a BA, we have an MA
What for, we say
There are no jobs to be had
But with your blessings
Everything is A-okay

Anger against the government was on the rise, and corruption had dug its roots deep into society. The song brought to the screen an honest portrayal of the growing antagonism of educated young men who had been buffeted by circumstances to a degree of utter hopelessness. Going beyond the reach of a film song, the lyrics were a statement by the lyricist of how he viewed and judged society. In 'Geet Gaata Chal', the article on his songs in *Filmfare*, Gulzar said about this song,

> In 1971, when the war to free Bangladesh was on, I had the occasion to watch Sukhdev's documentary, *Nine Days to Freedom*. The film deals with the bloodbath that ensued in a touching manner. At the same time, India was going through a very turbulent phase. I could not ignore the events taking place around me and in the rest of the country. I articulated this difficulty in the form of a comment through

the song, "Haal chal theek thaak hai" [Everything is tiptop!].

Thus, against the backdrop of the tumultuous social canvas of India, Gulzar adds the Bangladesh freedom war into his satirical song on politics.

The same satirical vein is evident once more in *Aandhi*, made four years later, which centres round the theme of political corruption. Aarti Devi, the film's protagonist, is fighting the elections, and when she goes to her constituency, using the song as a means to comment on politics, he paints a picture that in turn raises questions about the existing situation. The song goes thus:

Bow to him, the Revered One is here
To give an account of five years
He who does not bow to these gods is an infidel
Not a mere vote, our very lives are on offer
Many are the labels we have pasted and removed
Set up many chairs, and arranged tables
Give us an account, we have come in large numbers
Bow to him, the Revered One has come

The song parodies the election scenario, portraying satirically what happens before and after an election. If we read the song by itself as an indictment of the behaviour of politicians during an election, it holds as much meaning as a note of dissent from a citizen against the leader seeking his vote. Going beyond this, we see that Gulzar's mind is always alert to political events, despite being averse to politics. However, he limits his role and comments on politics to that of an observer who, watching from a distance, raises questions about its functioning, ideologies and participation. This can be seen clearly in many of his triveni poems too. A couple of examples can explain this more clearly,

Leaflets are being handed out in the bylanes
Choose your murderer
Elections are here, hard times are upon us

~

Bullets, dynamite, fire, bombs, slogans
Fireworks are warming the city
Throw the city open, for everything is 'bandh' today

The pertinent questions raised in a few words in his trivenis are an indication of the maturity and harmony with which the poet channels his thoughts. Yet, when we study those of his film songs centred around political or social issues, they show him at his satirical best, and often go beyond to reach the level of condemnation. The song sung by Nana Patekar's character in his much later film *Hu Tu Tu* should be studied in this connection:

There's fraud in flour
In trains and in petrol too
LIC is a swindle
The banks make a bundle
From jeeps and tanks they make four from two
Scams from army guns to boots
Scams stuffed like junk
In money-filled trunks
Scams all the way, brother

There is no need to explain these lines which are a powerful comment on the political corruption that permeates the social fabric. Similarly, the opening lines of another song from *Hu tu tu* are comment enough, 'Bandobast hai jabardast hai, bandobast hai jabardast hai/Khoon ki khushbu badi mast hai' (Security is forceful and ready/ Security is forceful and ready/ The scent of blood is heady).

In two later films, *Matru Ki Bijlee Ka Mandola* (2013) and *Haider* (2014) Gulzar's pen sketches the ebb and flow of social landscapes with a crusader's zeal. In two songs from *Matru Ki Bijlee Ka Mandola*, 'Dole dole…hat lootnewale' and 'Le suno bhaiyon/ Bhabiyon suno ri/ Katha chor ki re chori chori' (Come listen now brothers and sisters/ Boys and girls/ Listen/ Quietly to the thief's story), he highlights the troubles of everyday life. In the same way, in *Haider*, the song, 'Laal laal hua/ Laal-laal hua na Jhelum/ Jhelum laal-laal hua' (Red flows the Jhelum, red) is a statement on the 'gifts' politics and society have given to Kashmir.

It is also necessary to mention other films songs by Gulzar in films like *Laal Salaam* (2002), *Yahaan* (2005), *Raavan* (2010) and *Raajneeti* (2010) as political comments. Where the social and political situations have grown out of control, his songs are activist in tone, reminding us of his youth when, as a PWA member, he enjoyed listening to Ali Sardar Jafri's rousing poetry. A compilation of Gulzar's poems and songs and trivenis that have socio-political comments would be as weighty as a book holding the romantic writing that has earned him fame.

Examining the 'mukhdas' of the songs mentioned above gives us a different view of Gulzar use of language. 'Zara sa aao, baitho, watan ki baatein karen' (Come, sit, let's talk about the nation) from *Laal Salaam*, *Rajneeti*'s 'Boodha aasman, dharti de ghere/ Dhan hai dharti re' (The ancient sky cradles the earth/ Fortunate, fortunate earth is), the line 'Thok de killi' (Hammer the nail) from *Raavan* and from *Yahaan* the line 'Pooche jo koi meri nishani/ Rang hina likhna' (If anyone seeks my identity/ Tell them I'm coloured red' are worthy of note.

The song from *Yahaan* reads like a romantic number at first glance, but read against the background of Kashmir and the film's story, and the socio-political implications reveal themselves. The song from *Raavan* too has its own measure of weightiness:

Hammer the nail, hammer it willy-nilly
It's not too far, let's march to Delhi
The dictator has the evil eye, scares all silly
Oh you rebel, hammer the nail, hammer it willy-nilly
Let the chips fall, ply the billy

If we examine the songs that have a social concern, here too the sense of satire comes through strongly. They reflect those issues that existed aeons ago and continue to plague the middle class living in metropolitan cities. For instance, the problem highlighted in this song from *Biwi Aur Makaan* (1966):

Give me a house to live in
A floor on the roof, or a roof over the floor
Give me a house to live in...

Similarly, this song from *Gharonda* discusses the hurdles in finding a suitable house:

In this city
Two people in love
Through the day, and the night
Seek sustenance
A home

Ranging from topics that concern everyday life to those that evoke questions and satire, Gulzar's songs deal with them all. Besides his poems, his songs too reflect this tension evocatively. Whether it is 'Golmaal hai bhai, sab golmaal hai' (Everything is topsy turvy, my friend, everything) from *Gol Maal* (1979) or 'Kash lagaa, kash lagaa/ Zindagi ke kash lagaa' (Breathe, breathe deeply of life) from *No Smoking* (2007) or even the song 'Kabhi chand ki tarah tapki/ Kabhi raah mein padi payi/ Athanni si zindagi...yeh zindagi' (It dropped like the moon/ I found it lying by the wayside/ This half-rupee of a life...This life) from *Jahan Tum Le Chalo* (1999), every one of these songs reflect social problems and solutions to find harmony. This is no easy matter for Gulzar, for the life of ease that he seeks through his poetry is often transformed into social accountability when he encounters these concerns.

It's only natural that these concerns that are reflected in his songs and poems should also filter into his stories. He does not play the reformist or advisor in his stories, but placing his fingers gently on the source of pain etches it out into a story that communicates it perfectly. He stories 'Rape Market' and

'Hilsa' on rape; 'LOC', 'Tumbe' and 'Kuldeep Nayyar Aur Pir Sahab', inspired by the tensions between India and Pakistan; and 'Atthaniaya', which concerns the footpath dwellers of Mumbai, are some examples that must be read.

Using the wide spectrum of genres at his command, Gulzar expresses his involvement and engagement with social issues. The short, three-line trivenis and also his most recent poems written over the past few years continue to signal the need for social change. 'Parinde Hain Ya Parcham?', 'Lakeerein', 'Bahut Se Masle Lekar Gaya Tha', 'Kabbadi', 'Muhafiz', 'Ek Manzar', and 'Jalsa' give us glimpses of his socially alert persona.

Let those borders be
Someone must have drawn them in anger
Make them into 'pala'
Come, let's play kabbadi...
When, with a 'kudi kudi' I enter your 'pala'
You can take a hold of me
Do not let me touch the lines of the border
Which someone had drawn in anger.
Make them into 'pala'
Come, let's play kabbadi!'

(*Kabbadi*)

56.

I have often heard Gulzar-sahab talk seriously about the crafting of his songs, their structure and the light that emanates from the meaning hidden in the words. At such times he seems to me a seer who, rifling through the fire of his songs, is gathering embers with a pair of tongs.

Gulzar has always explored his own present, where time has wrought its changes. Though the question which follows below seems to be out of date now, as almost two decades have passed since work on this book was begun. But, since Gulzar is responding to the questions, it is only right that I put them down here.

To why do we no longer see India reflected in our songs these days, he responds with, 'How will you see India in songs? When even in films you do not see India, then how will you see Indianness in songs ?' Taking the thought forward, he adds, 'You must understand that songs do not shape society, it is society that is reflected in its songs. The speed of life has changed today. You can see how every film features New York, Washington, Europe, London. Where is India in them? How will you find that which you have stopped showing in the songs?

'Torn clothes are part of your lifestyle, they are your fashion statement, which you wear and show off proudly... then will you not find songs too in poor condition, as they have turned their noses up at their roots? When time has turned you into a fashion victim, then songs too will follow the same fashion. It's poignant that you nostalgically seek Indianness in songs after having rejected that way of life. Why would anyone be like Pandit Pradeep and write a song for you that says, "Get away, O people of the world, Hindustan is ours." Or, "Come children, let me show you a glimpse of Hindustan?" Why do you have such aspirations from the songs of today?' I listen to him talking about music in amazement, and quietly change the question.

57.

On December 15, 1978, Gulzar-sahab wrote an essay titled 'The Journey of *Meera*: From Idea to Screen', about the making of the film *Meera* which was later published by Radhakrishan Prakashan in 1979.

This essay held the answers to the many questions that were raised about renowned playback singer Lata Mangeshkar not being a part of the film. I still believe this essay to be an important document in his film journey. Which is why I am presenting some of it in my own words.

The idea of making a film on the Krishna-devotee poetess, Meerabai, came to Gulzar from the producer, Premji. Gulzar was overjoyed at the idea, wondering why he himself had not thought about making a film on the saintly poetess. Once the decision to make the film was taken, Premji suggested that the mahurat, the auspicious first clap, of the film should be done at the hands of Lata Mangeshkar, as she alone held the status of a Meera in modern times. Gulzar was happy with the idea, and he was able to convince Lata-ji too, to give the mahurat clap. Even as she agreed for the mahurat, Lata-ji also conveyed softly to Gulzar that she would not be able to sing for the film. The mahurat for *Meera* took place on October 14, 1975, on Dussehra.

Gulzar did not think it necessary to discuss with Lata-ji, her refusal to sing for the film. He told himself that the mahurat had just taken place, when the screenplay was written and the film went on the floor and the time came to record the songs, he would convince Didi at that point.

The script took a year to write and shooting began on June 19, 1976. Even before this, Laxmikant-Pyarelal had been signed on as music directors. They had decided that 'Mere Toh Giridhar Gopal' would be the first song they would record. Gulzar had already intimated the music composer duo that Lata-ji had refused to sing for the film. Both Laxmikant and Pyarelal believed they would be able to convince Lata-ji at the right time but destiny decreed otherwise. Despite their requests, Lata-ji was completely unwilling to sing for the film. The music director duo were in a fix, as they could not think of a voice other than Lata-ji's to record Meera's bhajans in. At this, Gulzar approached Lata Mangeshkar again.

Gulzar said that when he heard the reason for Lata-ji not wishing to sing for the film, he found it to be quite reasonable. Lata-ji explained that she had already sung Meera's bhajans for two private labels. She felt that after having sung the bhajans with great devotion and feeling, it was not right for her to sing the bhajans for a commercial film. Convinced by the sentiment behind this thought, Gulzar repeated Lata-ji's statement word for word to Laxmikant-Pyarelal. He also requested them to choose another singer so he could start recording. However, Laxmikant-Pyarelal were unwilling to go ahead without Lata-ji and bowed out. Gulzar was now faced with the problem of finding a music director who would agree not only to compose songs for a film that was so dependent on music without Lata's voice but would also have to find a singer to sing the Meera bhajans for an LP record.

Perhaps this is the only film in Gulzar's career in which the film went on the floors before the music was ready. Gulzar admits that his best friend, Pancham, too refused to compose for the film. He did not wish to court controversy by recording songs without Lata-ji. Gulzar wondered what would happen to *Meera* if it lacked both the right voice and the right music. Would he have to abandon the film?

Often, in times of trial, a hope shines bright. That hope grew brighter when, during the shooting, the film's art director suggested the name of Pandit Ravi Shankar, the famed sitarist who had composed music for a few films. The name filled Gulzar with confidence. He felt that Pandit-ji, being such a learned exponent of music, would perhaps readily agree to the idea of composing music for the film once he heard the concept. Pandit-ji was living in America at that time, and had distanced himself from composing for films. That was another hurdle Gulzar would have to cross as the music and soundtrack for the film had to be made in India. Even if he did agree, how should they set the music so that he could be called to India to record all the songs at one stretch. Then there was the worry over what Panditji's response to Lata-ji's refusal would be.

After some effort, Pandit-ji's America and London

numbers were sourced, and Gulzar spoke to Pandit-ji about *Meera*. Gulzar says that even as they were talking, he was sure Pandit-ji would agree. He had only one condition, 'Please narrate the script of the film to me. If I like it, I will surely compose the music for it.'

Gulzar says he narrated the script of *Meera* to Pandit-ji, face to face, across the space of three hours. After listening intently, Pandit Ravi Shankar gave his consent. Hiding nothing, Gulzar frankly shared the fact of Lata Mangeshkar's refusal, and that Laxmikant-Pyarelal had withdrawn from the film due to this. He also mentioned that R. D. Burman had refused to score music for the film for the same reason. Pandit-ji made no comment, but he did say regretfully that had Lata-ji sung for the film, it would have reached other heights altogether.

Around the same time as when Gulzar was in America confirming the project with Pandit Ravi Shankar, Lata Mangeshkar was in Washington DC in connection with a concert. When Gulzar informed Lata-ji that Panditji was composing music for the film, she was pleased.

After this, Gulzar and Pandit Ravi Shankar worked for ten to twelve days on the script and the placement of Meera's bhajans in it, and Panditji kept making notes speedily. Gulzar was amazed at how efficiently the great musician conducted his work. By August 1976, when Gulzar returned to India, they had decided that Vani Jairam would sing the songs for *Meera*.

In in his autobiography, *Raagmala*, published many years after the film, Pandit Ravi Shankar states that he felt great joy in composing the music for the film. Despite being beautifully and movingly crafted, the film was not a commercial hit. He has also stated that he felt Vani Jairam was the right voice for the film, as she was one of the foremost singers in South Indian films at that time.

Pandit Ravi Shankar came to India in September 1976.

The rehearsals for *Meera*'s songs started on November 22, and Vani Jairam as well as the entire musical unit were present. The complete album was thus recorded in the fifteen days between November 30 and December 15. Pandit Ravi Shankar was present throughout and was assisted by Vijay Raghava Rao.

Thirteen of Meera's songs and an alaap in the voice of Pandit Dinkar Konkini had been recorded. With Vani Jairam's voice, Pandit Ravi Shankar had created a great musical experience for *Meera*, marking a high in his musical career. The music of *Meera*, composed by Pandit Ravi Shankar to take forward his tradition of classical music touched with spirituality was thus completed. And shooting commenced again.

With Hema Malini, steeped in the role of Meera, climbing into her palanquin to depart from her parental home with her bridegroom, Bhojraj, Meerabai's story was imprinted on celluloid to become a part of film history forever, as one of its most beautiful visual compositions. Hearing Vani Jairam singing this song in the background still fills us with amazement:

Bala, I will become a hermit
Whichever garb my lord likes
That form I will take...

58.

From many points of view, Gulzar's *Namkeen* (1982) is an unforgettable film. Based on the novel *Akaal Basant* by Samaresh Basu, it is a screenplay of endless poignancy. Of special interest is the fact that, at this point in his film journey, Gulzar seems to have recreated the genius of his guru Bimal Roy on a new canvas. The film attempts to deal with all aspects of human singleness and solitude.

This intense film revolves around four women and a man. But after negotiating with ease the long stretch of two-and-a-half hours, one hardly feels one has sat through a film of such intensity.

The relationship that is created between Jugni (played by Waheeda Rehman), Nimki (played by Sharmila Tagore), Mittu (played by Shabana Azmi), Chinki (played by Kiran Vairale) and Gherulal (played by Sanjeev Kumar) within the shambles of a house situated on a small hilly hamlet, depicts the many shades of the tragedy of life. Gulzar relocates Basu's story, taking it from Bengal to the hills of Himachal Pradesh. The landscape he has chosen, with its evening mists and filtered morning sunshine, adds its own shade of melancholy to the story.

The story of *Namkeen*, salted with sorrow, is a relentless exploration of the unravelling of life. As Jugni, Rehman plays a nautanki artiste who is embittered after being betrayed by her instrumentalist lover. She no longer finds joy in her art. Through her character, we also glimpse the life of the dancing girls and courtesans who were considered mere tools for entertainment in the princely states and in the British colonies. Some of the dialogues in the film ruthlessly shine the torch on reality.

Gulzar portrays Jugni as an interesting character. Hurt by her husband's betrayal, she finds herself worrying endlessly about her three adult daughters. Her elder daughter, Nimki, is the film's principal heroine and also plays the role of narrator. She spends her days tending to her sisters and living in the hope that some day, someone will come and change her life. The shambles of a house the four women live in also seems to be deteriorating, stuck as it is somewhere between the past and the present.

Gulzar's narrative shows the middle sister, Mithu, as a mute girl, as a result of some mishap that occurred during her childhood. She is reckless, a happy spirit, full of empathy, sometimes secretly stealing away to eat paan without her mother's knowledge. Complete in her solitude, she writes poetry. About the clouds, the rain, the swans...

> *Come again, O clouds*
> *With pearls I shall embed your wings*
> *Fill my pond before you leave*
> *Near the pond's edge will I be waiting*
> *Under oath of my lord, Kali Kamli Wala*
> *Come again, O clouds...*

There is pain in the fact that she meets no one at the edge of the pond who can relieve her loneliness and suffering. All she knows is suffering and hardship which drive her to madness and prematurely end the spring of her life.

Gulzar sensitively creates all the elements required to piece together the character of Mithu. The film's hero, Gerulal, views Mithu's poetic persona with a paternal gaze and goes back after gifting her a diary to write her poems. In a way, *Namkeen* seems to be an unfinished diary of life's hardships, in which all relationships stand in confrontation with one another. Each one in a relationship fans the hope of gaining something from the other. The relationship between Jugni and her daughters is as fragile as a house of cards. Nimki's statement in this regard seems full of compassion, 'If I leave, no one will survive.'

The relationships in the film are indeed like pearls strung together on a string, which will break and scatter if even a single pearl is removed. A scene in the film shows us this. In the scene Sharmila Tagore responds to Sanjeev Kumar's question, 'Should I come back?' with, 'Come back, but not for my sake,' thus taking the poignancy to a much higher pitch.

Gulzar uses his sensitivity as a director to create small collages of human interactions. You hardly realise how entwined you get in the events of the film, which enter your heart and seem to be part of your own experience. Whether it is in the handing across of a cup of tea or the filling of water in the pitcher, the scene of food being served, to that of the sisters putting out the lantern at night before they sleep...the warmth of a family can be felt throughout. When the sisters enjoy a bit of mirth, laughing and giggling as they prepare to sleep, the scene brings home the fact that Gulzar has learnt well from Bimal Roy the art of depicting joy and sorrow in correct measures.

Waheeda Rehman's character's habit of hitting out harshly in her bitter state of mind also gives a lesson about life, wherein a reference is made to how language and words can bring about a change in society. Waheeda-ji's role in the film is that of one whose best years are over, with no understanding of what she should do with the years that lie ahead. It often happens in life that we waste our concern over matters that we later find are of no use to us. The ending of the film has been filmed poetically, with the director touching on both, separation and meeting, in a simple way. This dialogue by Sanjeev Kumar lingers in memory, 'Nimki, you had said then that you cannot go away and leave everything behind, but everyone has left you and gone away. This time I will not leave you behind. There's nothing here to take with you. Let go of what has passed, save what is left.' Nimki does go away with Gherulal, her truck-driver lover, but continues to carry with her the tribulations of the family she has left behind.

Despite the storyline, *Namkeen* is not just a tale. Rather it is knitted from strands of emotion, in which life takes new forms with every moment. Film critic Saibal Chaterjee has rightly observed, 'This film is a human drama, in which heartrending moments leave you stunned.'

On a different note, Pavan Jha, a student of Gulzar's films, says about the film's music:

> In Gulzar's *Namkeen*, the song, 'Aankhi chali, baanki chali' gives evidence of the director paying tribute to his guru, Bimal Roy, and Pancham paying tribute to his father. Hark back to the song from *Bandini*, 'O panchi pyare', which a woman prisoner inside the jail sings while pounding

> spices. The mortar and pestle and the rhythm of this song are completely reminiscent of that song. The sound of the rice being winnowed against the cane-implement (supda) is also prominent in *Bandini*. There is no cane implement in this song in *Namkeen*, but Gulzar and Pancham manage to add the sound. It's like a mismatched blend of fresh and stale food, which turns out to be unusual and enjoyable—just like the partnership of the characters of Jumman miya and Juniyabai are in the song—mismatched but enjoyable.'

The song referred to by Pavan Jha is set in the hills of Himachal. This song too has its place among the great songs in the history of film music:

Aanki set out
Baanki set out
A tableu set out in Chowringhee
With panta bhat and fresh brinjal curry

A girl was born in Jhumman's house
Her cheeks like red apples
Jhumman went out, twirling his moustache
Reached his wife's home
Speaking Persian at every turn
Asking for water with 'Aab'
Jhumman-miyan did die of thirst
But he did not quit his high horse, his 'Taab'

'Panta bhat and fresh brinjal', the combining of Punjab and Bengal, is as much a reflection of Gulzar and Pancham working together as the mismatched Punjab and Bengal traditions coming together to form a unique harmony in *Namkeen*. Just as leftover rice and fresh brinjal give a different flavour to a meal, in the same way, the melancholy permeating *Namkeen* and the stale relationships that Gulzar attempts to fill with new hope create a unique film.

Namkeen stands alongside Shyam Benegal's *Hari-Bhari* (2000) and Mrinal Sen's *Khandhar* (1988) in which films too the middle class finds ways to live between tears and laughter. The weeping over the tribulations besetting this section of society can be heard within the walls of the home. In exactly the way the four women of *Namkeen* cry silently, trapped in their lives.

59.

We can analyse the appeal of Gulzar's film poetry through a different prism too. If we examine the variety of imagery he uses, we understand that they adopt different forms to highlight different emotions. Like the scientific concept of the merging of the senses, the experiencing of emotions takes a different path in his songs.

There are countless examples where he talks about experiencing touch through colour. And being able to see through smell. Sound can be worn in the ears. With such word-play he creates a surrealism much like Franz Kafka created in his writing. We can witness some of the poet's 'Gulzarana' through these examples,

'I have seen the wafting fragrance of these eyes' (*Khamoshi*)

'When the eyes call out' (*Seema*)

'Someone plays the flute of their eyes' (*Kinara*)

'Succulent/juicy words from sour-sweet eyes' (*Griha Pravesh*)

'The dream of your lips placed on my breath remains still.' (*Asoka*)

'The fragrance of tobacco in your words' (*Bunty Aur Babli*)

'Make a veil out of the rays of light' (*Jhoom Barabar Jhoom*)

'Insipid, tasteless nights' (*Guru*)

'Musical-eyed man' (*Veer*)

This usage is unique to the poet's writing, and results in adding a new dimension to film songs. In this connection we should also look at the writers of unconventional poetry, who use symbols in a manner that imparts a newness to their songs. There is no trickery in the way in which Gulzar uses images in his lyrics to change the meaning of the content. Nor any desire for a status to be bestowed on him by those who read and understand his songs. It is but an obsession to find new experiments and routes that express themselves through his altered images. Just as, when writing this song from *Sadma*, he says:

I too have, every single sorrow of yours
Embraced, haven't I?

To embrace an abstract emotion like sorrow as if it were a friend is to give it a personification. This is his 'Gulzariayat', that he believes in giving emotional experiences a persona. Often this leads him down a mystical path. It is an ability to describe sensitive emotions visually, or colour moral ideas with romantic overtones. Examples of this dexterity are countless in his songs for Hindi films. And the same is true of the non-film songs, his poems and nazms. 'Pukhraj', 'Raat Pashmina Ki', 'Raat, Chand Aur Main', 'Kuch Aur Nazme', 'Pandra, Paanch, Pichattar' and 'Pluto' are rich with these experiments.

Countless examples of Kafkaesque surrealism can be encountered in Gulzar's songs. In the song from *Rockford*, 'Aasman ke paar shayad aur koi aasman hoga' ('Perhaps there is a sky beyond this sky') the following lines reveal his 'Gulzariayat':

On these long roads, everyone must be hurrying
Like a notebook's pages, the days must be flipping...

The antara of 'O dil banjare' (You nomad heart) from *Maya Memsaab* (1993) too effectively divides the content into unusual similes. This creates a different beauty and the song that swings between alternating forms gives a unique pleasure:

I want to fill the hollow of my hand

With the shade that filters through sunlight
I want to taste with my lips
The dreams that filter through the eyes

This merging of the senses that takes place in Gulzar's use of imagery makes his style of expression much loved among film goers, who recognise his style easily. Though newer song writers have tried to imitate this and created clones, it is interesting to study if they have achieved the same measure of success.

60.

The lullaby, 'Do nainon mein aansu bhare, nindiyan kaise samaae' (Tears fill the eyes, how will sleep ever come to them...) in *Khushboo* (1975) was composed by R. D. Burman and sung by Lata Mangeshkar. Gulzar tells an interesting story about the making of this song, which is sung in the film by Hema Malini for Master Raju, whom she loves as her own son. The scene is a simple one of a lullaby being sung by the heroine to induce the child to sleep. When the song was being recorded, Lata-ji, as was her habit, acquainted herself with all aspects of the song including whom it was being recorded on, the situation and mood etc. so she could modulate her singing accordingly. Gulzar's screenplay, based on Saratchandra's novel, had written the scene as a lullaby to be sung in soft tones.

Some songs have a destiny of their own. And the situation, their recording and the way they are filmed finally changes the plan completely. As it often happened when Lata Mangeshkar sang, this song, in her voice, acquired a layer of compassion and feeling. Yet it left Gulzar dismayed when he heard it after the recording. Where he had wished for a low pitched song that could lull a child to sleep, the song had been sung in a high pitch, and would have sat awkwardly on the scene. The two friends were at a loss about how they should tell Didi about this discrepancy.

Didi was always, on her part, ready to understand the signals of the composer and director and re-record a song to suit their needs, regardless of having given it her best in the first recording.

In fact, there had been an instance when, on the urging of a music director, she had given many takes of a single song. A well-known incident happened during the recording of 'Tere aakhon ke siwa duniya mein rakha kya hai' (Nothing exists in the world but your eyes) for *Chirag* (1969), music director Madan Mohan made her sing through many takes. And each time the playback singer unhesitatingly and with complete professionalism attempted to give exactly those nuances to the song that the music director had envisaged.

So, the difficulty was not about whether Lata-ji would sing it again to suit Gulzar's idea. The problem was that the song, in its high-pitched version, had appealed to the two friends. They could not however, find a way to justify the song being fitted into the scene.

The story is that R. D. Burman did not have the temerity to ask Lata-ji to record the song again at a low pitch. Gulzar said, 'Let us try asking once. If she says no, we can think of what to do next.'

So Gulzar went to Lata-ji with the intention of telling her that she had sung the song at a higher pitch than the situation in the film demanded. According to the scene, the song had to be subdued enough to maintain the calm of the night and enable the child to sink into slumber easily. Lata-ji immediately agreed to record the other version of the song.

Gulzar says her readiness helped mend the situation immensely. The song was recorded then, in a lower pitch, without music and with only the vibraphone playing in the background. Lata-ji sang this version too with her usual degree of perfection, and the song was fitted into the film.

Later, the high-pitched version was included in the disc. Thus, R. D. Burman and Gulzar got two versions of a lullaby for *Khushboo*, which added to the delight of listeners.

While talking to me about this for my book, the smile of delight on Gulzar's face revealed to me his joy at being able to obtain two amazing versions of the same song in the singer's incomparable voice. To experience this, you may listen to the high-pitched version on the LP and then visit the scene in the film to listen to Lata singing the song as a low-pitched lullaby. I can say with confidence that the song will entrance you in both versions.

61.

Through the 1970s and '80s, the term LP not only meant 'Long Playing' record, but was also used to refer to the music directors, Laxmikant-Pyarelal, as most of the popular songs of that decade were composed by them. There is little doubt that, together, Laxmikant Shantaram Kudalkar and Pyarelal Ramprasad Sharma created more popular numbers as a team than any other music duo in the history of Hindi films. We can also place the duos of Shankar-Jaikishen or S-J and Kalyanji-Anandji or K-A alongside L-P, as creators of everlasting melodies.

Gulzar is almost missing from the superhit run enjoyed by Laxmi-Pyare. In fact, through the seventies and eighties, two parallel streams can be observed in music. One of L-P and Anand Bakshi, and the other of R. D. Burman and Gulzar. Most of the emotional songs of this period were created by these two teams; a fact that can be checked by visiting their filmographies.

Obviously, while L-P were cementing their bond with Anand Bakshi in popular music, Gulzar was finding ways to express his artistic lyricism along with Pancham. Neither team impinged on the work of the other. And one notes how while Gulzar became the thought behind RD's music; Anand Bakshi, in much the same way, became the popular 'voice' behind Laxmi-Pyare's songs.

Gulzar's collaboration with L-P rests mainly on two films: *Palkon Ki Chaaon Mein* (1977) and *Ghulami* (1985). A journey of seven songs through the two films, with one song in *Ghulami*, 'Mere pi ko pavan kis gali le chali' (To which lane did the wind take my beloved) has been used in snatches, thrice, through the film. This composition with Gulzar and L-P working together is among their best offerings, with the duo composing the song with a different spin. The popular version of this song that has been set into the film has Lata Mangeshkar singing in a high pitch with the sound of the ghatam added to the support given by the synthesiser, violin, sitar, santoor and flute. In the interludes between the stahi or opening stanzas and the antara or following stanzas, the ghatam and flute add a strange poignancy to the lilting cheerfulness of the song. The jugalbandi between the sitar and santoor through the song's flow is in keeping with the signature the composers have used in their emotional compositions. In the sad segment of the same composition, based on a blending of the Bhupali and Desh raags, the violin and sarod play their parts evocatively. Here the daff is also heard faintly, while the flute sings along right through as it has done in the earlier version too. The sound of the wind that is blended into the music adds its own colour to the sad version, fitting itself into the scene that is unfolding on screen. In this superlative collaboration between Lakshmi-Pyare and Gulzar, the poet's lyrics etch out life's joys and sorrows in a picturesque manner:

I had seeded time, sowed it for him
Every moment I had threaded for him
Taking the light from my days and night, she left...
Which lane did the wind take my beloved

Someone stop her, she's carrying away my life

The other song of *Ghulami* is famous too:

Look not at this helpless heart with anger
This poor heart is suffering the sorrow of separation
The beats that can be heard
Are they of my heart or of yours...

A song that today's generation not only searches out on YouTube but also listens to intently.

Gulzar has always been an expert at writing songs that are enriched by other languages, of which this song is a prime example. The song which has its mukhda based on Amir Khusro's Arabic composition, 'Zehaal-e-miskeen makun tagaphul, duraye naina banaye batiyan' (Do not overlook my misery/ By fluttering your eyes and weaving tales) has been set to music by Lakshmikant Pyarelal with the same orchestration used successfully by them through the eighties while composing music for dance numbers. We can see here the blending of synthesiser, violin, shehnai, piano, dafli, dholak, and flute in the orchestra. 'Wood blocks' have also been used at times to create beautiful effects in some portions of the song. The effective arrangement of the instruments gives the song its unforgettable nuances. The repetition by Lata Mangeshkar and Shabbir Kumar of the line towards the end of the film, 'Tumhare palkon se gire hain shabhnam/ Hamaari aankhon me ruk gaye hai' (The dew dropping from your eyes / Has pooled in mine) carries the song to a perfect ending.

Apart from *Ghulami*, the film *Palkon Ki Chaaon Mein* also displays a variety of work. Of the five songs in the film, three which include 'Allah megh de/ Paani de re' (Allah give us clouds/ Give us the rain), 'Daakiya dak laya' (The postman has brought the post) and 'Ghungta gira hai, zara ghungta utha de re' (Your veil has fallen over your face, lift it up my dear) became popular numbers. 'Dakiya dak laya' has become a song associated with the post office, and draws on the events that surround the sighting of a postman going through the village delivering letters and money orders. Kishore Kumar's singing of the song in his inimitable style ensured its immortality. The village ethos, the memories of those who have left it for life in the city, and the messages of longing and sorrow of the wives left behind by young men who are earning a living in the cities are created in the song by Gulzar through word pictures. One stanza is worth reading in this connection. Also noteworthy is the fact that despite its popularity, this song did not feature in Binaca Geetmala's list of winning songs, but was included in the list of 'Chhaou geet', or songs that were overshadowed by the winners. But here is the stanza:

How will I spend these nights of separation
The rain recounts wet-soaked stories
In drops of fire I burn, I burn maddened
Let go the job, come back my love
Come back my love, come, the baisakh has come
The postman brings the post, the post has come

Lata Mangeshkar's song, 'Ghungta uthe de…' is also just as pleasant. Gulzar gives the lyrics a rustic feel to add a punch to the folksy tune. It is worthwhile to pay attention to the last lines of the three stanzas which go, 'I look like a bride, turn me into one, re', 'Add the fire of mehendi to my feet, re' and 'shake some imaginary doors/windows, re'…This song which seems to echo an age-old refrain is yet another example of how the lyricist is able to use his pen to create empathy and give his lyrical ideas new wings.

In my opinion, the most important song of the film is 'Allah megh de/Paani de re' which the poet has taken from East Bengal (now Bangladesh). This rain evoking song was first sung by the folk singer of yore, Abbasuddin Ahmed. The song was taken in its exact form and set to music by S. D. Burman who also sang it for *Guide* (1965), directed by

Vijay Anand. Under Laxmikant-Pyarelal's baton, with the lyrics adapted into his poem by Gulzar, the song was sung for the film by Asha Bhosle and Kishore Kumar. Whereas the version in *Guide* used the original lyrics, this version has many changes. Keeping the original lines and thought intact, Gulzar add new aspects:

Allah give us clouds, give us rain
Give us rain, give us gur and grain
Allah give us clouds, give us rain

Give rain and I will give alms
In charity a cow
A cow will help me cross into heaven
By swimming across your waters...

Laxmikant-Pyarelal set Gulzar's words into a tune that had the tones of a universal chant, and turned into a prayer for every person in the village.

The two other songs of the film, 'Surme wale saiyaan hamaro ji' (My lover, he with the surma-lined eyes) and 'Ladkhadane do mujhe hosh se ruswaiyee hai' (Let me stumble, I have a grudge against consciousness) are worthy of note songs rich in lyrics and composition, but, for some reason, have not been much appreciated or discussed.

62.

Bawarchi (1972), *Chupke Chupke* (1975) and *Khubsoorat* (1980) are films with screenplay and dialogues written by Gulzar that still tickle audiences with their wit and humour. The comedy in these three films, all of which were written for Hrishikesh Mukherjee, is of a high order, with no slapstick or vulgarity. The three films mentioned above not only entertain, but also carry a social message.

While writing the dialogues for *Bawarchi*, the screenplay and dialogues for *Chupke Chupke* and the screenplay and songs for *Khubsoorat*, Gulzar wove in some unusual, small comic incidents that were based keeping in mind the interactive timing of the actors.

However, Gulzar ensured that the weight of the screenplay was not affected by his focus on the dialogues. Rather, the dialogues helped to tighten the structure of the entire film. Some of the characters in these films were drawn in such a way that they created funny situations and evoked laughter the moment they appeared on screen. Harindranath Chattopadhyay's character in *Bawarchi*, Om Prakash's character in *Chupke Chupke* and Ashok Kumar and Dina Pathak in *Khubsoorat* make this possible. Using dialogues as his vehicle, Gulzar quite easily made these films into complete comedies. To the extent that, while writing the songs of *Khubsoorat*, he kept in mind that his songs should help the effort to keep the comic moments bubbling throughout the film.

You will remember all the exchanges between Pyare Mohan alias Dr Parimal Tripathi (played by Dharmendra) and Raghavendra Kumar Sharma (played by Om Prakash), where the former teases the older man by adapting the syntax and translation of English grammar to his chaste Hindi speech. In the same way the interactions and dialogues between the characters played by Rajesh Khanna and Harindranath Chattopadhyay as the cook and the cantankerous grandfather left the audience rolling with laughter in the aisles.

This is highlighted in *Khubsoorat* too, when we see the entire family unable to find joy in even the small things of life because of the strict discipline imposed on the household by the oldest member, Nirmala Gupta (played by Dina Pathak). The entry of Manju (played by Rekha) at this point and the comedy that ensues in her interventions in the life of each character is remarkable for its perfect timing. Remarkably, even three decades after these three films were made, their freshness and ability to raise laughs remains inviolate. They continue to provide a real balm for the senses in times of stress. This song from *Khubsoorat* depicts the ease with which Gulzar is able to create moments of joy and laughter:

Break all the rules
Stop living a life of discipline
Eat, drink and make merry
Laugh loud with no restraint
Worry about tomorrow when it comes
Live today for today...

63.

In his films, Gulzar has created women characters who are not just bold by nature, but are brave enough to face life head on. Yet, despite being rebellious, his women protagonists do not raise slogans about resistance, as often happens in films. Even if they participate in a rally, they remain aware of their principles. Every voice of the women created by Gulzar's pen has its own identity. Even if she exists only in a tiny frame of the film, she can upturn the stakes of worldliness. The ambitious politician of *Aandhi*, Aarti Devi, stakes her political career to return to her husband and her home. *Sitara*'s Dhaniya alias Sarita, in the eyes of the world, erases her existence as Sarita and returns as Dhaniya to the village because she does not wish to sacrifice her love.

Aarti Sanyal, the heroine of *Kinara*, regrets and blames herself for failing to understand her friend who wishes to honour her fiancé's last wish, by publishing his book. *Khushboo*'s heroine, without losing her self-respect, is able to make her husband understand the reason for his inability to assert his authority over her openly. And Chaya of *Gharonda* sacrifices her love for a life of ease.

Thus, there are many instances wherein Gulzar gives his women characters the ability to be human. There is no taboo in his world on unfettered love, nor are they any controls over the expressions of love. Significantly, Gulzar creates his characters, both men and women, as real humans, complete with their failings and mistakes. They are not idealised or cloaked in greatness. Every one of his characters is someone like us, and it could well be that you are not watching them in a film, but are witnessing something that's taking place in the neighbourhood. The actresses portraying Gulzar's female characters are not required to lose control of their temper beyond reason, or be buffeted by a flood of emotions. To the extent that even when picking up the character of Meera from the pages of history, she is presented to us as a real person. Meena Kumari, Suchitra Sen, Hema Malini and Sharmila Tagore transform the characters of Anandi Devi, Aarti Devi, Kusum and Nimki from the screenplay to real women on screen.

64.

Gulzar and R. D. Burman were featured together in an episode of *Vishesh Jaimala*, a programme meant for our brothers in the army on Vividh Bharati, the radio station, is which both of them discussed some favourite songs created by them. I am referring to this episode because of the banter that they exchanged, as they usually did.

R. D. Burman tells Gulzar, 'When you come to the music room, you bring some crazy stuff you have written, which I cannot accept. And I keep singing strange things that you do not like. And we start arguing about it.' Gulzar responds to this with, 'The reason for this is that you speak Bengali. When I translate something to explain it to you, it gets difficult. For example in this song, "Beeti na bitai raina", we argued over the meaning of "biraha ki jaai", in the line "Biraha ki jaai raina". Nobody had used this phrase before this. Writing "Biraha ki beeti" was not enough to express the idea of a night spent in the sorrow of separation. It took me at least an hour of me breaking my head over explaining this to you.' Both laugh and the song is then played over the radio.

Gulzar continues to add that when R. D. Burman is unhappy with his lyrics, he addresses him as Gulzar-sahab instead of the usual, fond 'Gulu'. He adds, 'Whenever I would bring a song to you and you felt that a line or word was difficult, you would address me as Gulzar-sahab, and I would understand that something was not right with the song.' R. D. Burman laughs in response. Gulzar continues, 'Once, when I brought a song about the saawan, you said, "You dwell too much in saawan-bhadon. Write something new at least sometimes." "But, the season is the same, so is everything about it; I had to find new ways of presenting it through my words. So when I brought this song to you, I told you, 'You have worked on three or four songs about saawan with me; now show me a new tune.' 'Do you mean I repeat my tunes?' Pancham retorts. Gulzar's response to this is interesting. 'No! I mean I have started understanding music to an extent now, and you, poetry! Which means we are a good team.' In the background, Lata Mangeshkar's sad song from *Kinara* starts playing:

Let the monsoon not come this time
This year my eyes will rain instead
Let the monsoon not come this time...

65.

Gulzar wrote the screenplay and dialogues for *Sitara*, directed by Meraj, just as he had done for Bhimsain's *Gharonda*. *Sitara* is the story of a pair of lovers living in a village. The screenplay writer gives the course of their love all the freedoms possible within the framework of a society where all are considered equal. The story is based on the middle-class social milieu. Gulzar knows well that emotional needs do not stay confined to any social class, but can find ways to reach out to the like-minded in any strata of society and forge links with them. Like many popular films, this film begins with a poor village girl's dreams and her journey into the city in an effort to fulfil them. The young girl suddenly finds success and becomes a heroine.

In his traditional style, Gulzar unfolds the love story. The hero and heroine do not meet through a romantic scene, but have been together since their childhood. The ease and closeness of their friendship easily turns into love. There is no magical moment of love blossoming in the film, rather it shows a love that grows out of caring for and understanding each other's needs that are part of daily living. In this way, *Sitara* depicts a realistic picture of life.

Gulzar is able to psychologically analyse the man-woman relationship in a way that makes the romance realistic. The mature relationship between Zarina Wahab and Mithun Chakraborty in the film, if viewed from a modern perspective, can be called a live-in partnership. However, there is no casualness in their relationship. Rather, they share laughter and joyousness, and are partners in the true sense. Gulzar shows us the complexity in human relationships beautifully, but also makes a case through his dialogues for male and female characters to be viewed equally. To the extent that when his innocent heroine becomes a successful actress, she still loves the hero with the same fervour she had known when they were living in the village.

The writer does not let their love tarnish but, through the flow of the story, creates many layers of understanding between the man and the woman for each other. This is a delicate balance that Gulzar tries to capture in every frame of the film.

It is to Gulzar's credit that he changes the Indian tradition of tragic love stories to give *Sitara* a happy ending. He successfully pens songs of the uncontrolled joy of love. This is filmed in the most natural way, as Zarina Wahab and Mithun Chakraborty sing in the voices of Asha Bhosle and Bhupinder,

My beloved's bangle
A diamond in the bangle
I'll swallow the gem and die
Shall I die once, or twice
Or thrice, or die how many times...

Despite the emotional canvas that *Sitara* is set in, Gulzar attempts to embed satire too into the film, through the role of well-known character actor Kanhaiyalal. The song written for the heroine, 'Yeh saaye hain, yeh duniya hai' (These are shadows, this is the world) has been composed very delicately by R. D. Burman. I present here a few lines from the song which show us the ups and downs of life in the movies very clearly,

Every face here seems borrowed
The tears in the eyes seem tacked on
The path to the top is immoral
These are shadows, this world is made of reflections
In the midst of crowds, of loneliness
These are shadows, this is the world...

All three aspects of Gulzar, as screenplay, song and dialogue-writer are in evidence in *Sitara*, which can indeed be studied as a text on honing these skills.

66.

Lekin, directed by Gulzar for Lata Mangeshkar's banner Dinanath Kala Mandir is remembered not just for his brilliant direction but for the unusual dialogues too. It is a musical film with classical music at its base. The film was made on lines similar to *Mahal* and *Madhumati*.

Keeping in mind the mystery encapsulated in the film's theme, the dialogues Gulzar wrote for its heroine, Dimple Kapadia, have a literary flavour.

The story of this off-beat film concerns Rewa, a female spirit. Entangled in the space between life and death, she is seen trapped in some invisible meeting point between the two. It is perhaps only because Gulzar has written the dialogues that Rewa's imaginatively crafted metaphysical presence seems real enough.

The film's hero, Sameer Niyogi (played by Vinod Khanna), is a government employee who comes to Rajasthan to collect antiques for government museums from an abandoned haveli. In the haveli, he meets Rewa repeatedly, who tells him the story of her past. Listening to her sorrowful story and meeting her time and again, he finds himself sympathising with her.

In the course of a conversation, Sameer tells Rewa, 'Though you have shed your body, you have not been able to free yourself from that moment that hangs between life and death.' The dialogue continues and reaches a conclusion when he says, 'Leave behind that moment of death, Rewa. Or else you will keep repeating this story and keep dying with every telling.' Of course, Gulzar, while adroitly blending this supernatural aspect with real life, writes some exceptional dialogues.

Gulzar controls the supernatural story with great empathy. The release of Rewa's spirit is not effected through magic tricks or rituals but through love, acceptance and a feeling of companionship that finally helps her cross the desert. Gulzar, in Rewa's state of being trapped in a moment in time, evokes the psychological state of trauma in which a person becomes a mere shadow of his real self. This agony also refers to the innumerable moments of pain the poet himself has experienced. One of the best remedies to heal trauma is to share the pain as the coachman did, in Chekhov's story, 'The Lament'. With no one to confide in, he tells his sad story to his horse. Like Rewa in the film, Gulzar tells the story of his sorrows through his literature and his films. In a dialogue with author Joginder Paul that appears in the book *Footprints on Zero Line: Writings on the Partition by Gulzar*, he says, 'The horror of the Partition had settled so deeply into me that for years I would wake up with nightmares. If I had cried at that time, shed endless tears, perhaps I would not have been able to write and express myself. My writing helped me. Not all at once, but little by little, gradually...'

In the beginning of *Lekin*, Sameer has a dialogue which can be reproduced in toto. When he reaches Rajasthan and visits the abandoned haveli for the first time, his friend, Shafi Ahmed Siddiqui (played by Amjad Khan) asks him, 'What do you smell?' And he replies, 'I can smell time.' In this way, *Lekin* tries to capture a special mood. The film has to be seen to understand how the period it depicts has been captured poetically and through music. The manner in which the dialogues cast a spell when viewed through the hero's perspective adds an intimation of the extraordinary nature of Rewa's persona. Most of the film's songs were well received, but in the context of the time-frame they occupy in the film, in which Rewa is trapped, Gulzar crafts some extraordinary lyrics. To understand their emotions, one needs to enter a different dimension:

I have been waiting for an aeon
No one has come this way
Some chariots of the moon did go past
But no one stepped down.

The two wheels of night and day
Have rolled past throwing up dust
I kept sitting in my mind's courtyard
No one crossed the threshold...

The desert is like a character in the film. The instruments like the tanpura, sur-mandal, pakhvaz, ghungroo, tabla, sarangi, sitar and sarod play their roles in making it mysterious and romantic. Gulzar amplifies and impresses on us the nature of the forsaken, lost soul through music.

Madhumati was directed by Bimal Roy, based on a story written by no less a genius than Ritwik Ghatak. In *Lekin*, Gulzar pays his guru a tribute.

67.

There's a meaningful story behind the making of *Lekin* too. As it happened, Lata Mangeshkar had been unhappy for a long while over the fact that film songs had deteriorated and were no longer based on classical music. She also regretted the passing of the era when films like *Mahal* (1949) and *Madhumati* (1958) were made. The songs of these films, despite being romantic, were haunting and melodious. They were much loved, and the suspense they evoked held no fear for the listener. With these thoughts in mind, Lata-ji once told Gulzar, 'These days it seems as if the songs emerge from some grocer's shop.' She then added that films like *Mahal* and *Madhumati* should be made once more with music playing a major role and songs that had seriously crafted lyrics that were worthy of being sung.

She laid down the caveat that the director of such a film should be none other than Gulzar, and he should also write songs that would become classics and recreate the magic *Madhumati* had wrought in its time. Thus did a film which echoed *Madhumati* in mood and tenor come into being, with Gulzar as its director, screenplay writer, dialogue writer and lyricist. *Lekin* also presented classical music in an acceptable form. And Lata Mangeshkar sang the songs to ensure there was nothing that could ever connect them to the sounds emerging from any grocer's store.

Lekin unfurls on screen at a leisurely pace, like a khayal in slow tempo. Gulzar's pen took on the role of the creator of a bandish that was entirely new in concept and execution. Though he had in the past too stepped on new ground, writing lyrics that reflected his knowledge of both folk and classical musical traditions. Songs like, 'Bole re papihara' (The songbird sings) (*Guddi*), 'Mitwa bole meethe bain' (My beloved speaks sweet words) (*Parichay*), 'Meethe bol bole, bole payaliya' (The anklets speak sweet music) (*Kinara*) are some such examples.

But with *Lekin*, Gulzar created the ground for writing original songs that, like bandish compositions, held the seeds of melody in them. Each of the film's songs qualifies; 'Main ek sadi se baithi hoon,' (I have been waiting for an aeon), 'Jhoote naina bole saachi batiyan', 'Yaara seeli seeli birha ki raat ka jalna' (My love, this stale night of separation burns with a slow fire), 'Kesariya balma, mohe baawari bole log' (My comely lover, people say I am lovestruck) and 'Suniyo ji ek araj mhari' (Hear this plea of mine).

A song in the film sung by Asha Bhosle and Pandit Satyasheel Deshpande, renowned exponent of the Gwalior gharana, 'Jhoote naina bole' is notable for the way it has been set into the mould of classical music.

Pandit Satyasheel Deshpande narrated to me that he would often sing 'Wahin jao-jao balma', a classical bandish set in Raag Vilaskhani Todi to entertain his friend, Hridaynath Mangeshkar, who was so impressed by it that he adapted the song for his film. When Gulzar-sahab was requested to write a new bandish based on the mood and concept of the traditional song, he ensured that it was as close to the meaning and mood without falling short of the beauty of the original.

At some point there was a doubt whether the word in the opening stanza was 'joothe' or 'jhoote'. Most listeners would distort the word to 'jhoote'—deceiving—whereas the poet has written 'joothe', as in 'tasted by another'. Though the term may be non-poetic in origin, it is layered with poetic implication, with the poet saying that even the eyes that are steeped in love for another are considered 'joothe', and yet, strangely they reveal every secretly experienced sensory delight clearly. When we look at the history of film music or at contemporary songs, 'jhoote naina' as in deceiving eyes, or eyes speaking falsehoods are commonly encountered; eyes that are 'jhoote' are only seen in *Lekin*.

Apart from the wizardry with words, the composition of the music is remarkable too. Starting with Pandit Satyasheel Deshpande's voice singing the opening lines 'Neeke dhundariya thumak chaal chalat hai' in Raag Vilaskhani Todi, it has Asha Bhosle interjecting with Gulzar's lines 'Jhoote naine bole saachi batiyan'. As her rendition nears its end, Pandit Deshpande comes in again with a harmony in the same raag. The two voices in contrasting content and manner create a melodious aura.

The song, 'Suniyo ji ek araj mhario' too gives the same feeling that one experiences while listening to the melody of a the 'thumri' or 'dadra' styles being rendered at a traditional musical soiree. Setting the song in the Punjabi theka taal, which has sixteen beats. Pandit Hridaynath Mangeshkar has used the violin, sarod, sarangi, tabla-tarang, pakhvaj and tabla to create the background support. The use of the ravanhatha, an ancient bow and string instrument, adds its own flavour. Listening to the song one gets the complete feel of a bandish being sung in Raag Mand in the traditionally classical way, with snatches of Shudh Kalyan glistening through. The entire melody sparkles when Gulzar adds lyrics like:

Why have you forgotten me,
After sending me to an alien land
Call me back, father
Send me a palanquin
Four men to lift the palanquin
Hear my plea,
O father of mine
The rains have come, take me home
O father mine...

68.

Illiyaraja, a student of T. V. Gopalakrishnan, the mridang exponent and doyen of Carnatic music, is seen as the man who transformed Tamil film music and made it contemporary. *Sadma* (1983) was his first foray into the world of Hindi films. The film stands apart from among the handful of Hindi films that he directed music for. Though Illiyaraja had worked on a few other Hindi films before *Sadma*, none of them won the interest of fans or music lovers. Among them were forgotten films like *Kanyadweep* (1982), *Sandhyadeep* (1982) and a few others.

Gulzar wrote the dialogues and songs for *Sadma*. The songs of *Sadma* written by Gulzar need analysing, as does the music of the film. Illiyaraja's music in *Sadma* has a pattern of its own; with the singing style, orchestration and rhythm patterns blending the modern with traditional elements.

The typically Gulzarana imagery of the song, 'O babua yeh mahua mehekne laga hai' (O darling, the intoxicating mahua spreads its fragrance) is set to an entirely new kind of tune that converts a dance song into pure sensuousness. Despite that, the song never descends into vulgarity. This is also evident in Asha Bhosle's rendition, as she sings along with the chords of the guitar and the percussion instruments, with pauses timed perfectly at just the right places. This results in the romantic verses getting erotic and ecstatic overtones to suit the visuals. Gulzar-sahab too, to suit Iliyaraja's style, creates a word play between the sthai, the octave, and the antaras of the song,

Whenever the evening smoulders
Thoughts of you come to me
My desolate, bare, white arms
Are suffused with smoke
The winters hang heavy
The poisonous moon won't move

Without you...
O darling, the intoxicating mahua spreads its fragrance

Iliyaraja uses the traditional analog pattern to create all the songs of the film, but one can clearly see the weaving in of electronic elements. 'O babua yeh mahua' uses the technique of the 'panning sound' to great effect. The kick-drum takes the sound from the left to the 'shaker' on the right side. And the shaker sound on the right, like chan-chan, chun-chun, chuh-chuh etc are given a clear expression. The music created by the synthesiser, flute, guitar and saxophone besides being pleasant also give the song an innovative structure. Asha Bhosle takes the line 'tere bin' to a new level in the way she expresses the words. It is a good example of the perfection of her craft as a singer.

Gulzar's imagery in the lines, 'Whenever the evening smoulders/ Thoughts of you come to me' is in perfect sync with other images of the evening, elsewhere. And yet this intoxicating song can be read as poetry that evokes quite a different mood.

Much later, A. R. Rahman uses a similar technique to that of 'O babua yeh mahua' in *Guru* (2007). Having been a part of Ilaiyaraaja's group as a keyboard player biding his time while he developed his own style, Rahman created his own canvas of electronic music which would cause the past three decades to be identified as the 'Rahman Age'.

Guru has an intoxicating dance song 'Maiyya-maiyya gulabi taare chun le' (Maiyya-maiyya, pick rose-like stars) written by Gulzar. Listening to it brings back the memory of the song in *Sadma* and its music director.

The most pleasant song in *Sadma* is a lullaby that the music director has set in Raag Pilu. This song, 'Surmai ankhiyon me, ek nanha munna sapna de ja re' (Leave behind a small dream in these kohl-lined eyes) is among Gulzar's best lullabies. This song, brimming with maternal love, also highlights the beauty of human relationships. As in these lines,

Gift me a real dream
Give me someone of my own
A stranger, yet somewhat known
Lighter than the dew
Softer than the softest silk
O birds of sleep in flight
Come my friends, into the eyes...

The 'ra-ri, ra-ri, o ra-ri rum' refrain that closes each stanza adds a softness to the lullaby. Ilaiyaraja often uses the violin and the flute in his interludes. Here, he creates a delicate fusion tapestry through the tabla, synthesiser and flute. The composition also has an interesting beat structure, in which the 'dhang' and 'tak' sounds can be heard adding their beauty. The song, in Yesudas' voice, gains a new dimension thanks to the blending of his classically trained voice with the folk-based tune. Gulzar, while reminiscing about this lullaby in an article in *Filmfare* said:

> I believe that Yesudas' voice is most suited for singing lullabies. Listening to him, I feel happy about writing lullabies. Personally, I have always felt that if a lullaby has to be sung, let the father sing it, because then Yesudas would be singing it. I don't think mothers, grandfathers or grandmothers should sing lullabies. I think this is the best song of the film *Sadma*.

Two other songs of *Sadma*, 'Ae zindagi, gale lagaa le' (Life, come embrace me) and 'Ek dafaa ek jungle mein' (Once upon a time in a forest) are also interesting numbers. Sung with feeling by Suresh Wadkar, the former is a song in which Gulzar takes one out of the depths of despair towards the brightness of hope. The many instruments and the interplay between the synthesiser, guitar, bass guitar, sitar, tabla and flute add to the song's beauty. Ilaiyaraaja does full justice to the song 'Ek dafaa ek jungle mein' sung in the voice of Kamal Haasan.

In order to create a soundtrack that moved away from

the customary, Ilaiyaraja blended folk music and traditional classical music through the orchestration. The long-playing record of the film is evidence of the effectiveness of the blend of rhythm and symphony in the compositions. The music of the Tamil film *Mundram Pirayi* on which *Sadma* was based, also created a new wave in the film music of the eighties.

69.

Gulzar had inscribed the fly-leaf of his collection of short stories, *Raavi Paar*, to his wife, Rakhee, which read, 'The longest short story of my life'. This statement is an expression of his personal relationship, of the love story between the filmmaker Gulzar and the actress, Rakhee, which began towards the end of the 1970s. The two met for the first time in Calcutta (now Kolkata) when Gulzar was assigned to write the screenplay of Tarun Majumdar's film *Rahgir*. The year was 1968. Tarun Majumdar was crafting a Hindi version of the Bangla film, *Patal Lok* starring Biswajeet and Sandhya Roy. Rakhee was a close friend of Sandhya Roy's, and had been living in her house for the past seven years.

The easy friendship that developed between Rakhee and Gulzar slowly transformed into a deeper feeling. Gulzar was working on a few scripts and dialogues for films, among which were *Aashirwad*, *Sunghursh* and *Khamoshi*. Around the same time, Rakhee's career was launched in Hindi films with *Jeevan Mrityu* under the Rajshri banner. Even as their individual careers soared, Gulzar and Rakhee got married on 18 April, 1973.

The details of the wedding are quite interesting. No less a personage than the queen of ghazals, Begum Akhtar, added her voice to the sangeet ceremony. While I was writing my book *Akhtari*, her student, Rita Ganguly said in an interview that she had accompanied Ammi, as her students called the singer, to Rakhee's house 'Muktangan' in Santa Cruz for the sangeet ceremony. She also added that, 'I remember clearly that Ammi had sung a chota khayal in *Raag Darbari* and also a "mubarakbadi" which had the following words, Congratulations on a marriage/ Granted as a blessing by Allah Rasool himself

Actor Sunil Dutt took on the role of Rakhee's brother throughout the wedding ceremonies while producer N. C. Sippy took upon himself the task of ensuring all the necessary arrangements on Gulzar's behalf, including the sending out of the invitation cards from his office.

In her book about her father, titled *Because He Is*, Gulzar's daughter Meghna writes the interesting fact that both parties missed inviting a pandit to conduct the ceremonies. With no other recourse, a Gujarati pandit was hastily brought over from a nearby temple. The net result of this was that all the ceremonies were carried out in Gujarati, which Rakhee understood nothing of, and of which Gulzar too could not make much sense.

Rakhee's presence as a wife in Gulzar's life was brief, but those who know both closely know of the deep understanding that still exists between them. To the extent that both ensured that the fact that they lived separately did not have any ill effect on their daughter, Meghna.

Meghna has found an emotional aspect with her father's life as reflected in his films, in the fact that in most of his films he conceptualises a home as a broken home or a ruin. Perhaps this was a reflection of his own married life, which he translates into the homes in his films. This can be seen in *Mere Apne*, *Khushboo*, *Kinara*, *Aandhi* and *Namkeen*. However, there is no denying that Rakhee's role in Gulzar's life has been an important one, as friend and fellow-traveller.

Gulzar has always rated Rakhee highly as an actress. He considers her role in Avtar Kaul's film *27 Down*, based on Ramesh Bakshi's novel, *Atharah Suraj Ke Poudhe* as the best example of her effortless acting style. He has also appreciated the Yash Chopra-directed entertainers, *Daag*, *Trishul*, *Kaala Patthar* and *Kabhi Kabhie* as fine examples of her acting prowess. He believes that there are some sensitive actresses from whom some directors manage, within a time frame, to capture their best work. Yash Chopra is one such brilliant director who gave Rakhee really good roles in his films.

Often he also chooses such films as examples, that go beyond their commercial success to be successful in every way. He refers to Subodh Mukherji's *Sharmilee* in which Rakhee excelled herself in playing a double role portraying two very opposite characters. Gulzar wrote the dialogues and songs for Ramesh Talwar's *Baseraa*. Rakhee's character in the film is written to portray how she goes through events and emotional upheavals to reach a climactic point. As someone who always refers to his wife with respect and admiration, in 1990, at the *Filmfare* Awards function too, Gulzar acknowledged his feelings publicly. That year she was awarded the Best Supporting Actress Award for her role in Subhash Ghai's *Ram Lakhan*. When Gulzar was called on stage to announce the winners and present the award, he opened the sealed envelope and without taking any name he called out, 'Aji sunti ho…'

Three beautiful faces create the perfect reflection of the relationship between the two of them…Meghna, Govind and Samay…

At times the desire arises to ask Rakhee whether the universe that exists in Gulzar's poetic temperament, including the rising moon, the tiny planet Pluto, the galaxies and the innumerable stars that rise as evening makes way for the night, were all created for Rakhee. To give expression to the relationship where, as fellow travellers, like the two banks of a river they enjoy the ease of flowing together.

Even today, if you sit with Gulzar-sahab at breakfast or lunch on the first floor of his house, Boskiyana, the presence of large collages of family photos bear witness to how family oriented he is. Look at the photo of Samay, Meghna and Govind's son, in which he is sitting on his grandmother, Rakhee's lap. In another she is playing with him. Drenched in the colours of Holi each one is looking at the other with affection shining clearly. I have seen the love for Samay shining brightly in Gulzar's eyes, but even as I glimpsed the love and respect he feels for Rakhee, he quietly shielded it from my gaze.

70.

The room where Gulzar reads and writes. In some ways his office, where he sits to write his film songs and dialogues, his screenplays. When you climb the Nargis Dutt Road on Pali Hill in the western suburb of Bandra, you will see Gulzar's verdantly decked bungalow 'Boskiyana'. It is on the ground floor of this house that the space exists in which Gulzar creates his magic with words. This room is lined with books on all sides. Innumerable books, with impressive, thick binding; statues and busts of Buddha, some small, some large, collected from different parts of the country. The calm face of the Buddha and his peaceful demeanour has always had a strong influence on Gulzar, and he has been collecting, for years, Buddha images made of various materials, wood or metal, or stone.

Gulzar refers to the act of sitting in his reading-room chair as sitting down to work. On one side is a very realistic half-bust of his favourite poet Mirza Ghalib wearing his typical cap. On the next wall are drawings and various caricatures of Gulzar's many moods made by his friend, the artist Gopi Gajwani. In this methodically arranged room, everything assumes a poetic colour, its mystery intensified by the low lighting that Gulzar prefers.

To sit there and talk to Gulzar is to feel that you have

encountered a Sufi poet in his monastery.

Alongside his room is that of his assistant and also the chair where Farhana, who looks after his work, sits. Whenever Farhana meets you, the fact that she has been learning her work from Gulzar will be immediately obvious. On asking Gulzar which of his poems he considers his best, he says with a wicked twinkle in his eyes, 'A poet's best has to be looked for in his dustbin, after writing which and finding no joy in it, he has torn up and consigned to the rubbish bin.'

71.

Readers and critics will find themselves at a loss if they try to find a metaphor to describe Gulzar's poetry, because there are almost no figures of speech that have not been used in unusual ways of expression by him. Whether it is romance, or scenic descriptions, a touching picture drawn from past memories, or a hilarious exposition of life's philosophies, his creative mind has converted even the commonplace into something typically his own through the infinite possibilities his extensive vocabulary opens up for him.

It seems as though, throughout his journey as a writer, the various personae in him take turns to show themselves as they travel together. Just as he says here:

Come, let us all wear mirrors
We will all see our own faces
And the soul? Who has seen even their own?

The yearning to don all the mirrors is at the heart of Gulzar's poetic talent. By creating sorrowful music and placing his finger on the pulse of all of life's troublesome issues, he arrives at the eternal truth. Through his poetry Gulzar orchestrates vast symphonies that allow us to read that which transports us to a point where we can look into ourselves more clearly. With creative honesty he admits that this is his reality:

Nothing is unchanging, nothing at all
That which is permanent, is but me, myself
I, who change with every moment...

72.

He has introduced a new form into Urdu poetry, the triveni. Trivenis first appeared in 1972–73 in *Sarika*, the magazine that was edited by Kamleshwar. It was no great challenge for Gulzar to define a new genre in writing. That too a form whose foundation he laid. He says this about the trivenis he has composed:

> When I first created this form, I was unsure about which Sangam it would end at. I called it triveni because the first two lines describe a thought and form a pair, like Ganga and Jamuna. But flowing under these two rivers is yet another, the Saraswati. Hidden. Invisible. The idea behind triveni is to show Saraswati. The third line is a secret hidden in the first two.

The poems Gulzar writes that personify the meeting of Ganga, Jamuna and Saraswati have the first two lines leading from one to the other, like the lines of a ghazal. The third line gives a new twist to the first two lines. Creating thus, a flexible interpretation of their meaning, or hijacking what seems to be a commonplace verse to mean quite something different. As if the unseen Saraswati wishes to impose the truth of her existence on Ganga and Saraswati.

This form of composition is a result of Gulzar's fundamental train of thought, and he has written a countless number of them for his fans. The narrative structure becomes clear in this example:

Ghalib bestowed this blessing on me
May you live for a thousand years
This year went by in a matter of days

73.

Short stories like 'Dumbe', Hilsa' and 'The Stone Age' that deal with turmoil and tensions across the border delineate the terrors of war and chill the heart with the ruthlessness of cold on a wintery night. 'Dumbe' is based on the daily skirmishes that take place between Suchitgarh in India and Sialkot in Pakistan. Gulzar writes, 'The fight between Hindustan and Pakistan! They fight like schoolchildren. Broke this one's slate. Snatched away that one's plank. Sometimes poked a nib into another. Sometimes spilt ink. Remember as kids we used to go to watch the rams fight.'

'Hilsa' too is a report with news of rioting when a girl's picture is published in a newspaper. The victim of a gangrape, she bleeds to death. Gulzar deepens the terror created by this by comparing the eyes and face of the dead girl to those of a dead hilsa fish.

'The Stone Age' also refers to how the minds of young people stray towards violence. How in this age of hardening sensibilities, young people suddenly change their thinking and way of life. Gulzar repeatedly affirms, 'In the beginning, man made weapons out of stone. They hunted and lived in caves. Those communities that had fire were considered superior. They lived in open areas, and travelled to different places and captured lands…'

Gulzar exposes the injustices of the present through his stories. They mirror the wrong direction that we are steering society towards. It is known that Gulzar experienced such events in his childhood, the fearsome effects of which not just cause tears, but remain embedded deep in the mind as a permanent wound. These stories have been written to help people understand human relationships; an urgent need of the times.

74.

Libaas (1988) is the only film made by Gulzar that is based on a story by him, titled 'Chaabi'. This story was later included in his collection *Raavi Paar* as 'Seema'. Based on three characters, Sudhir (played by Naseeruddin Shah), Seema (played by Shabana Azmi) and TK (played by Raj Babbar) the story is themed around a woman finding ways to lead an independent life. Two men come into Seema's life and neither of them can offer her a means of improving the quality of her life. She lives in the quandary of knowing how much her former husband, who was her friend and fellow stage actor, still loves her, just at that point in her life when she exits her first marriage and marries TK. Living with this commercial-minded and opinionated man, she cannot but think of her former relationship with its joyful events and memories.

Though *Libaas* revolves around the complexities of a breaking marriage and the welding of new bonds, the film takes its plot through the relationship of mature individuals who work in theatre and takes the measure of their interactions, partnerships and trust for each other.

Sudhir, an ambitious theatre director, treats his wife on the same level as other actors. He trusts Seema and loves her too, but fails to convince her about how much he cares for her. Seema constantly grapples with the feeling that she is nothing more than a character in a play for her husband. She accosts him about this many times, but his commitment to theatre is far deeper. At one point, while rehearsing a play, when Seema forgets her lines, he says in anger, 'Now look...read from this and remember it I can forgive you if you forget to cook, but not if you forget your lines.'

The tone of this reprimand makes Seema believe that her relationship with Sudhir is going nowhere, that it has stopped growing. There is no beauty left in it. This tension in *Libaas* moves at many levels to unravel the complex nature of relationships; and like cards from a pack shuffles Sudhir, Seema and TK, about and scatters them in different directions. *Libaas* is the emotional exposition of a mature story with the images from theatre as a backdrop, which in turn add colour to the story.

Music has always formed a major feature of Gulzar's films. Going beyond entertainment, the songs take the story forward and also expound the central theme in their own way. The treatment of the subject of *Libaas*, keeping in mind its relevance at the time it was made, created occasions for many complex picturisation of songs on Seema's character. All the songs of the film have been sung by Lata Mangeshkar, whose voice was capable of revealing the complex emotions with ease. Three songs sung by her, 'Phir kisi shaakh ne', 'Seeli hawa choo gayi' (The stale breeze caressed me) and 'Khamosh sa afsana paani se likha hota' (You might have written a silent story in water) give meaning to Seema's emotional state at different moments. It might indeed seem possible that all the songs of the film add layers of meaning to the story, as the director wanted to use poetry and music to reveal the mental turmoil resulting from each situation. Like this song which tells us about Seema's internal confusion:

You might have written a silent story in water
You wouldn't have told it, I wouldn't have heard it
I stay quiet, scared, as the day comes to an end
A lamp goes out
A lamp burns
If only you had
Lit a lamp

Yet another song that became very popular and is considered a part of Lata Mangeshkar's playlist, is also among Gulzar's own favourites, which he connects to the theme of *Libaas*. He says: *Libaas* is a different kind of garment, a story set against the background of theatre. It was hidden earlier in a bouquet as 'Chaabi'. Stage characters have a strange energy.

Their mood too keeps changing, like *Libaas*, or clothes. In the same way, they wear the day and take it off. Some of this is captured in this song:

A stale breeze touched me
Bruised my drenched body
Across the river blue
Bloomed a soaked moon

Also deserving of mention is the fact that some outstanding plays from the world of theatre, complete with the point of view they present, have been woven deftly into *Libaas* and through their dialogues and visuals add to the film's seriousness. Besides scenes from Mohan Rakesh's *Aadhe Adhure*, Girish Karnad's *Hayavadan*, the screenplay has references to Girish Karnad's *Tughlaq*, Vijay Tendulkar's *Sakaran Binder* and *Shantata, Court Chalu Aahe*. It is good to know that while adding in aspects of such serious plays, Gulzar gave no thought to the effect they might have on the commercial success of his film. Gulzar considers this film among his most mature. Sadly, the film was only shown at a few film festivals and never made it into theatres. Not only Gulzar's fans, but fans of Hindi cinema were deprived of the chance to see a brilliant experimental film.

75.

I was asleep when you touched me
And I nearly fell into your arms
Perhaps I stumbled upon a dream
Let me float along in my dream
Thirsty I am, let me so remain

Ijazat (1987) holds a special place among the films made by Gulzar. This is an example of a mature film that can be read on the screen as one reads a poem. Based on the well-known Bangla novelist Subodh Ghosh's story 'Jatugriho', this film about a love triangle is a complex rendition of the tensions that rise out of the relationships between Sudha (played by Rekha), Mahendra (played by Naseeruddin Shah) and Maya (played by Anuradha Patel).

The story of *Ijazat* is not as noteworthy as the treatment of the narrative is. The parallel presence of a third entity who has had a live-in relationship in the married life of a photographer and a well-educated teacher at the Panchgani school is evident. This third persona is that of Maya, a free-spirited bohemian who is Mahendra's beloved. This creates a triangle between husband, wife and the other woman, and explores the relationships between them.

Critics have recognised *Ijazat* as a serious and meaningful film. With the very first scene where a husband and wife meet as strangers in a railway waiting room, it is evident that the story will, as it unfolds, open every possible strand of their relationship. Maithili Rao's essay, 'Rebels Without a Cause' in the *Encyclopaedia of Indian Cinema* which talks about the period between 1976-1989, is noteworthy,

> *Ijazat* underlines the controversial elements that are recognised as part of married life...but the interesting thing about this is the character created by Gulzar of the other woman, who is unfettered and will not be bound even by her love; much like an Isadora Duncan.

This is an interesting angle from which to explore the film. When, in the waiting room, Mahendra and Sudha alternately revisit their past, they also try to understand those gaps in their relationship that have caused them to become strangers to each other. Looking beyond the attraction that draws the three into a complex knot, one sees the vast emptiness that occupies their lives.

With the deftness of a practised filmmaker, Gulzar creates a metaphor using the image of water, right from the starting credit roll of the film. The free flowing river, the gurgling mountain stream, waterfalls that break free of the restraining slopes and the ceaseless rain are used to convey to us the mental states of the two women and the man caught between them. It brings to mind the poem 'Pani Ke Sansmaran' (Memories of Water) by the Hindi poet, Raghuvir Sahai, in which the water falling on his back evokes all kinds of memories. Gulzar reveals the role water will play in the film in the very first song that accompanies the credits,

A small story
The monsoon rain
Fills the entire valley
I do not know why my heart feels full
I do not know why my eyes spill over

Ijazat also brings up the subject of live-in relationships, which Gulzar handles in a delicate manner. The dialogues are thus rich with meaning. The best dialogue is spoken by Sudha, and reflects her intelligence and her evolved personality. At one point Mahendra tells Sudha that despite being engaged to her, he is in love with someone else. He cannot see how to navigate the road ahead. Sudha's response becomes the high point of the film, expanding the scope of the narrative. Rekha tells him, 'Do what is right and correct.' Despite this, the contradiction in the story is that Mahendra is unable to do the right thing and caught in the pressure imposed by his father and the undecided behaviour of his beloved, he marries Sudha.

When, much later, Mahendra and Sudha speak openly, the man -woman conflict rears its head once again. When Mahendra realises his mistake, he asks Sudha for forgiveness. At this point too, a dialogue spoken by Sudha brings out the poetry inherent in the film. She says, 'Habit wears off, but rights never go.' This is a frame that allows one to understand the mature relationship between a man and wife. Viewers are not partial to either character, but understand more clearly that however strong and understanding a relationship may be, the presence of a third person cracks it.

Every frame of the film, the picturisation of songs and the high level of acting by all the characters, main and supporting, makes the film a delectable viewing experience. Filmmaker Ashok Mehta's camerawork adds to the effectiveness of Gulzar's perception of the film. The film brings to mind these lines from famed Japanese filmmaker Akira Kurosawa's memoir *Something Like an Autobiography* (translated by Audie E. Bock), which are reflected in every other frame of *Ijazat*. Kurosawa writes:

> There is something that can be called cinematic beauty. This can only be created in a film, and without it a film cannot touch the viewer; when this is very well presented, then deep emotions are experienced while watching the film.

These lines seem particularly apt when we watch *Ijazat* not just as a film, but as a work of art.

I would like to highlight two songs that are picturised so beautifully that they stand on a different level from most songs. 'Katra katra milti hai' (You come by it in scraps) and 'Mera kuch samaan' (Something of mine) are the two songs that, besides the popularity they have achieved, also tell us a lot about Anuradha Patel's character as a rebellious free spirit who lives life on her own terms. Asha Bhosle adds her impeccable rendition to the incomparable composition by R. D. Burman.

> *One hundred and sixteen moonlit nights*
> *The mole on your shoulder*
> *The fragrance of damp mehendi*
> *My few mock complaints*
> *All your false promises, let me remind you*
> *Send them all back*
> *Return all that is mine to me.*

If I am not wrong we see in the casting of the balanced personality of Sudha and the rebellious Maya a similarity to the casting of the simple and grounded Vidya (played by Nargis) and the independent-minded Maya (played by Nadira) in Raj Kapoor's *Shree 420*. Though the Maya in that film was portrayed as rather too materialistic, and the person who leads the hero to wrong ways. The Maya of *Ijazat* is neither materialistic nor does she wrongly influence the hero. Despite this, the contrast between Maya and Sudha plays like the central theme of the film. *Ijazat* gains its novelty also from the way it explores the relationship between these two women.

The relationship is an invisible one, without any frivolousness, and neither do the two have any animosity towards each other. Both women, while evaluating each other's natures, express their opinions; which is quite natural. When Maya hears Sudha's voice for the first time over the telephone, she excitedly tells Mahendra, 'Do you know, Didi's voice is sweeter than yours, as if it is emerging from a throat made out of glass.' And on the other hand, Sudha says of Maya, who meets her husband while they are in the plane, 'One feels sympathy for this crazy child, and love too…'

Ijazat revolves around the tensions between Sudha and Maya and their relationships with Mahendra, and the gap that exists as an unsolvable issue of the claim each has over him. If for Rekha it manifests as 'Khaali haath shaam ayi hai/ Khaali haath jayegi/ Aaj bhi na aya koi/ Khali laut jayegi' (Empty-handed the evening has come/ Empty-handed she will return/ If no one comes even today/ She will return empty) then for Anuradha it is, 'Jhoote-moote ki shikve kuch/ Jhute-moote ke vade bhi sabh/ Yaad kara doon/ Sab bhijwa do/ Mera woh samaan lauta do. (My mock complaints/ All your false promises, let me remind you/ Send them all back /Return all that is mine to me.)

R. D. Burman's music composition adds its own magic to Gulzar's cinematic adaptation of Subodh Ghosh's novel. 'Mera kuch samaan' is a once-in-a-decade creation. Ashok Mitra's cinematography brings the film closer to art. Even as Rekha, Naseeruddin Shah and Anuradha Patel bring their roles alive,

Shammi Kapoor in the rôle of Dada and Sulaba Deshpande as the mother, do their bit perfectly too. *Ijazat* holds its place in Gulzar's filmography as a delicately crafted film. This film symbolises every such moment when we cannot, despite our desire, live out our dreams. Even as we realise that we create dreams that appear like bubbles and vanish. Gulzar's line, 'The dream was trampled underfoot', acknowledges this. Despite this, it is mandatory to spin dreams.

76.

Gulzar made *Maachis* on a very different note from his other films. This film, steeped in political consciousness, looks with empathy at those youth who, misled by terrorists, follow the path advocated by them. Both *Maachis* and *Hu Tu Tu* are strong comments on the state of affairs of their time. A thread of romance runs along with the main story of *Maachis*, which helps identify the film's political intent more clearly.

Based against the background of terrorism, the film examines the fact that innocent youth, when harassed beyond a point by the police, end up becoming criminals in spite of themselves. The axis on which the film revolves is the troublesome idea of suffering crime quietly. The film looks closely at terrorism and tries to suggest logical solutions. Gulzar makes his point clear, speaking like an observer, without making proclamations of any sort. He makes no differentiation between two people; even if one is living the life of an honest citizen and the other has, due to circumstances, adopted a life of crime. He repeatedly makes us probe the reasons why an innocent young man has turned into a terrorist.

One of the important characters in the film is that of the terrorist, Sanatan Singh (played by Om Puri), who seriously expresses some phrases apportioned to him by Gulzar in his role as screenplay and dialogue writer. As an example, when the hero, Pali (played by Chandrachur Singh) asks him, 'Where are those brothers? Where are your family members?' in a response that causes goosebumps, Sanatan Singh says, 'Half were consumed by '47, and half by '84.' By encapsulating the agonies of the two riots—Partition in 1947 and the anti-Sikh pogrom of 1984—so simply, Gulzar conveys a strong message.

In fact, throughout the film he puts forth one idea or the other in the form of a question. Gulzar is aware that there have been many aspects to the problem of terrorism and that the government's strategies too, have an influence on this. *Maachis* tries to look at all these aspects, and grapple with circumstances to find a solution.

At the start of the film, the police falsely accuse Jassi (played by Raj Zutshi), Kripal Singh's friend, of being a terrorist and take him away. When there is no further news of him, Kripal Singh's lawyer reveals the truth. Nothing has changed still. His remark, which is relevant even today, continues to haunt us, 'Son, yes the law exists. It always has existed, but those keys no longer open those locks. That's why people have started breaking them.' This is indeed one of the reasons why storms beset this country. The innocent who have been punished wrongly forget the line between right and wrong and seek revenge for their circumstances, wrongly, in the name of jihad. This is what has strengthened the roots of terrorism.

Gulzar looks at this with empathy and gets a mujahideen to say, 'I am not fighting any religion or country. I am fighting against my constraints and helplessness.' However, despite these statements, the film does not espouse the cause of terrorism. It just underlines the circumstances that force normal people to take up wrong ways.

Though they have embarked on a do-or-die mission, these revolutionary youth also get nostalgic about their homes and families. Two songs of *Maachis*, 'Chappa-chappa charkha chale'

(Chappa-chappa runs the spinning wheel) and 'Chhod aaye hum woh galiyan' (We've left those lanes behind) showcase Gulzar's touching depiction of this mental landscape. When the film's heroine, Veera (played by Tabu) suffers agonies of separation from her fiancé, alone in the quiet of her home, it is as if she is converting her sorrow into physical pain. The song, in the background, in Lata Mangeshkar's voice, is a lament capturing the moment:

Send bearers and summon me, my love
Through many nights I lie awake
Lying useless in the gatehouse, the palanquin
Seems like a bier...

The songs of this film were given to debut music composer, Vishal Bhardwaj, who has created superlative tunes for the film. Gulzar writes lyrics for the songs that in some way emotionally sympathise with those walking the wrong path. 'Chappa-chappa' based on folk elements in music is an example where the gentle lyrics add emotion to the song. Gulzar has a penchant for the Punjabi folk vernacular, and through his journey in song writing, he has imbued many songs with the fragrance of the soil of Punjab.

It is worth reading some lines from the song to understand the emotions underlying the seriousness of the film,

The fair damsel who fed us from a bowl
She who every Friday applied kohl to her eyes
Under the leafy arches...
With false excuses she beckoned me to the kitchen
With iron tongs she hit me for embracing her
Oye biba, your fire burns...
Chappa-chappa runs the spinning wheel
Friends meet together under the ber trees...

Maachis has been presented as a metaphor for the youth of any nation who, rebelling against politics and police, burn their weapons and annihilate themselves in the process. Though the film has a line of dialogue that says, 'Damp matches cannot set a revolution ablaze'. *Maachis* investigates that phase of the 1980s when a majority of youth, rebelling against the violence against the Sikhs, became a comprehensive mass of angry young men who revolted against the system. Many of these became terrorists while others, though innocent, were forcibly termed as such. It is the life of these unfortunates that Gulzar's *Maachis* looks at with sympathetic eyes.

The scene where Veera takes off the cyanide capsule that Pali keeps tied around his neck is beautifully filmed. She does not want her fiancé to die by suicide, or die at the hands of the police who capture him. But the possibility of death is very real for those who walk the path of terrorism. That there is no hope of escaping death for terrorists is a lesson Gulzar illustrates in the film. The tragic end of the film shows us with due seriousness, and compassion how every member of this youth brigade gets into a chakravyuh-like maze, from which it is impossible for him to emerge.

77.

An interesting statement was made by actor Naseeruddin Shah in his autobiography, *And Then One Day*. The issue concerns *Mirza Ghalib* and is also linked to Gulzar, the filmmaker. As it emerges with a measure of emotion from Naseeruddin Shah's memories, it is worthwhile to note it as a significant point in the journey as sharp-witted artist of the cinema as Gulzar.

It so happened that when Naseer was studying in St. Stephen's, it was being said that Gulzar was planning to make Ghalib with his favourite actor, Sanjeev Kumar, playing the title role. Naseer was not in consonance with this. Sanjeev Kumar playing the role of Ghalib! The thought pierced his mind with the force of hot needles.

Though till then he had not even read a single couplet by Ghalib, he could not come to terms with the fact that Sanjeev Kumar would play Ghalib. Then, one day he heard the news that Sanjeev Kumar had suffered a heart attack, and the shooting of the film had been delayed. On learning afterwards that Sanjeev Kumar was not playing the role, he procured Gulzar's address through the help of his friend Vikram Mehrotra, and wrote him a long letter, listing his capabilities. Let's read about it in Naseeruddin Shah's own words:

> Actually, I am that actor whom he is searching for. I counted out the capabilities that made me perfectly suited to play Ghalib's role: I am from Meerut (true) from where Ghalib procured his wine. I have lived in Kansimjaan in old Delhi (half truth, I had only visited it) and I am fully conversant with Ghalib's poetry (a complete lie). I convinced him that it would be to his advantage to choose me. I am a very skilled actor.

He posted the letter to Gulzar, but had no hope of getting a reply. And that was what happened. No reply came. Naseeruddin Shah would often wonder what effect the letter might have on Gulzar. Yet, what was the harm in trying? Even if he got irritated, he would at least remember him.

By then, *Nishant* (1975), his well-appreciated film with Shyam Benegal, had been released. Naseeruddin Shah was hoping that perhaps Gulzar too had watched the film. After some efforts, he managed to get an appointment to meet Gulzar at his Pali Hill office. He was surprised when Gulzar greeted him with sincerity. He even praised his work in *Nishant* but made no mention of their working together. Naseer, though impressed with him, was a bit disappointed by the fact that Gulzar had not made any reference to the letter he had sent earlier. He felt it was impertinent on his part to ask about the letter, and held his silence.

The film on Ghalib did not get made but, many years

later, when Gulzar made a serial on the life of Ghalib, he chose Naseeruddin Shah for the role. A happy and confident Naseer could, through the shooting on the serial, delve into the character of Ghalib and live out his dream role. It was the realisation of a long held desire. By then he had established an affectionate relationship with Gulzar. This gave him a confidence very different from the bravado of the young actor who had written the letter years ago.

Finally, he picked up the courage to ask Gulzar about the letter. Looking sincerely puzzled, Gulzar-sahab said to him, 'I never received any such letter...'

78.

It is important to take note of the symbols inherent in the films made by Gulzar. Some such emblems that, without any loud proclamations, make the intent behind the whole scene clear. Examine the scenes in his films closely and you will get many such instances of the thought or idea behind a scenario being revealed through an image or symbol. This is Gulzar's style: the discipline of not emphasising anything but keeping his perspective as undertones.

We can examine some examples. In *Kinara*, while Aarti Sanyal (played by Hema Malini) is performing a dance on stage, her fiancé, Chandan (played by Dharmendra) dies in an accident. Gulzar shows this symbolically by focussing on her ankle bells from which a bell breaks free and rolls away. This signal is to let the viewers understand that the hero has lost his life. Similarly, in a scene from *Mausam*, Sharmila Tagore in the role of the daughter Kajli is raped. While showing this symbolically, all that happens is that the bottle of medicine slips from Kajli's hand and shatters on the floor. In *Koshish*, when Haricharan (played by Sanjeev Kumar) and Aarti's (played by Jaya Bhaduri) infant child ventures out of the house and dies after getting soaked in the rain, the director heightens the emotional impact of the scene by showing how, inside the house, the child's bottle falls and breaks, spilling the milk on the floor.

In *Parichay*, to signal the fact that the days of hardship thanks to the tough love that disciplinarian Rai Sahab (played by Pran) imposes on his grandchildren are coming to an end, we see Ravi, the hero, (played by Jeetendra) playing the sitar. The carefree and felicitous way in which he plays and the way the sound of music reverberates through the *haveli* after years of silence, is a clear indication that change is in the air. In *Mere Apne*, the visual of Anandi Devi's slippers lying overlapping each other is a symbol of the fact that she has embarked on a journey into the other world.

Interpreting these symbols is a fine way of understanding the craft of a master film director. In this ability to express an idea in a single image, Gulzar owes much to his guru and mentor, Bimal Roy, and Gulzar uses it successfully in film after film, making it his own in the process and expressing succinctly what would otherwise require many scenes to be filmed as explanation. Gulzar uses this ability to maximum advantage to add crispness to his direction, making tedious explanations unnecessary.

79.

In Kalpana Lajmi's *Rudaali*, Bhikhni (played by Rakhee) tells Shanichari (played by Dimple Kapadia), 'The sorrow in your heart has turned to wax. No one has fomented it, which is why it has not melted.' This dialogue holds the essence of the film.

When the motherly Bhikhni says this to Shanichari, who has been unable to shed tears over all the tragedies life has cursed down on her, the damn of her tears bursts like a sweeping flood. The screenplay, dialogues and songs of the film are by Gulzar. As we take in the *bandish*-like compositions of the many small lines of dialogue, it becomes obvious that the screenplay knitted into the life of *Rudaali* has been woven by a poet.

Gulzar instils a soft fragility into the friendship between the two women that makes us forget for a while that the film revolves around the professional mourners, or rudaalis, of Rajasthan, who beat their chests and wail at death ceremonies. He depicts the tender mother-daughter bond between the two women in a masterful manner, and the actresses do their bit to make it ring true. By the end of the film, it is made evident that the relationship is in reality that of a mother and daughter.

The film is also about two women trapped in a chauvinistic patriarchal society and the narration of their sorrowful stories to each other, some of which is rendered through the visually beautiful song picturisations. The song 'Dil hoom hoom kare, ghabraye' (The heart weeps, and cowers in fear) is heard in the film every time Sanichari finds herself in love. She has never been loved since childhood, which is why any proximity to love scares her. Which is evident when she says, 'Bhikhni, my attachment to you makes me afraid...'

Gulzar also comments sarcastically on society, using irony to convey his thoughts. Whether it is referring to bargaining to pay less for the funeral rites done to earn spiritual merit, or the practice of slandering someone even after their death, his sabre-sharp writing cuts through it all. At the same time, he refers with irony to the practice in Rajasthan of hiring women of a particular caste to lament at deaths.

Kalpana Lajmi, Gulzar and Bhupen Hazarika have an equal share in making *Rudaali* a film that is delicate, trembling with emotions yet also a gritty and harsh reflection of reality. However, the harshness is smoothed away by Lata Mangeshkar and Bhupen Hazarika through the film's songs. A song delineates the thought hidden in the film, that time is still, and only human emotions flow. In Bhupen Hazarika's voice, the song becomes almost prophetic:

Go slow, O time
The shade has vanished from the pathways
Far away still, my beloved's town
Go slow...

There have been many fans of this film, including the Bharatnatyam and Odissi exponent, Sonal Mansingh, who believe that *Rudaali* is a film that can be enjoyed and appreciated as many times as it is viewed.

80.

Gulzar's poetry and Bhupen Hazarika's music flow in perfect sync in the song 'Samay o dheere chal...' in *Rudaali*. It's interesting to see how the folk tunes of Assam that energise Bhupen Hazarika's music, and which he uses to shape the song's tunes, give a new flavour to Gulzar's lyrics. The following lines from the song should be read as the writer's statement of opposition against superstition and magic:

This wind has taken everything
Even whisked away all signs of the caravan
Where will those who fly in the wind be found
Somebody tell me my lover's whereabouts
O Time, go slow
The shade has vanished from the path
Far away, my beloved's town

Like in most of his songs, in these lines too, Gulzar creates a secret bridge between life and reality, where by infusing an ordinary situation with suspense, he creates mysteries of meaning. This typical style of his has added a new dimension to film songs. Many such songs can be listed. Like, 'Mere saath chale na saaya' (No shadow walks with me) from *Kitaab*,

'Jeevan se lambe hain bandhu, yeh jeevan ke raaste' (Longer than life, my friend, are these roads of life,) from *Aashirwad*, 'Jaane kaise beetengi yeh barsaatein' (Wonder how I will live through these rains) from *Baseraa*, and 'Main ek sadi se baithi hoon/ Iss rah se koi guzra nahi' (I have been waiting for an entire aeon/ No one has come this way) from *Lekin*. The play between mystery and philosophy can be seen in each of these songs.

The song in *Rudaali* has Lata Mangeshkar, Asha Bhosle and Bhupen Hazarika himself adding to the tune's alluring quality and the powerful effect of Gulzar's words. Gulzar too realises the power of Bhupen Hazarika's magic, and has commented on his abilities as poet and music director. Gulzar says:

> This poet, whose name is Bhupen Hazarika; how easily he hears the sound of people's hearts. How completely justified it is to call him a people's poet, for whichever person he talks about, it seems as if that person himself is speaking. The sigh that emerges from his words becomes a part of the poet's own utterance. There is no difference between them. Like when he talks of a boatman on the Brahmaputra, he speaks with the emotions of a boatman. Hope and faith never let go of Bhupen-da's hand. Not in his folk songs that he sings, or in the songs that he writes and composes music for. To the extent that even when alone, he is never lonely. His shadow stays with him, keeping hope alight.

As must be evident, like 'Samay o dheere chalo', there are all the other songs of *Rudaali* too which are the result of the combined imagination of Gulzar and Bhupen Hazarika. They go beyond being beautifully filmed songs to a testament that, through emotion and tunes, is an acknowledgment of each other's talents. Evidence of the perfect synchronisation of their 'jugalbandi' could be seen even before *Rudaali* in their first collaboration, *Ek Pal*, in which the duo displayed the same virtuosity and newness in their creations. The background to this song too is interesting, as the heroine sings of her quandary on realising she is pregnant by her lover. Gulzar explores the depths of a woman's mind to write the lyrics and Bhupen Hazarika composes the tune of the song with the same sensitivity. Singer Bhupinder expressed surprise about how well Gulzar had interpreted the mental state of a pregnant woman. The song:

Wonder what it is, that makes my heart afraid
My heart wants to weep
Of my own self, I am afraid
Afraid of what may be
My breath is not my own, it seems borrowed
I thirst, but my thirst is fragmented
My life seems to be shared with another
Afraid I am, of what may be...

81.

Gulzar also crafts songs with an intellectual edge to them. It is an aspect of his creativity that can be seen along with his softer, emotional creations. I wish to highlight here how, even as he seems to be writing a song steeped in playfulness, he can infuse it with a strong dose of satire.

Gulzar's pen picks up new concepts and expresses them in unusual ways through his poems. It's not unreasonable to think that there is a significant body of poems that give us glimpses of his philosophy. Here I am discussing just a single song that stands apart through its words, structure and intention. In the very first lines the lyricist manages, keeping in mind the situation of the film, to say what poets writing in diverse languages have been highlighting in different ways. This song, from Ramgopal Varma's *Satya*, has these lines:

Put a bullet into your brain
Your mind makes the most chatter

Should you give in to the chatter, Kallu,
Your life will shatter

It is necessary to understand the meaning of what Gulzar says, using the slang that the underworld converses in. If you listen to your mind and do what it says, you will always be tense. What an idea this presents! Any thinking individual suffers from the fact that he cannot rid himself of any tension, or dilemma by thinking about it. Instead of trying to run away from one's thoughts, the poet suggests, 'Put a bullet into your brain'.

Through the playful antics of goons which make for entertaining viewing and listening. Gulzar suggests that society can survive only if the noise in the brain, and the fears that rise from it, are quietened. Though he has written it sarcastically, it is also quite true that an active mind looks for solutions to a problem through all available routes. If the solution is not possible, what option is there but to shoot the brain?

82.

One song needs closer examination. It is a milestone as, in the writing of it, Gulzar lets us get a glimpse of his times. This song from *Maya Memsaab* (1992) is unusual in the fact that while coping with society and life's issues, it seems to also hark back into the past where our memories dwell. At that point if you turn to look ahead again new memories seem obliterated. The song is:

Come, live in this heart and see
This is an ancient city
In every breath a story rests
In every breath lives a tale
This is an ancient city
This heart, a village

Some pain here, and some regret
Razed many a time
And rebuilt once again
This heart is an ancient city

Lata Mangeshkar who has sung this song opined that Gulzar-sahab has written it very well, with remarkable lyrics. To quote her, 'Gulzar-sahab has worked wonders in the *Maya Memsaab* song. His style is completely different and he presents life's philosophies in novel ways.'

83.

Don't turn back to look, my love
Didn't you hold my finger and
Teach me to walk
This doorstep is too high
Help me over it
Baba, I am your queen
A piece of your heart
Help me once more
Over the doorstep
Don't turn back to look, my love

(*Raazi*)

Overflowing with emotion, this bidai song is written by a lyricist who, if viewed as a father, would seen as being ninety years old now. Though he wrote the song for a film, *Raazi*, it is difficult to separate the feelings he has as a father for his daughter, Meghna, from what he creates for the character in the film.

'Mudh ke na dekho, dilbaro', echoes the traditional saying that a girl leaving her parental home after the wedding ceremony should not look back. If she does, she will not be able to shake off the love for her maternal home but will carry the sorrow of separating from it into her husband's home.

It is after a gap of many years that a serious and emotional bidai song that can evoke tears has been written, in which the daughter's bond with her father has been expressed so clearly. What also needs our attention is that any connection with the mother is absent in this bidai song. Keeping the mother in the background, the entire song is centred around the father as the bride leaves her home.

Gulzar puts forth the emotional leitmotif of the song and the daughter's feelings from the very first stanza:

When the crop has been cut
It does not grow anew
Daughters who are wedded
Do not turn back to look
If it's such a sending-away
If it is such a long separation
Then, this threshold of pain too
Help me across...

Of course, if we look at the song in connection with the film, then *Raazi* is communicating her story at many levels. Besides being the emotion-laden bidai of a bride, it is also the secret voyage of the character playing a spy going from India to neighbouring Pakistan. And again, in 'Dahleej oonchi hai, paar kara de,' refers to her integrating herself into the life of a family in a country that would not normally welcome her. Daughters do go after a bidai from one country to another soon after marriage, but here the allusion is to leaving her country to go to a neighbouring one to play informant, which heightens the drama. The mental tension of the heroine at this point gives the song a meaningful twist. The music by Shankar-Ehsan-Loy too expresses the seriousness of Gulzar's narrative.

Incidentally, it is also necessary to refer to that moment when his daughter was giving birth and he could only watch her suffering helplessly. It gave rise to a poem about pain and suffering titled, 'Meghna'.

Recollecting that time Gulzar-sahab says he could hardly think of anything beyond wishing that Meghna would somehow emerge safely from trial and that her baby would be healthy and well. The line 'Mudh ke na dekho, dilbaro' seems to be written on the same note as that poem which was written for Meghna, when Samay, Meghna and Govind's son, was born. 'If it's such a sending-away/ If it is such a long separation/Then this the threshold of pain too/ Help me across…' It seems to be the articulation of his own agony while witnessing his daughter's suffering. Here are a few lines from that poem too:

I was watching the sea
My pot of nectar was to emerge from the sea
Sporadically the sea would toss and turn
Making the water convulse in pain.
As spasms racked my daughter's delicate womb
I was afraid of asking for the nectar

So it is that the bidai song that is woven into the relationship between a father and his daughter creates a churning of emotion in spite of its melodic quality. 'Baba, mai teri mallika/ Tukda hoon tere dil ka' are lines that ring true for a daughter at any time of her life. If we look at the song along with all the other poems written by Gulzar-sahab for his daughter, it would not be negating the value of the film song, but lifting it to a song which universalises and embodies the father-daughter relationship across the world. Including Meghna's Pappy, and Gulzar's Bosky.

84.

I find it motivational that when Martin Freeman talks about the multi-character series *Sherlock* he credits his success to the fact that he understood his audience to be intelligent. The significance of this statement is deep, and effective, despite the lack of details. Do you not agree that most highly creative people across the world have placed their faith in those who appreciate their work and respected their intelligence? Just as Martin Freeman infuses a fresh perspective into a timeless character and in the process gives Sherlock a fresh lease of life among the intelligent public as a much-loved character.

Gulzar walks the same path when he chooses the stories of India's much loved writers to make them into films. In the making of *Khushboo*, *Namkeen* and *Ijazat* based on the works of Sharatchandra, Samaresh Basu and Subodh Ghosh, we can see a reflection of Martin Freeman's appreciation of and respect for his audiences; who in turn have lauded Gulzar's work as that of a consummate director. This standard also applies to his film songs and private poetry in which simple lines and incidents are used to reference significant concepts. He can take a simple incident to its extreme limit, to justify it. Like Sherlock, he alone can find a story in the witnesses and evidence that the police might have in its possession. Who can identify your addiction to snuff from the discoloured sleeve of your shirt. Which is probably why he has stayed relevant through changing times. We can thus say that Gulzar understands every fold of his characters' shirt sleeves. He can even make out if one of them has a cold.

It is an artiste's responsibility to move beyond popular themes and use his art to lift the tastes of his audiences and readers to a new level. Along with *Sherlock*'s writers, Steven Moffat and Mark Gatiss, Gulzar too understands this.

85.

Some opinions I have gleaned through the numerous interviews of Gulzar that I have read in print and social media, in the ten years of researching this book, have left a deep impression. One such interview was conducted by Sunaina

Kachru for the *New England News*. Here I am presenting a small opinion contained in it.

Sunaina asks Gulzar, 'Why do we find it so difficult to define life?' Gulzar's restrained and simple response is memorable. He says:

> Since civilization began, we have been trying to invent processes that could help explain the meaning of life. Actually, for centuries we have been trying to understand the secrets of life. This way, we try to fathom what lies ahead of us through some formulae. If the rains are near, best to buy a raincoat beforehand. Fill the cracks in the roofs. Mend your umbrellas. But if you never get drenched in the rain, and never experience the rain fully, both with mind and body, then what is life all about? In an attempt to find formulae to save ourselves from any sort of pain and discomfort, we miss out on a deeper experience of life. Pain and sorrow do not always cause distress, they can also be a reason for immense joy.

In Gulzar's responses we can sometimes find ways to understand the philosophies of life. A reference to a letter written by Rainer Maria Rilke to a young poet is justified here, in which he tries to assuage his sorrow:

> Only that sorrow is bad and dangerous which a person tries to suppress by sharing with another. Like those illnesses that one tries to treat superficially, and which subside only to relapse with greater impact. They continue to collect within us. They are but a form of life. They are lives that have not been lived, that have been laughed at, that have been ridiculed.

Lost as we are in emotional desolation, we find courage in these words. A ray of light opening up a way in the darkness that can lead us forward...if this were possible, perhaps we would look beyond our limited understanding into the past to understand the wisdom of our ancestors. Then perhaps we would trust our sorrows and our joys; for these are the moments when something new evolves within us, something unmarked and new.

The concept that Gulzar shares with Sunaina Kachru as his definition of a meaningful life echoes what Rilke said nine decades ago to a young man to help him shake off his sorrow. Each one has one's own ways of coming to grips with life, absolutely one's own, varied and secret.

86.

Many years ago, when Gulzar, on a visit to Delhi, stayed at Delhi's India International Centre, I met him there in connection with my book. He always stays in the deluxe room on the first floor of the main building of the IIC. I was recording him in room number 48. We were discussing many things when we were told that his friend, the eminent cartoonist Gopi Gajwani had come to meet him. I had been introduced to him through Gulzar-sahab, so I was happy he was sitting with us. Quite quickly, Gajwani joined the conversation saying, 'I will also ask Gulzar-sahab some questions.'

The recording, which I had started on another subject, was soon embellished with stories and incidents. While listening to that recording as I worked on the book, I was happy that I had been present at the pleasant interchange of conversation between Gulzar and Gopi Gajwani. I reproduce it here:

Gopi Gajwani: It often happens that if I draw something abstract, a common man comes to me and says, I can understand nothing of it. He says for me an abstract picture is one that tells me it portrays a sunrise or a sunset...that I understand. I tell him you are using the term understanding wrongly. He is not understanding, but identifying himself with the image.

Gulzar: Absolutely right! This is simply a matter of identification.

Gopi Gajwani: And I want to add that there is no rule that if you make a face, only the colours of the face must be used in it. Consider a portrait of Vincent Van Gogh, in which he has used mustard yellow to draw his face. Now it is a part of history, on why he used mustard to paint the entire face. It is important to understand this.

Gulzar: This is similar to writing a description of the cosmos, while writing about it. It is necessary to understand the reality of the cosmos, which contains the entire universe, and also those pulse beats within which the entire creation exists. Man and women exist, animals, plants, flowers—an entire globe, complete with its biology, exists. And say, you start from zero, then, you will reach that point of abstraction, where everything in the universe exists beyond the biological.

Gopi Gajwani: But you paint with words so beautifully.

Gulzar: No, I cannot speak like a painter. Pardon me for this. I understand the rhythm of lines; I can grasp the melody of colours. I can comprehend why you have used a colour here. But I can hear in me the entire song, the complete rhythm, and the complete melody, when I look at a painting rich in colours.

Gopi Gajwani: It is necessary to be a poet, to be able to read a painting.

Gulzar: This is a myth. I don't know how many people will agree with me. The pen is a poet itself; this is the easiest form of fine art.

Gopi Gajwani: Poetry is not as easy as you make it out to be. I sometimes think: a blank canvas is in front of me. We open a drawer, sitting in a small space, and it is full of colours. Then we think about what can be mixed into this blue. I believe exactly the same thing must be happening with words; what shall I use from where, what elements shall I mix together, and where shall I place it. What goes ahead, what follows, meaning, if I reduce this, then how much should I condense it, and if I need to expand on it, how much...Gulzar-sahab, it seems working with colours and words is rather similar.

Gulzar: This is true. While choosing words for poetry, one must also select the sound; this happens often with you too.

Gopi Gajwani: The entire palette has to be exposed...the palette of words, the complete palette of colours...

After this Gulzar asks me to call for tea and his favourite ajwain straw biscuits. I undertake to heat them in the microwave. This small conversation which was recorded into my recording system seemed to me, when I heard it years later, to be interesting enough.

87.

> The spaces, the silences, that which remains unspoken even after it is articulated—that is cinema. To listen to silence and express it, is to create cinema. What the writer says between the lines, cinema reveals. You have a chance of expanding on it. Whichever flourishes you wish to use as decoration, is possible in that space. As a director, I know which point to hit.
>
> —Gulzar in an interview
> with journalist Yashwant Vyas

Gulzar explains the process of creating cinema with a poet's sensibility of saying things succinctly. Cinema is, for him, shaping images out of silence. So we can try to understand his approach as a director who gives voice to that which is latent, and silence is the pause in which myriad images can take shape.

He brings even darkness into the realm of light, of which the American poet Mary Oliver says, 'Someone I loved once gave me a box full of darkness. It took me years to understand that this too was a gift.'

Keeping aside the gifts of darkness he has received from the world, Gulzar frequently moves through those areas of light while making his films, where any emotion gifted to him becomes a thing of value for him.

The flourishes in film making that he refers to is the expression of the artistic ideas that crowd into his mind. And he takes it to the perfect 'sum' or conclusion that leads to the next idea. Thus joining scenes that seem unrelated to create a new lexicon in cinema. Which is why his statement holds effect:

Everything before and after is broken
Life was contained in unbaked pots.

88.

In 1984, Gulzar took a detour from political and socially themed films to write the screenplay and songs for *Hip Hip Hurray* and direct it, a film based on football. Making a sports-themed film was a risky business in the 1980s, as only pure entertainers were considered the benchmark for success. Prakash Jha, along with his friends Manmohan Shetty and Pradeep Uppur hatched a plan over a cup of tea and snacks that a film should be made on sports. In Prakash Jha's words, 'It must have been 1982–83 when we started the discussion, as at that time there was a trend of making smaller films. Manmohan Shetty imported a 16 mm machine on which one could shoot, which negatives could then be blown up to make a 35 mm print. This is about the time when the formula was created that along with *Damul*, another popular film should be made, so both could be released at the same time. Around the same time, I was introduced to Gulzar-sahab at some function.

'I met him. What can I tell you about how big a fan of him I was. Of course, we were all his fans. We had watched all his films. We decided that we would request Gulzar-sahab to write the dialogues of the film. I took an appointment with him and went across and narrated the idea of the film to him. It will please you to know that when he started talking, we felt he should also write the screenplay of the film. Just dialogues would be inadequate. To ensure the minute details, if the screenplay too were written by him, it would work well.'

Prakash Jha continued, 'As one knows, Gulzar-sahab sits in his office every morning wearing a starched, well-pressed kurta and pyjama. He attends office with the discipline of a "brown sahib".

'So it was decided with Gulzar-sahab that he would write all three: screenplay, dialogue and songs, for the film. Though thirty-eight years have elapsed since, I remember clearly, his office was in Pali Hill. We would go to him every day. His lunch would come from home. He would sit with us, share his lunch and continue to chat. After lunch, I would have some tea and leave; and he would continue to write. My experience in interactions with him was special. The minute details in *Hip Hip Hurray*, and some important points raised by the songs, were all made possible by Gulzar-sahab.'

On my asking Prakash Jha what he felt was Gulzar-sahab's most notable feature, he replied, 'I have never heard him speaking loudly. He always speaks gently, on any issue. He is such a fount of knowledge; the references to Urdu, his knowledge of poetry, his creativity, everything is quite amazing. In spite of this, he never made me feel I was young, new, and would not understand any of this. I never had this feeling. I think, with regard to this film, this was a great partnership resulting in good and memorable work.

'Later, when I made *Rajneeti*, many lyricists were writing the songs for it. I felt we needed a song by Gulzar-sahab too. I met him and told him you are always in my thoughts. My request is that you contribute a song to this film. He then wrote, "Budha aasmaan dharti dekhe re" [The ancient sky gazes upon the earth].

Talking to Prakash Jha, it becomes evident that two creative people, consummate artistes in their respective fields worked together to make an off-beat, worthy film like *Hip Hip Hurray*. Even today its songs stand apart: Yesudas' 'Ek subah ki mod par' (At the crossroads of a morning), Asha Bhosle and Bhupinder's 'Jab kabhi mudh ke dekhta hoon' (Whenever I turn around to look) and Shailendra Singh's 'Maidan hai sari zindagi' (All of life is a playground). Renowned playwright Ramgopal Bajaj played an interesting cameo as the school principal in the film.

Hip Hip Hurray was the only film to be made in the 1980s with sport as a backdrop. Later, a slew of big budget sports films featuring stars were made. Among them, *Jo Jeeta Wohi Sikandar* (1992), *Lagaan* (2001), *Iqbal* (2005), *Chak De! India* and *Goal* (2007), *Kai Po Che* (2013) and *Gold* (2018) were worthy of note. *Hip Hip Hurray* really set the ball rolling for films based on sport.

89.

Among the slew of new music directors, Anu Malik's work falls into the popular category. Though he has also created some noteworthy tunes for Gulzar's lyrics. It is interesting to note that spanning from R. D. Burman to Shantanu Moitra, Gulzar has also contributed his lyrics to remarkable songs, among which Anu Malik's work is also present. Keeping the popular flavour of his tunes intact, this musician has worked with Gulzar on *Fiza* (2000), *Aks* (2001), *Ashoka* (2001), *Filhaal* (2002) and *Jaan-E-Mann* (2006). A close look reveals that some of the songs in these films were popular and appreciated critically too. Also worth noting is the fact that wherever Gulzar writes lyrics to take the idea of the film and its story forward, Anu Malik, even while keeping his popular style in mind, adds a lot of melody to the composition. Though he has been criticised for either lifting western tunes or basing a lot of his music on popular western songs, there are times when he sparkles. For example, the title song of *Filhaal*—the depth of feeling that Asha Bhosle adds to the meaning of the words makes it hard to believe that the music, which is serious and measured, has been composed by Anu Malik. The addition of the piano and the way it has been used in the song add to its appeal considerably. Though the tune is an example of new age music, the song still sounds sweet, when Asha Bhosle singing softly, the line, 'Yeh lamha filhaal jee lene de' (Let me live this moment) moves into louder tones. The lines that expound the philosophy of life are beautiful,

Life, let me live this moment
Nothing you have written in my fate
Remains
Each day you write
Something new
Whatever you wrote I have lived to the fullest
Let me live this moment

Gulzar talks about the writing of this song in *100 Lyrics*, translated by Sunjoy Shekhar:

> I credit Meghna for this song. She was the director of the film—-and I thought the word *'filhaal'* was not suited to poetry. I wrote the song in many ways. But it was not complimenting the situation. But she had the song in her mind, though she was unable to explain it. Finally, she wrote a full elaboration of her idea in English and gave it to me. She had already finalised the tune with Anu Malik. I managed to write it, but was not completely satisfied—the satisfaction came only when the song came out and remains popular till today. But even now I find phrases in it that seem to be hanging somewhere between poetry and prose.

Anu Malik composed great music for Santosh Sivan's film, *Asoka* (2001) which was matched by Gulzar's lyrics. Among these, 'Raat ka nasha abhi/Aankh se gaya nahi' (The headiness of the night/ Hasn't yet drained away from eyes), 'O re kanchi, kanch ki gudiya' (O kanchi, you glass doll) are remarkable. Gulzar amazes with the imagery he creates in 'Raat ka nasha abhi'. Here are some of the lines that explore the design of the song delicately:

I revel in you, though you aren't by my side
I dream a new dream as I turn on my side
When thoughts of you come, time skips along
My body, lying underneath a coverlet of water, burns

Similarly, the songs of passion in *Fiza* too were composed by Anu Malik. 'Tu hawa hai, fiza hai, zameen ki nahin' (You are the breeze, the splendour, not of this earth), 'Na leke jao, mere dost ka janaza hai' (Don't bear away the coffin with my friend) and 'Aaja mahi mere aa/Aa dhoop malu mein tere haathon mein' (Come my love/ Let me caress the sunlight into your hands) are by Gulzar. Though all three songs, composed with care by Anu Malik became popular, 'Na leke jao' by Jaspinder Nirula is unusual. The composition, lyrics and the way it has been sung all contribute to the mood it evokes as a song of mourning. The poem brings out the sorrow that remains after bidding a final adieu to a departed soul. Anu Malik's music deepens the pathos with its slow movement. The song needs to be read in full; for leaving any line out of the song belies the sorrow being expressed.

Do not bear away that coffin with my friend
The clay is still warm, the body fresh
His breath is entangled, unravel it
The words that wait at the lips, let him complete it
Hope is still alive, the pain is still fresh
Do not bear away the coffin with my friend
The clay is still warm, the body fresh
Wake him, let me embrace him and see him off
What a farewell this is, what manner of goodbye
Each wound on my heart is still fresh

If read as just a poem and not as a film song, this is a dirge in which pain and emotions are at their peak. Anu Malik uses the drum and percussion with such aptness at the 'sum' that it gives the song the feel and rhythm of a dirge. Playing the dhol loudly along with high pitched singing is also a feature during Muharram, a glimpse of which can be caught in this song.

The songs of Rakeysh Omprakash Mehra's supernatural thriller, *Aks* add substantially to the film. Gulzar has written all nine songs for the film, using imagery quite differently. Anu Malik too has excelled, with no song in the film sounding like any other. Among these, 'Aaja gufaon me aa'(Come into the caves), 'Yeh raat' (This night), 'Hum bhool gaye' (We have forgotten), 'Rabba-rabba', and 'Banda yeh bindaas hai' (This fellow's carefree) are notable numbers. We can easily call the music of this film experimental.

The strong Caribbean instrumentation used in 'Banda yeh bindaas hai' places the tune somewhere between traditional Indian music and western symphonies. The song seduces one to dance, thanks to the adept singing by KK. Some lines of the song can be read to assess how Gulzar adds those elements to the heady song that increase its tempo:

This fellow's carefree
For the nectar always thirsty
This fellow's carefree
A bee he is, he is a bee
Greedy and crafty
Two masks has he
And a sword, ready to parry
This fellow's carefree

Two songs from *Jaaneman* are notable, because they fit into his familiar style of poetry, and have been set melodiously to music by Anu Malik. These songs are, 'Sau dard hain, sau raahatein' (There are a hundred ills, and a hundred easements) and 'Humko maloom hai, ishq masoom hai' (We know, love is innocent).

90.

Gulzar has created lyrics that are quite unusual with Shankar-Ehsaan-Loy too. In the latter part of Gulzar's long journey as a lyric writer, there are only a few music composers who have collaborated with him to create good songs across many films. We can count Shankar-Ehsaan-Loy, Anu Malik, Shantanu Moitra and A. R. Rahman among them. With Shankar-Ehsaan-Loy, the films that come to mind are *Rockford* (1999), *Bunty Aur Babli* (2005), *Jhoom Barabar Jhoom* (2007), *Mirzya* (2016), *Kill Dil* (2014), *Surma*, *Raazi* and *Mere Pyaare Prime Minister*, all in 2018, and in 2020, *Chhapaak*. This trio of film directors use traditional instruments to create a new kind of fusion music. Shankar Mahadevan, on his part, seems to find ways to blend the classical music traditions of north and south India. Ehsaan Noorani is the group's guitarist. He has studied music abroad and deftly handles the orchestration. Loy Mendonsa, the third member of the group, is an accomplished musician who plays the piano, bass guitar and harmonica among other instruments.

Mirzya is a good example of the effective collaboration between Gulzar and the trio of music makers. Also remarkable for the fact that most of the songs have been sung by folk singers, who bring their own lexicon into play to create pleasing effects. Besides Mame Khan, the Nooran Sisters—Jyoti and Sultana—and Daler Mehndi, classical exponent Kaushiki Chakraborty have also sung for the film. One of the songs, 'Aave re hitchki', a soulful number, has been sung by Shankar Mahadevan and Mame Khan. This song evokes the folk tunes of the nomad Banjaras and is scented with the flavour of Rajasthani music. Gulzar's words bring in his own phrases beautifully, and Mame Khan's voice sings out with unparalleled clarity. However, this folk-based tune also uses electronic music in good measure, including the synthesiser, bass guitar, violin and other western instruments. Keeping in mind the Rajasthan background, Gulzar has also used words from the language of the region. The orchestration adds a unique element to this composition.

Similarly, the song 'Ek nadi thi' (There was a river) by the Nooran Sisters and Mohan Kalyan is steeped in indigenous expressions. When the song begins with Mohan Kalyan singing at a high pitch, the low tones of the Nooran Sisters singing the refrain offer a pleasing contrast. Gulzar writes this song in his well-known fashion, but gives it new meaning and direction by which it gains a visual dimension. The lines go thus:

A river, bound by its banks
Flowed slowly
If she broke it, floods would follow
If she changed course, all of earth would wash away

In 'Doli re, doli re' from the same film, Mame Khan starts singing at a high pitch and colours the song with the special flavour of his Rajasthani style. Along with this, mixing into the tune as a parallel tune, we hear sounds of jazz that, without disturbing the folk element, brings in the piano, trumpet, harmonica and the instruments of percussion. It is a beautifully balanced tune on which Gulzar gently places his poetry. Gulzar is a seasoned writer of bidai songs and here he creates one that is unprecedented:

My master has sent word, I shall do his bidding
You cannot delay coming, if you don't come, I die
Linger no more in your father's house
Linger no more in your father's house
Belonging to her husband, she goes,
Belonging to her husband, she goes...
The doli goes, the doli is goes,
What the husband says, goes...'

The music directors have moved away from their usual style to fined new expressions for each of the songs of *Mirzya.*

Two other songs from this film are in a class of their own thanks to the composition and the rendition. 'Kaga re, kaga re' (Crow, oh crow) sung by Kaushiki Chakravorthy and 'Chakora' by Mame Khan, Shuchismita Das, Akhtar Chinnal and Shankar Mahadevan are remarkable as much for their melody as for Gulzar's lyrics. In 'Chakora' the song's rhythm moves smoothly along as the song progresses, with all the voices blending and keeping the beat perfectly to create great impact. The composition of 'Kaga re' has a blend of western music with classical traditional music, where Kaushiki proves her mastery in the short span of three minutes. Gulzar too writes striking lyrics, as seen in this stanza:

Crow, oh crow
Give me news of my love
Let me not die of thirst
Bring me a beakful of water
Crow, oh crow
Give me news of my love

We can think of other great songs besides the experimental compositions of *Mirzya*, that show us the brilliance of the collaboration between Gulzar and Shankar-Ehsaan-Loy. 'Dekhna mere sar se aasman udh gaya hai' (Look, the sky has vanished from above my head) (*Bunty Aur Babli*), 'Dhaage tod lao chandni ke noor ke' (Bring me silver strands of the moon) (*Jhoom Barabar Jhoom*), 'Pyar ki baaziyan/ Na jeetiya na haariya' (The games of love are/ Neither won nor lost) (*Surma*), 'Zindagi yun gale aa lagi hai' (Life has come upon me) (*Kill Dil*), 'Ae watan, watan mere aabaad rahe tu' (Nation, O my nation, may you always flourish) (*Raazi*) etc are examples.

Two songs from this combination of lyricist and musicians were viral phenomena. One of them, 'Kajrare kajrare' from *Bunty Aur Babli*, was composed as a dance number but set in the mode of a qawwali. The second, from Meghna Gulzar's *Raazi*, is in the form of a Kashmiri bidai song. The title song of *Chapaak* too is a good result of their collaboration and Arijit Singh sings the touching lyrics that highlight the mental state of a victim of an acid attack with feeling. These lines say it all:

He who erased a face
Removed it from sight
Splashed a few drops of corrosion
Snatched away an identity
A face crumbled
Like a pawn tumbled
Like the sun eclipsed
Snatched away an identity

These songs give us a good glimpse of the chemistry between the trio who carve a path between Indian and western music to create melodious tunes. That these modern musicians worked so comfortably with a veteran songwriter like Gulzar can be compared to the time when Gulzar, as a young lyricist, partnered with veterans like S. D. Burman and Madan Mohan.

91.

Gulzar's partnership with A. R. Rahman, one of the most prominent music directors of our time, has flourished. The compositions they created together for *Dil Se* (1998), besides being experimental, had a Sufi flavour to them. Gulzar admits that he worked in a 'Sufi' mode for the first time to collaborate with Rahman and create songs for the big screen. Rahman, who uses influences of western music, Latin American and Middle Eastern music, creates electronic music. His music is modern and fresh. Till date, this duo has successfully worked together on ten films: *Dil Se*, *Saathiya* (2002), *Guru* (2007), *Slumdog Millionaire* (2008), *Yuvraj* (2008), *Raavan* (2010), *Jab Tak Hai Jaan* (2012), *The Hundred-foot Journey*, the Hindi-dubbed Tamil film, *Linga* (2014) and *Okay Jaanu*

(2017) creating songs that are a cut above the tried and tested in film music.

The beauty of Rahman's compositions for his first Hindi film *Dil Se*, with his unique orchestration, lay in their departure from the pattern followed by traditional Hindi film music. Thus opening a new vista with songs like, 'Chal chaiyya chaiyya', or 'Ae ajnabi tu bhi kabhi awaaz de kahin se' (Hey stranger, give me a sign), or even 'Tu hi tu satrangi re' (You, the seven-coloured one) Apart from this, the song, 'Jiya jale, jaan jale' (My heart, my soul is on fire) has its own story in which, along with Gulzar's lines, the interludes of the song are sung in Malayalam by Girish Puthucheri, preempting the music ahead. Lata Mangeshkar brings her own innovations into the rendition. Rahman uses the mridangam, violin and flute here alongside the electronics. The sorrowful sound of the violin that intercepts the music casts its mood over the entire song. When the Malayalam chorus comes in after Lata-ji's portions, led by M. G. Srikumar, it changes the nature of the track. This exposition of Rahman's recreation of Raag Bhairavi remains the high point of his experimental music. Also interesting is the way the lyrics of the song, popularly considered a wedding-night song, have been crafted. Some lines that bring out the romance and passion are significant:

> *Sparks of pain sparks flash all over my body*
> *Masses of butterflies scented with bruised flowers*
> *All night the mehendi is crushed under my feet*
> *What can I do, whom can I tell, how the night was spent...*

Talking to cinema expert Nasreen Munni Kabir for her book, *Jiya Jale: The Stories of Songs*, Gulzar has this to say about the making of this song:

> Rahman had recorded it in a completely different way. He asked the background singer to sing the same line repeatedly, which he would record onto varied tracks. Thus, Lata-ji kept singing and each time Rahman recorded her

> singing in different ways. It's quite likely that while singing the same line over and over, the singer will change it slightly with each repetition. This is natural with any artiste. Then Rahman presented the entire recording to Lata-ji, asking her to choose her best lines from it; though he himself chose the lines that he thought were Lata-ji's best.

The Malayalam lines of 'Jiya jale' which echo folk music have the electronic music blending with the main voice, creating a deep resonant sound. This song from *Dil Se* is noteworthy for being the first modern, experimental collaboration between Lata Mangeshkar and A. R. Rahman with Gulzar's delicately wrought imagery making it a very poetic and evocative film song.

'Ae ajnabi, tu bhi kahin, aawaz de kahin se', is another of Rahman's successes. Technically, the use of the kick-drum helps to add emotion thanks to its slow rhythm and low sound. The violin playing at many levels in the background adds its own pathos, and Mahalaxmi Iyer's voice interjecting 'Paakhi-paakhi pardesi' (O bird, bird from strange lands) in the midst of Gulzar's lines makes the song a listening pleasure. It makes us imagine that the song emerges from the depth of emotion that rests mainly on sorrow. In such songs expressing sadness, Gulzar is able to effortlessly evoke the emotion in listeners. The violin and the choral singing mingle in the interludes to great effect. The music director has worked hard at giving the Bhimpalasi-based *raag* a unique beat. Udit Narayan and Mahalaxmi's voices are effectively used to enhance the pain of separation. Throughout the album, the separation that is evidenced as an emotion is equally thanks to the contribution of A. R. Rahman, through his music, and Gulzar, through the writing.

Electronic music plays a star role in the song, 'Tu hi tu satrangi re', based on Middle Eastern sounds of an Arabic hue. Udit Narayan balances this song on a level between desire and spirituality, with Kavita Krishnamurthy adding a short alaap and a reading of a couplet by Ghalib. Gulzar, while embedding a mystical element in the lyrics, creates the possibility of myriad interpretations. The words and music of the song blend and yet seem to stand out separately. The Sufi elements in the music elevate the track out of the level of the ordinary. A few lines to illustrate:

The limpid silence of her eyes
Touches me like a whisper
I kneel in prayer
Aware, but also unaware
Shadow of my heart
My companion clad in the rainbow
You colour my mind...
Are you the light, why so far away
When you are near, like a feeling
Are you a dream or a shadow are you,
O seven-coloured one...

The same Sufi colours tint the song, 'Chal chaiyya chaiyya' in which the percussion joins in the rhythm of the train running on the rail tracks. This song is a prime example of how a Sufi thought can be laid over a modern tune to create a new musical dimension. Though basically composed as a dance number, the percussion takes on a role of its own. Sapna Awasthi and Sukhwinder Singh sing it with a passion to create emotions not commonly evoked in songs with a spiritual theme. Enough to say that in all such Sufi themed songs that followed, even penned by other writers, the focus has been on creating music that enters the listeners' minds with great impact.

Many other creations of Gulzar with Rahman fill us with astonishment at how a musician working with electronic sound can create such melodious music to express typically Indian emotions and thoughts. Rahman's style has always been to break his own rules, and structure a song according to its subject. The tune takes its form accordingly. We can examine many songs in which, moving away from his usual style, Rahman uses folk or classical elements. At such times percussion is minimally used, and the harmonium, tabla, *mridangam* and violin come into focus. His tunes often break the traditional metre to seek unusual ways of arriving at the 'sum', finding a new definition of melody in the process. *Saathiya*'s 'Chalka re, chalka kalash ka paani', (The water splashes out of the kalash) *Guru*'s 'O humdum' (O my fellow traveller), 'Ranjha ranjha kardi ve main/ Aapne Ranjha hoi' (Calling out to Ranjha, I have become Ranjha myself) from *Raavan*, and other songs from the same film are some examples of how Rahman, according to their themes, uses Indian references. The popularity of all these songs rests on the fact that Rahman has woven his tunes taking in the full measure of the weight of their words.

Speaking about the chemistry between Gulzar and Rahman, it is important to add that the collaboration between them is far from over. Who knows how many more films they could partner in to give us some unparalleled compositions.

An observation that emerges from the examination of their partnership to date is the ease with which Gulzar, a poet with a Sufi bent of mind, and a singularly gifted musician like Rahman collaborate. Gulzar writes songs that resonate with the younger generation; Rahman, on his part, has created experimental music to match the words and created immortal songs. In this popular list we must mention 'Jai ho' from *Slumdog Millionaire* which won the lyricist and composer the Oscar in 2008 and the Grammy in 2010, which was also awarded to Tanvi Shah.

92.

In writing some songs, Gulzar has created serious challenges for himself. These songs stand a distance apart from his normal usage of words. It appears as if he has abandoned his unique style and metre and embarked down a new path where his imagery takes on new forms. These are not romantic songs, nor do they express the feelings or thoughts of the hero or heroine. Neither are these romantic or sad songs in the popular mould, through which, over the years, Gulzar has evoked a range of soft feelings in listeners. In these songs, Gulzar has created something off beat, keeping the situation in mind, using contemporary language, modern imagery and metaphors.

The first song in this genre that needs discussion is 'Yeh raat' (This night), composed by Anu Malik for *Aks*. The emotion of the song that tries, in this dark film, to depict negativity through a description of the night that Gulzar's pen finds new imagery for,

This night...this night
Like a chameleon
This night
Like a venomous cobra
This night
Not to be chewed, nor spat out
This black poisonous night...

Night is presented in new ways in this song: 'a chameleon' and a 'venomous cobra'. In two more songs of *Aks*, 'Aa ja gufaaon me aa' and 'Banda yeh bindaas hai', the same quality of novel word play is evident. Anu Malik creates off-beat tunes with percussion used interestingly.

Besides *Aks*, Gulzar creates a wonderful image in *Satya* for music directors Vishal Bhardwaj and Sandeep Chowta where he writes a song of celebration that has family and neighbours participating. Though this is a duet, the setting is the criminal underworld, where people express their love in a different way making it a song with special references. In this connection, a song like 'Sapne me milti hai, o kudi meri' (She meets me in my dreams, my girl) has to be heard for its words, its composition and the expressions of its playback singers. The song also has the path-breaking image of the empty rickshaw following the woman around; an image possibly used for the first time in Hindi cinema. Some lines from the song are presented in this regard:

I meet him in my dreams
This man of mine, I meet him in my dreams
Like an empty rickshaw
He follows me on the roads
Through the day

Simple she is, yet fiery
She's descended perfectly finished
Sometimes she meets me
This girl of mine...

Yet another song, based on a Russian folk tune has been also composed by Vishal Bhardwaj, for which he requested Gulzar to write the lyrics. The carefreeness of this song is equally evident in the words as Gulzar, keeping in step with the brilliant orchestration and the fast tempo of the song, matches it with his words. Listen to the song from *Saat Khoon Maaf* and you too will be caught up in the flow of the words and the melody and end up humming it. Right at the start of the song, before the mukhda can begin, Gulzar lightly invokes the memory of the Russian litterateur Alexander Pushkin. The lines flow thus:

He's walked from afar, over many a mile
A Pushkin from Russia
For me he left Moscow
In love, this too is possible.

Then the rest of the song starts on a fun note:

Darling, let our eyes meet
Stop me not, let me love you
The spring is listless, my life restless
Let the bulbuls wait a bit

Darling, let our eyes meet

This song, with the arrangement in western music, has been sung superbly by Rekha Bhardwaj and Usha Uthup. Also worthy of mention is Shantanu Moitra's song from the film *Yahaan* which is a sensitive film set against the background of Kashmir. The song, 'Naam adaa likhna' (Write my name, Adaa) is a testimony to Gulzar's ideology, where his sensitivity merges with the plot of the film. The song has many hidden references which are revealed if the song is heard outside the context of the film. This song too is many steps away from Gulzar's usual style. To move away from one's chosen metre, and to create a new structure while writing on a new theme is not only a huge step for a writer, but also a significant milestone for Hindi film music.

Should anyone ask about my identity
Write that my colour is red
With a finger on my fair body
Write my name Adaa
At times, the moon lingers nearby
At times, the evening stands nearby
Come
Let us float in the Jhelum
Our circumstances
Some day will surely change...

93.

Let us examine his less popular songs. It can be a surprising study to discover why despite the literary qualities and the melodious content, these songs did not capture the attention of music lovers. In Gulzar's long list of the songs he has written for films, there are some which slipped from notice and did not get the attention they deserved. If we look at it from the perspective of Vividh Bharati and its programmes

on radio, then these songs made a brief appearance like shadow songs, or 'Chaya Geet', in Gulzar's career, and were then forgotten. Though they can be heard on and off on Vividh Bharati, hearing them infrequently creates a desire to listen to these songs yet again and appreciate them. This opinion is valid, for an artiste as versatile as Gulzar who, in his ninth decade, is still creating fresh songs for any number of characters essayed by young actors and actresses.

There must be a dozen or so films that did not make their mark in which Gulzar wrote as lyricist. Among them are: *Bhool Na Jaana* (unreleased), *Prem Patra* (1962), *Poornima* (1965), *Biwi Aur Makaan* (1966), *Sanatta* (1966), *Rahgir* (1969), *Anokha Daan* (1972), *Doosri Sita* (1974), *Shaque* (1976), *Griha Pravesh* (1979), *Ratnadeep* (1979), *Baseraa* (1981) and *Hip Hip Hurray* (1984). Even among these films, one song often found favour while the rest languished.

Bhool Na Jaana was made in the sixties and remained unreleased. The music was composed by Daan Singh, a Rajasthani composer, who was best known for two songs he composed for *My Love*. Sung by Mukesh, these songs were 'Jikr hota hai jab qayamat ka/ Tere jalwon ki baat hoti hai' (When the end of days is discussed/ Your magnificence is spoken of) and 'Woh tere pyar ka gham' (The grief of your love).

We find only one song by Gulzar, sung by Mukesh, in *Bhool Na Jaana*, 'Pukaro mujhe naam lekar pukaro/ Mujhe tumse apni khabar mil rahi hai' (Call out, call out to me by name/ From you I receive news of myself). Despite its poignant words and the heartfelt, simple rendering, the song did not catch on. On examining the tune, it reveals itself to be a beautiful composition based on Raag Misr Bhupali and expounded beautifully by the sitar and flute. It is surprising that even though most of Mukesh's songs gained great popularity and he was a singer loved by many, this song remained unnoticed. Perhaps because the film was never released and thus the song did not reach viewers and listeners in the normal way, through the film.

Gulzar holds a special place in the history of lyrics in Hindi cinema with fans educating themselves using his lyrics. His measure of success stands at par with Shakeel Badayuni, Sahir Ludhianvi, Majrooh Sultanpuri, Shailendra and Anand Bakshi. Studying those songs of these successful lyricists, which never made it to popularity or gained it only to flicker out like a brief candle, can be an interesting exercise. It is heartening to note that there are, in Gulzar's case, only a handful of songs that did not get universal appreciation. I would like to highlight the songs of two films which had noteworthy music created by the music directors. The first song is from *Anokha Daan*. Composed by Salil Chowdhury in his usual style, and presented as a background song, 'Madhbhari yeh hawaein/ Paas aayen/ Naam lekar mujhe yeh bulayen' (The heady breezes/ Come close to me/ Call me out by name). The entire song is supported by Western instruments, and slide soft and loud, like a golden design etched on enamel, over the words to create a pleasing and melodious whole.

At first glance this seems an easy enough song but the deftness with which Lata-ji sings it, climbing up and down the notes effortlessly, and melodiously stressing chosen words in each line make it obvious that this is no easy song to hum along, or copy. This song also deserves a closer look at the arrangement of the music. Sadly though, this gem of a song went by with almost no recognition.

The second example is from Basu Bhattacharya's *Griha Pravesh*, the music for which was composed by Kanu Roy. A classical music composer, Kanu Roy got only a handful of films but all the compositions he created were sweet and original. The time is right to mention here the chemistry that worked between Gulzar and Basu Bhattacharya. Both learned their art at the school of Bimal Roy, and it can be said of both that when these veterans worked together as a team, the result was of a completely different level of excellence. Gulzar worked with Basu Bhattacharya in three films: *Anubhav* (1971), *Griha Pravesh* (1979) and *Aastha* (1997). All the songs by Gulzar indicate he was writing them from a level of comfort and peace. A similarity of thought on creative issues is evident in the friendship between the two. Perhaps that is why Gulzar gave of his best for his friend's films. Though, it remains sadly true that this did not seem to help in winning popularity with the masses for the songs that resulted from their working together.

In fact, *Anubhav* is the only film in which two songs by Gulzar, 'Mera dil jo mera hota' (If only my heart were mine) and 'Mujhe jaan na kaho meri jaan', (Do not call me jaan, my love) became immensely popular. Gulzar wrote all the songs as well as the dialogues for *Griha Pravesh*. The song, 'Boliye sureeli boliyan' (Speak sweet words), based on classical music is as good as any other raag-based song for which Gulzar has written lyrics. Sung by Bhupinder and Sulakshana Pandit, in Raag Bihaag to lyrics that have a traditional ring to them:

Speak sweet words, speak sweet words
Tuneful words for sweet and sour eyes
Heady words for salty eyes
Speak tuneful words, speak tuneful words...

It always saddens me and makes me wonder why it did not get the same measure of acclaim as Gulzar's other lyrics based on classical music like 'Beeti na bitai raina, birha ki jaai raina' from *Parichay*, 'Abke na saawan barse' from *Kinara*, 'Badi der se megha barse ho rama' (This rain has been pouring for a long time O Rama) from *Namkeen* and 'Na, jiya lage na' (My heart is not in anything) from *Anand*. In fact, this question is relevant to all the eight songs of the film. A second song from the same film is a good showcase of Sulakshana Pandit's voice. Listening to this soft composition is as pleasurable as dwelling on the import of its delicately wrought wordings. However, this is one of Gulzar's invisible creations. To the extent that there is not a single mention of it in the compilations of Gulzar's best songs released by music companies.

Were you not you, who would you be
People say you would have been a messiah of stone

If on the face carved of marble
The manner of your style remains the same yet
When you drop your gaze
Who cannot lose their heart to such bashfulness

Were you not you, who would you be
People say you would have been a messiah of stone

Every line of this love song written in praise of the lover is pure poetry. The beauty of the composition is that Kanu Roy lets the poetry express itself by keeping the interludes brief. There is no explanation for this song not finding favour, though Vividh Bharati does keep its memory alive by occasionally playing it.

It is quite a coincidence that three years after this song, the song that Gulzar wrote on a similar theme for Shekhar Kapur's *Masoom*. 'Huzoor iss kadar bhi na itrah ke chaliye/ Khule aam aachal na lehrake chaliye' (My lady, walk not with such style/ Do not display your charms so freely) did get to be a very popular number and the R. D. Burman creation rings out even today.

Other songs of *Griha Pravesh* too have been forgotten, though neither the poetry nor music was found wanting in any way. Chandrani Mukherji's 'Pehchan to thi, pehchana nahin/ Maine apne aap ko pehchana nahin' (I may have known you, but I did not recognize you), Bhupinder's 'Zindagi phoolon ki nahin/ Phoolon ki tarah mehekti rahe' (Life may not be a bed of flowers/ Yet may it forever give off their fragrance), the song by Yesudas, 'Logon ke ghar mein rehta hoon/ Kab apna koi ghar hoga' (I live in others' houses/ When will I have a dwelling of my own) and Bhupinder's 'Machal kar jabh bhi aankhon se chalak jaate hain do ansoo' (Whenever two teardrops fall from the eyes) deserve to be heard and appreciated afresh.

The identity of an expert lyricist also lies in the fact that a decade after his writing a song, some trained ears latch on to his meanings and the old sentences burst with new significance. In this, many of the sad songs that have been forgotten could gain a new relevance. This is indeed what transpired with the songs of Basu Bhattacharya's *Aastha* (1997). With poetry in all its colourful word power matching the experimental music given by Sharang Dev, every aspect of the film was sound. Two songs deserve special mention: 'Tan par lagti kaanch ke boondein' (Droplets like glass strike the body) and 'Labon se choom lo/ Aankhon se thaam lo mujhko' (Kiss me with your lips/ Hold me in your eyes). The latter song has Gulzar's voice interspersing to give a twist to the tune. Yet the film, despite its songs, failed to woo the public. The sad part was that playback singer, Sriradha Banerjee too did not get her due.

I am convinced this is not just Gulzar's experience, but one that every artiste, however big his reputation be, has gone through. And there has been no conspiracy behind this, just a falling short of being able to grasp and communicate a concept properly to society at large. Narendra Sharma, Rajinder Krishan, Sahir Ludhianvi and Shailendra are among the lyricists who have known this. As also playback exponents like Lata Mangeshkar, Mohammad Rafi, Kishore Kumar among others. Yet, such is the autonomy of art, that independent of time, art finds its own way. Some literary text comes into focus years after its publication, and very often a forgotten film suddenly gains relevance, and the narrative comes to life again. This can be seen through some films in the context of Gulzar's songs. Especially, *Doosri Sita*, *Sannaata*, *Ratnadeep* and *Shaque*.

While the song, 'Din ja rahe hain, ki raaton ke saaye/ Apne saleebe aap hi uthaye' (The days are passing/The nights shall bear their own crosses) by Lata Mangeshkar in *Doosri Sita* found fans, two other songs sung by Asha Bhosle, 'Tu jahan mile, wahin mera doonon jahan' (Where I meet you, is where my two worlds are) and 'Aye re, aye re, nanhe munne raja ko nindiya sulaye' (Aye re, aye re, the little prince will be rocked to sleep) were ignored. Yet, both these songs from the trio of Pancham-Asha-Gulzar are worth listening to. Asha Bhosle with her seductive voice creates a vista of sound in 'Tu jahan mile…' Asha-ji's voice opens in a way that one imagines a vista where words, like lines of blossoming flowers, wait impatiently to be to be expressed. Much the same can be said of the song from *Ratnadeep* that the trio have created. 'Aisa ho toh kaisa hoga', which tempts you to play it again and again. Yet again, Lata Mangeshkar's song for *Sannata*, 'Aisa hota toh nahin/Aise ho jaye agar/Tumhi mil jao' (This doesn't happen/ But if it did/And I found you) and 'Koi bechara, dil ko kho kar khoj raha hai' (A poor soul has lost his heart and seeks it) did not make it to the superhit ranks despite the soulful rendition and content.

Some duets too fall into this category. Salil Chowdhury's composition, 'Saawan ki raaton mein aisa bhi hota hai/ Raahi koi bhoola hua toofanon me khoya hua raah pe aa jaata hai' (It happens on monsoon nights/A traveller lost, confused by the storm/Finds his way again) set in the style of Rabindra Sangeet for *Prem Patra* is one such. This, despite the silken rendition by Talat Mahmood and Lata Mangeshkar. 'Humsafar, mere humsafar, pankh tum parwaaz hum' (My fellow-traveller, you are the wings and I, the flight) from *Poornima* too, despite being a beautiful number in every way, has never been counted in the top list of love songs. The Asha Bhosle-Kishore Kumar duet, 'Kabhi kabhi sapna lagta hai' (It sometimes feels like a dream) from *Ratnadeep* is part of the same small list of duets by Gulzar that went unappreciated.

Some unknown voices as well as those voices that have so beautifully cast their spell over the world of playback music have sung the songs that are getting their due years after their release. Examples of these include the Lata Mangeshkar song, 'Mitwa re, bhool gaye the raahen' (Oh love, my love lost his way) (*Rahgir* [1969], music by Hemant Kumar) in which the chorus adds a special charm. Another song sung by Lata and chorus from the same film, 'Bairi aanchal pag pag uljhe hamaar' (Like an enemy, my veil trips me up at every step) is almost completely forgotten. But even the endearing elaboration of the rural dialect did not add to the song's popularity. 'Bas ek chup se lagi hai, nahi udaas nahi' (I am only silent, there's no sadness in me), from *Sannata* with Hemant Kumar's musical score, as well as all the songs of *Biwi Aur Makaan* suffered the same ignominious fate, though the latter film had some good numbers. The duet by Lata Mangeshkar and Asha Bhosle, 'Dabe labon se kabhi to koi salaam le le' (If only in silence, accept my salutations), can be placed among the everlasting duets by the sisters. Though the song sounds like a dance number composed by Lakshmikant-Pyarelal, it was actually Hemant Kumar who swung the baton to create this popular and melodious duet.

Some lost-to-us songs that exemplify Gulzar's superb penmanship include 'Do nainio ke pankh lagaakar/ Man paakhi udh jaaye' (My mind takes flight upon the wings of my eyes) from *Shaque* which had music by Vasant Desai. This song was sung by Kumari Faiyyaz. The singer's classical style that mingles with some elements of ghazal singing add to the song's appeal. Also forgotten are Lata-ji's 'Saaware sunao bansuri' (Play your flute O Dark-Skinned One) sung to R. D. Burman's music in *Baseraa*, and 'Ek subah ek modh pe' (One morning at the crossroads) set to music by Vanraj Bhatia for *Hip Hip Hurray*. And even Yesudas' wholly original way of singing could not save the song from *Daayra*, released about thirty-six years ago, the opening line of which was, 'Palkon pe chalte chalte, jab unghne lagti hai' (Stepping along on eyelashes, when she gets drowsy).

It eludes reason why, despite modern technology that makes it possible to download any song from any one of the countless available sites, some good songs remain hidden in the mist of neglect. This is true even of some recent songs which have been written by Gulzar. Among them, 'Piya tora kaisa abhimaan' (What pride is this, my love) from *Raincoat* (2004) and 'Ret udawe re naina rookhe' (These eyes that don't cry raise clouds of dust) from *Maqbool* (2004), 'Humko maloom hai ishq masoom hai' (We know love is blameless) from *Jaaneman* (2006), 'Ji na jalaiyo, jalaiyo na rasiya/ Ji me jaan basi hai re' (Do not trouble my heart, beloved/ My heart lives in it) from *Das Tola* (2010). Other songs in the list include, *Teen Patti*'s 'Thoda thoda sawaab hai, thoda thoda gunah hai' (A little bit of good, a modicum of bad) released in 2010, 'Jo dikhte ho/ Wo lagte nahin' (You are not what you seem like) from *Kya Dilli, Kya Lahore* (2014), 'Bhide re bhide naina/ Naina banjare' (The eyes collide/ These wandering eyes) from *Pataakha* (2018). Gulzar's lyrics for a song he wrote for Vishal Bhardwaj's *Rangoon* (2018), which is an adaptation of the classic C. Ramchandra number for *Patanga* (1949) is a study of his craft. The original song went, 'Mere piya gaye Rangoon/ Wahan se kiya telephoon...' Gulzar's adaptation:

My beloved has gone to England
Heralded by a band
Wonder where he will land
That Hitler does not get startled

And the song, 'Pavan udave batiyan.../ Kanha, bairan hui bansuri' (The breeze spreads the word/ Kanha, your flute has become my rival) from *Veer* (2010) shows folk music in a new garb. Rekha Bhardwaj has sung both songs with verve, yet listeners did not take to it like they did to those songs of Gulzar of that time that went viral as experiences of a new style of expression. 'Hamari atariya pe aaja re saawariya' from *Dedh Ishqiya* is enough proof of his immense popularity.

It is also necessary to mention two songs sung by Jagjit

Singh and Vishal Bhardwaj to complete this list of half-appreciated, undeservedly neglected songs. The songs are, 'Jaag ke kaati saari raina' (I spent the whole night sleepless) from *Leela* (2002) and 'Aur phir yoon hua' (And it so happened) from *Striker* (2010). Gulzar's lyrics are as well-crafted as always:

And it so happened
A dream woke me one night

And it so happened
The moon dimmed
And it so happened
The dream scattered
I kept burning in the radiance of the darkness
And lying there with my smouldering heart
Couldn't sleep for an age

Vishal Bhardwaj's music and rendition did complete justice to the poetry in the words, but the song faded without a trace. In the same way, only true fans of Jagjit Singh hold the *Leela* number dear. Both songs have been sung by their composers. Jagjit Singh had improvised on the original poem, 'Ulti ho gayi sab tadbeerein/ Kuch na daawa ne kaam kiya' (All plans went awry/ No medicine worked), written by Mir Taqi 'Mir' which had been set to music by Khayyam and sung by Begum Akhtar. He kept the same detailing as in Khayyam's original. Both compositions, by Khayyam and Jagjit Singh, are classical and have intimations of Raag Chayanat and Nand. Let us also take a look at Gulzar's poetry here:

The entire night was spent in waking
Dew filled the eyes yesterday
Love's fire would not be put out
The flowing river would not be stalled
Two eyes flowing to the sea
The entire night was spent in waking...

For such songs, that languish without love from listeners,

despite their near perfection in all aspects, this paraphrasing of the lines by John Keats are most fitting, 'Heard melodies are sweet, but those unheard are sweeter.'

94.

Things that lie beyond a direct link to his poetry, song-writing and film direction also form a part of Gulzar's genius. At one point in his creative journey, Gulzar created three serials, *Mirza Ghalib*, *Tehrir Munshi Premchand Ki* and *Kirdar* for Doordarshan. All three were eminently successful. This was at a time before India had access to 24-hour digital television channels.

Fans of his films might be unaware of the fact that he is a nonpareil translator too. He enjoys translating all those poems of poets from around the world whose works create an impression on him. Besides translating Rabindranath Tagore's poetry, he has also translated the poems of celebrated Marathi poet Kusumagraj and the autobiography of APJ Abdul Kalam, the former President of India. Titled *Parvaj*, the book also has an audio version. A few years ago, he translated and edited a collection of poetry by poets from India, Pakistan, Bangladesh, Sri Lanka and Nepal for Harper Collins, in a book titled *A Poem a Day* containing 365 poems, one for each day of the year. This was a task that kept him immersed for nine years. It is an indication of how he keeps his interests and ideas relevant through changing times.

One of his favourite assignments has been the curation of countless non-film music albums of some of the topmost singers and music directors, where he also speaks about the artiste and his work. The first in this series was on playback singer, Bhupinder, in 1979 titled *Yeh Jo Shayar Tha*. Though as early as in 1967, an album titled *Hemant Kumar Ke Geet* has been made along with the singer-musician. Actually speaking, this run of successful albums on artistes started in 1987 with *Dil Padosi Hai*, with songs composed by his dearest friend R. D. Burman and sung by Asha Bhosle. A dozen and more albums followed, of which some must be mentioned. Prime among them, his partnership with Bhupen Hazarika to make *Mai Aur Mera Saaya* (1992), *Marasim* with Jagjit Singh in 1999 and again *Koi Baat Chake* in 2006, *Sunset Point* with Chitra, Vishal Bhardwaj and Bhupinder in 2000, and *Visha* with Ghulam Ali in 2001. In 2007, a very evocative record titled *Amrita Pritam* was released, containing some of her poems. He also created, in partnership with Abida Parveen, the Sufi singer from Pakistan, *Abida Aur Kabir* in 2003, an album that continues to echo even today. Also notable is the 2011 release titled *Barse-Barse* with Vishal and Suresh Wadkar.

Gulzar celebrated his friendship with Bhupinder and his wife, Mithali with *Chand Parosa Hai* (2008) and *Surmai Raat* (2013). That he can deftly capture portraits of his friends at some beautiful moment of their lives is evident in these albums. This also holds true for his work with Vishal and Rekha Bhardwaj in the album *Ishqa-ishqa,* considered one of their best. The album *Gulzar in Conversation with Tagore*, created in 2016 along with Shantanu Moitra, with Shaan and Shreya Ghoshal singing the songs, was hugely appreciated. Shantanu Moitra also composed for an album of Gulzar's translations of Tagore's children's poems, in the same year. The album was titled, *Tapur Tupur.* To his credit also goes the contribution in making documentaries on two legendary classical exponents: the sarod maestro Ustad Amjad Ali Khan and the superlative singer Bhimsen Joshi. Both documentaries, made in 1990 and 1992 respectively, won the National Film Award for Best Documentary film in their respective years.

For the Commonwealth Games, Gulzar composed the lyrics, 'Dilli chale, chalna hai, chal-chal, Dilli chale', set to music by Shankar-Ehsaan-Loy. For Roop Kumar Rathod, he composed inspirational songs like 'Jan Gan Vande'.

He finds great pleasure in writing songs, poems and stories for children. The books he wrote for his daughter, Bosky, have been a favourite with other children too. *Samay Ka Khatola*, a book of songs, poems and stories written for his grandson, Samay, a few years ago, resonates with his desire to engage with children and share ideas with them. One can thus say this of Gulzar, that his bag of creativity has something to beguile the whole world, in different ways.

95.

Exactly in the way that classical singers are able to suspend time while they delve into their craft, often taking their listeners with them into a quiet, different world, poets too know how to connect two artists through the medium of words. A binding in which the stitches are invisible, yet two very individual minds, time periods and landscapes are bound together as one thought.

By doing so, a classical singer or poet can at some point create a hiatus from where his fans can appreciate the rare truths hidden in his art. Not just Kabir, who wove his words to help society move towards a moral consciousness, but even Gulzar has helped, through his pen, to make countless people aware of their moral strength. If, living in the present, we can find inspiration to colour our lives with the colours of an idea contained in a poem, then it is just as possible that an accomplished musician can create a new design of sound to fill life's empty spaces. Every age has played with the idea of keeping the body and soul as innocent as the day it came into being. Gulzar presents the idea thus:

Often have I seen you weaving the cloth
When some thread breaks or finishes
Tying it again

And adding some new bit to it
You continue weaving
Yet in your cloth
Not even a single twisted knot
Can anyone perceive...

96.

A traveller am I, friends
No home nor destination
I have to keep walking
Keep walking...

(*Parichay*)

Gulzar's poetic journey has started out on such a long trajectory that it is as if even the poet himself doesn't know which road his next step will lead him to, or in which city or town he will be spending the night. Wandering through such roads is a never-ending journey for Gulzar's poetry, and unknown even to himself, bonds are created with the nearby environments. And it often happens that, on this winding but fascinating journey, new connections and relationships are created.

As he navigates this meandering journey, he often has to look back and gather to himself the many aspects of emotions and relationships. Throughout, Gulzar has identified himself with Nature, giving it a living presence and keeping the relationship as alive and close as happens between human beings. Which is why there is an abundance of the personification of Nature in his poems. To him, a ray of sunshine is infused with human emotions, and a shred of a cloud can enter your room at any moment bearing human feelings. The entire universe, rivers and streams, seas and mountains, and plants and flowers add their presence to extend the scope of living things. 'Do Parinday' is a poem to be read in this context,

The sun which entered through a window
By that same window left
Leaving, it paused at the pane
Turned around and examined the room
Then it slowly went out
And settled on the lawn like a frightened bird

The sunlight which takes breath like a living thing comes alive here. We seldom see such a creative humanisation of a flowing river in Urdu or Hindi poetry. This poem is well known, but it is worthwhile to revisit a few of the opening lines

The river flows mumbling, grumbling to itself
Some small desires held within its heart
A lifetime has passed crawling over sand
To flow over the bridge is the ache in its heart!

Gulzar himself admits that before writing such a poem, it is necessary to understand the voice of the river. After understanding this voice, the picture of the river that he adds to the scene is similar to that of the lover who had once glimpsed the face of a girl in the water. Gulzar crafts these poems very carefully, creating new metaphors to create a link between Nature and humans.

'Come let us peel all the layers off the cloud and see.'

'I heard what the river said.'

'Separated from the mountains, when I return.'

'A treasure stood outside the door.'

'Blemished and dappled, the morning rose.'

'When the fingers of the sun comb through the branches.'

'The day you took off is still hanging in the lawn.'

'There was a peepul.'

'Nature seemed like an old woman.'

This is why everything that features in his poem floats away like clouds in the sky, dissolves like colour in water, and scatters like many-coloured leaves and flowers in all directions. Like a wise fakir giving instructions, he adds new perspectives to the poems. This small example of one such poem will make it clearer:

When the leaves start falling in autumn
What would they be telling the branches?
We are going after living out our season
You stay happy—
You have to tend to children through every season
And bid them goodbye.

('When the Leaves Start Falling in Autumn')

97.

When, for his serial *Mirza Ghalib*, Gulzar decided on Jagjit Singh to be the voice of the poet, there was consternation and the question, 'Mirza Ghalib and Jagjit Singh?' Even Salim Arif who was working on the serial as his assistant mentioned to me that he too had wondered about what had made Gulzar decide on Jagjit Singh. Gulzar was at peace with his decision that if anyone could do justice to the serious and meaningful verses of Ghalib, it could only be Jagjit Singh. Adding to this was the fact that he had planned the entire music of the serial as a complex project. According to the biography *Baat Niklegi To Phir* written by the respected journalist Sathya Saran, Gulzar said with regard to the music, 'I did not allow Jagjit to use any instrument that was not prevalent at that time, and a lot of arguments resulted between us because of this. Jagjit Singh would say, "Where is the freedom to create the music?" He was not prepared to abandon his electronic instruments.'

Besides this there was the fact that many masters had beautifully sung Ghalib's songs before Jagjit Singh. K. L. Saigal's name comes first in this list, whose rendition of

Ghalib still commands attention. After Saigal, Talat Mahmood and Suraiya had made Ghalib's songs popular in the film *Mirza Ghalib* (1954) by Minerva Movietone. Besides films, Mehdi Hasan, Begum Akhtar and Lata Mangeshkar had each sung Ghalib's songs and released LP records which were considered benchmarks. Naturally, Jagjit Singh must have worried over the fact that he would have to find a way to recreate Ghalib and make his music different from all that had been created before.

Gulzar's experiment of not using any modern instrument in the songs proved successful. The songs were recorded using only traditional instruments. Later, he had Singh overlay the sound of the sarod and other instruments recorded on a separate track onto the recitation, so that the ghazal would sound melodious. Thus an album was created in Jagjit's voice that created history in the 1990s. The music of the album still garners as much attention as the serial itself. Jagjit Singh and Mirza Ghalib have become almost synonymous, partly due to Gulzar's idea that only if Jagjit Singh imbibed the tones of Ghalib's voice, would the poetry ring true.

Of all the ghazals sung by him for the serial, 'Bajeech-ay-atphal hai duniya mere aage' (This world is to me as a child's playground), 'Har ek baat pe kehte ho tum ke tu kya hai' (At every turn you ask what are you worth) and 'Aah ko chahiye ek umr asar hone tak' (A sigh needs a lifetime to take effect) come to mind. Listening to them, Jagjit Singh's baritone and the tiny embellishments he brings into his rendition on completing the couplet strike one as quite amazing.

98.

The friendship between Gulzar and film director-musician Vishal Bhardwaj has created a niche for their music in Hindi films. Their partnership is similar to what Gulzar shared with R. D. Burman in the past. Vishal has given shape in his unique style to a huge cache of Gulzar's songs. Among the successful results of their collaboration are *Maachis, Chachi 420, Satya, Jahan Tum Le Chalo, Hu Tu Tu, Chupke Se, Maqbool, The Blue Umbrella, Omkara, No Smoking, Kaminey, Ishqiya, Striker, Saath Khoon Maaf, Matru Ke Bijli Ka Mandola, Ek Thi Daayan, Dedh Ishqiya, Haider, Drishyam, Talvar, Rangoon, Pataakha, Darlings* and *Kutte,* with almost every song in these films finding favour with listeners. Vishal Bhardwaj brings to his music shades of the music of eastern UP, which he has adapted seamlessly into Hindi cinema's needs. He has also gathered from Indian folk music, expressions and pure rural elements and given them a new flavour; something that few contemporary musicians have done. Vishal has also competently given Gulzar's words new expressions, thus placing the veteran writer in a contemporary setting and cementing his own place as a musician in the process.

Earlier chapters have, under different contexts, discussed the work of these two collaborators. So whether it is the Russian folk song, 'Darling', of *Saat Khoon Maaf* or the use of Kashmiri instruments in 'Jhelum' from *Haider*, Vishal has pushed the boundaries at every point to prove himself a new-age composer.

I am trying here to highlight the fact that the body of music created by these two minds proves that if a contemporary musician decides to experiment, he can create the same level of art that geniuses like Salil Chowdhury, Khayyam, R.D. Burman or Jaidev did. And not surprisingly, we can see a considerable body of Gulzar's work with these four composers too. And a bouquet of beautiful songs among them. I personally think that of all the wonderful work Gulzar and Vishal have produced together, the songs of *Maqbool, Omkara* and *Haider* are superlative. Of course, keeping in mind that their creation for *Maachis* has achieved cult status. I do not think that the songs, 'Chappa chappa charkha chale', 'Chod aaye hum' and 'Pani pani re' will ever be forgotten. Vishal Bhardwaj and Gulzar joined hands many years after the bond with R.D. Burman was snapped with the latter's death.

The music that Vishal and Gulzar created spans the emotional spectrum. If the songs of *Omkara*, *Maqbool* and *Haider* are serious and weighty, the numbers in *Chachi 420* and *Makdee* are light-hearted and comic or dance-inspiring numbers.

Being a poet himself, Vishal Bhardwaj is able to understand the nuances of the senior poet's writing and embellish it with tunes accordingly. Gulzar, on his part, keeping Vishal's experimental music in mind, writes lyrics that maintain the balance between words and sound.

Yet, the first meeting of two men was nothing short of filmi. As it happened, Gulzar was making a documentary on the sarod maestro, Amjad Ali Khan, and a music segment needed to be filmed. Khan-sahab wanted to have the music dubbed, for clarity's sake, and a studio had been booked in Delhi for the recording. Gulzar had arrived in Delhi for the same purpose. Coincidentally, Vishal Bhardwaj was at the same studio and he learnt that Gulzar was expected there late in the evening. He decided to hang around as long as was necessary so he could meet Gulzar. It was a Sunday, and as evening descended, and the nearby shopkeepers pulled down their shutters and left, Gulzar was unable to locate the studio. He called the studio from a nearby medical store, hoping for someone to come and guide him to the studio. The call was answered by Vishal Bhardwaj. Telling Gulzar to wait there, he reached the shop in five minutes. As the two wended their way to the studio, Vishal in all eagerness introduced himself as a musician and confessed that he had been hanging around the studio since morning, hoping to meet Gulzar. He added that he dreamt of composing music for films, and wanted to meet Gulzar in Bombay. Impressed with his passion, Gulzar told him to visit him whenever he next travelled to Bombay.

A few months after this meeting, the two met in Bombay with Suresh Wadkar's help. Of course, subsequently, a deep friendship would develop between the two men, and result in some superlative songs for Doordarshan and cinema. On being questioned about Vishal Bhardwaj, Gulzar says, 'Till date, he has maintained the liveliness, the enthusiasm, and it is infectious.'

If we consider just one film, *Omkara* as a measure of their collaborative success, we can see all aspects of what went into the creation of a unique album. So, whether it is 'Dham dham dhadam dhadaiya re', soaked in vir rasa and sung in the folksy Alha metre, or the folk element introduced into 'Bidi jalaide', or the hint of a *dadra* that touched the composition of 'Namak ishq ka' (The salt of love), or the developing of the emotional 'O saathi re' in a soft undertone, every song is unusual and unique. Indeed, after *Maachis*, the duo seem to have hit a new high with *Omkara*. Both films stand apart due to the variety and melody of their songs. Shreya Ghoshal and Vishal Bhardwaj have created magic in the song, 'O saathi re', to which Gulzar's poetry adds its own share:

O my companion, the day must not wane
Come, let us stop the day
Run behind the sun
Allow no shadow to fall
O my companion...

Rekha Bhardwaj, on her part, uses her effervescent voice to take the song, 'Namak ishq ka' to another plane. Rekha Bhardwaj adds flavour to a song much like Asha Bhosle, Mubarak Begum and Sudha Malhotra did in an earlier era.

Of course Vishal Bhardwaj knows fully well which voice will suit a particular song. Working like a team, Gulzar, Vishal Bhardwaj and Rekha Bhardwaj create the old world mood in songs like *Maqbool*'s, 'Rone do, jiya kare' (Let me cry, my heart wants to), *Ishqiya*'s 'Badi dheere jali raina' (The night smoulders slowly), 'Hamari atariya pe' from *Dedh Ishqiya* and 'Mere piya gaye England' from *Rangoon*, among others, including, 'Darling', the song sung along with Usha Uthup for *Saat Khoon Maaf*.

Some aspects of Vishal Bhardwaj's compositions for Gulzar's songs come through strikingly. These include the minimization of orchestra to give the words prominence, and the careful selection of the playback singer for each song. In this Vishal Bhardwaj holds a similarity to the approach followed by R. D. Burman, whose attempt was always to ensure these aspects were carefully looked into. When he would not understand a word, he would without hesitation ask Gulzar its meaning. In Vishal's case, Gulzar himself took on the responsibility of explaining the import of the words of his song to the composer and sharing the meaning in detail. He has said in interviews that before the composition of every song, he would engage in lengthy discussions. It would be only after discussions that Vishal would commence with the creation of the tune.

Choosing from a host of melodious and popular songs, we should revisit this song from *Pataakha*, composed by Vishal Bhardwaj, which belongs to where he hails from, and in which Gulzar and Vishal use language and folk music effectively and create a memorable song,

You have a lover, and I have one
Yours is a goon and mine a saint
I will cover mine with veils
Yours will roam on the streets, naked

99.

Gulzar has a special relationship with Salim Arif. A courteous relationship that is linked through theatre. Collecting many of Gulzar's stories, portraits, sketches, opinion pieces and poems, Salim Arif creates a beguiling presentation. This friendship revolves around the stage, and results in some serious theatre that combines literary and cinematic aspects. Memories, and a document that holds all life's joys and agonies. It is not without reason that the three famous theatre productions that Salim Arif has brought out of the collage of all his writings are a strong statement about society today. Of these works, *Kharashein*, *Lakeeren* and *Athanniyan*, Salim Arif has this to say:

> Gulzar-sahab is very careful with his words and ideas…he well understands his personal and creative responsibility. Which is why he speaks slowly, after some thought. He is very sparing with both his words and opinions; yet his poems and stories are spontaneously dramatic. Like he can get the owner of a brothel in *Mausam* to say that, 'My daughter is not for sale,' or have a cancer patient say, 'I cannot even say, may the years of my life be added to yours,' or yet again at the ending of *Ijazat* have the line, 'This time I am leaving with your permission.' Her saying this and then taking his blessings before leaving seems to me a very dramatic moment. And it is this dramatic quality that I have extracted from his poems and stories and collected to present to viewers of theatre.

Salim Arif has, after close scrutiny of Gulzar's work and the correct understanding if its meaning, presented some stories based on Gulzar's writings. In *Kharashein* he has used 'Hilsa', 'Ravi Paar' and 'Khouf' to highlight their social and political content. The fourth story in this play is a script by Gulzar of Samaresh Basu's 'Khuda Hafiz', which was titled 'Adaab' in the Bangla original. Similarly, in 'Lakeerein' he has chosen

'LOC,' 'Over' and 'Kuldeep Nayyar and Pir Sahab' as they are linked by theme and thought. In *Athanniyan* he has included the stories 'Jhadi', 'Atthani' and 'Baas' along with a few poems.

While adapting the stories to create a theatrical project, Salim Arif was secure in the idea that if separate stories on a political or social theme could be presented together, then Gulzar-sahab's political statement would become clear to viewers. When this was combined with his poems as a collage and presented, it became obvious that Gulzar was indeed a contemporary poet whose poems with political comment hit home. But why, one wonders, would a poet who dwells in romance and explores delicate relationships delve into political comment? Like Pablo Neruda and Bertolt Brecht, he holds in his mind political dreams that have the power to change society and the world. And it is this attempt to change the state of things that shines through, 'Koshish', 'Lakeerein' and 'Atthaniyan'.

Even before he started on these projects for theatre, Salim Arif had collaborated with Gulzar on his films. He had worked as an assistant director on *Maachis* and *Hu TuTu*. In fact, his first association began when he worked for Gulzar's *Mirza Ghalib* for Doordarshan in 1987. Working with Gulzar, Salim Arif tried to understand the thoughts of the poet who through literature learned to comment on the hardships unleashed by politics. Salim Arif was aware that the poems of Raghuvir Sahai and Bhawani Prasad Mishra had been adapted for the stage. But it was insufficient from the point of view of being a commentary on political issues. By the time he got Gulzar's approval to adapt his poems, he had a clear idea how to do so, to make them suited for theatre. He believes that 'Kharosh' was the first project through which poetry was effectively communicated. The positive response he received for it made clear to him the true role of politically themed poetry.

Gulzar, on his part, has, besides converting a considerable number of stories and plays, also written some original scripts for him. Salim Arif has successfully staged the nine plays gifted to him by Gulzar. Salim Arif says, '*Sunte Ho* was the name of the stage adaptation of "Streer Patra" which was a story by Rabindranath Tagore. He has also added the present day story, "Mard" as a second part, to show that things have not changed much since Tagore's days. The theme that women alone are answerable; sometimes to the husband, sometimes to the brother, and sometimes to the son highlight the many faces of men who shackle a woman down. Yet another significant play that Gulzar wrote is titled, "Pansa". This was a short adaptation of Pavan Verma's long, sonnet-styled poem, "Yudhisthira and Draupadi". Gulzar wrote this in blank verse and edited it and I presented it on stage. I believe that this comes second only to Dr Dharamveer Bharti's *Andha Yug*, in plays that deal with themes from the *Mahabharat*.'

Gulzar has also adapted three stories as plays for children, for Salim Arif to present on stage. Among them is *Agar Aur Magar*, an adaptation of Brecht's play for children titled, *He Who Says Yes, He Who Says No*. Brecht's play questions the validity of traditions. A song in the play written by Gulzar is interesting. The words of it go, 'Agar yoon hai, magar kyoon hai' (If it is so, why is it so). Similarly, there is *Nuclear Sher*, a modern adaptation of the *Panchatantra*. Besides which he has written a long poetic version of *Pinocchio* under the same name, and a play based on Satyajit Ray's grandfather, Upendranath Ray's story 'Goopi Gyne Bagha Byne' which he titled, 'Gugly Jhanak Jhayen'. Salim Arif shares the fact that Gulzar calls him a 'jebkatra', a pickpocket, who takes away things from his pocket for his own use. In reality Salim Arif takes only those poems, stories and diary entries to embellish his plays, which in fact are given to him by Gulzar himself.

Watching the partnership that leads them to walk together down the long road of creativity, makes the link between literature and theatre very clear. Anyone who has watched these plays and understood the issues and the meanings of the lines will realise that Gulzar has mindfully extended himself into this sphere.

100.

I wandered down many paths while writing this biography. I used to think I understood him completely, but I was wrong. As I delved into his work, new windows kept opening. If I worked on his poems, the film songs would slide away. If I concentrated on the stories, the screenplays would seem to range up and beckon me to give them my attention. And encountering his name in film after film as dialogue writer was the last straw added to my impending madness. Sometimes, the songs, dialogues and screenplay would all be his…and he would have directed the film too! Then I would find a film where he had written only one song! And it needed analysing! Often I felt that his career is a well into which, should you lower a brass vessel tied to a rope, you would never hear the sound of it touching the water.

Much like the story of Hatimtai, I felt that each time I tried to find an answer to a question, a series of new questions would open up to befuddle me. Watching his films late into the night, I felt like a student struggling to complete the syllabus so he could pass the exams. Then there was the added injustice of having to cope with Urdu that was woven into the Devnagri in his writings. To say it succinctly, Gulzar is like the light that makes that which is hidden in the darkness glow.

Understanding his magic with words, his temperament, is like a child trying to catch a butterfly. If I have indeed managed to capture a few butterflies, then the journey must have taken me through garden paths. Only I know of the countless nights through which the scent of these flowers kept me awake. These sleepless nights spent tracing the life of Gulzar are now bestowed on his countless admirers.

गुलज़ार निर्देशित फ़िल्में...

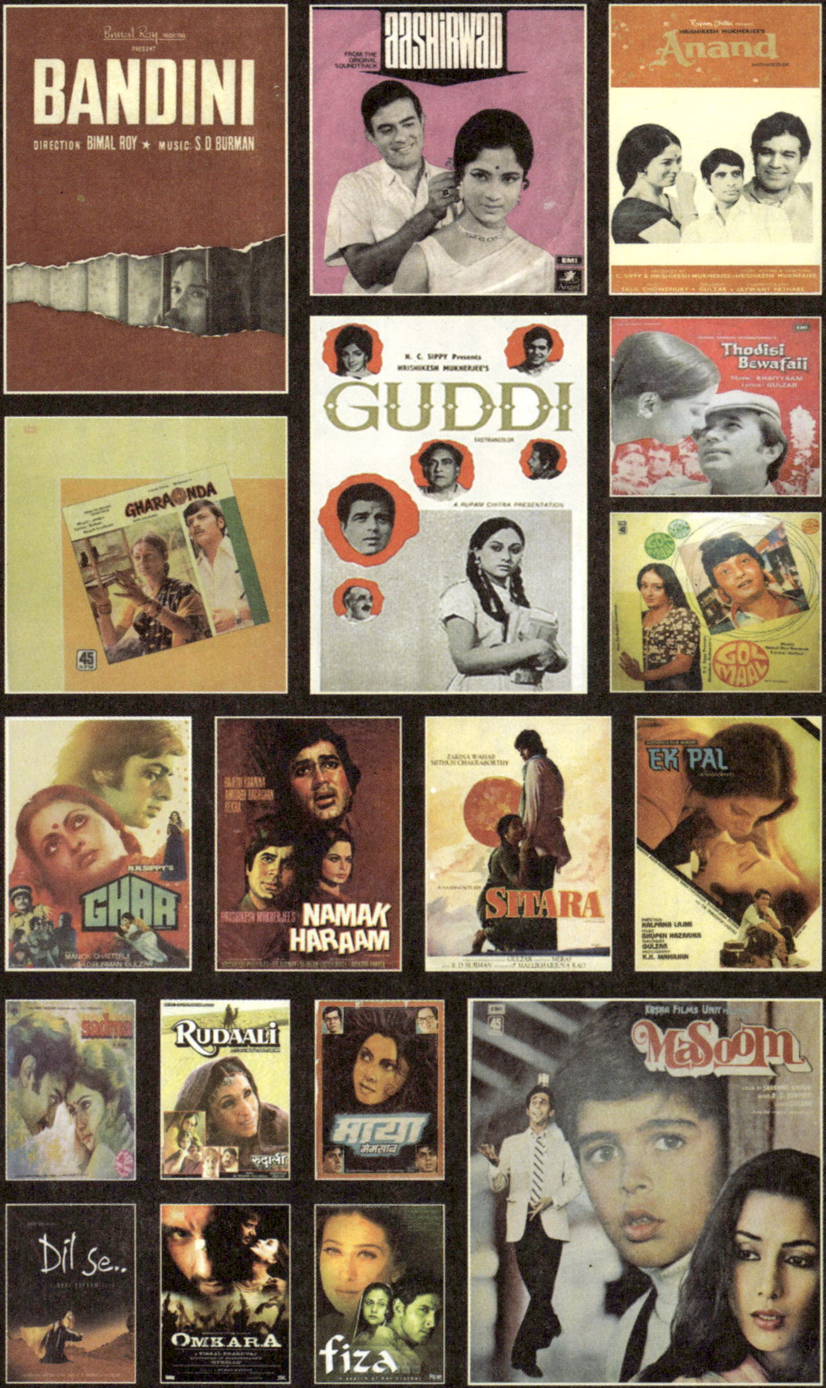

संवाद, गीतों और पटकथाओं के कुछ यादगार मुकाम...

Gulzar Sa'ab

Thoda sa Baadal Thoda sa Paanee...

A Dialogue with Gulzar

Yatindra Mishra: What memories of your childhood do you still carry that can take you back into the past?

Gulzar: Here I cannot name any one person. But I can name a country, which is Hindustan, and which I hold very dear. I have been brought up here, and in my upbringing there was a smaller portion of religion as compared to culture. I came from the Punjab and grew up in Old Delhi. So you can understand, I hailed from the place from where the Pir, Murshids, Sai and the dervishes who would sing Sufi poems hailed. I have listened to their compositions, it's like my legacy. But I grew up speaking the language of Old Delhi, though old Delhi has now become Punjab. Our house was just outside Roshanara Bagh. Our address used to be Roshanara Bagh, Sabzi Mandi, Delhi. It was opposite the clock tower. There was a room in the shop too, where I would often sleep. I would get up and come for my bath from there.

We used to call them 'rais', those contractors who would take up contracts for the fruit gardens. We would play gilli-danda with the sons of the rais in Roshanara Bagh, throw stones and bring down the jamuns and spoil our shirt pockets with their stains. We would get thoroughly scolded at home, but those days remain in memory. When the women who worked at the Birla Mill would go in a group, carrying tiffin carriers on their heads, singing in the Rohtak and Karnali dialects as they went, we would understand that the shift had changed at the Birla Mill. The workers would sing songs, in the form of questions and answers; I still remember one of those songs.

It went something like this, 'Aree choti sali kahvann lagi ek raat aur datt ja' (My younger sis-in-law started to say, stay back one more night'). The songs in this dialect were pleasing. My house was in this Hindustan, which I still remember, and is very close to my heart.

Yatindra Mishra: You have started with a very beautiful reference. I don't remember if any contemporary from that time has ever remembered his past like this, with references to dialects changing with changing shifts and times.

Gulzar: Yes, neither have I read any reference to this anywhere. I am surprised why no one has described or mentioned life at that time in these places, where such things were prevalent. I remember very well in my childhood that on Saturday nights, Delhi's Connaught Place would be shut to Indians. Where there is a market now, there used to be a maidan, and in the middle of it there was a big platform on which a band would play. British couples would dance to the tunes played by the band; that was 'Saturday Night'. Whosoever got a permit could stand in the verandahs and watch the dancers. One needed permission even to watch the dancing. At that time, Khushwant Singh's father, Shobha Singh, was well respected and he was in charge of the entire area. I remember my father would get a permit from Shobha Singh. Then my father would take me and my younger brother to listen to the Saturday night music.

Yatindra Mishra: You mentioned the verandahs of Connaught Place. There's a poem by you titled, 'Baramde'. In that, there are verandahs surrounding the courts. Could it be that the memory of watching the dancing from the verandahs, or some such childhood memory has filtered into that poem, though the poem has no reference to those romantic evenings.

Gulzar: Those are the verandas of the present-day courts, where justice does a continuous merry-go-round of the courts. There is war, fighting and argument everywhere. In the courts of today, the verandas surround justice, in which justice itself shuttles silently from one veranda to another searching for itself. It goes something like this:

The poor oppressed caught in their teeth
They surround, these kho-kho playing verandas
Verandas, running all around the courts, verandas!'

Yatindra Mishra: In recollecting your childhood, the reference you made to the Hindustaniyat of yore, does it still come to mind?

Gulzar: Of course! The fragrance of Hindustaniyat holds me in its grasp even today.

Yatindra Mishra: Do the songs and languages that link India and Pakistan still trouble you, or do you see them as a link to your birthplace?

Gulzar: They do not haunt me, but it does hurt. It hurts because it is present somewhere. If it was not present then possibly it would never bother me. I slip into the past and view them. This nostalgia and the reason for revisiting the past are seen clearly in my poems. It is like a clear truth seen in most of my ghazals too. There are so many wounds of my childhood on my subconscious mind that I am scared to even touch them. That's how it is, and I repeat my childhood in my writing and relive it.

Yatindra Mishra: In all this, is there something that still remains incomplete, which torments you and disrupts your peace of mind?

Gulzar: Let's put this somewhat differently. If I try to search for that one person, then the person my mind captures is my father. I spoke to you about Connaught Place; it came to mind because of my father. If I think of Dina, then he was leaving us at Dina station and taking a train. I was standing there and he was in the train. He was leaving the station and going further and further from me. Then he sent for me. When we were in Paharganj, Delhi, he would braid my hair, as my hair was very long then. My thoughts are about documenting my father's existence. I can say it thus too, that my father is very intensely present in my memories. To come from there in 1947 and accept the conditions here despite his own bedraggled state. To see violence upon violence. To see bloodshed. The shrieks and wailing of those being brought in by the truckloads, and hear the same sounds from those leaving from here in trucks. I have seen all this. You will be happy to know that despite all this, there has been no fundamentalist in our family. The reason rests with my father; his stature was such that at no point through that time did he give us any wrong advice, despite the fact that our birth place was lost to us. Though he would sigh deeply and say in Punjabi, 'Qayamat has arrived, it will pass.' He understood everything. He would take a deep breath and let out a long sigh. I still have trouble understanding that long sigh of my father.

Yatindra Mishra: I do not know why the song 'Chhod aaye hum woh galiyan' (We've left behind our lanes and bylanes) from *Maachis* was repeatedly coming to my mind when you were remembering those times. In many poems too the same emotions arise when you reminisce about your childhood, Dina and the Partition. A poem, 'Memory' starts like this:

We were all running away
As refugees
Mother had worn all the jewels she owned
Bundled them up...

And the ending of the poem goes like this:

But often in the silence of the borders I have seen
Often in the desert I have seen
A memory that still dances
And a top that even now is spinning...

The pain that seeps into songs and poems is justified. Do we need to view these writings only in the light of your childhood travails? Or do they have any other meaning?

Gulzar: Yes, that does happen. You spoke of 'Chhod aaye hum woh galiyan' then that comes in the film *Maachis* in another context. There he is a lover, and he sings with his friends, personifying his town as his beloved. In a way this song also tells us the story of the characters. Mostly, the stories of the characters' suffering become songs.

Today the characters have changed, times have changed. Many of the old memories have been buried deep within. I have also moved away from the old prejudices, and the most significant thing is that after a long time has passed, we have found release from some aspects of many of those issues. Today, I view myself as a responsible citizen, far removed from my childhood. And in the form of a responsible and alert poet.

Yatindra Mishra: What is your reading of the political reason for the Partition?

Gulzar: With the division and the creation of two countries, a strange ethos is created, where trust and the ability to be carefree vanish. Faiz-sahab [Faiz Ahmed Faiz] speaks for all poets when he says:

This stained and dirty light

This dawn bitten by the night
This is not the dawn
We were waiting for...

Yatindra Mishra: The memories of your youth are overshadowed by the Partition. Despite this, you have never made a film with Partition as the theme.

Gulzar: This is a debt I carry. My very first film was based on the Partition, and Hemant-da [singer, music director Hemant Kumar] was to produce it. I had even completed the auditions of my actors. All preparations were complete, and the story was ready. This story was that of a truck-driver who, during Partition, drops some refugees near the border and returns. The film revolves around the small stories pertaining to the various characters. Like who, and in what condition had to leave his home behind; who has come from across the border and who accompanied him, and who had he left behind. In this way I had created the story line. It was my story which I wanted to make into a very emotion-laden film. But circumstances at that time so transpired that the film could not be made, and the film was stalled while it was still at the level of the script.

Years later, when I watched Govind Nihalani's long serial *Tamas*, which painted a very real picture of the Partition, I folded the screenplay of my Partition film and stowed it away in my cupboard forever. I even told Govind-ji, 'This fire smouldered in me; for years I had a screenplay in my mind which I hoped to make as a film on the Partition someday. This fire has been extinguished after watching your *Tamas*.'

Yatindra Mishra: Amongst all your memories, which one memory about Old Delhi still rises to the surface?

Gulzar: Old Delhi existed even when I was young. Today, it is much bigger than it was then, and is yet still called Old Delhi. Earlier Sabzi Mandi used to be part of it, now that vegetable market has been shifted elsewhere. In our letters we used to write, simply, 'Roshanara Bagh, Sabzi Mandi, Delhi.' If someone wanted to add more detail they might add, 'Opposite the clock tower,' because that was the main square. The rest were side lanes and small squares. From here, one road would lead to Roshanara Bagh, one towards Jawahar Nagar.

Jawahar Nagar is where I would go to learn cycling. Everyone would go to the empty maidans there to learn how to ride bicycles. It was also ideal for playing gilli-danda, being an open space. Now that area has become a part of Delhi University. The Hindu College, which was earlier in the Kashmiri Gate area, has also been shifted here. After Matriculation, I joined St. Stephen's College.

Yatindra Mishra: When did you study at the United Christian School?

Gulzar: From the fifth to Matriculation. I had studied through primary at the M. B. Medial School. I would say with great pride, M. B. Medial School. When I grew up, I realised it was the Municipal Board school near Roshanara Bagh.

Yatindra Mishra: Is the school still there?

Gulzar: Yes, it is. In the same place. But its name has been changed to some vidyalaya. I cannot remember the exact name. But it is a girls-only school now.

Yatindra Mishra: May I ask why your studies were interrupted and why you could not complete your B.A.?

Gulzar: It's a long story. When we came away to Delhi after Partition, our house had become a small refugee camp of sorts. Father was not able to afford it, yet he would catch hold of any stranger in the refugee camp if he was from our village. And thus a new member would be added to our home. So you can understand that our house was overflowing. It became impossible to live there, which my father well understood. He decided then that I should go to Bombay where Jasmer, my elder brother, lived.

Yatindra Mishra: You have spoken very little about your

mother. If you can refresh your feelings about her, your readers will be happy.

Gulzar: I have no image of my mother in my memory because I was only a few months old when she passed away. She is only a bubble, a vacuum. It is true that I wrote a poem about my mother, and said in it, 'If I should recognise you, how can I recognise you?' The only solution is that I search for her in my face, she will be somewhere in it.

Yatindra Mishra: You have shared your pain by remembering your mother. Your story, in this context, is very similar to Maqbool Fida Husain's. He too never saw his mother. Whenever he painted his mother's face, he left it empty because he did not know what his mother looked like.

Gulzar: What can I say about Husain-sahab? I can understand how many questions must lurk behind his painting a blank face. Though if I had been in his place, I would have abandoned the question of how my mother might have looked and painted whom I had seen, meaning, my father's face and painted the memory of my father instead.

Yatindra Mishra: What do you remember of your grandfather's home?

Gulzar: I do not remember my grandmother's name, but my grandfather's name was Bhag Singh. I remember faintly that my maternal grandfather never visited us. If we met on the road, or saw him somewhere, well, that's how we met. My grandmother too we would meet if only she came somewhere nearby to visit some relatives. Whenever my maternal grandfather came, he would gift me one anna. My grandmother would give two annas on meeting me. The one-anna coin was round, the two-anna coin, square. My step-mother Vidyavati would often tease me,

Punni's grandfather came, gave Punni a single anna
Punni's grandmother came, gave Punni two annas

Yatindra Mishra: Did you address your father as abbu?

Gulzar: No! In the house I would call him Pappa-ji. Later, when I became a writer and correspondence began, abbu somehow happened. I have already mentioned that we spoke in Hindi and Punjabi as well as Urdu at home. We had all grown up absorbing the Muslim way of manners and culture, as I had explained earlier. We grew up with this language. Phrases like 'Subhan Allah' and 'Masha Allah' came easily to us, we used the terms very naturally. Which is why when I referred to him in my writings, it was always as 'abbu'.

Yatindra Mishra: What was your grandmother's name? Do you have any memories of her?

Gulzar: They called her Gurudai or perhaps Guruditti; meaning, a gift from Wahe Guru. In my memory she is a very weak, old woman. Abbu took care of her and looked after her. People of the same age as him would say to him, 'You are so very fortunate, that you are getting a chance to perform seva.' And truly, my father did a lot for her. Her image is surely somewhere in my mind.

Yatindra Mishra: It's very necessary for me to know all this, Gulzar-sahab! Mainly because I want to link all this to your creative journey, in which you have been giving us glimpses of yourself in your films, screenplays, poems and all the other aspects of your creativity.

Gulzar: When I look back I see a connection...That book of Tagore's, *The Gardener*, which I got when I needed it most. After that I kept reading Saratchandra's books. I feel that in some way, my past is attached to stories from Bengal. As you can see, you find all the characters in Saratchandra's stories. The dadi, her relatives, the nani, step-brothers and sisters, all kinds of relatives present in a joint family are found here. So, countless characters in their different shades can be found in Saratchandra. Though you also find a variety of characters in Premchand too. But my past is linked to Bengal's literary story tradition.

Yatindra Mishra: You said it! Bangla literature has traditionally been able to explore and delineate human tensions and contradictions.

Gulzar: Yes, that exists in Bengali literature. This might be one of the reasons I am so close to Bengali literature. Even in Bangla, there are different shades. We see more melodramatic scenes in Saratchandra while Bibhutibhushan Bandhopadhyay's stories do not have such high dramatic moments in them. They reveal everything slowly and simply before laying bare the entire story. In *Pather Panchali* you will see the entire spectrum of his craft of story-telling.

Yatindra Mishra: After listening to all this, I am beginning to somewhat understand your poem, 'Putla', better. Please share the poem.

Gulzar: Sure! It is my past which I need to keep fresh in my memories. Then there is a creative purpose to it too; which you transfer into your story or poem and distance yourself from.

An unformed thing
Made of mud, baked in the oven
The face of a statue
Kept there, in the drawing room
The eyes would catch sight of it, mid-conversation
Had to be slid, to be moved from one place to another
Tried keeping it on top or below while cleaning
Behind the door, in front of it
No place seemed to be right.

It wouldn't even break, that it could be thrown away
For years, after placing it here, there, left and right
When placed outside the house
It ran away!

Often they ask me at the crossroads
Made of mud cooked in the oven
A visage...was that you?'

Yatindra Mishra: Did you ever get a chance to meet Mahatma Gandhi?

Gulzar: Yes! I was lucky enough to see him from close quarters when I was young. Gandhiji had come to the Sis Ganj gurudwara in Chandni Chowk and even delivered a speech there. I remember clearly that I could see him and hear him from up close. I remember the day, it was Gurpurab. Tensions had been rising between Sikhs and Muslims in Delhi, and Gandhi had fasted to calm things down. It was in the same gurudwara that he broke his fast unto death.

Yatindra Mishra: You developed a love of reading in childhood. Do you have anything that connects your reading with social or family memories?

Gulzar: In those days, in my childhood, the only newspapers were *Pratap*, *Jang*, *Veer Bharat* and *Milap*. The image of the Second World War is still fresh in memory. When we were in school, we would see the elders reading. They would read in the sunlight or sit outside in groups. They would discuss politics, contemplate the doings of the British and discuss the headlines about the War.

Yatindra Mishra: You belong to Punjab and your native language is Punjabi. Yet you write and speak Urdu and your Hindi is as good as those who belong to the Hindi-speaking belt. How did this come about?

Gulzar: Arey bhai! I learnt Urdu in school from a maulvi sahab, Mujibur Rehman-sahab. I don't know where he was from, but he taught Urdu with great dedication. That is useful to me even today.

Yatindra Mishra: When you were a part of the PWA group meetings, would you also participate in other literary events?

Gulzar: For sure! I would definitely attend PWA meetings. We would also go to the Punjabi Sahitya Sabha. The three of us, meaning, Lajpat Rai who is a writer and wrote in *Midday* and was studying with me, and Sagar Sarhadi. Just the three of us would go. The PWA meetings were held on Saturdays, and the Punjabi Sahitya Sabha meetings on Sundays. After that we would go to a Marxism class in Matunga, which was held in a tent-like pandal. There was a party called the Revolutionary Socialist Party that organised the classes. Sheila Madhok would take our class on Marxism. The three of us were less interested in Marx and more in her teaching. She was very intelligent and beautiful, which is why we were very interested in attending that class.

Yatindra Mishra: Did you ever try to make this into a story as part of a film?

Gulzar: It is not necessary to use every little thing in cinema. Often things from our youth or childhood enter involuntarily into cinema, or into literature. The scenes of jalebi being made, the madaari who comes with dancing bears in *Kitaab* have all been part of my experiences. After all, life is the source of inspiration.

Yatindra Mishra: In what way do you remember Bimal Roy?

Gulzar: I remember Bimal Roy in many ways. When he took me out of the motor garage and made me his assistant, he seemed to be like a father who was worried about my future. The motor garage was not the right place for me. No one in my family had thought thus about me. So he had a definite influence on me. He was the complete director.

It's not that there were only a handful of people making meaningful cinema in his time. Guru Dutt, Amiya Chakravarty, Zia Sarhadi, Kishore Sahu and Asit Sen were making good films in their respective styles, films that had a realistic approach. However, with films like *Do Bigha Zameen*, *Bandini*, *Sujata*, *Kabuliwala* and *Parakh*, Bimal Roy was standing at a point where realism and imagination were held in a fine balance. It was a part of everything. From choosing the story to recording the songs. Bimal-da was a perfectionist. He draped himself in cinema.

Yatindra Mishra: Has there been any other influential person in your life besides Bimal Roy?

Gulzar: After Bimal Roy's death, producer and singer Hemant Kumar was the one who supported all of us. He knew Bimal Roy's unit was in danger of getting scattered, that everyone needed some work or the other. He made a magnificent gesture. He entrusted Bimal Roy's personal secretary, Mukul Dutt, with the task of writing songs for Bengali films. In the same way, keeping in mind each one's talent and need, he got each person employed somehow. Around the same time, he introduced me to Hrishikesh Mukherjee, who was then working on *Aashirwad*. Hrishikesh Mukherjee had left Bimal Roy while I was still there, and started working independently.

I remember till today that it was because of Hemant Kumar's introduction that Hrishikesh Mukherjee entrusted me with writing the songs and the screenplay of his film. And later, he asked me to write the script of *Anand*. In the same way, Hrishi-da introduced me to the producer of *Anand*, N. C. Sippy, who gave me a break in 1971 by producing my first film.

Yatindra Mishra: The sensitivity that Hema Malini shows in *Khushboo*, was it a vital part of the screenplay?

Gulzar: The sensitivity in Hema's character in *Khushboo* is amazing. The sense of pride that the character has in the film is because of Saratchandra. Saratchandra brings in emotion where necessary. But in the novel, the emotion is quite loud. One finds a unique kind of melodrama in his stories and novels. But there was something amazing about him. Look through his writings and the films made on them and you will find that special quality in his female characters. You can call this self-confidence, or pride or to an extent, ego...You will find that ego in all the main female characters in his work. You will see it in Paro and in Chandramukhi. In *Khushboo*, the sense of pride in Hema Malini comes in automatically, because it's in her personality.

Yatindra Mishra: Do you not feel that you somehow try to look at women's self-respect through the prism of Saratchandra's female characters? Using the medium of literature to get a grasp on this character?

Gulzar: I believe this is correct in connection with *Khushboo*. When you understand a temperament quality, and agree with what it stands for, it becomes your responsibility to internalise it before endowing your character with it. That is why in most films one looks at the women characters through one's own ego and creates their persona from a new perspective.

On a different note, I would also choose *Ijazat* as an example. The character of Rekha in it is, I feel, a paragon of calm, dignity and grace. A quietude and a seriousness laced with a different kind of dignity. Watch *Ijazat* and see the calm and patience that Rekha's character shows, despite having loved and lost, and you will be reminded of Saratchandra's female characters.

Yatindra Mishra: With regard to *Khushboo*, what would you say is new in the story and screenplay that brings in a new dimension to this discussion?

Gulzar: I do not look at this film as different from Saratchandra-ji's. If you read his story, 'Pandit Mahoshay', you will find it has a very involved plot. But in cinema you have to have a feasible story, even if it is only a part of the whole. I felt the first three chapters of 'Pandit Mahoshay' very useful, and added them separately to the story of *Khushboo*. I thought the most beautiful element was the relationship between Kusum, the heroine, and her beloved, Brindavan, the hero. I was fascinated by the fact that the relationship between them was very different from that in traditional stories. This novel of Saratchandra is very long and complicated. So I only took up that section of the story that focuses on their relationship and made it the theme of my film. I found Kusum's nature and her self-respect, and her refusal to accept defeat that keeps her apart from her beloved and yet linked to him very interesting. The theme of *Khushboo* revolved around this aspect. In the film, a very unusual relationship develops between the hero and heroine about their rights. The hero's son whom Kusum considers her son, is also a part of the relationship. There is no calculation, no keeping account. The heroine knows the boy is the mistress' son yet she loves him as her own.

Yatindra Mishra: With relation to commercial cinema, what was the issue that you felt in your heart that I must surely make a film on this, even if you only thought about it but did not find the time to make it, or it just floated away?

Gulzar: If I look into the prism of my work, then *Devdas* was a film that I had started work on but it could not be made. This novel by Saratchandra always fascinated me and I felt I should picturise it my way. Though I was well aware that before me, Saigal-sahab and Dilip Kumar had starred in two big productions. K. L. Saigal was a huge legend and, in the same way, in his time Dilip Kumar-sahab too. This is what would bother me in cinematic terms, that *Devdas* was no legend, then why were these giant actors cast for the role. A marvellous part of the *Devdas* novel is that Saratchandra-ji made the character of Devdas an ordinary man but his presence in the novel comes across like a legend. If you have read the story you will agree that in comparison with Devdas, the two women are more important and laudable.

Also an important fact is that when Devdas falls in love, he is an adolescent. He is still young when he returns to the village and realises his love for Paro. His naïveté and impetuousness are his character's most impressive aspects, through which his character's innocence sparkles. Sarat-babu has done a superlative job. I was keen to capture this, which is why I considered making *Devdas*.

Yatindra Mishra: Is this the reason why you wished to cast

Dharmendra in the role to show the purity and honesty present in Devdas' character?

Gulzar: That's correct. Dharmendra is an adolescent even today. Even today there is an honesty in the man, which can be seen in his entire personality. A pure gentleman by nature. Look at him, and you still see romance in him. You can read what he is saying in his eyes. He is still a romantic man.

Yatindra Mishra: Behind your idea of making *Devdas*, I can see the thought of recreating Paro and Chandramukhi. How do you see it?

Gulzar: Paro is a girl who becomes mature in a single night when she is married off to a big landlord who is not only of her father's age, but has two grown-up sons and daughters. She is a carefree girl as long as she is in love with Devdas. Immediately after her marriage, as the responsibilities of her new home press upon her, her entire childhood, youthful mind and love all get left behind and she suddenly seems to be a mature woman. On the other side is Chandramukhi, who is a woman. She sits at the kotha, but when she falls in love with Devdas, she spontaneously abandons the character of a woman and enters a state of girlhood. What a fantastic contrast the writer has created. The transformation of a girl into a woman, and a woman becoming a girl as she yearns for love.

This, in my opinion, is the most beautiful aspect of the novel, which I believe no film director has focussed on while making *Devdas*. With due humility I will say that both Bimal Roy and P. C. Barua made their films from Devdas' perspective.

Yatindra Mishra: What was the reasoning behind choosing Hema Malini for Paro's role, when it would have been more prudent to cast her as Chandramukhi, as she is a dancer?

Gulzar: When I started somewhat understanding the novel, I realised that the characterisation in the novel was somewhat like what I have just explained to you. Which is why I chose Sharmila Tagore for the role of Chandramukhi. As a filmmaker I felt that when Sharmila Tagore, playing the role of Chandramukhi, would sit at the kotha and sing, she would be seen as a woman who, after she falls in love with Devdas, transforms into the personality of a girl. And similarly, Hema-ji's simple and intelligent personality would, in some way, match Paro's dignified life who transforms after marriage into a responsible woman. That is why I planned the casting of *Devdas* in this manner.

Yatindra Mishra: Had the songs of this film also been recorded?

Gulzar: Yes, two songs were recorded. One was the very beautiful 'Kuhu kuhu bole koyaliya' (The koel coos) and the other, 'Sehma-sehma daraa sa rehta hai/ Jane kyon ji bhara sa rehta hai' (Cowering and afraid/ Why is the heart so full) which was a sad song in Bhupinder's voice.

Yatindra Mishra: Who sang 'Kuhu kuhu koyaliya'?

Gulzar: Who else would sing it but Lata-ji?

Yatindra Mishra: When we look at the graph of your song-writing for films, there is no deviation. If we look at your journey over the past sixty years, the songs are not forcibly or artificially created, but are presented in all naturalness. The harmonious quality you have of bringing in poetry into your songs has been present like a continuous stream. How do you look at this, when you listen to these songs sometimes?

Gulzar: Rather, I often say it like this: look how the times keep changing. One possibility is that I am changing and time remains the same. Can it be so? The other is that all around me times are changing, and with it, expressions, language, films too are changing. The characters in the story have started changing, so some transformation will happen in my communication too. But it is not possible that poetry disappears from it. When your expressions change—with films, with characters, with stories and with your own circumstances—but that the thought itself changes in this, that is not possible. You have to look at the destination. Your existence, the place you are at, and what it is that you are doing. Whatever you are doing today, are you doing it of your free will, that needs to be looked at.

Yatindra Mishra: What you are saying is reasonable, and the condition of writing freely is a very important condition for songs to be written for the film industry...But this industry views everything from a commercial angle. If we evaluate the past two decades of the new century, this reality comes to the fore. Due to this, the songs for films too are being conceived differently. As an example, producers do not feel the need for a composer to create a beautiful composition; instead, they try to ascertain that the tune that is being made can be adapted as a short tune that can be sold to mobile phone companies.

Gulzar: True, but the question here is, for whose survival is this being done? Is it for the survival of art, or is there some other reason? Where there is the question of me as a lyricist, I am vigilant: if the thread slips out of the grasp, then why did it slip out? I try to hold on to it, and every single word or note which slips away, I try sincerely to catch it. That is the reason I have made my films sincerely and on my own terms.

Yatindra Mishra: Do you think that every artiste works on his medium with such serious thought? Does he not lust after success, prestige and getting more and more work? In today's mad race is competition still honest, clean and simple?

Gulzar: It is very necessary to face oneself, because every time one is answerable to oneself. The question of others and how you will compete with them arises later. If there is filth outside, what stops us from keeping the inside clean and tidy? You or me, or anybody, cannot write with an eye on the market. Nor should we keep the critics in mind when we write.

 Yatindra Mishra: Lata Mangeshkar and Asha Bhosle have

sung some amazing numbers in those of your films where R.D. Burman has composed the music. These songs became very successful and are even today counted among Hindi cinema's immortal songs. A question rises in my mind that if the writer is the same, if the composer is the same, why does the appeal of the full composition change in the voices of the different playback singers. What I mean is, listen to, 'Do nainon me aansoo bhare hai' (Tears fill the eyes) from *Khushboo* in Lata-ji's voice and at the same time, listen to Asha-ji singing 'Bechara dil kya kare' (What will the poor heart do)—the songs appeal to the emotions at different levels.

I'm trying to understand if the songs sung by these two singers are interchanged, then what effect would Pancham create? Or what effect would it have on your poetry. Meaning, if Lata-ji sang 'Mera kuch saaman' and 'Yeh saaye hai, yeh duniya hai' and Asha-ji sang, 'Abhke na saawan barse' and 'Seeli hawa choo gayi'.

Gulzar: There's another side to this question too, that before choosing if we can decide who could sing it the best. Or to turn the question on its head and ask, if in my films, instead of Pancham, Madan Mohan-ji or Khayyam-sahab had scored the music, what might have happened then? You will get into trouble here, because the moment you think of these names, the composition changes completely and the style of singing too takes a new route.

Yatindra Mishra: Do instances arise in playback singing in films where the singing is more than that is demanded by the film or it lags behind the demand?

Gulzar: Lata-ji sang the 'lori', lullaby, in *Khushboo* in such a high scale that we were at a loss: how could we film a lori sung at such a high pitch. Because of this, despite Didi having sung it so beautifully, we had to record the song again without much music.

Yatindra Mishra: Have you ever tried to see if you could change the expression of a song? Some such possibility where the lines of the song could be altered, or once the song was ready, you felt that the imagery used, as well as the form and situation, could have been expressed differently?

Gulzar: If you are a creative person, this thought will occur repeatedly. If I give you the example of the song, 'Mera kuch saamaan tumhare paas padaa hai' in which there is a line, 'Aur usme lipti raat padi hai/ Woh raat bhujha do/ Mera woh saman louta do'. Now that night is burning, the one that is being referred to. I see the burning of the night like that of a candle. We snuff a candle to put out the light. People put out the day with a blow of the breath and bring in the night. But the night is still burning within me, blow it out, extinguish it. Perhaps another poet will not think like I do, and search for another expression.

In Sahir-sahab's song, 'Pedon ke shaakon pe soyi soyi chandni/ Aur thodi der me thak ke chali jayegi' was an expression I heard for the first time, that moonlight could get tired and go away. Perhaps this was Sahir's way of expressing the night. I had never thought of it. I had never imagined the moonlight getting tired; so it all emerges from your life, and how you present the night. And see how Shailendra has described the night. In *Awara*, he writes, 'Dum bhar jo udhar muh phere/ O chanda/ Main unse pyar kar loongi, baatein hazaar kar loongi'. The moon turning its face away is such a beautiful image, but it had never occurred to me. Yet, it is not necessary for me to think in the same way as some other poet. Songs should be viewed in this way, that what comes from within you is the most beautiful. The way other poets express themselves belongs to them, and must be appreciated.

Yatindra Mishra: This is a vital point you have made, that one must stay with the imagery that one has fashioned according to one's understanding. And one must welcome and appreciate the expressions of other poets.

Gulzar: Yes.

Yatindra Mishra: Which screenplays have caught your fancy? Whose screenplays and dialogues have you considered perfect? And also, which are the stories and novels which, when adapted into a screenplay, seem to be perfect to you?

Gulzar: Now, I cannot name just one, there are so many whose work is marvellous. I do not look at every piece of fiction as a possible adaptation for cinema. Some adaptations however, by their very presence, seem perfect. Like Bimal-da's *Devdas*, where the screenplay by Nabendu Ghosh and Rajinder Singh Bedi is of a very high standard. In the same way, when I watch Krishan Chopra's *Char Diwari*, I find it a brilliant film. Krishan Chopra appeared with this film when I was working with Bimal-da. It became clear how much work has gone into the script. That impression still remains. I also remember the black-and-white film *Jogan* with Dilip-sahab and Nargis-ji, which was released at that time in Liberty Cinema. That film too, because of its subject, lingers in the mind. Kedar Sharma had directed this film, which was produced by Ranjit Movietone. The screenplay has been very efficiently crafted. Such films have been giving an idea of how any script can be successfully written.

Yatindra Mishra: Which is the element which has the possibility of disrupting a good script?

Gulzar: We have a tradition of creating drama. An attempt to make every dialogue and situation dramatic, so it does not seem as if any character in the film is speaking in his own manner. The dialogues seem stilted and false. That is why I stay very alert where dialogues are concerned. Prakash Jha's *Damul*, in the matter of dialogue, seems to me the best example. Watching the film you do not feel at all that people are mouthing dialogues. There's such felicity in the use of real life conversations that you forget you are watching a film. It has been our habit to make dialogues that are not natural.

At some point of time, in films influenced by Parsi theatre, dramatic dialogues sounded good, as the subject was itself dramatic.

Like the dialogues in *Yahudi* by Bimal Roy, a film adapted from the famous Parsi play *Yahudi Ki Ladki*. Wajahat Mirza had written the lines in a very dramatic mode, which was then spoken by Sohrab Modi in as dramatic a manner on screen, 'Your sorrow is sorrow, the sorrow of others is make-believe. Your blood is blood, our blood is water...' this was suited to the subject. But if today dialogues are written in a similar dramatic way, they hold no meaning, because the times have changed.

Yatindra Mishra: Which recent films have screenplays worth mentioning?

Gulzar: In the years that followed, most of Shyam Benegal's films were notable for their screenplays. There is no grammar being followed in the screenplay; despite that, in *Manthan*, the landscape and dialogues hold you captive in every scene as the story progresses. Shyam Babu's *Suraj Ka Saatvan Ghoda* is also a wonderful film, which he adapted from Dharamveer Bharti's novel, and justified the adaptation completely. *Bhoomika* and *Nishant* too are excellent delineations of their subjects. These are good examples. Goutam Ghosh's *Paar* is also a unique film, whose script I really liked. I specially keep in mind the fact that Goutam Ghosh created such a crisp and meaningful screenplay from Samaresh Basu's short story 'Paar'. One more film comes to mind, M. S. Sathyu's *Garm Hava*, which was made with great care, based on Ismat Chughtai's short story. This film needs to be remembered for its excellent story, screenplay and direction. Shama Zaidi worked very satisfyingly on the screenplay.

In contemporary times, I find Vishal Bhardwaj's screenplay of *Saat Khoon Maaf* very good. Though you may think I am prejudiced in his favour, I do believe he has adapted Ruskin Bond's story very well. To make the subject of land grabbing, which is what the film *Matroo Ki Bijli Ka Mandola* is about, into a musical is no easy task, but Vishal managed it successfully. That was a good screenplay. Here I also view Meghna's script for *Filhaal* from another perspective. Only a woman can think of making a full film on the subject of surrogacy. If any man had tried to come to grips with it, he would have never succeeded in communicating it the way Meghna has done.

Yatindra Mishra: Cinema is a commercial medium. How does a filmmaker manage to keep his creativity safe in it?

Gulzar: In this connection I wish to mention something concerning Meghna. As screenplays go, the screenplay of *Raazi* is very mature. It deals with many strands of the subject yet never loses its focus. Meghna has responded to some questions about the film's screenplay thus, 'This film is not for everyone. The audience it is meant for understands the script's narrative.' This is a beautiful thought, which she transformed into action. Those who watch cinema or are linked with in other ways need to know that cinema is not just entertainment, it is something far beyond that. We need to choose our audiences.

Yatindra Mishra: Is there any screenplay which you wished to make as a film yourself, but which someone else made beautifully?

Gulzar: For a long time, the story *Telenapota Abishkar* (In Search of Telenapota Village) by Bangla writer Premendra Mitra, was stuck in my head. When I read the story I was very keen to make this into a film. I was however unable to understand how to make a screenplay from the story. I liked the story, understood it, but could not find a way to adapt it into a screenplay.

Later, when I watched Mrinal-da's [Mrinal Sen] *Khandhar*, I immediately understood that this indeed is the correct way of giving the screenplay a form. After watching *Khandhar* I understood that I could easily write the screenplay. Meaning I understood the tone and the point where the screenplay should start from. The basic thought of *Khandhar* is interesting, but the excellent way Mrinal Sen has created its screenplay is worthy of admiration.

Yatindra Mishra: Have you liked any other work by Mrinal Sen?

Gulzar: There is a lot of his work, many films that I have liked immensely at one time. Especially *Bhuvan Shome*, which I believe is his best film. Suhasini Mulay and Utpal Dutt have worked beautifully in the film. I also like his *Akaler Sandhane* immensely. I saw a much later film of his, starring Nandita Das, *Amaar Bhuvan*. It is a very good film, short but very powerful. I thought it was an excellent creation.

Yatindra Mishra: Did you work with him at all?

Gulzar: He would often tell me in jest, one day I will work with you. I was afraid that Mrinal-da would say this only to scare me. I would tell him too, 'You kept me under the threat for a long time, that you will give me a chance to work with you, but you never did.'

Yatindra Mishra: Almost all the screenplays and dialogues you have written have been for Hrishikesh Mukherjee or other worthy banners. Was it a conscious choice to be so selective? And which are those films which you wanted but could not work on due to shortage of time or any other reason?

Gulzar: Yes, it is true that I have made very few films for others besides Hrishi-da. One reason for this is that I was making my own films. That cut into my time, and I wanted to do my work with excellence. Though I did write films for my friends, like *Griha Pravesh* for Basu Bhattacharya. Later, too, I did other films including for Shekar Kapur and Shabana Azmi.

Yes, but there is one regret. There was a proposal to write Shakti Samant's *Amar Prem* and we had discussed it. I was keen too. But I had just started on *Mere Apne* at that time, and Shakti-da himself told me, I understand, it's your first film, pay attention to it. That's how I missed *Amar Prem*, and I still regret it. I still think it is his best film.

Yatindra Mishra: Can you remember anything from the period when you were writing screenplays and scripts that still holds relevance?

Gulzar: A film called *Sunghursh*, made by H. S. Rawail. It had Dilip-sahab, Balraj Sahani and Sanjeev Kumar in it. It was a very elaborate story and script based on Mahashweta Devi's Bangla story, 'Layli Ashmaner Ayina'. I enjoyed working on the dialogues and being a part of this film. I worked very diligently for it. The film was well made.

There's something interesting about this film. In the wake of my friendship with Sanjeev Kumar at that time, I found it exciting to watch the scene between him and Dilip-sahab. I cannot forget how, after each scene that starred Sanjeev Kumar and Dilip-sahab together, Sanjeev would touch Dilip-sahab's feet. I really liked his idea of showing respect to his senior. Also because that respect was due to Dilip-sahab and Sanjeev himself, by his behaviour, earned respect in the eyes of others.

Yatindra Mishra: Do you have any interesting memories about being in the company of Dilip Kumar during the *Sunghursh* days?

Gulzar: You will be surprised to know that when the film was being made, Dilip Kumar and Vyjayanthimala had stopped speaking to each other. Dilip-sahab would call me and send Vyjayanthimala a message that he was going to rehearse with me and that she should understand his movements, dialogues and entry etc according to the scene. Then he would say, 'Kudi nu das de, mai ki keh reya ha,' and I would take the message to Vyjayanthimala. He would always speak only in Punjabi.

Slowly I built a good rapport with him. He would talk

about and discuss each scene in detail. While *Sunghursh* was being made, I was working on Hrishikesh Mukherjee's film *Aashirvad*. He was also shooting *Bairaag* in Bengal for Asit Sen. He had come to meet Hrishi-da on the sets and called out to me, 'Gulzar-sahab! Please come here, why are you feeling shy?' When I went up to him, he said to Hrishi-da, 'Arey, you have a really good assistant. He's a very capable man.' I received this love and blessing from Dilip-sahab and I value it immensely. From this point of view, working for *Sunghursh* was a valuable experience. That I could write all that which Dilip Kumar, after some alteration, shot for the screen, was a huge achievement for me.

Yatindra Mishra: Are there other unusual aspects of your friendship with Dilip Kumar that you would like to share?

Gulzar: Yes. I knew that he was involved in social work. He was always doing something to help the blind and the deaf and dumb. I invited him to speak for a documentary, and he came readily and gave a shot exactly as I wanted it. Later, while he was shooting for *Bairaag*, I requested him to give me a shot for *Koshish*. To which he said, 'Come to where I am shooting.' I said I would come with the camera and all the other equipment and take the shot during his free time. To which he replied with great affection, 'Gulzar, come. The work will be easily done here. You will unnecessarily lug a camera and other things. Just come and I will give you the shot as you want it.' When I reached, he told Asit Sen, whose film he was shooting, 'I will give the shot for Gulzar on your camera. Later, please send the negative to him.' The shot was taken for *Koshish* and Asit Sen later sent me the negative. He too felt no discomfiture.

Yatindra Mishra: How did you feel writing screenplays for Hrishikesh Mukherjee?

Gulzar: I wrote a whole lot of films for Hrishi-da. I enjoyed watching films with him, it gave me the feeling of being in a classroom. We would all be fully absorbed, but would keep thinking about what he would find to his liking and what could earn us a rebuke. I thoroughly enjoyed writing *Khoobsurat* and *Chupke Chupke*. The subject of these films were good, and the films too. One small film which flopped was *Sabse Bada Sukh*. This too, I wrote very carefully, and it was made well, but it just did not run. Do look for it and watch it on YouTube. You will realise that a lot of work was expended on its script. Writing *Arjun Pandit* gave me the satisfaction that I had tackled a serious subject well and written competently for it.

Yatindra Mishra: If you had to choose one from among the films you have written, not only for the screenplay, but because the subject too has been tackled well, which one would it be?

Gulzar: I would mention *Meera* in this regard. For the script and the period. For the entire story to be justified in the present, the narrative was developed so that *Meera* was not confined to any particular time period, but was universalised to represent a woman…

Yatindra Mishra: Who should we remember as the screenplay and dialogue writer who influenced you to walk down this creative path?

Gulzar: There were such brilliant writers at that time. I am referring to fifty years ago, when visionary directors, each one better than the other, were making films. Right at the top one must remember K. Asif's *Mughal-e-Azam*, and the entire team of writers who worked on it: Wajahat Mirza, Kamal Amrohi, Amanullah Khan and Ehsaan Rizvi.

Yatindra Mishra: Besides these accomplished writers, are there others whom you remember?

Gulzar: There is a complete tradition in Hindi cinema, in which we can see many people who have worked together to create successful writing. As an example, you can see the work of Khwaja Ahmed Abbas with Raj Kapoor—what wonderful work has been accomplished. To romanticise a realistic screenplay to such an extent that, at a different level, it brings in socialism and Nehruvian society; *Shree 420* and *Awaara* are some examples of this. Raj-sahab's later, semi-autobiographical film, *Mera Naam Joker* and his adolescent love story *Bobby* are also worthy of detailed examination.

In the same way, Rajinder Krishan also plays an interesting role. Though most people know him as a lyricist, in his time he had written for Hindi films, especially for AVM Productions, Madras. Such was his stature that he would write a scene at night, and early in the morning of the following day it would be sent by plane to Madras where a studio assistant would pick it up and rush with it to the studio. He was so adept at this that I never once saw him anxious or worried. Mehmood-sahab's *Padosan* is a fine film based on a script written by him.

Yatindra Mishra: Is there, in your estimate, any filmmaker who is significant in relation to Indian themes?

Gulzar: Shantaram-ji [V. Shantaram]. He has a style all his own. He came from Marathi theatre and made films in his own fashion. He used to work in Kolhapur, but even after he came to the city from that small town, he did not lose his sensitivity. Look at his early films; from them I consider *Aadmi*, *Padosi* and *Duniya Na Maane* as classics. Later, he brought the complete theatre tradition of Kolhapur into his films: the same behaviour pattern in his characters and the colours of Kolhapur in his costumes. The same style in acting and dialogues. He lived Kolhapur in Bombay.

He also made a few experimental movies. In which *Dr Kotnis Ki Amar Kahani*, *Do Aankhen Barah Haath* and *Jhanak Jhanak Payal Baje*, the last based on classical music and dance, are remarkable. You will find that the most important point in Shantaram's films is social commitment. All these films are socially relevant. He is one of the pioneers who featured an English song in *Duniya Na Mane*. He was the first director who, through *Aadmi*, *Padosi*, *Dahej* and *Duniya Na Mane* created the belief that he could bring about social change through cinema. He said, 'I can reform society or cinema should reform society. Cinema has to be purposeful, educational and meaningful.'

Yatindra Mishra: Your response makes me think that because Shanatram-ji made films that were concerned with social reform, he is still relevant today.

Gulzar: That is why Shantaram-ji is Shantaram!

Yatindra Mishra: What do you think about S. D. Burman's music? Especially since your career in music began with him.

Gulzar: This is a very personal opinion, but I consider him a banyan, a very big banyan tree. It has countless branches, some swinging and swaying. So, just as the branches hang from the tree, in the same way a great many people are linked to S. D. Burman and influenced by his music. And if you want to see what influenced him, you will find it in Bengal's folk music, in Baul songs, in the Bhatiali songs of the boatmen.

Yatindra Mishra: Indeed, he was a veteran artiste who has influenced an entire generation. Which aspect of his composition do you find most beguiling?

Gulzar: 'Ab ke baras bhejh bahiyya ko babul' (Father, send my brother to fetch me home this year) from *Bandini* is Dada's most touching song. The duet with Lata and Rafi in *Abhimaan*, 'Teri bindiya re' seems to me one of Dada's signature compositions. Besides this, two songs sung by Dada himself for *Sujata* and *Bandini* respectively: 'Sun mere bandhu re' (Listen, O my friend) and 'Oh mere maajhi, mere sajan hai uss paar' (Boatman, my love is on the far bank) have always been among my favourites. And of course, the songs of *Guide* are at another level, and have taken S. D. Burman to the highest stature in the history of Hindi film music.

Yatindra Mishra: After S. D. Burman's *Bandini*, you did not work together, but you had a close friendship with R. D. Burman, and so you must have continued to meet him, and visit his home. In this connection I am eager to know what you think of the technical aspect of his music and how his music stood apart from that of the others of that time.

Gulzar: I have not learnt music, so how can I judge Dada? That would be wrong. He hailed from the royal family of Tripura and his personality was steeped in the soil and music of the region. One aspect in his music that is prominent is the chemistry that exists between him and his accompanists and his fellow musicians. Remember that song from Dev-sahab's *Kala Bazar*, 'Apni to har aah ek toofan hai' (Each sigh of mine is a gale). It was filmed inside a train compartment, and Rafi-sahab had sung it with great gentleness. Listen to the song carefully and the flute that can be heard in the interludes where the instruments take over is quite unusual. Dada used the sound of the flute there to give the effect of the train's whistle. Only Dada could have created this magic, that a classical instrument that is played along with bhajans or while delineating a tender love song, is adapted to stand in for a running train's whistle. Very large-hearted and fun-loving, he was a man who could easily get angry too.

Yatindra Mishra: If you have any interesting anecdotes of his anger, do please share them.

Gulzar: Oh, there are plenty. Which should I remember? I will share one or two incidents related to this interesting side of him, by which you will get an insight into his nature. I had heard of an incident between Dada and musician Kanu Roy. Kanu Roy was a great football fan. He made a request to Dada that he should take him to see some big match. When Dada had an extra ticket for some match, he took Kanu Roy with him. Two prominent teams, Mohun Bagan and East Bengal, were playing. Both were leading opposing teams and the funny thing was that the fan of one team would berate the other team, even if the other team was playing really well. The interesting aspect of Dada's personality starts here. As soon as the match started, Dada came to understand that Kanu Roy was a Mohun Bagan supporter, while he himself favoured the East Bengal team. When it was half time, both went out of the stadium. But when the match resumed, Dada left Kanu Roy outside and went back in and watched the match alone because both the tickets were in his pocket.

Not just that, Dada used to carry a small tin of paan with him, and God forbid that anyone should try to help himself to a paan from it. Majrooh Sultanpuri had said about him in a jocular way, 'He is a child-like rascal.' Dada was really like that, and constantly worried about whether the tune he had made would be rejected. In fact, an argument broke out between him and Bimal Roy over the song in *Bandini*, 'Mora gora ang lae le', about how it was impossible for Kalyani, who lives with her father and reads Vaishnavi verses, to go out alone at night and sing. Dada flared up at this saying, 'How can it be, the tune I have made is for the outdoors. If you change the situation, my tune will be spoilt.' Bimal-da was stubborn about the point that she would sing inside the house. Fighting like children, they finally came to an agreement that she would leave the house singing. Dada had used his ultimate weapon, 'If she does not go out, I will not compose the song.' Bimal-da who anyway spoke very little agreed with a 'hunh' and retreated into silence. With a tendency to wrinkle his face in anger at the smallest provocation, and also let go of his anger almost as quickly, S. D. Burman was a very loveable human being.

Yatindra Mishra: The songs composed by S. D. Burman and R. D. Burman, were they similar in some way or different? How different was the music of the son's from the father's, despite their belonging to the same musical tradition?

Gulzar: Both were legends in their time. The simple truth is both made music in their own way. What I found most loveable was that both would add almost similar dummy words to the tunes they created. Meaning, Dada in his tunes and Pancham in his, used the same dummy words repeatedly and made their compositions.

This line in Bangla was their favourite, 'Chand uthe chelo gagane/ Amaay deri holo je' (The moon is up in the sky/ I am late). Besides this they would also create some funny rhymes. Look at these dummy words Dada used for a composition, 'Bap-bapu ji, bakery ka doodh peeta hai…' This was a line based on Gandhi-ji, and he would pronounce 'bakery' in a typically Bengali way. The most important thing is, what beautiful tunes he composed with such nonsense words! He created this wonderful composition for *Insaan Jaag Utha* on these lines, 'Janun janun re, kaahe khanke hain tora kangana' (I know, why your bangles tinkle).

Yatindra Mishra: There was a time when cinema and culture were following two principal streams, where one school of thought was 'Lahore' and the other 'Delhi'. These are two significant places bracketing your birth and your growing-up years, and one can read, as one traverses between them, the story of your struggles. Have you tried to understand your life from the angle of being someone caught between two cultures: your birth place, Dina, which is close to Lahore on one side, and Delhi where you grew up on the other?

Gulzar: When you talk about the cultures of Lahore and Delhi, it is also clear that they have existed from the beginning and can be viewed as two big centres of education. This trend existed in the Mughal era and after that, even in the British period, both Lahore and Delhi were considered prominent centres. Though there was a distinct culture in Bengal too, and along with Lahore and Delhi, Bengal too was considered a prominent centre for education.

You will also realise that in Lahore and Bengal, reading and writing, culture, language, cinema, music were all very vibrant. Apart from these, Delhi gained prominence as the seat of government. Though Delhi too developed as a centre for Urdu, the echoes of which continued to be heard for a long time. At the second level, Lucknow too is seen as developing as a centre for Urdu studies.

Yatindra Mishra: Could you explain in detail how the elements of folk entered your music and how you developed them?

Gulzar: Folk is a very precious part of one's memory, which seems just as beautiful when you revisit it. I have listened to Maharashtra's lavani, Rajasthani songs, Punjabi heers and Bulleh Shah. I have heard the magic emanating from the ektara of the Baul singers of Bengal. I can say that in a way that a part of me exists in the vast treasure house of folk music.

In the beginning of my career, I visited Calcutta quite often, accompanying Hemant Kumar. In those days Hemant Kumar would have programmes in far-flung villages through Bengal. They would go on through the night and that's how I steeped myself in the music of Bengal. I prepared my mind to understand Bhatiali songs, and Hemant Kumar and Salil-da helped me a lot in this. Hemant Kumar's programmes would start late in the night, around 1.30 or 2, and if I felt sleepy during the programme, I would go to the back and fall asleep. Thanks to these programmes, folk music filtered into my consciousness. At Salil-da's, no music sitting was complete without the presence of Baul music. I have heard a lot of it in his company. This is how I got acquainted with the country's folk music, and it settled in me.

Yatindra Mishra: Is this why there are so many elements of folk music in your songs?

Gulzar: Perhaps I have also received a huge share of folk music from the earlier generation too, and it is seated deep in my consciousness. In today's generation, villages are almost disappearing and migration to the cities has become a trend. But folk music, in the true sense, lives and thrives in the heartbeat of villages even today. You have to go to the villages of India to experience true and pure folk music.

Yatindra Mishra: Continuing on this, I want to ask about the many geographical references that crop up in your folk songs. For example, in the very unusual song that you have written for *Ek Pal*. In this bidai song, as the palanquin keeps travelling further, you get to see the scenes and culture of the village in all its entirety. How did you connect with rural life to write this song? You must remember the whole song, but I am sharing it here anyway:

A bit slowly, a bit carefully carry the doli
Very delicate is my my innocent sister
When past the kanchi pond goes the doli
Two tears dear girl, leave behind
How will she dry the sheet after bathing
Into the shade of the courtyard, lead her
When past the peepal tree goes the doli
An auspicious red bindiya leave behind
When over the Lohit bridge goes the doli
A golden toe-ring leave behind
A bit slowly, a bit carefully carry the doli onwards
Very delicate is my my innocent sister.'

Gulzar: Thank you for thinking of such a beautiful song. Endowed with Bhupen-da's wizardry, this song emerges completely from the background of Assam. While making *Ek Pal* we listened to so many songs with Bhupen-da which were infused with the natural beauty of Assam and the sound of the Brahmaputra. While I was writing this song, more than just suiting it to the theme of the film, I crafted it to match Bhupen-da's folk tunes and paid close attention to ensuring that I chose words that would help understand the geography of Assam.

Now that you have reminded me, the song's tune has started echoing in my ears. The chorus of this song too has been presented so well.

Yatindra Mishra: This can also be understood through examples from later films, in which the folk base brings in a mystic element, and the song seems to be intentionally visual. I am referring to the songs of *Lekin*, *Rudaali* and *Daayra* in which the visual and the suggestive together create a new expression. 'Main ek sadi se baithi hoon' (I have been waiting for an eon) from *Lekin*, 'Samay o dheere chalo' (Travel slow, O time) from *Rudaali* and the song, 'Choote nahin choote na maati ka yeh chola' (This carapace of clay, it does not let me go). What would you say about these songs?

Gulzar: These need to be seen against the background of the script, and as songs in themselves. It is true that I have taken the liberty to be a bit mystical and spiritual, which lifts the song to a new level. There was also an element of classical music in the songs of *Lekin*, and the songs alluded to a tale of secrets. It's possible that there was scope to be a bit mystical here. The *Rudaali* song, 'Samay o dheere chalo' is indeed a philosophical song, and Bhupen-da had made three versions, sung respectively by Lata-ji, Asha-ji and Bhupen-da himself. When it comes to the song from *Daayra*, 'Choote nahin choote na', I find it is like a Baul song because of its metre. And the mystic is a necessary element in Baul thought, which comes into their songs too.

Yatindra Mishra: Is there a touch of the mysterious and the spiritual in this song from *Rudaali*, 'Jis tan ko chua toone/ Uss tan ko chupaoon'?

Gulzar: In this, when she refers to 'Jis tan ko chua toone/ Uss tan ko chupaoon', the heroine is talking about the body you have touched and which I hide from society, from the world, from worldliness. But what you have touched within me, who can I show that to? I can only show it to you. So it is a delicate expression of how a down-trodden woman shows her body and soul to the man she loves, who comes from a higher strata of society.

Now when you ask about the image of her reaching the moon, it is a tradition of choosing a metaphor big enough to describe the depth of one's love. A tradition wherein we refer to Radha and Krishna to speak of our love. Then we add a layer to it to make it mystical and Sufiyana. We surround the song with layers so that it operates on two levels, spanning two worlds. Meaning both, physical love between mortals on earth as well as love for the divine beyond the heavens. Through the medium of lover and beloved, cleverly speaking of love gives songs a rhythm, which adds a mystical shade to even simple, everyday words. That is the reason what was said in relation to inner and outer self becomes so personal that its meaning, when explored, seems to be mystical.

Yatindra Mishra: In my opinion, the songs of *Rudaali* and *Daayra* were the first time that the mystical element entered your song writing. Or was it later, while writing the songs of *Dil Se*? There are three songs in *Dil Se* which are immersed in the Sufi mood which include 'Chal chaiyya chaiyya', 'Ae ajnabi' and 'Tu hi tu satrangi re'.

Gulzar: It is true that a frank Sufiyana colour came into my songwriting for the first time in *Dil Se*. But I would like to add that all this was possible because it was linked to A. R. Rahman. At Rahman's place, writing Sufiyana lyrics was easily possible. I could openly give rein to Sufiyana lyrics which he would set into tunes that had the same mood and flavour. Though my temperament has always had an element of the Sufi in it, and if you look at my very first song, then 'More gora ang laile' for *Bandini* too has philosophical overtones. But with *Dil Se*, I discovered Bulleh Shah up close for myself, and a song like 'Chaiyya Chaiyya' has been written in his metre.

Yatindra Mishra: When you write songs of sorrow and depression, do they come out of any particular moments of turmoil, or is it your inner conscience that adds the Sufiyana element to such songs of pain?

Gulzar: If you are asking whether the songs are written in depression, then it's a no. The simple truth is that there is a story, a character. When I am writing, I am living with that character in the script. And whatever her feelings can be, I recreate them, and feel them.

Yatindra Mishra: Does this mean that there is something in the past, a sorrow, that a poet expresses in his own way in his poems?

Gulzar: A poet writes his songs through his life experiences. Another aspect is that if you are going to base the sorrow of the character you are writing for on your own experience, then you must evaluate how deeply you can plumb your own emotions. How deep is the well inside you and how far into it can you go? The sorrow you are asking about, I can only say that I had deeper levels and could go even deeper. I went as far as I did with the character.

Yatindra Mishra: Would you like to give any example of this?

Gulzar: An example is of the song from *Gharonda* in which, in empathising with Amol Palekar's character, the poet in me wrote a song of loneliness and depression into which I delved to bring out the feelings of the character. It can be seen in the antara of the song:

The days are empty vessels
And the night a sightless well
In these desolate, dark eyes
Smoke rises instead of tears
There's no reason to continue living
Searching for an excuse to die...

You will see the same thing in my poems on death. Like, 'Take down from the spirit the pretty jewel of the body/Rise from prayer, say amen and give up the spirit.' That is a side of death that I have an experience of. It is true that depression exists there. Death has been cleaned up and made antiseptic. This is a gift from our sacred texts, that death must never be dirtied. This has come into my poem, 'Pakeeza':

Move, but let there be no movement anywhere
Rise in a way that no leaf stirs
Putting down each fold of the dress, rise so that the sound doesn't
touch
...Take care that no wrinkle from life
Go with the pure, clean face of death...

It is a gift from our culture, our religion, our sacred texts that we make death a huge and beautiful thing. That is why, even entering deep into the well and encountering death, one does not experience depression. Maybe you have not felt it because you have not yet even touched this surface, and you will feel, ' This is such a depressing thing being said here.' If some day life gives you some such experience, then you will feel, 'Yes, I have seen this sorrow before'. It's possible you may even go further than this, but this point you have already seen. Then perhaps it will be of use to me too, because somewhere or the other, I too will keep showing it through my poems and songs, stories and characters.

Yatindra Mishra: You have explained life, death and the depression that comes from it so succinctly, from the point of view of a creative person. Can we then, attaching your idea to many such poems and film songs, read the acceptance of depression in the pure and clean face of death?

Gulzar: Undoubtedly! If it is my poem, then many aspects of my life along with the pain experienced are present there. The thing I had mentioned...about going deep within and entering the well where even water is not present, and the level of sand exists...to reach there and turn around to look at life again, makes everything clear and comprehensible. As for examining the depression and sorrow present in the songs I write for films, in them, much more than my existence there, is the issue of the depression felt by the character in the film. There should be no expectation from a film song that it is derived from the writer's past experiences. It is fully a part of the story of the film, whatever be the situation of the song itself.

Yatindra Mishra: A lot of detailing goes into the creation of characters in a film. It is through minute details that we can create a true picture when we picturise a character according to the screenplay. In this connection, while designing a character did you have any interesting experience which drove home the importance of detailing?

Gulzar: I remember an interesting story. It so happened that Maharaja Karni Singh-ji of Bikaner, who is a very renowned marksman, wrote me a letter. This is in connection with the film, *Meera*. He wrote, 'For the first time I have seen in a film based on Rajasthan, the difference between the Sisodia and Rathore clans is so clearly defined. For the first time a director has shown the difference clearly,' For that he heaped praise on me. It was a great compliment. He praised my work for its detailing, which pleased me immensely. I think I must still have his letter lying somewhere safe.

Yatindra Mishra: That way, you must have countless letters praising your work. Do you not think that just as the young are throwing light on the aspects of your screenplays for films, you should also place these letters before your readers?

Gulzar: I am not in favour of bringing out all the letters. If it is something special, then that's fine. This tradition that started with Ghalib has become a quite unnecessary custom in Urdu. Ghalib's letter-writing style was unique. People passionately collected his letters and, with the same fervour, wished to publish them. And this is how a new practice in Urdu prose started. There was a beautiful quality in Ghalib which I call arrogance, because it was a notch higher than ego, which made his ego remarkable. Every artiste lives by his ego. But this ego has a beak which pokes people. Which is why where Ghalib is concerned, I call it arrogance.

This ego's beak, to me, is like the crested feather on

Ghalib's cap. What an understanding that man had, that he started a new trend with his letters. Due to him, a whole lot of books of collected letters were published. The thing is that if there is a reason for letters to be published, then they must also reach the common man.

But at this point it is necessary to add that if there are a lot of personal things in the letters, and it is like a conversation between two people then I am not of the view that those letters should be made public. Every artiste has the right to live his life privately. I personally believe that every creative person needs his own personal space.

Yatindra Mishra: This is a reasonable opinion, and it should be so.

Gulzar: It should be so because that space is necessary to move about. The most difficult thing to handle these days is that everyone has a camera at hand, and it is always open. If you are eating, your throat is seen swallowing. They sit right in front of you, without as much as a by-your-leave. There is no courtesy left. Camera, video, everything is in the mobile phone. This is switched on. Even if you are sitting far away, they zoom in and try to invade your personal space. This is very bad. It should be a part of courteous behaviour that you do not enter anyone's world without knocking first.

Yatindra Mishra: You have created portraits of famous people of the world of literature, cinema and music. From Rabindranath Tagore to Bimal Roy and Salil Chowdhury to Jagjit Singh, all are present. How did you get the idea of writing portraits on these personalities?

Gulzar: It was not a tough job for me, because I am familiar with painting. I often went to see exhibitions, and sometimes even picked up a brush and sat before a canvas to paint. Now, there's been a gap for some years. To put my thoughts on paper or canvas and play with those colours is a completely novel sensibility, and I love it.

You know I used to work in a motor garage, and my job was to match the colours and paint the cars that had been damaged in an accident. Thus I had the experience of the motor garage too, through which I understood this form. Then whether you make a pretty painting or write a poem about it, it's quite the same thing.

Yatindra Mishra: Can we then understand that through the portrait, the complete nature of that person is contained in the poem? Meaning, does one get a glimpse of his life ?

Gulzar: When you comment about a character in a social media post, the comment may not describe him fully but does reveal something about him from an angle, which throws light on his personality.

Yatindra Mishra: Do you think the written word will survive?

Gulzar: Yes, words will survive, and so will books. However numerous the technical advances, the importance of the written word will remain. In fact, with changing times it will increase. It could be that books change their form. Like we see more and more books in the form of audio books and e-books. Words will remain safe, because it is through them that we can continue to remain civilised.

Think on my words, that even before there were printed books and printing presses, there were poets and poems, shastras and Puranas, as also the songs of classical singers and saints. Everything was learnt through words and language and through the oral tradition, passed from one generation to the next. I think, and it is my hope, that the times ahead will be such that books will be well respected.

Yatindra Mishra: So the power of words will continue unchanged and only the ways of presenting them will change. And society will have to keep up with the changes in form.

Gulzar: That will happen. Take a look and see how even today handwritten books and manuscripts are still in good shape. When paper was invented, the tradition of imprinting thought and ideas and knowledge on it started. If you look back at a thousand years of tradition of the many languages of our country, how many things exist that were found, and which publishing houses, after restoring them, published and brought to light with great care. In the same way, when printed books seem like an old and outdated idea then the world of books will easily find a new form for itself. Just think how many things are not on paper, but all of us in our everyday life, store on the computer's hard drive. You do not need paper to communicate with anybody. Everything has become digital now. A simple click on the computer and anyone in any part of the world can receive your letter or news of you. We must welcome this technical change. If it is so useful in our daily life, why would it bring harm to the act of propagating our poetry and story collections?

Yatindra Mishra: Is there one person among those whom you have learnt from, and those whom you came into contact with to understand your existence, who, above all, you consider your teacher?

Gulzar: It's a good question but I do not have a simple answer for it. One has many gurus in life, not just a single one.

Yatindra Mishra: In your own words, you have expressed what Pandit Bhimsen Joshi said! He said that the knowledge of music a singer of any gharana garners through dedication and practice also contains elements stolen from other gharanas. 'One needs to add some metal to make jewellery out of twenty-four carat gold. In the same way, in my singing, besides the Kirana gharana, I have included whatever I liked from other gharanas.'

Gulzar: What Panditji said is correct. See, what happens is that you learn from many. And often it happens that you have learnt something but paid no attention to it. Much, much later you realise that this thing that I have learnt, I got from there, that person.

If I just talk about cinema, then besides Bimal-da, there are all those who held me by the hand and taught me. Shailendra, Debu Sen, Hemant Kumar, Hrishi-da, each of them opened doors in cinema for me that only a teacher opens for his student. As for literature, right from the beginning till today, I have been a student of all the good poets and by reading them I have understood the grammar of poetry. I am still tasting the sweetness of Mirza Ghalib and Gurudev Rabindranath Tagore's kindness.

Yatindra Mishra: Do you ever feel the need to rewrite a poem, ghazal or story?

Gulzar: Yes, I do. And I keep doing it too.

Yatindra Mishra: This means that there are always newer versions of your stories and poems. Will you share something you have changed?

Gulzar: This is what I do. If I find a line or two is extraneous, I trim it off. Before I send something for printing, or before reading at a big gathering, I definitely edit my work. If I feel I have said too much, then it's a problem. Any poet who reads his previous writing feels that he might have said too much. Over-saying is the problem in writing, and this is not just my problem. Every poet has to deal with this, masters too.

Yatindra Mishra: How do you deal with this process?

Gulzar: Quite a few of my poems, even today, remain unfinished. In some, I have said more than necessary, and some are such that, being unable to edit them properly, they lie as they are and I have not published them.

Yatindra Mishra: How long does the process of fine-tuning the unpublished poems go on? When do you finally feel that you have taken it to a point where you can say it's done, and leaving it there, move on?

Gulzar: I do not start a story, poem, legend, short story if it does not seem complete in my understanding of it, and is not fixed in my mind. This process can even continue for years.

Yatindra Mishra: What do you see in your own poems that you have tried to do differently from other poets?

Gulzar: I have not made any such effort! I think I bring in a very different imagery of the cosmos in my poetry, which is scattered all through my poems and songs in a marked manner. In fact, once even Dr. Gopichand Narang had hinted to me saying, 'The cosmos has no role to play in Urdu poetry. Despite this, your poetry is full of it.' When I thought about what he had said, I felt he was right in a way. The favoured subject of my poetry has been an attempt at grasping the consciousness of the entire universe. I thoroughly enjoy doing this. You might be surprised to know that I read about NASA every single day, and enjoy the papers and journals they bring out. I find their attraction magnetic, and think about how I can understand the many secrets of the universe and place them before people in my words.

I often think working in space is similar to what a poet does. Just as a poet keeps registering his time, and writes down what comes into his mind in a flash, or keeps collecting all emotions and stories, a space rocket does something quite similar. Going beyond its domain, it collects new data and objects in a flash, and through the energy created by the constantly changing mysteries of the universe, something new keeps happening.

Yatindra Mishra: In the 1980s, when the standard of film music went down and music deteriorated into noise, lyrics too took a sudden downward dip. If we take the period between 1981–1990, some really good songs were also written though in very small numbers. I am quoting a few examples that include Javed Akhtar's 'Yeh kahaan aa gaye hum' from *Silsila* in 1981, Jan Nisar Akhtar's 'Aye dile nadaan' from *Razia Sultan* in 1983, Vasant Dev's 'Bela mehka re mehka' from *Utsav* in 1984, and your song, 'Mera kuch saamaan' from

Ijazat in 1987. How was it that a few stood at their point without compromising with the demands of changing times?

Gulzar: All the poets whose names you have taken are steady people. They never need to compromise on their work, regardless of whichever medium they are writing for. Jan Nisar Akhtar had no need of cheap popularity, neither did Vasant Dev or any of the other lyricists. If there is a new wave of writing, and if a poet feels he does not belong to it, why would he write for it? He will retire for a period into his reading room, blow away the dust that has settled on the books of learned writers, and find solace in them. He will find his way leading out from there, some forgotten journey that he can embark on. I am fortunate in that I have always listened to my heart and feelings and tried to write as they dictated. I found the same joy I had experienced in writing the songs for *Aandhi*, *Mausam*, *Kinara* and *Parichay* in the 1970s when in the following decade I wrote for *Sadma*, *Ek Pal*, *Masoom* and *Ijazat*. I felt no difficulty in writing these songs.

Yatindra Mishra: Two distinct traditions of lyric writing for Hindi cinema have been obvious all through; one of Urdu poets and the other of those who come from the Hindi-speaking states. If Shakeel Badayuni, Sahir Ludhianvi, Jan Nisar Akhtar, Majrooh Sultanpuri and Raja Mehdi Ali Khan were on one side, then the other had Pandit Pradeep, Kedar Sharma, Pandit Narendra Sharma, Saraswati Kumar Deepak, Gopal Singh Nepali, Pandit Bharat Vyas, Rajinder Krishan, Indeevar, Neeraj and Yogesh. What contradictions do you see in this entire canvas? And which flavour did the most for Hindi cinema?

Gulzar: I think where cinema is concerned, the writing of a song gains significance depending on the story and period. If you are making a film on a period where Hindi was spoken, then of course it becomes necessary to use words from the Hindi language. Similarly, if the story has an Urdu base, the songs must have the flow and cadence of a ghazal, only then will they be relevant. The simplest rule is to write the songs in the language spoken in the film. The two groups you spoke of do exist, but you can see that all have adapted their language according to the need of the films they worked on. For example, check out Sahir-sahab's language in Kidar Sharma's *Chitralekha* which was a period film. How beautifully he has used the Hindi language: 'Man re tu kaahe na dheer dhare' (O heart, why are you so impatient.) You tell me, has his being an Urdu poet made any difference?

I have always said that cinema alone represents the shape and language of the songs in it, regardless of the language the song writer favours. Another example I want to share is that of Indeevar, who wrote his songs mainly in Hindi, using a mix of Urdu and Hindi. In the song from *Malhar*, he says, 'Bade armaan se rakha hai sanam, teri kasam, pyar ki duniya me yeh pehla kadam' (Upon you I swear, my love, I have set foot in the world of love with great hope). I call this mix of Hindi and Urdu flavouring, Hindustani. If you see all of Pandit Pradeep's work, the Hindustani flourishes in his Hindi writing will not leave you unimpressed. Think of any of his huge cache of songs, and all of them are flavoured with Hindustani. 'Door hato ay duniya walon, Hindustan hamara hai' (Stand aside, O people of the world, Hindustan is ours), 'Aao bachchon tumhe dikhaoon jhanki Hindustan ki' (Come children, let me show you a glimpse of Hindustan), 'Dekh tere sansar ki haalat kya ho gayee bhagwan' (Look, god, what your world has come to), and later, the hugely famous, 'Aye mere watan ke logon/ Zara aankh me bhar lo paani' (My fellow citizens/ Summon the tears into your eyes). Now you tell me which of it is in Urdu and which in Hindi. This is a gift from cinema that it has given us the Hindustani language.

Yatindra Mishra: Can we accept the Hindustani that exists in cinema as a language that links us with one another?

 Gulzar: This is an important thing that when a Hindi or Urdu writer writes for cinema, he exercises his authority over the language which carries the accents used by the common man. There is no language that is foreign here. Hindi speakers know Urdu, and Urdu speakers know Hindi. I think the gift of Hindustani given to us by cinema has united the entire country. And if this language can be made the link language, a lot of knotty issues will be easily solved.

Yatindra Mishra: Who are the lyricists whose songs you find yourself close to? While writing songs for Hindi films, whom have you found closest?

Gulzar: I have never tried to reach close to anyone, but those poets whose work I admire, I gravitate towards them. I watch them, learn from them, admire them. Shailendra is one. He is very significant. I see the same Hindustani flavours in his accents. 'Mila hai kisi ka jhumka/ Thandi thandi, hare hare neem tale' (I found someone's dangler/ In the cool, green shade of the neem tree). This could only have been said by Shailendra. The way he says, 'Hare hare neem tale/ Mila hai kisika jhumka', is from the folk tradition, and in such beautiful Hindustani! To romanticise it in this way and then add a folk element to it is no mean feat. Sahir-sahab too makes romantic expression into everyday speech. See how beautifully Sahir-sahab writes this, 'Chand maddham hai aasman chup hai' (The moon is fading, the sky quiet). This is the first time anyone has said, 'Chand maddham hai'. Till date I don't know if anyone has said anything like this in any language.

There are countless such examples that can be quoted in the poetry of Shailendra and Sahir-sahab. I am thinking of the song from *Shagun*, how beautifully expressed it is. 'Parvaton ke pedhon par, shaam ka basera hai/ Surmai ujala hai, champai andhera hai' (The evening roosts upon the mountain trees / The light is inky, the darkness tinged with yellow). Now unless you have experienced this, where will you find the language for expression that can be transformed into the language of the masses and presented back to them. So I find the language and expression of Shailendra and Sahir-sahab, their capability, their sensibilities, and emotions very close to my heart.

Yatindra Mishra: One of your relevant observations concerns Lata Mangeshkar and Asha Bhosle is that both have reached the moon together, but Lata-ji placed her feet on the moon first, just like Neil Armstrong was the first to set foot on the moon. Asha Bhosle, sitting on the other side of the same vehicle, stepped after Lata-ji on the moon and like Edwin Aldrin, she was the second to reach the moon.

Gulzar: I can understand why you want to raise this issue again. Let me take the idea forward and say that they are two sides of a cassette tape. You can call one A and the other B. But by habit you hear A first before you hear B. Now Lata-ji is A because she started singing first. Asha-ji sang after her, so she naturally goes on side B, but they are the two sides of the same record. You can listen to either first; but being A, one tends to start with Lata. And it's her right too, being the senior.

Yatindra Mishra: You have given a very good evaluation of the two sisters.

Gulzar: Absolutely. Both are legends of our time. And great voices too. Meaning they have legendary voices. This is a huge gift to cinema.

Yatindra Mishra: What would you say about other voices in this connection?

Gulzar: If we look, we will find some voices in folk songs. Voices to sing the heer in Punjabi, for songs accompanied by the dholak, and voices to sing Rabindra Sangeet. I did mention to you that I have listened a lot to Surinder Kaur and Jagjit Kaur. Jutika Roy had a unique voice and was very popular in her time. Jaddan Bai, Begum Akhtar and Shobha Gurtu were excellent, forceful voices. But I can say with confidence that if for this entire century you needed to pick representative voices for film songs, they would undoubtedly be Lata-ji and Asha-ji. There are many other wonderful voices, among which we can quote Ameerbai Karnataki, Parul Ghosh and Geeta Dutt.

Yatindra Mishra: What about the male voices who represent film music?

Gulzar: Here, too, the situation is similar. The first and most prominent name is that of K. L. Saigal. He is the biggest legend of the century in cinema. If I look through the entire century then, after placing Saigal-sahab on the highest level, I can only see two representative voices, Rafi-sahab and Kishore Kumar. I will say this much, they will remain the representative legends of the first century of cinema.

Yatindra Mishra: Is the evocative poetry that existed in the music of yore on a decline? Or can we say that after an interval, the era of melodious songs will return, where songs will be created that will have a long shelf life and a lingering effect?

Gulzar: The fault is not that of the changing times, nor of the singer, but in the system. It's not as if there are no good poets today, or a dearth of composers. And it's not that there are no singers. There's a huge amount of talent. It's the system that has changed. Things have changed so quickly that there has been no time for them to grow with you. One song comes, then another. Then one more and yet another. Fourteen songs come one over the other in the course of a day. If one hundred and fifty songs are launched in a month, where is the time to consume them? They can't last, they need time to be understood and to seep in. Everything today is so very commercial. If a voice with potential enters the field, it gets involved in so many stage shows that it gets burnt out in no time. Everything is done at such speed that even what you do gets burnt out. It has no time to develop and enter the memories of listeners to remain there.

Yatindra Mishra: This stops an artiste from developing his art.

Gulzar: Only an artiste can care about himself in such a way that he progresses. To become S. D. Burman or Pancham, a Lata-ji or Rafi-sahab or Kishore Kumar, you have to grow in your art. It takes a lot of hard work. I remember very well that though he was so well established, Burman-dada would still worry about a director rejecting the tune he had created.

Yatindra Mishra: Is this true of other art forms too?

Gulzar: Of course! Creativity needs leisure. Some patience too is required. See, we are waiting to be able to do something good. In such an environment it is possible to create something which can stand at par with the work of greater artistes. Ghalib knew what he was talking about when he said, 'Dil dhoondta hai phir wahi fursat ke raat din' (The heart seeks once more those days and nights of leisure).

Yatindra Mishra: Was there something that you could not learn while working with Bimal Roy and which still troubles you when you think about it?

Gulzar: This question needs a bit of tweaking. The two things I needed to learn, filmmaking and patience, I managed to learn. But the artistic concept cannot be learnt or taught. That is each one's own. But I can never become Bimal-da. There's a saying, 'Where the master is, that space is always completely empty.'

Yatindra Mishra: You have lent your voice to many albums by prominent singers and have shared your opinion on the text too, to present some new thought. For example, on the songs of Kabir sung by Abida Parveen, or when you talk about Amir Khusro and heer in connection with Bulleh Shah and Baba Farid. Is there a poet, saint or a traditionalist you still wish to record something about?

Gulzar: The moment you mentioned the albums, Meerabai's name popped into my mind. There has been no thorough exploration of the numerous ways she can be interpreted. 'Ay re main to prem diwani/ Mera dard na jaane koi' (I am love-maddened/ No one know my pain) If this line is read superficially, it will elude you. If you pour into it the emotions of a poet, a woman suffering separation from her beloved, a rebel, then many layers of meaning unfold. The power of the verse will overwhelm you. This is a classic.

Abida Parveen can do great justice to Meera's poems, if she sings them. The work of a great poet will find a great, powerful voice. If this happens, it will be a huge boon to music.

Yatindra Mishra: In your film music one sees that along with the words, there's also a play on sound. I have discussed this even at the start of my book in my notes. Is the use of sound-linked words like 'chappa-chappa charkha chale' a technique you consciously use, especially while writing songs?

Gulzar: This has been prevalent even earlier in Hindi cinema. I have only taken forward the tradition of sound-centric song writing. Look back at old songs and you can hear the sound of lightning dancing in 'Lapak-lapak ke aa re badarva' in the song from *Boot Polish*. The song 'Jhanak-Jhanak payal baaje/ Payaliya ke runak-jhunak par cham-cham manava naache' mimics the sound of ankle bells or ghungroos. In the same way you can hear tears falling in a song, when Lata-ji sings Madan Mohan's composition, 'Naina barse rim jhim, rim-jhim' for *Woh Kaun Thi*. Such a beautiful song.

In my songs, there is yet another another sound, like the rhythm of a train climbing into the mountains, giving the song its rhythm, in the song from *Dil Se*, 'Chal chaiyya chaiyya'.

Yatindra Mishra: Have you ever felt that a composer has done complete justice to the words you have written for a song?

Gulzar: It happens quite often. An issue came up during the creation of the now very popular song, 'Kajrare-kajrare' for *Bunty Aur Babli*. Ehsan and Loy asked me, 'Gulzar-sahab, what do the words "Dariban" and "Ballimaran" mean?' I explained to them that these were places in Delhi where

Ghalib used to live. They were surprised, and said, 'You are a writer, therefore you know this, but those who will be listening to this song, how will they know where Ghalib used to live and what his connection is to this song?' I replied, 'If people can make this song such a big hit without knowing this, how much more would they do if they knew?' Though I said this in jest, I did explain the meaning in the context of the song's situation.

In the same song I have used the word, 'lu', as in 'Tera aana bhi garmiyon ki lu hai' (Your arrival is like the hot wind of summer), though we do not have the 'lu' blowing through Bombay.

Yatindra Mishra: There must be more such examples.

Gulzar: This danger will persist in the entire cinematic field if composers do not take the trouble to fully understand the lyrics. In my own film *Aandhi*, first Pancham and, later, Sanjeev Kumar were curious about the word I had used, nasheman. Today, when someone gets excited and ask and involve themselves in the full process, I like it a lot. When I was working on *Devdas*, Lata-ji, while singing the song 'Kuhu kuku' asked me the meaning of 'saroli'. I explained that it was a mango of great sweetness. She was pleased and said, 'I wanted to know how sweet, because it is important to bring that feeling into the song.' So you can understand, if Lata-ji, Pancham or Sanjeev Kumar asked about anything, how deep their involvement with the song and the entire film was.

There is also A. R. Rahman, who has full faith in me and keeps asking me questions. I too keep explaining to him the meaning of the words used in my compositions. Once, Rahman was discussing a word with me on Skype. Rahman wanted some dummy lines for his song, and suggested a word like 'sanam', as he felt it would fit well. I quickly stopped him, saying the use of such words needs to stop. He got worried, asking, 'Does it have a dirty meaning?' I said, 'I will give you some beautiful words. And we should stop using words that have become cliches in film music.'

Yatindra Mishra: Has there been any incident regarding the words used in your songs which gave you joy? That you felt you had written a song that helped someone?

Gulzar: In the song from *Fiza*, 'Aa ja mahiya' a line goes, 'Aa dhoop maloon main tere haathon pe.' A young girl from Canada wrote asking me, 'Uncle, why do we call the soap, sun?' And I thought, what a good idea, there should be a soap called Dhoop, or Sun. I thought it was beautiful and her mother must have explained the meaning to her. On another note, there used to be a soap called Sunlight Soap.

Yatindra Mishra: What is your view of the tradition of Sufiyana poetry in the current context?

Gulzar: If we examine this concept of 'Sufiyana', the first question is, is it Sufiyana? For that which we say is spiritual, does it speak of spiritual concepts? Spiritual writing, which at one level refers to the beloved. It is obvious in Rumi, in Shams Tabrizi, Bulleh Shah, Baba Farid. It has come travelling from Central Asia to us.

Talking to the divine in a Sufiyana way was already prevalent among us. In the Sufiyana tradition, the middle person is removed from the communication and one communicates directly with Allah, becoming the beloved. Talking to this beloved has been with us through centuries. The poetry regarding Radha and Krishna has been Sufiyana for centuries. Considering ourselves to be Radha, we place our feelings before Krishna. Dharamveer Bharti's 'Kanupriya' comes to mind. All his poems have been coloured by the love of Radha and Krishna. We find it expressed beautifully by Kabir too.

Yatindra Mishra: Your Ghalib also talks of love. You have made a superb serial on Ghalib, written a book, *Mirza Ghalib*, and written poems too. Why does he appeal to you so much? How do you, as a poet, view his qualities?

Gulzar: You might have heard often enough, how every time I refer to him, I call him *Chacha* Ghalib. Have you heard anyone else saying this? *Chacha* Momin, or *Mamu* Momin, *Tau* Dagh or *Chacha* Mir, it has never happened with anyone else. Pt. Jawaharlal Nehru whom the entire country knew as *Chacha* Nehru, and called him so with respect, is an exception. With Ghalib however, chacha becomes a more personal term, and that's why I call him chacha. He is absolutely down to earth.

Yatindra Mishra: You have a beautiful way of looking at Ghalib…

Gulzar: Ghalib experienced the reality of life in ways that triggered his poems and writings. Without these experiences, he would never have been able to say all that he did. You cannot find that voice within yourself, that level of art cannot arise, nor the irony that Ghalib possessed. When he spoke, he surpassed all his contemporaries.

He never regarded Kafiabandi as poetry. It is also exemplary that all his imagery was inspired by Hindustan. There is no Persian influence discernible in it. You can say that though he inherited Persian traditions, he identified with Hindustan. You might insist that the Vedantas belong solely to Hindi or Sanskrit or that they are an intrinsic part of Eastern philosophy, but Ghalib's Sufiyana philosophy is as much of our daily life and culture. This couplet is such a close reflection of our philosophy:

These matters of the soul you discuss, Ghalib
We would consider you a saint were you not a drunkard.
What cure is there for life's worries except death
The flame burns in all colours till the coming of day.

Yatindra Mishra: I consider this his best couplet:

Where is the second step of desire, O God,
We found the desert of possibility has just one footprint.

Gulzar: This is the culture I was referring to.

Yatindra Mishra: You took a couplet of his, 'Dil dhoondhta hai phir wahi fursat ke rast din' as the opening lines of a song for *Mausam* and expanded it beautifully. I would like to hear again the story of the making of the song.

Gulzar: Undoubtedly there is a beautiful poem on which this song is based. Ghalib had written it as 'Jee dhoondta hai phir wahi fursat ke raat din'. I took only the opening lines because I felt they contained a story. There must have been some story in mind which could be found lying in the courtyard in the gentle winter sun. Of how does it feel when the warm winds of summer waft at night. This is the concept that, with due respect to him, I tried to elaborate on, on his behalf. Consider these well-written lines:

On any pretext, I must spend the days and nights on your street
Finding someone to talk to, someone to greet

While writing this script I felt that this man (Sanjeev Kumar) had experienced something that needed to be added into the script. I felt that every mood searches for an anchor. And so I composed the same song in many versions to bring out different moods through the film. You will be surprised to know that Madan Mohan-ji made four versions of the tune for this song, of which two were used. Both are marvellous.

Yatindra Mishra: I think this song was also filmed quite uniquely.

Gulzar: The most interesting part of the picturisation was that we used the masking technique, which, at that time, was considered quite novel. I think this technique was used for the first time in a film song.

Yatindra Mishra: What are the requirements of poetry that a poet imposes on himself?

Gulzar: If we turn this question around and ask, which is the aspect that must be imposed on a poet? It's true that each will have his own opinion, which has to be written in his style for the poetry to be honest and sincere. Think of it, is it possible that I start writing like Nazeer Akbarabadi? There is a famous Hindi poet, whose lines I have never forgotten: 'For days, the hearth wept, the mill was sad.'

I do not possess this tone, but I can express the same subject in my way, and so can someone else. If I could write like Nagarjuna, at least his political satire, I would write nothing else. I would write exactly like Nagarjuna writes.

Take what I am saying as praise for him. If one has to quote Nagarjuna, one must mention where the feeling arose that it was necessary to quote him. A poet must aspire that he at least impose on himself that he keeps improving his work, keeps learning, and maintains the ability to praise the work of others.

Yatindra Mishra: How beautifully you have put it! Your response jolts a memory. Sajid Hussain, the composer, once phoned R. D. Burman and said, 'Burman-sahab, the song you have composed for *Sharmeelee*, 'Megha chhaye adhi raat' (Clouds gather at midnight)...what a wonderful song it is. I can give up all of my music for this one song by you...'

Gulzar: Absolutely! That's exactly what I am saying. Praise those who praise others for excellent work. Otherwise this custom will be lost to us, and no one will speak up when some good work is created.

Yatindra Mishra: If you had to choose a single song sung by Lata-ji, which one would spontaneously come to mind?

Gulzar: Is it possible to remember just one song of Lata-ji's?

Yatindra Mishra: And your favourite song written for Asha-ji?

Gulzar: The same question again?

Yatindra Mishra: Your all-time favourite song?

Gulzar: At this moment the one that comes to mind is 'Ghabrake jo hum sar ko takaraye, to achcha ho' (It is befitting that we bump our heads together in fear).

Yatindra Mishra: What an incomparable song you have remembered, Gulzar-sahab! This was written by Nakhshab Jarchavi. In fact, he wrote all the songs of *Mahal* (1949). It has a stanza that is so amazing it must be reproduced here:

Let him too witness the sinking of my heart
Should tears fill my eyes, that would only be right

Gulzar: Wah! Thank you for reminding me of Nakshab.

Yatindra Mishra: Any other important singer whose voice brought to a song the same intensity and beauty as Rajkumari gave to 'Ghabrake jo hum sar ko takaraye, to achcha ho'?

Gulzar: Dada Burman's voice. There is a magnetic quality, a saltiness in the tone of his voice. The song from *Sujata*, 'Sun mere bandhu re' (Listen to me, my friend) is sung from the heart. The nasal quality of the song pierces the heart like an arrow. One more amazing quality that you can learn from Dada's songs is knowing where a word can be broken while singing. It is inherent in his tunes that he makes the singer break or pause a word according to the composition and the metre. As an example, let's look at his composition for *Guide*, 'Wahan kaun hai tera, musafir, jayega kahaan' (Who waits for you there, O Wanderer, where do you go). Listen to the word 'musafir' and the number of different ways Dada uses it. You will be hypnotised by the idea of how to sing a song in so many ways to emphasise the words.

Yatindra Mishra: Colour is a strong part of the imagery in your songs. From 'Mora gora ang laile, mohe shyam rang dai de' (Take away my fair skin, Lord, colour me in your deep blue) to 'Neeli nadi ke paar, geela sa chaand khil gaya' (Across the blue river, a wet moon blossomed)...Do colours feature so often because at one time you were so connected with colours that the entire day would be spent dabbling in them?

Gulzar: It's not necessary that I should have been a painter to be able to speak of colours. Or that colours find a presence in my song because I worked in a motor garage painting dented cars. The colours in my songs come naturally. Maybe I make my imagery through colours. If they were made of black and white then, I would not say, 'Neeli nadi ke paar.' If you can understand it, look towards the moon. It is yellow, when a golden yellow moon emerges from the water it seems as if it is coming out of the blue water.

In 'Jhoote naina bole, saachi batiyan', there is a line, 'Nit chamkaye, chand kali rattiyan' (The moon forever brightens darkened nights). There are such nights too, and you realise your relationship with the moon. Because I also paint, it does occupy a portion of my creative mind, and the description of a colour in any song is quite natural.

Yatindra Mishra: Is there any song that you had to be cajoled into doing for a musician, or had taken up with hesitation, but which became extremely popular afterwards?

Gulzar: That has not happened. All the people I have worked with, all have been great masters. Madan Mohan-ji, Jaidev-ji, Khayyam-sahab, Bhupen-da, each of them has composed what I gave them beautifully. Yes, discussions would definitely take place. Often to get a song to fit the metre, one or two words would need to be changed, or shifted here and there.

But Pancham would definitely make a face when presented with blank verse. His usual refrain was, 'You write songs that sound like the news.' In such cases there would be improvisations, but the songs that resulted would be beautiful. I told you how he wanted words to be changed in the song from *Ijazat* too, but later composed it as it was. He had initially rejected, 'Mera kuch saamaan'.

I remember one song, also composed by Pancham. When I was working on *Kinara*, the line 'Ek hi khwab kai baar dekha maine' (I dreamed the same dream many times) came to me spontaneously, and I gave it to Pancham. As was his habit, he kept that page aside. Whenever I would remind him after we had recorded one or two songs of the film, he would say, 'Why do you repeatedly want to go back to that song?' He kept delaying the recording in this way. I had no idea why he was behaving like that, but it was obvious that he had no interest in recording that particular song. Finally, after countless reminders, the day for the recording dawned. Anyway, the song was finally ready, and Bhupinder played the guitar beautifully in between his singing. Pancham had, as always, created a beautiful composition. Later, he also started liking the song. Remember how popular, 'Ek hi khwab kai baar dekha maine' became. Even today it is considered a relevant song in love situations.

Yatindra Mishra: I remember a story. Usaad Bismillah Khan said of ghazal singer, Begum Akhtar, that the slight crack that would develop in her voice while singing extended *taans*, rather than being a mistake in the grammar of music, increased the beauty of her style. He used to say, 'This was the tyranny of her voice.'

Gulzar: Perfect! You used a perfect example to take the conversation forward. In a voice like Begum Akhtar's, any composition she sang would become her signature, and her style would shape the text and the grammar of the song.

Yatindra Mishra: If you had to name someone special from the formidable tradition of Hindi film songwriters, who would it be?

Gulzar: D. N. Madhok was a great songwriter, very accomplished. In the early 1950s the language of his songs was worth noting, where he would use folk imagery and pure local dialects to convey something. 'Jab tum hi chale pardes/ Lagakar thes/ O pritam pyara/ Duniya me koun hamara' (If you go away/ Having hurt me/ My love so dear/ Who in this world is mine?) or 'Mil ke bichad gayi akhiyan, hai Rama' (The eyes met and went asunder, hai Rama) in *Ratan* are songs where you can sense the fragrance of his words.

He has a special place in my mind, and it is above all other songwriters. The heights he achieved with K. L. Saigal's song in *Bhakt Surdas*, 'Nainheen ko raah dikha prabhu/ Pag-pag thokar khaoon main' (Show this blind one the way, O Lord/ I have obstacles every step of the way) is significant.

Yatindra Mishra: You place Dina Nath Madhok at the forefront of all the early lyricists?

Gulzar: Yes, D. N. Madhok is a pioneer lyricist, who started in 1931 when songs first came into Hindi films. At that time the tradition of songs came from the stage, in which the plays written by Agha Harsh Kashmiri, the influence of Parsi theatre, and the gharana-themed classical music and ghazal singing styles played an influential role. Around the same time, Urdu poetry also entered the Hindi film scene. Films were being made on mythological themes, and the trend of bhajans had also started. All these influences were harmonious and helped the nascent film music to flower. At this point, D. N. Madhok came into the spotlight as an important songwriter and created his identity with his very first film, *Radhe Shyam*. This film was released in 1932. You may be surprised to learn that the film had twenty-nine songs about Krishna and his life events, and Madhok-sahab wrote all of them in a charming, unique way. Which is why I hold him as the leader of the early tradition in Hindi film music. Also because the style he used to write his songs in set a trend that was followed for years afterwards.

Yatindra Mishra: And Pandit Pradeep?

Gulzar: Pandit Pradeep came just after Madhok-sahab. He was also a lyricist who wrote countless songs of inspiration for films. Pradeep-ji's songs were of a different metre, and he would sell them set to his own tunes. Nationalism was a constant undercurrent present in his songs. Of course, the most important of them is 'Ay mere watan ke logon', which brought tears to Pandit Nehru's eyes.

He was a milestone of the 1940s. Very often, his philosophical songs, like those of Kabir, send out warnings. 'Dekh teri sansar ki halat kya ho gayi bhagwan, kitna badal gaya insaan' (Look, O Lord, what has come upon your creation, how man has transformed), is such a simple but eloquent message; every song of his speaks of the philosophy of life. His vision converts his thoughts and expresses them in an Indian context.

Yatindra Mishra: What about Kedar Sharma?

Gulzar: Kedar Sharma was as good a poet and songwriter as he was a director.

Yatindra Mishra: Do you have any memories connected with Sahir-sahab that you want to share here?

Gulzar: Sahir-sahab used to live in the Four Bungalows area. Those days, the area was very far away from Bombay city. The roads were not in a condition that any bus or other vehicle could navigate them. He was among the few songwriters of the early years who had a Morris car.

Sahir-sahab lived on the second floor, and around the same time, with a few of my friends, I was staying in the outhouse of the same building. The rent was twenty rupees a month. Now looking back, I feel blessed that even in my early days of struggle I stayed in that part of Bombay where Sahir-sahab had chosen to reside.

Yatindra Mishra: What memories do you have of Shailendra?

Gulzar: I met Shailendra when he was already writing for films. The names of Shailendra, Lata Mangeshkar, Shankar-Jaikishen were constantly on the radio, repeated like the names in a rosary. He was part of a duo with Hasrat Jaipuri, but one felt that he wrote most of the songs for Shankar-Jaikishen. My earliest meeting was in 'Bapu Nivas', a small place with a room, a kitchen and a verandah where Basu Bhattacharya, Debu Sen and Himadri lived. Shailendra had taken this place to be able to write in peace. Basu Bhattacharya and Debu were assistants to Bimal Roy. As they had no place to stay, Shailendra had given them this space. Salil Chowdhury would come there to meet Shailendra, and the meetings of the Bombay Youth Choir would often be held there. Till today I have not been able to find out when and how Shailendra wrote his songs for films. Once he said to me, 'The time from morning to lunch is for Shankar-Jaikishen. That discipline cannot be broken. If it is broken, there will be big trouble.' It had been decided that he would write the script for *Pinjare Ki Panchi* and that I would write the songs. But lack of time changed that decision. I wrote the script and he wrote the songs. He knew the difference between poems and songs. He knew how to convert a poem so that it becomes a song.

Yatindra Mishra: Can we discuss the works of some of the others?

Gulzar: Prasoon Joshi's name comes in front of me first; he has grasped the metre of poetry and musical sensibilities very well. Many of his songs are well liked, among them, the songs of Rakeysh Omprakash Mehra's *Rang De Basanti*. He shows many shades of life in a single album. If I look at the tradition started by D. N. Madhok, I must add Swanand Kirkire's name to it. One sees the use of such words and language that stem from the same source. The journey of Irshad Kamil has been interesting too. He uses Punjabi in a novel way. He displays a naivete in the way he pushes the boundaries of Sufi poetry. But I feel he will go even further if he hones the literary writing he uses. He is still on the journey. I see these three as important song-writers who will remain even after this era passes. Apart from all of them, one more name that must be mentioned is that of Kausar Munir, who writes sensibly and is adept at using new idioms. Amitabh Bhattacharya is an innovative lyricist, I like his work too.

Yatindra Mishra: Where do you see A. R. Rahman's position in today's context? He is also counted as one who has wrought changes in Hindi film music.

Gulzar: A. R. Rahman has the quality that sets him apart. The sound of his drum at one level sounds Indian. In fact, it is an Indian folksy sound which he has used very well. His most important contribution is changing the structure of songs.

Yatindra Mishra: Do you feel his breaking of tradition to create a new song structure is a big achievement?

Gulzar: He has made songs akin to free verse. He has broken the rhyming pattern which songs were written in, moved the songs away from the rhymes, something they had been using for years. It has come closer to blank verse.

Yatindra Mishra: This is a good way of understanding Rahman's technique. You are also adept at writing poetry in free verse, so it must be an easy task for you to match the music or to write the words to match the music he has composed.

Gulzar: It goes beyond that. For this you need to understand blank verse well; just as you need to understand free verse.

Yatindra Mishra: In this, Rahman comes through as a great artiste.

Gulzar: Undoubtedly so. He is a milestone of this era, in the same way as Pankaj Mullick was of his, or C. Ramchandra. I call him a milestone, because it takes time to become a legend.

Yatindra Mishra: Kishore Kumar has been a prominent voice in your films. You, R. D. Burman and Kishore Kumar have been a great team. There are innumerable everlasting songs created by the three of you. 'Musafir hoon yaaron' (I am a traveller, my friends) from *Parichay*, 'Koi hota jisko apna, hum apna keh lete yaaron' (I wish there was someone, someone to call my own) from *Mere Apne*, 'Jaane kya soch kar nahin guzara' (Wonder what thought stopped the night from passing) from *Kinara*, 'O maajhi re, apna kinara, nadiya ki dhara hai' (O boatman, my shore is the river's perennial flow), from *Khushboo* come to mind immediately.

Gulzar: Some songs of his that I would like to remind you of: *Do Dooni Char*'s 'Hawaon pe likh do hawaaon ke naam', or 'Aane wala pal, jaane wala hai' from *Golmaal.* Actually, my meeting with Kishore-da happened during the making of *Do Dooni Char*. He was a big artiste in all aspects. During the shooting of *Do Dooni Char* he had a rule that he would shoot all day but leave, at any cost, at 5.45 p.m. We used to think he was eccentric, which is why he had this strict rule.

Yatindra Mishra: Among the new composers, whom would you place on the same level as the great composers of music you have had a long association with?

Gulzar: At present the most prominent among all is Vishal Bhardwaj. Vishal is from Meerut. He understands poetry and the sensitivity of poetry. He has grown up in the courtyard of the accomplished poet, Bashir Badr. The vibes that Vishal has for poetry have not been there earlier with others.

Earlier on Hemant Kumar was among those who wrote his music after thoroughly grasping the poetry, just as Vishal does now. The reason for that was Hemant-da had sung a lot of Gurudev Tagore's songs, so he could feel the flavour of the poetry he had imbibed. Today, when I see the same thing in Vishal, it makes me happy.

Yatindra Mishra: The songs made today have created a fashion of including English words. A line of a song is framed half in Hindi and half in English. What is your view on this?

Gulzar: This is decided according the character who is speaking the dialogues. He will sing the same way, won't he? Today, every single character speaks English. If a person sings the way he talks, it seems more natural. It just cannot be feasible that he speaks English the rest of the time, but when he sings, he sings something like Ghalib's ghazals.

Yatindra Mishra: While writing the songs for *Gharonda*, what was your experience of working with music director Jaidev? He has been a very accomplished music director and the film is known for its serious subject and the serious content of its songs. What do you want to share about Jaidev? Which of his compositions do you like immensely?

Gulzar: All the songs of *Hum Dono*. And especially the one sung by Lata-ji, 'Allah tero naam, Ishwar tero naam' (Allah is your name, your name is Ishwar). His approach was a mix of the traditional and the modern.

An interesting fact that I want to share with you: Jaidev-ji and R. D. Burman were two composers who were learning by assisting S. D. Burman...how different from their guru and how unique and successful they became.

Yatindra Mishra: The composition of 'Ek tha bachpan' (There was once a childhood) is very complicated.

Gulzar: Yes, it is my most difficult song. If I have had any difficulty with a song in my entire career, then it was with 'Ek tha bachpan'. I found the song very tough. The reason was that Babuji is singing it to a child, and when she grows up and sings it on radio, it must still be relevant.

Both of *Guddi*'s songs were made under pleasant circumstances. 'Bol re papihara' was a classical bandish which was given to me saying I should take it further and compose a song along the same lines. So, I made a classical song accordingly.

The other song from *Guddi* which is a prayer, 'Hum ko man ki shakti dena, man vijay kare' (Grant our heart strength, that it may emerge victorious). While composing it, very innocently, Vasant Desai said something very nice. I still remember that innocence. He told me while laughing in his childlike way, with his elbows on his knees, 'Song must move along like this, propelled by the story.'

The prayer-song later became so popular that many schools in Bombay took to playing it during morning assembly. Composing for a song, it was as if Vasant Desai would create visuals out of his compositions. Listen to the music he has composed for Shantaram-ji's films and you will agree that he has merged the screenplays with the soul of his music.

Yatindra Mishra: What was your experience with Kanu Roy? Though it was limited to *Anubhav* and *Griha Pravesh.*

Gulzar: Thinking of Kanu Roy makes me feel regret over the fact that he was given such few films despite being such a good composer. I do not remember him working for anyone besides Basu Bhattacharya. And there was some injustice done to him. Meaning, the producer would say, I will only give you seven musicians, you have to manage with that. Actually, Basu used to feel that nothing much happens through music; all one hears is the flute, or the sitar. Composers bring in all these other instruments for no real reason. Which was why Kanu Roy was forced to work with a limited number of accompanists.

But it must be said that Kanu Roy was, in his own right, an accomplished musician. Very melodious. He used to be a welder on the Howrah Bridge, in Calcutta. He was fond of music and contacted Salil-da. Salil-da saw something in him and made him his assistant. That is how he came into the film industry. Where did the film industry have songs like 'Meri jaan, mujhe jaan na kaho meri jaan' before? It is thanks to Kanu Roy that we can listen to this song now.

Yatindra Mishra: Who is the director you regret not having been able to work with, and who might have enriched your film journey?

Gulzar: When I look back I realise I never managed to work with Guru Dutt-sahab. Without him, who would have seen films on such imaginative subjects like *Pyaasa, Sahib, Bibi Aur Ghulam* and *Kaagaz Ke Phool*? All these films are writer's films, made from the writer's perspective.

Yatindra Mishra: I want to talk about the stories behind the composing of songs for *Ijazat*. I want to hear the stories about the other songs.

 Gulzar: During the time *Ijazat* was being shot, I went across to meet Pancham. That day he played a phrase of a western song to me, which he wished to include in a loop in his song. Pancham believed the loop would fit beautifully. The phrase he was playing for me had a metre like this: 'tee, ree, ree, ra ra ree ree'. He asked me to write some words for it. Something immediately came to my mind and I wrote, 'Choti si kahani se, baarishon ki paani se/ Saari wadi bhar gayi' (With a small story, with rain/ The whole valley brimmed). I was writing and he would keep humming to match the words. Gradually the song started taking shape. By the time it dawned fully on us, the composition was ready and fitted into the tune he had chosen. And the strange thing was that the song was created with no song situation present in the film.

When the song was ready, Pancham suggested I should create a suitable situation in the film. I kept trying to explain to him that all possible situations where a song could be used had been finalised. There was no scene in the film where a new song could be fitted. But he kept insisting. I too was quite taken with the song. Finally I could decide that the song could be used in the titles. I told the film's cameraman, Ashok Mehta, that to justify the song, he needed to shoot the raindrops through different moods. Ashok Mehta caught on immediately. We went to the interiors of Khandala in the monsoon and returned after shooting the many aspects of the rain. Thus, through Pancham's stubbornness, we found our title song.

Yatindra Mishra: 'Katra katra' is a song with unusual lyrics. What was the story behind the making of this song?

Gulzar: A funny incident took place with Pancham regarding 'Katra katra'. As Pancham was not very familiar with Urdu he asked me, 'Have you heard any such song till now that starts with katra katra? You write anything at all and come to me to make it into a song, please find two other words instead of these.' Pancham was looking worried, so I told him not to worry. I gave him options like 'boond-boond', 'saawan-bhadon'; and he seemed to like them. He brightened up and said, 'Yes, these sound more musical.' And he started composing the song with the new words in place. But he began to feel the new words were not fitting with the movement of the song. Soon enough he abandoned the new words and returned to the old lyrics. Then we found the perfect tune, through which the song was finding its true expression. Though 'Mera kuch saamaan' is the milestone of *Ijazat*, 'Katra katra' too could be composed parallel to it as a beautiful song.

Yatindra Mishra: What was the process of the creation of 'Mera kuch saamaan'?

Gulzar: You know the story of the making of this song, but let me repeat it. When I handed him the song his first reaction was, 'Good scene.' I explained, 'Pancham, this is not a scene; it is a song for which you have to compose the music.' For some reason, Pancham got angry and said, 'Yaar, tomorrow you will bring the *Times of India* and hand it to me saying, compose a tune for this.' Saying which, he threw down the paper on which the song had been written.

Asha-ji, who was present, picked up the paper and started reading. Just as she entered into the mood of the poetry, she picked up the phrase 'Lauta do' and started humming. When Pancham heard it, he asked her to hum the phrase again. Asha hummed the tune. Pancham felt that it sounded really nice. Taking the paper from Asha-ji, he immediately started composing a tune on the harmonium. You will be astonished to know that the song that had made him angry and which he had turned down, was composed and ready in just a few minutes. I just cannot tell you what a genius musician Pancham was. Once he got the hang of a song, and caught a strand of the meaning, it took him just the span of a few minutes to compose the song. I am lucky that I found Pancham, and my songs got a composer like him. Touch wood!

Yatindra Mishra: The song 'Khali haat shaam ayi hai' (Empty-handed the evening has come) in the film for some reason seems like a veneration of Madan Mohan-ji by R. D. Burman.

Gulzar: Pancham too felt that 'Khali haat shaam aye hai' had shades of Madan Mohan in the tune.

Yatindra Mishra: *Dil Padosi Hai* is a necessary stage in understanding how the three of you worked together…

Gulzar: *Dil Padosi Hai* was made in such a way that it should sound different. The same old teenage romance songs cannot do justice to a mature love story. In this respect, 'Raat Christmas Ki Thi' is an experimental song, in which two people meet but he is not her husband, nor is she his wife. Yet they meet and get involved in an affair. This comes through clearly in these lines of the composition, 'You were not alone, I was not lonely either' which is a very common situation yet no one wants to deal with this subject. So whether it is a film or a private album, I did it in this way and that song became popular.

A composition on a similar theme is 'Jaane do mujhe jaane do' (Let go, let me go). This song is about a woman who is ill-treated by her husband; he beats her. Now this is such a complicated situation where the woman does not want to continue the relationship. She wants to be free of it and go far away. When she remembers the hurt she has received, then the line follows that says, 'Gehre kharashon ki gehri nishaniyan hain/ Chehre ke neeche kitni kahaniyan hain), 'Of deep wounds there are deep scars/ Behind the façade of the face lie many stories). That is how I wrote this song.

Yatindra Mishra: 'Majhi re majhi' (Boatman, O boatman) is a composition that is at a different level in this album, both from the point of view of words and music. Is there anything you wish to share about it?

Gulzar: The basis of this song was that a woman wants to run away with her lover and the excuse she makes is that a mendicant has come to the opposite bank of the river, whom she must visit. This is a song with a strange situation, and

Pancham added a whole lot of experimental music while composing it. Even today, listening to the song, you will realise what a brilliant composition it is. I still feel deep regret over the fact that the album did not do too well at the time of its release. Sometimes, some albums and songs only get their due much later.

Yatindra Mishra: Is there any actor or actress with whom you could not work and which opportunity was simply lost forever?

Gulzar: Smita Patil.

Yatindra Mishra: You have mentioned the most gifted of personalities in acting…It is indeed regrettable that she is not a part of your filmography.

Gulzar: Smita never got a chance. Life did not give her time to flower to her full potential. She has done wonderful work in Shyam Benegal's films. She was at her best in *Manthan*. *Nishant*, too, was one of her memorable films, but I saw her brilliance in *Bhumika*. I found that Amol Palekar too was equally wonderful in *Bhumika*.

Yatindra Mishra: Do you regret missing out on a chance to work with artistes from areas beyond art and commercial cinema, or from the stage, who might have brought in a new way of expressing what you wished to say, had you directed them in a film?

Gulzar: If I name him, it is likely that you will ridicule me, but I repeatedly wished to take him in my films.

Yatindra Mishra: Pray tell us who he is…

Gulzar: Our own Amjad Ali Khan-sahab, the sarod maestro. I had made a film with him that was based on his life and work. He is still handsome, and we cannot even guess how good-looking he must have been in his youth. While working on his documentary, I felt a great inclination to work with him in a film.

Yatindra Mishra: When Ustad-sahab comes to know of this, and when people read this, they will be amused that you wished to cast Ustad Amjad Ali Khan as a hero!

Gulzar: Yes. That was a miss, because I met him rather late. I met him the first time at Sharmila Tagore-ji's house. This was at a time when he was in love with Subhalakshmi-ji and was to marry her soon. I saw the restlessness in him at that time. He was a close friend of Sharmila-ji, and when he would talk, we would see glimpses of the love that dwelt in his heart. He is a romantic soul. Seeing this, I often thought that I could frame a story around his handsome personality and character.

Yatindra Mishra: This gives rise to another question. Was there a singer, male or female, whom you could not work with. Some voice that made you wish would sing your songs.

Gulzar: Mehdi Hasan-sahab was that voice. The title song of *Lekin* was 'Kesariya baalam aao ji padharo mahre desh', and I wanted him to sing it. He was visiting India at that time, and staying in a rented flat in Bombay. Since it was the title song, there was no situation, and I thought I would use it as the background song. However, Hridayanath-ji had a change of mind and he decided, no, Didi will sing this song, and the matter ended there.

Yatindra Mishra: There is an impressive history connected with the musical traditions of courtesans. Their singing at their kothas, or the concerts they staged at the royal courts, has a long tradition that had a big influence on Indian classical music. Did you ever consider making a film on this way of life?

Gulzar: No, never, because I did not think on these lines at all. Yes, but I did somewhat base the character of Waheeda in *Namkeen* on these women, on the nautanki dancer Jugni. That is the only cameo which you can say comes close to these characters, but it does not really amount to anything.

Yatindra Mishra: Which artiste in Hindi cinema stands apart due to his art? Who seems the best if looked at holistically from the point of view of actor and director?

Gulzar: Pancham used to sometimes call me 'Gullu'. You can call me Google. Ask anything. Answer everything.

Yatindra Mishra: You wrote a song for Shyam Benegal's film, *Mammo*, 'Hazaar baar ruke, hazaar baar chale' (I stopped a thousand times, started a thousand times). Is this the only song you wrote for Benegal-sahab?

Gulzar: He had asked me to write a song for *Mammo* for a situation that gave voice to the Partition. Vanraj Bhatia had composed it, and it was sung by Jagjit.

Yatindra Mishra: Which was the best time you spent with your friend, R. D. Burman?

Gulzar: Of course when he was composing my songs. But to tell you the truth, both he and Asha-ji were great cooks. They often had contests over their cooking. Pancham liked making European dishes, but used a lot of chillies. In fact he grew green chillies at home. He would call for chilli plants and seeds from Burma and Singapore. His garage and terrace were filled with chilli plants.

Whenever we were recording background music, and if Asha-ji was present too, we would eagerly wait, once the recording was done. I would know for sure that Asha-ji would bring something she had cooked at home to eat after the recording session. What amazing food she would make and how lovingly she would serve it to her friends!

Yatindra Mishra: Which is higher: literature or cinema, and why?

Gulzar: It is clear that till date our cinema has not managed to achieve the intellectuality of books. It's like how we use literature to testify that the scenario was such at that time because Shakespeare in his plays, and Sarat Chandra or Premchand in their novels were reflecting the times in their work. I have always considered literature to be streets ahead of cinema. Also, cinema stands on base of the literature. Cinema must produce its own literature in its own language of moving images.

Yatindra Mishra: Your song 'Do nainon me aansoo bhare hain, nindiya kaise samaye' (Two eyes brimming with tears, how can sleep settle in them) has no rhyming lines, but there is a rhythm that is created by the metre. How do you manage to make your songs read like poems even without confining them to a metre?

Gulzar: I've cheated a bit in this song, so that the music director does not realise that I have made the lines run free. When you read 'Do nainon me aansoo bhare hain, nindiya kaise samaye', it seems complete in itself. There are many such songs in which some lines are long, some short. Some are based on the metre of Hindi poems, some take their metre from the Urdu temperament. Some are somewhere between Hindi and Urdu too.

Yatindra Mishra: In the song, 'Aye ajnabi, tu bhi kabhi aawaz de kahin se' (O stranger, call out to me sometimes) the words 'Pakhi-pakhi pardesi' are heard in the background in Mahalakshmi Iyer's voice. Did you write this in the original song or was this an improvisation added in to beautify the song while the tune was being created?

Gulzar: Rahman had a big contribution in this. In classical music you have a base on which you start the bandish, and then define the raag, and then, as the song follows, you add paltas in the middle and take taans...in other words, you start unveiling it and double the speed or increase it by four times. Rahman started doing the same thing in film music. He breaks the structure of a song and then plays around in the heart of it.

Rahman asked me to give him a word with the 'pa' sound in the middle of the antara. He asked me a cute question, 'Is this only a sound or does it have meaning?' I explained to him that pakhi meant bird and the word was used in both Hindi and Bengali. Later, he added the line in Mahalakhsmi Iyer's voice, above and below the antara, and I think it adds to the seriousness and depth of Udit Narayan's voice in the stanzas.

Yatindra Mishra: Where is the point you can reach the 'sum' from in a tune which has been made by breaking the traditional movement of a classical song? In blank verse, where does the right point to catch the sum come from?

Gulzar: Yatindra, you have consumed the milk and the cream. Only the dregs are left. It's the horizon line one looks for. I learnt this from painting. Look at a painting; regardless of how abstract it might be, or whether it has lines or faces drawn crookedly, the painter would still have created a horizon line where your eye will stop. Even in modern paintings the horizon line will be visible somewhere, balancing the entire picture.

Yatindra Mishra: Your film, *Libaas* could not be released. You must still feel regret over this. When you think of the film now, what do you feel?

Gulzar: *Libaas* was a very mature film. If it had been released, you would understand how a very unusual subject had been treated with utmost sensitivity. What else can I say about my own film? Yes, the music was released and became very popular.

A few years ago, the screenplay of the film was also published. This film was based on a story written by me, titled 'Chaabi'. Later it was added into my story collection, *Ravi Paar* under the title of 'Seema'. The famous script and dialogue writer, Javed Siddique-sahab even based a play on it titled *Kachche Lamhe* (Vulnerable Moments). This film with a theatre background had some scenes from classic dramas included in it.

 Yatindra Mishra: Folk theatre has not had the same success in cinema as folk music has. Do you have an opinion on why this is so?

Gulzar: There was no market for it. Cinema is dominated by the market. When art cinema had a market, some good films were made and some big names emerged from this. The case of folk theatre and children's cinema is the same. Amol Palekar made *Paheli* (2005) which was somewhat successful, but this one example cannot be considered good enough to make a claim for more such films. Even in theatre, the story is quite similar.

Yatindra Mishra: In *Meera* you portray Meerabai as a woman who reaches unusual heights on the strength of her character. You have not made her a legend or a mythical person, a fact which I think is the film's biggest strength.

Gulzar: This is what everyone who has read 'Meerabai' on their own, and then saw her as a character in my film. If I could take you into Meera's era, I would like to say, if Meera's in-laws could have known that one day she would enter the annals of history and make her own story a legend, perhaps they would have treated her more gently.

The members of her family had a clear and simple idea: if you are a Krishna worshipper, there is a proper temple made for him. Worship there as much and as long as you wish to. But what behaviour is this that, despite being a member of a royal family, you go to the riverside and cohabit with the sadhus and the nomads there? In any age, not just in princely households, if even a middle-class woman sets about behaving in this way, there would be much clamour.

But Meera goes beyond all this. Beyond the ties of social norms. This rebellion is her great strength, making her one of the strongest characters of her time. She cares little for poor or rich, caste or creed, or the environs she moves about in. She goes straight to Raidas' cottage. She thus does something that shocks society. When she talks of devotion, of spiritual love, of worshipping Krishna, no one in the large social milieu she belongs to, sides with her. She is completely alone.

Yatindra Mishra: Meera is still alone, even today.

Gulzar: That is one hundred per cent true. If Meera comes back to stand before society today, this era too will harass her to conform to the norms of the present and create hurdles in the path of her good work. Also worth pondering is the fact that she was born during what we call the Bhakti period. It was also a period of conflict. Haridas belonged to that period, as did Surdas and Raidas. Poets who sang devotional songs, saints and mendicants were everywhere in the country. And she represents this aspect of that age. This aspect pleased me immensely and I filmed *Meera* keeping this as her real image. I left out all those aspects that would have made her seem legendary or great. I felt her greatness lay in herself, her poetry, her rebellion. That worked for me.

Yatindra Mishra: You took a rational approach to presenting Meerabai. The entire film is based on this sincere effort, and that is what takes the film to a different intellectual level.

Gulzar: Take the case of Sukrat (Socrates), or Meerabai, who was given a cup of poison to drink. Gandhiji was killed by a bullet. Has anything changed even today? What happened in our time with Gandhi is similar to whatever transpired with Meera during Akbar's time. All the great spiritual tomes our nation possesses have not made us as spiritual as we should be.

Yatindra Mishra: This is stuff to be understood and absorbed.

Gulzar: Cinema is not just entertainment. However much we may improve our technique or use what we learn from the West in our films, the original thought stems from the thought process that we wish to express by making a film or writing a book. The obsession to find the truth existed then and continues to exist even now. Falsehood was prevalent even then, and is spread all across society even today. The aim should be to say something extraordinary about the character, the historical event or a historic personality and let society know the truth. If you are doing this, then whether you are writing a poem, making a film or working for theatre, you are creating a radiance somewhere.

Yatindra Mishra: Do you not feel that all those who did indeed bring radiance into society were harassed in their time? That their advice and ideas were accepted by society only many years after they had passed?

Gulzar: This happens. We were talking about Meera. From Kabir to Guru Nanak, this is exactly what happened. When Nanak sang his bhajans and Bala and Mardana played something on the ektara and sarangi, how many people would have felt appreciation stirring in their minds or thought that something worthwhile was being said, by worthy people. How many among those who sat in the groups around him and sang along really thought that they were in the presence of a guru. We only created 'panthis' and encased the words of such illustrious people in it, saying, here is a religious book, venerate it.

Yatindra Mishra: What do you think about Guru Nanak's poetry?

Gulzar: Whenever I read Nanak, I find his language difficult. It is tough. I see an effort in his compositions. It makes me feel he has a lot in mind, a very big image which he wants to condense and show. I think his wandering about for twenty to twenty-two years was something that expressed his restlessness and marked his internal journey. His travels are called his 'udasiyan'. All other jogis would go with him wherever he went. I felt it was a huge thing that he travelled far to spread his word. The inner restlessness would trouble me immensely. I would feel time and again, why does he not sit and meditate instead? Why does he not stay in one place? That is the reason his imagery too is not confined to a single place. It is very beautiful, and as magnificent as his journey was.

You can call Nanak's poetry scholarly, like Ghalib's poetry. He says, 'Nanak's name is a ship, he who boards, alights on the other side.' I think it was a significant thing; to use the ship as a simile in that period. It places him as a modern poet in his time.

Yatindra Mishra: The aarti in Raag Dhanashri in the Guru Granth Sahib, 'Gagan my thal ravi deepak bane tarika mandala moti' has so much inner meaning. It imagines the entire universe to be the plate that holds the lamp that performs the veneration of the Divine. This is, in a way, the worship of Nature's creations.

Gulzar: What a beautiful thought you have expressed. The bubble of pain that you can see in it, the bubble continues alongside throughout. A pain that is visible; that travels with you, or me, or with other poets. It is not visible in Kabir. Not even when he realises that he does not know the mother who gave him birth, who abandoned him. What was her face like? That relationship of pain, linked to the umbilicus, how can it fade away in anybody? But it disappears in Kabir despite the fact that he is also searching for the same thing. On another level, the searching call from his heart reaches Allah.

He presented his poems before the suspicious world without any hesitation. And continued his journey in peace, not feeling hurt, or anger or letting himself get affected by their taunts. The facelessness he assumed when he said, 'Ghunghat ke patth khol re, tujhe piya milenge' (Take off your veil, you will find your beloved) became a philosophy in itself. This is so beautiful. The art that his expressions hold is known only to him…that which connects him to his pain, which stays with him and reaches out to trouble our conscience too.

Yatindra Mishra: Kabir's poems too are based on familiar elements.

Gulzar: His region was from Banaras to Maghar. Every common sight that we see but take no note of: from a brass vessel to the grinding wheel, the river bank to the bird picking grain, he mentions all of it.

Through his long journey he crafts his imagery around ordinary objects. This makes him a formidable poet. Meaning, though he is roaming about in the world, he returns to the grinding stone in the house and the hearth in his poems. He is a true Sufi, whose words evoke your trust. That if Kabir says this world is quite useless, forsake it, you agree that indeed this is a philosophical poet who has his finger on the pulse of truth. Whether it is his Hath Yog, or his couplets, Kabir's presence is evident all over the world.

Yatindra Mishra: You have evaluated Kabir so well. Which aspect of him do you find the most interesting?

Gulzar: His ability to bring spirituality into the heart of his sorrow-filled poems. His poems reflect things that can be seen anytime in daily life. It can be with a hawker or a man selling sweets. It can be found in the hands of a child flying a kite, or with the mender of clocks. It can also be found in the hands of your mother who is taking the roti off the stove.

Kabir is a tradition who scorches your mind and heart. He is like someone who catches you in a wrong-doing. And it is his poetry that will save you from guilt and guide you away from the wrong path.

Yatindra Mishra: Who is your favourite Sanskrit poet?

Gulzar: Bhartrihari. Who is called Bharthari in folk culture. There is a couplet by Allama Iqbal:

The heart of a diamond can be cut by a leaf
But even a saw cannot sever the umbilical cord

Through Iqbal's poem, I can say of Bhartrihari that a diamond can be cut by a flower, but the saw cannot cut the umbilical cord. Relationships are so firmly made that, if linked to the navel, they may get knotted but won't get cut off. Bhartrihari is one such poet who stands at such a height that he cannot be ignored. He alone is a poet who after seeing all the shades of life, writes poems on *Shringar*-customs-separation.

Yatindra Mishra: What would you like to share with us your views about Amir Khusro's poems?

Gulzar: Each of them is beautiful. He was a great poet. Reading his poetry, you don't even realise what important points he makes. His language is very appealing too. Khusro has a huge influence on Hindi poetry, which reaches into our film music too. Who, today, can write anything to match his bidai song, 'Kahe ko byahi bidesh?' (Why did you marry me off to a foreign land.)

Khusro is a torch-bearer, countless poems find their light lit from the flame of his poetry. His Sufi poetry set the tone for writers of Sufi poetry through the ages that followed. It confounds us to realise how modern his thought was almost a thousand years ago. His relationship with his guru Nizamuddin Auliya, and the many poems that resulted from it, are quite amazing. His close bond with his Auliya resulted in his writing and composing songs in the same vein in style and thought. First he composed riddles then went on to create kaimurkiyan.

He amazes us in the way he uses language as a tool to negotiate through the raags and raginis in his compositions. He was the only intellectual who was a part of the durbar of seven emperors. He witnessed so many sultanates changing. What an exalted space he occupies as a poet; the very thought astounds us.

His was the earliest voice to shape Urdu. And there's a folk belief that he improvised and shaped the sitar and table too.

Yatindra Mishra: And Bulleh Shah?

Gulzar: I can only say of him that he must be singing in abandon somewhere. I might have told you this before; once

Bulleh Shah's teacher, Inayat Shah, was angry with him. The amazing thing in this is that if your guru is upset with you, your life becomes meaningless. You are crying, you are sinking in sorrow. He was in love with his guru. That love also encompassed the Almighty. Standing on the road to the masjid that his master would emerge from, Bulleh Shah started singing:

Your love makes me dance madly
Like from a cup of poison have I drunk
Come my healer, or I will surely die
Your love makes me dance thaiya thaiya

To dance thus, to reach a stage of a disciple dying for the love of his guru is very spiritual. Despite reading it so many years later, its power can be felt.

Yatindra Mishra: Leaving aside Meerabai in *Meera*, which character did you enjoy developing the most in your films?

Gulzar: Vinod Khanna would say to me, I understand Meera's emotions so well, I wish I could have played the role. I could understand his mind because he was passing through that phase when he was thinking of leaving the film industry. He had fallen in love with the philosophy that Osho propounded. Vinod Khanna was such a genuine person that he was leaving the industry only after completing all his commitments. When he said that he could understand Meera completely, I could understand that it was his love for Krishna expressing itself.

He comes across in *Meera* in a very beautiful, gentle undertone. He portrays Bhojraj's character perfectly. He did not present himself like a hero, something that most actors tend to do. The personality of Bhojraj is overshadowed by that of Meera, and Vinod Khanna let that happen most naturally through his acting. Today I believe that this was also possible because of the feelings he was experiencing; all if it was reflected in his characterisation.

Yatindra Mishra: In the film, *Asoka*, there is a line in the song, 'Raat ka nasha abhi' that is so typically Gulzar. 'Karvat badalti hoon, to sapna badal leti hoon', (When I turn on my side, I change my dream). We find countless such lines in all your songs right from the beginning till the present. I want to know if what started with 'Humne dekhi hain in aakhon ki mehekti khushboo' (I have seen the shimmering fragrance of your eyes) of *Khamoshi* becoming more effortless now?

Gulzar: One cannot force this into a film. Film is a director's medium, after all. Even if one wants to, one cannot think anything is effortless and write it. Even when I was making my own films, the songwriter did not have the freedom to think like a poet and go beyond the script. I have been writing songs for years. My effort has always been to read the entire script, then understand the situation and then write the song.

Yatindra Mishra: This is a valuable insight concerning film songs. Can we look at this communication beyond films too? Meaning, if taken out of the film, are these songs just words and music?

Gulzar: It depends entirely on how you look at a song by itself; not as part of the film. Just as you felt one line of the song could be spoken about in the context of poetry. Communication is paramount in classical music. If you see different shades in the singing of a raag by Kishori-ji (Kishori Amonkar) and Bhimsen-ji (Bhimsen Joshi), it is their different ways of communication that is expressing itself differently to you. At what level they are able to present their work to you, and at what point it touches you and what it evokes in you, that is what the singing style is all about. In the same way, whether it is me writing or someone else, if a single line manages to touch you, the writing has done its job. Then it matters little who has sung it or for which film it was written.

Yatindra Mishra: You are talking about that grammar in which a lyricist writes standing outside himself. Does the personality of a lyricist somehow get reflected in film songs too?

Gulzar: Why not? If that didn't happen, then it would not matter who was writing; it would all be the same thing. You know, of course, how the singer or the lyricist sometimes moves away from the frame that was given to them as the area of expression. If you leave the frame, you create a new expression. If you do not risk moving out of the frame, nothing can be accomplished. If Kishori Amonkar or Bhimsen Joshi had not developed their styles individually, would they have become so accomplished, or their music so successful? Only those who find their own language can make a mark. A songwriter too must do just this; he who finds his language, whatever the situation, even if he writes something ordinary, the meaning will be evident.

Yatindra Mishra: Which aspect of your life do you most connect your songs with?

Gulzar: I think of the moments that are meaningful. That moment is not by itself, every moment has a complete scenario surrounding it.

Yatindra Mishra: It is valuable to go back in time.

Gulzar: A huge vista opens up behind the moment. You can see the journey and a scenario reveals itself. Like in the song 'Seeli hawa choo gayi, geela badan chil gaya'. There's a complete story behind the way the breeze touches the skin, which includes scars and wounds that bruise and scrape at the skin. So this is linked to your thought which stems from your own experience and you find other means to express the emptiness it has left within you. If some feeling emerges from the long history of a moment, it holds a cache of emotions inside it.

Yatindra Mishra: Are there personal reasons for thinking this way?

Gulzar: As a poet and scriptwriter, my mind is shaped in such a way that I like to examine every moment in its entirety.

Yatindra Mishra: Is there any song written by you, written in connection with one such moment, that you think is most presentable?

Gulzar: The songs of *Sadma* come immediately to mind. First, 'Surmai ankhiyon mein nanha nanha sapna de ja re' and second, 'Ay zindagi gale lagaa le/ Humne bhi tere har ek gham ko gale se lagaya hai, hai na?'

Yatindra Mishra: When did films become an important part of society?

Gulzar: Even today there are people who know nothing about films. Who are the people involved? Which banners exist? They know nothing about this. So, this obsession with films did not exist earlier. Gradually, the popularity of radio pulled people towards films, when it started playing film songs regularly. When the television set entered homes, and there was a movie showing every Sunday, that made a difference too. I do not remember any big publication like *The Illustrated Weekly of India* publishing film news of any kind, though it did publish pictures of elite weddings.

Yatindra Mishra: Which are the publications whose influence can still be felt?

Gulzar: I have already mentioned *The Illustrated Weekly of India. Dharmyug*, under the editorship of Dr Dharamveer Bharti, had its day too. No other Hindi publication could match its glamour. Besides these, I can think of *Hindustan Patrika*, *Sarika* and *Madhuri*. The last dealt with cinema. Amrita Pritam used to publish a Punjabi journal named *Nagmani* in Delhi. All these were magazines published at a time when the reading and writing scene was such that even people in cinema would rifle through the pages of these papers quite seriously.

Abbas-sahab (Khwaja Ahmed Abbas) used to write for Baburao Patel's *Film India* magazine. It was mostly gossip, or his opinion on some film event or news, but made for pleasurable reading. R. K. Karanjia of *Blitz* was a character in his own right. He had charisma and, in his time, *Blitz* had its own place as a publication. In fact, K. A. Abbas wrote the Last Page for it for forty uninterrupted years!

An Urdu magazine called *Shahrah* used to be published from Delhi, and Sahir-sahab was its editor. Yunus Dehlvi's *Shama* too was a prominent magazine in Urdu. Besides stories, it also carried film news and writeups, and interviews. A very important Urdu magazine was published from Lahore. Called *Nukoosh*, it was started in 1948 by Ahmed Nadeem Kasmi-sahab and Khadija Mastur. Mohammad Tufail became the editor after Kasmi-sahab. Later, Kasmi-sahab brought out another good Urdu magazine in 1963, *Funoon*. These are some magazines that have stayed in memory and it is a matter of regret that most of these have shut down.

Yatindra Mishra: Who, according to you, is the one editor whose absence is a great loss to the magazine publishing world?

Gulzar: I had mentioned Shankar Pillai's name in connection with *Shankar's Weekly*. Besides him, Khushwant Singh was a magnificent editor; I see no one else of his stature. For a while Prakash Pandit also edited a good Urdu magazine, but I forget its name now. And in Hindi you will not find another editor like Dharamveer Bharti. Kamleshwar-ji took *Sarika* to great heights. And I think highly of Jabir Hussain, who currently brings out *Doaba* from Patna. In my view, these were all great editors.

Yatindra Mishra: Which publication seems the best from those published at present?

Gulzar: Some years ago, Amartya Sen's daughter, Antara Dev Sen had brought out a very beautiful magazine, *The Little Magazine*. It had everything in it, Ffom literature to cinema, science fiction to poetry, everything was published with due seriousness and care. I found this a very likeable magazine, from an Indian perspective. It used to carry good illustrations and have a good design and was printed on good paper. I think it's been years since I last saw a copy. This magazine too shut down, and I find that sad.

Yatindra Mishra: You have mentioned a really good magazine. I too had a chance once to be featured in it. I have a series of poems on classical singer Girija Devi, and an English translation of one of the poems was published in *The Little Magazine*.

Gulzar: Wah! That's wonderful. This means that some publications and magazines are such that you remember being published by them. The fragrance of the publication lingers for years. I still harbour happy memories of my 'Triveni' poems being published by Kamleshwar in *Sarika*.

Yatindra Mishra: What is your favourite pastime?

Gulzar: Taking long journeys. I have travelled a lot by car in Hindustan. I have gone by car from Bombay to Badrinath. And twice or thrice to Kanyakumari. Mandu is one of my favourite places, so I have been there often. If I have to reach a faraway destination, I stop somewhere on the way for the night and continue the next day. Like the time when I went to Kanyakumari, I stopped in Bangalore. I stopped in Bangalore for a day and reached Kanyakumari on the third day.

I have travelled a lot across the country scouting locations for my films. When *Lekin* was being made, we roamed across Rajasthan by car, sifting out locations. Mostly I prefer road journeys but, thanks to my age, I now find it more comfortable to take flights and save time.

Yatindra Mishra: Was there any particular reason for signing Meena Kumari as the protagonist of *Mere Apne*?

Gulzar: As it happened, when N. C. Sippy-sahab gave me my first break to make *Mere Apne*, he had called me to his office. He asked me straight away, 'Have you got any heroine in mind?' I replied, 'Chaaya Devi has done an excellent job in *Apan Jan* and she speaks Hindi quite well, so we should request her. To which he said, 'Name some actress in Bombay whom we can offer the role to.' Then I thought of Meena-ji and I said that Meena Kumari would be perfect for the role. Then N. C. Sippy said, 'Why don't you take Nimmi and make the film?' I did not think Nimmi was right for the role so I replied, 'Nimmi-ji will not suit the character, and neither will she be able to do justice to it.' Sippy-sahab was such a good man that he immediately said, 'Will you talk to Meena-ji or should I?' Then I laughingly told him, 'You are the producer of the film. The film will be made under your watch. It is best if you speak to Meena-ji.' And that's how Meena Kumari became part of the film.

Yatindra Mishra: Was there any special reason for signing on Suchitra Sen for *Aandhi*?

Gulzar: There's a story behind this. Producer J. Omprakash had called me to listen to a story that he wanted me to direct. The story was written by Sachin Bhowmik. It was a thriller that he wanted to cast Sanjeev Kumar and Suchitra Sen in. I was also informed that Sanjeev Kumar was very keen to work with Suchitra Sen. So Sachin Bhowmik had written the story keeping these two actors in mind.

When I went to meet J. Omprakash-ji, both Sachin Bhowmik and Sanjeev Kumar were already there. I found the story very mediocre. The plot was that of a mundane 'Bambaiyya' film. I said, 'It won't be a good move to call Suchitra Sen to Bombay for this story. Why will she take on a film like this?' Surprisingly it was Sachin Bhowmik who responded first to this bitter comment of mine. 'You are right. This is Bombay! You can sign on any actor for this, but if you call Suchitra Sen down, it has to be a different kind of story.' Everyone agreed with this. This was around the time that I was also thinking of *Aandhi*. I felt this was the perfect time to narrate the story to all those present. The film has two protagonists and it is about their relationship and how their bond breaks and the heroine goes on to become a successful politician. I only drew the outline, but everyone immediately understood the plot.

J. Omprakash asked, 'Do you have the story written out yet?' I promised him that I would send him the synopsis in two or three weeks. I said, 'If you like it, we can work together on it.' He was pleased by this and said, in the next two months or so, I have to meet Suchitra Sen. As promised, I sent across the synopsis in two weeks' time.

I had already started working on the story and that is how Sanjeev Kumar and Suchitra Sen became a part of this film.

Yatindra Mishra: The strange thing about *Aandhi* is that Suchitra Sen is the only female character. No other woman is in the film, not even in a small role.

Gulzar: Yes, that is so. But look, despite there being just one woman character, the film is well balanced. I do not think you will easily find another such instance in Hindi cinema. And yet, it is a feminist film.

Yatindra Mishra: Which is your favourite song from *Aandhi*?

Gulzar: I like all the songs. The duets have all been very popular, but from the point of writing, I like the political satire, 'Salaam keejiye, ali janab aye hain', that has been composed as a qawwali. Though the most ideal song, situation wise, is, according to me, 'Tere bina zindagi se koi shikwa to nahin'. Partly due to the picturisation, and partly to the tune created by Pancham, who had picked up the tune from the Durga Puja festival song. The fun thing about this song is the word play; if you take only the first line, then you get two parallel meanings. It is a pun. One meaning is: 'I have no complaint about life beyond my complaint concerning you.' The second meaning you can read is: 'Beyond your absence, I have no complaint to make about life.' This unfolds in layers.

Yatindra Mishra: What can you share with us about the qawwali song in the film?

 Gulzar: Nothing. You say it, or someone else will.

Yatindra Mishra: Which song of *Khushboo* do you still hold close to your heart?

Gulzar: We have spoken a lot about *Khushboo*. How long will you keep sniffing at the same flower?

Yatindra Mishra: Okay, if not the rose then the magnolia! Between screenplay and dialogue, which do you pay more attention to or give more weightage to? Do you prefer writing only the dialogues or the screenplay too?

Gulzar: In the beginning I wrote the screenplay and dialogues of most films together. Films like *Guddi*, *Sitara*, *Masoom*, *Ek Pal* and *Rudaali*. Though there were many other films in which I wrote only the songs and dialogues, but not the screenplay.

Yatindra Mishra: As a screenplay writer, you might have come across occasions when you have had to write a scene outside of the flow of the story. Some scene that is suddenly seen as necessary during the course of the shoot. What do you do in such cases?

Gulzar: It has happened quite often that a scene has to be written right away and added to the film. It often happened when I was working with Hrishikesh Mukherjee.

There were many occasions, working with Hrishi-da, when I had to write something at a moment's notice. This incident is related to *Guddi*. There was a shot in the scene where Mohan Studios is on fire and a photographer is hell bent on taking a picture. He says, 'This picture will not sell, it is your faces that sell.' Hrishi-da wanted me to write a scene to this effect. I said, 'This scene will in no way fit into the film. It will seem overly sentimental. Let it be, please drop it.' He got annoyed, 'What is this? I don't care, write the scene somehow and give it to me.' I wrote the scene. It was filmed. Even after the film was complete, I felt it was superfluous, stuck on, but we could do nothing about it as Hrishi-da wanted it. When the film was released, we went to the first show to check viewers' reactions. You will be surprised to learn that the very scene I had considered unnecessary was the one that the audience clapped loudest for. There was nothing more to say. Hrishi-da had communicated exactly what he had wanted to say.

Yatindra Mishra: You have made mature romances. One sees mature love stories in *Khushboo*, *Aandhi*, *Kinara* and *Ijazat*. Is there any special reason for this?

Gulzar: Because I have grown old before my time! I will mention three films in this connection, where love is more beautiful because it occurs between mature people: *Khushboo*, *Namkeen* and *Ijazat*. You can see how much variation there is in each of the relationships, and how many new ways of dealing with them have been discovered.

Yatindra Mishra: What is the effect of silence in films?

Gulzar: That's a very poetic question. One needs to see how much space has been left for silence by the writer of a story or novel.

Yatindra Mishra: You have made only one comedy, *Angoor*. What was the reason you never made another?

Gulzar: That is not right. I have written many comedies for Hrishi-da like *Bawarchi*, *Chupke Chupke* and *Khoobsurat*.

Yatindra Mishra: The abstraction you introduced into the song 'Humne dekhi hai in aankhon ki mehekti khushboo' in the film, *Khamoshi* went on to become what can be considered your signature style later. Do you agree with this?

Gulzar: I agree that it was the first time I underlined the abstraction, and people realised it was something new in my style. The song was written to suit a male singer. Because a man was to sing it in praise of his beloved's eyes. Hemant-da composed the tune but once it was ready he changed his mind. He thought Lata-ji should sing this song. Now you tell me, is it possible that a woman praises another woman's eyes? But it is the magic of Lata-ji's voice that she can even change the gender of any song.

Yatindra Mishra: Have you ever written anything for some upcoming or established theatre-director? Or were you ever requested to write a song or dialogues for any play?

Gulzar: Salim Arif has been with me for many years, he has assisted me in many films, and after making a request, took some stories from me. I told him, 'You have assisted me in films, do assist me here too. I will work with you. Let me see this form, let me check it.' This is literature, and story-telling too, and also readings. Otherwise, how can you introduce poems in the midst of stories? Salim would laugh at this and just say, 'Give them to me please.'

This turned out to be a learning process for me. This medium has its own attraction that pulled me towards itself. So, in this way, Salim made theatre possible.

Yatindra Mishra: How did you view the work that happens in theatre in relation to yourself and your work?

Gulzar: I was learning. I wanted to grasp this form. I find the direct contact with viewers very interesting. You made a film, publicised it; you called a few people and showed it to them. Some liked it, some did not, everyone reviewed it according to their inclination. If it's a book you write, well you published it. Here too, the same thing, just like with cinema. Some will like it, some may not. Someone will review it. Some people may come and tell you, we read your poems, liked them. But when you are called out to read your poem in a theatre, and there are hundreds of people sitting waiting to hear you read, that is theatre! This is the most attractive part of theatre. It's a one-to-one relationship with the audience. Wherever theatre goes, the experience of creating a relationship with the audience continues, and I find that fascinating.

Yatindra Mishra: You have described the transient quality of theatre wonderfully. It reminds me of a famous quote by Pandit Kumar Gandharv, 'When I sing, I die every day. The

Kumar Gandharv who sang Tilak Kamod, and Tilak Kamod itself, both die. Tomorrow, yet again, Kumar Gandharv will sing Tilak Kamod, but neither will be the same…'

Gulzar: What an amazing statement Pandit-ji has made! Absolutely correct. This is what happens in theatre too.

Yatindra Mishra: What has been your experience of reading poetry in a theatre, or sitting at a literary meet and reciting your poems and expounding on them? Are you just a poet or storyteller at such times? Or can you feel the presence of the film director, song writer and screenplay writer too on stage?

Gulzar: Everything has been written by me, so something or the other will be sensed by others. I do not venture into the world of poetry while working on a character in cinema. But I am sharing my experience. When, after an hour or more of reciting poems, comes the time for audience interaction, the questions people ask are, 'Why did you stop making movies?' 'How was that song of yours written?' Meaning, no question about poetry ever comes my way. If at all, it is related to the songs. I once asked a gentleman, 'Can you name three of my films?' He replied immediately. Then I said, 'Can you name three of my books?' He replied, 'One is *Pukhraj*, but I cannot remember any others right away.' Then I could only think that he had not come to listen to my poetry but to talk to me about my films.

Yatindra Mishra: Can we say of your films, that from *Mere Apne* to *Hu Tu Tu*, all are written through the point of view of a writer?

Gulzar: Correct! There's nothing to disagree with here. I want to tell you something related to this. It has been said about my film *Parichay* that it is based on *The Sound of Music*. I do not refute this. If indeed *Parichay* reminds you of *The Sound of Music*, that's a good thing.

I had read a story by Rajkumar Maitra titled 'Rangeen Uttariya' in a Bangla magazine *Ulto Rath*. Rakhee liked the story a lot and read it out to me too. I felt I should make a film based on it, sometime. I had not yet become a director, but thought it was a good thing to get the rights to the story. Hemant-da was constantly travelling to Calcutta. I told him, 'Dada, I want the rights to this story.' He said, 'What will you do with it?' I said, 'When I get the chance, I will write a screenplay.' He brought me the rights to the story. I translated the entire story into Urdu and felt, even then, that this man has surely been inspired by *The Sound of Music*. Especially in the part where the children force their teachers to leave by troubling them.

If the song in the English film is based on 'do re me', then 'sa re ke sa re' based on 'sa re ga ma' is not a copy. If you compare it with *The Sound of Music*, the father there wants his children to learn music but they do not wish to do so. In *Parichay*, the grandfather hates music and his son has left the house because he wishes to pursue music, and all the five children are kept away from any music. So, the circumstances of the *Parichay* song are completely the opposite. I mean to say that I made the film with a poet's sensibility. The glimpses of *The Sound of Music* you get are due to the story having some parallel elements. The focus of my film is on the younger generation and their right to enjoy the love of the elders. A poet decides how much of the story to keep and what to let go of ; that's how the film was made. You will see the same principles in *Koshish*, *Kitaab* and *Ijazat*.

Yatindra Mishra: What is your film-craft like?

Gulzar: Craft is one thing that is always with me. That is the reason why when I write the screenplay based on someone else's story, the story takes off. The story is no longer the same story. Other stories too join in. I want to sincerely confess something else too. From *Mere Apne* onwards, all my films are my very own, thought out in my own way, and structured as I wanted it...though I lacked confidence in the beginning. At the time I started making films, I was a writer, a story teller, but the self-confidence was somewhat shaky. Which is why I took the support of other writers' names, some names that could give me confidence.

Yatindra Mishra: Is this not a prejudice? That only established writers can write good stories for films?

Gulzar: Not at all! It is not so. It is not prejudice to feel that I am still raw. I was writing constantly. Please understand this. If a writer writes a story keeping the form of a screenplay in mind, then it will be exactly like a screenplay. No screenplay writer or filmmaker can claim that his screenplay was changed while writing the story, because the grammar of a story is different.

The same thing happens when writing a screenplay based on a story or novel. A scriptwriter often ignores many aspects of a story because he feels it is not necessary to the film. A film made on a superlative story can be a damp squib if the script is not properly worked out.

I worked on the stories of well-known writers to gain confidence. It was at that time a crutch, that because it is a well-known author's work, it is special. But I wrote all the screenplays of these stories, changing bits of the story as required. Even while filming, I improvised as I thought necessary. I think every director does the same. After all, cinema is a director's medium, he alone holds the reins of the other elements in the film, like music, songs, story etc.

Yatindra Mishra: So, in your view, is the screenplay the most vital part of making a film? Is it the central point from where the director takes the film forward?

Gulzar: Yes. Writing the screenplay is practically equal to making the film. The direction depends on how good a screenplay you can write is. A film is not made by shot-taking. It is the screenplay that shows the way. If someone else is writing it, then I am superfluous. Then he who has written the screenplay and given it to me is actually making the film.

Yatindra Mishra: Is there any such dialogue that convinced you that you had achieved distinction as a dialogue writer? Did the self-confidence you lacked while working on the early screenplays finally come to you?

Gulzar: This question reminds me of an incident. Once, we were coming out of the theatre after watching Ramesh Sippy's *Andaaz*. Music directors Kalyanji-Anandji, who had composed the music for the film, were also with us. I had written the dialogues for the film. As soon as we stepped out of the theatre, Kalyanji-bhai said something to me that was the biggest compliment I received concerning the dialogues of the film. He said, 'Gulzar-bhai, watching *Andaaz*, I kept feeling that not the actors in the film, but you yourself were speaking the dialogues. They did not sound like someone else's dialogues, they had your stamp on it.' I feel this analysis of my dialogue gave me the confidence that my dialogue writing was as worthwhile as Kalyanji-bhai had mentioned.

Yatindra Mishra: Did you ever feel any challenge writing film songs that were different from the experience of writing your earlier songs?

Gulzar: It has indeed happened many times. I can think of three films in this context. The first was writing songs for Illaiyaraja's *Sadma*. Second, the songs of *Dil Se* for A. R. Rahman. And third and the most challenging one, which was writing for Amol Palekar's *Daayra* for which Anand Milind had scored the music. The subject of *Daayra* was bold and ahead of its time. I felt I had to keep the window of my mind open while working with Amol Palekar. I remember well, he wanted an erotic song to suit a situation in the film. The trouble with our film industry is that the meaning of erotic or sensual is mostly confused with being sexy.

'Mera kaam karoge' sung by Asha-ji was filmed beautifully. Because Amol is also a painter,the picturisation of the song also carried a painter's sensibilities, with no obscenity in it.

Yatindra Mishra: The songs of *Daayra* portray a cruel reality where the music becomes complimentary.

Gulzar: Anand Milind did a fantastic job with the music of *Daayra*. The influence of their father, the veteran music director, Chitragupta, is strong in them. The most wonderful thing that happened while writing the songs of *Daayra* was the request from Amol that he wanted to design the cover page of my short story collection. I agreed quite happily. Later when my book *Raavi Paar* was published in English, the cover page for it was created by Amol Palekar.

Yatindra Mishra: What did you want to tell us about the challenge that you faced with Rahman's music?

Gulzar: One can talk endlessly about Rahman. There was great difficulty in finding an ease of interaction between us. If English had not been a common language between us, then it would have been impossible to explain to him which word needed to be pronounced in a certain way. I would always find it very difficult. Often playback singer Srinivas, who had sung Tamil and Telugu songs for Rahman, would help me in this. He would sing a sketch version and make it ready for Hariharan when he came for the final recording. After this, whenever I had to work with Rahman, I would call Srinivas to create a sketch version.

Yatindra Mishra: Do you consider any playback singer unique and different from all the others?

Gulzar: Hemant-da (Hemant Kumar) was quite unique. He was the only playback singer I have seen, who would light a cigarette in the course of a recording. Even while singing he would keep the cigarette in front of him and claim that it gave his voice a natural bass. Marlboro was his favourite brand, and sometimes he would also take snuff. He always wore a white shirt and a dhoti with a thin black border. In true Bengali fashion, the left side of his dhoti was always tucked into his pocket. And it would suit his personality very well.

Yatindra Mishra: You have made so many music albums which have been really popular thanks as much to your commentary as to the singers themselves. Who is the artiste with whom you are yet to record?

Gulzar: At one time I had a huge desire to make an album with the famous Pakistani singer Farida Khanum-ji. I admire her and appreciate her voice. I had even mentioned to her that if she came to India for a few days, I would like to work on an album with her. That day I realised that my wish was reciprocated; she also hoped to work on something with me. She even took some of my ghazals and sang them. Then she requested me to get them composed. But then the matter remained incomplete.

Yatindra Mishra: Among the characters you have created, which would you rate a favourite?

Gulzar: Some characters have been essayed beautifully by actors on screen. I would name Rekha and Naseer in *Ijazat* and Sanjeev Kumar in both roles in *Angoor* as the ones I like the best. *Libaas* could not get a release, but Utpal Dutt did a wonderful job in it. Besides them, Pancham has been a great support.

Yatindra Mishra: You have written some absolutely amazing songs for children in films. It is only your songs that are sensitive enough to actually essay the emotions of childhood. How are you able to do this?

Gulzar: One of the most important, in fact the most necessary aspect of writing for children, is, I feel, the need to be able to communicate within their IQ level. Unless you cloak yourself in that IQ, you cannot reach out to them. How will what you write sound right? How will you get the right words? Not unless you enter their minds and think like they do.

I cannot don a thick pair of glasses and look at children through them. Give the children a song in which they can recognise the sound of words that they use when they speak, which they can understand easily. Won't that be the song they love, then?

Yatindra Mishra: Do phonetics have an important place in the songs written for children?

Gulzar: Absolutely! 'Lakdi ki kaati, kaati pe ghoda, ghode ke dum pe jo maara hathoda, dauda dauda dauda ghoda dum uthake dauda.' The da-da-da sound in this is repetitive like a tongue twister, yet it is easily reproduced. This emphasises the role of phonetics. It is most important to give children a song that they can play with, toss around like a ball. Whether they bounce it on the floor, or on the wall, or on someone's back. A child must be able to play with your song.

The easier it is for him to play with your song, the more he makes it his own. That's what happened with these songs. For example, the 'lakdi ki kaati' did not remain just that, but children added their own words and made a game of it. This is the biggest quality of a children's song. Another example is Mowgli's story, the song I wrote for *Jungle Book*. 'Chaddi pehen ke phool khila hai'. Now look at Mowgli's story. All the animals that gather there see that there is a small basket in the forest, in which a child is lying, and he is wearing a chaddi, underwear. That's what they see, and when they report it to the king of the jungle, Sher Khan, their version is that a flower has bloomed in the forest and it is wearing a chaddi. They think it is a flower, and it is wearing a chaddi. I saw Mowgli from this perspective in *Jungle Book* and wrote:

Across the forest there is talk and song
A flower wearing knickers has just been born

I have not imported this image from the outside, it has come from the story itself.

Yatindra Mishra: This is a beautiful song that has been a part of our youth too. We hum it even today, and cannot imagine an alternative song that can describe Mowgli's character in a better way. I love these lines from the song:

There was a bird, oh so shy
For he was naked, oh my my
Happy had he been and well
Living inside his shell
Now he wonders why he emerged
When a flower had bloomed be-knickered.

Gulzar: See, even the bird thinks that I was at least wearing something when I was inside the egg.

Yatindra Mishra: Do you feel there are many lacunae in children's literature in our country? Especially among writers, because they think it is of lesser importance?

Gulzar: To an extent I do agree with you, that children's literature is not taken as seriously here...But I would surely like to add that my own experience has taught me that it is not an easy or simple task. Writing children's literature is more difficult than writing for adults. I feel distress about the fact that we have not given our children the respect that is their due. We always try to relive our own childhood through them.

We send a child to school, put him into a good school, spending a lot of money. But you have no time for your child...The society that believes it is doing things for the child, is actually doing it all for its own ego, because of pride. If you spared a thought for the child, you would not think of the building or bungalow, but of the playground, and whether there was a place for the child to play.

Yatindra Mishra: This is a sharp observation: that you think of access to a playground near the house...

Gulzar: When you yourself have not given enough thought to your own child's needs, why do you expect a writer to write keeping your children in mind?

Yatindra Mishra: The treatment too changes according to the age of the child...

Gulzar: That has to be. The imagery changes with every stage.

Your examples are different for each age. So too your subjects. The idioms and phrases you use will change and scatter to take on new meanings. You have to prepare your vocabulary differently for all the ages between three to twenty-five, and you are not ready for it. You have decided that you will sit on a chair, hook on your thick glasses and write something for children. Go and ask the child how he receives your writing. If you have not spent time with them, not spoken in the language they use, then all your efforts are a waste. Your entire work is then fake; and definitely not written for children.

Yatindra Mishra: Some excellent work has been done on children's literature in English. How do you see the scenario in English, compared to Hindi?

Gulzar: In India we have mostly duplicated whatever has come from the West. There has been very little original work. At one time there was good work being done in the Bengali, Malayalam and Marathi languages. But even that never reached the standard of the West. In this regard, the work of Satyajit Ray's father, Sukumar Ray, and of Ray himself is worth looking at. Only Ray's work is enough to show us how when he writes or makes films for adults, he is serious and yet, when he creating characters like 'Professor Shanku' for children, how the film goes beyond science fiction to become a vital part of children's literature. If there's *Charulata* at one end, there is *Goopi Gyne Bagha Byne* at the other; which would you say has less depth?

Yatindra Mishra: You have written books for Bosky, which are good examples of children's literature...

Gulzar: I could not do as much as I had planned to. Despite this, I had promised myself that I would present Bosky a new book by me on every birthday. And I did so too. Right up to her thirteenth birthday, I wrote a new book every year to gift to her. Many books like *Bosky Ke Gappe*, *Bosky Ka Panchatantra* and *Bosky Ki Ginti* were created this way.

Yatindra Mishra: It's such a beautiful thing that in the process of educating your daughter, you gifted your books to an entire generation, like a blessing!

Gulzar: Thank you.

Yatindra Mishra: The song, 'Kajrare kajrare, tere kare kare naina' from *Bunty Aur Babli* not only broke all records with its success and remained at the top of most radio station lists for a long time, but is still very popular with the younger set and can be heard at social gatherings even now, years after its release. How do you view this success, especially as a lyricist who does not easily agree to writing for item numbers?

Gulzar: Aishwarya Rai has a huge role in this success, as she gave the song a special feel. And she has also danced so well in it. The music by Shankar-Ehsan-Loy is also amazing. When all these factors meet, then a song reaches that place, where its success continues for years.

Yatindra Mishra: 'Iss mod se jaate hain' is one of your masterpieces about which we can talk on and on...Can we discuss the song?

Gulzar: Some of its appeal is because of the poetry, and some due to the way Lata-ji and Kishore Kumar have sung it.

Yatindra Mishra: How do you celebrate moments of success and joy in your life? What is it that, far removed from the film-related world, gives you much happiness?

Gulzar: Firstly, I do not remember ever throwing a party to celebrate my success. I had the desire to make good films and to read a lot of good literature...So that's what I kept doing. I find joy in being in the company of literature. All the whisky bottles I have opened to party with friends have been to celebrate Sunil Gavaskar hitting a century. You cannot estimate what a great fan of Gavaskar, I am. My friends were all aware of the fact that the day Gavaskar hits a century, they must go to Gulzar's place.

I had the occasion to meet him once, and I expressed the desire to take a photo with him. Later, when Lata-ji made *Lekin*, it was Gavaskar whom we invited to give the mahurat shot. As both Lata-didi and I were such ardent fans, we decided the film's muhurat should be done only by him.

Yatindra Mishra: How interesting...the reason for your celebrations!

Gulzar: I like Sachin Tendulkar immensely. And I watch other cricketers too avidly. But I am totally a Gavaskar fan.

Yatindra Mishra: What disturbs your mind?

Gulzar: The question, why is there a border between two countries? My mind wants to rub out all the borders all over the world. If it exists in people's minds, then some effort should be made to erase that even more quickly.

Yatindra Mishra: What are your expectations as a citizen from your fellow countrymen?

Gulzar: Who am I to make such demands? I can only tell the new generation that they should read as much of world literature as possible. And listen to world music and watch world cinema in the same way. This will push the horizons of our thinking further.

Yatindra Mishra: What is your positive point?

Gulzar: I am positive about life...And I say to the youth that they should stay positive.

Yatindra Mishra: And your negative point?

Gulzar: Now tell me why I should tell you that!

Yatindra Mishra: Any such song that you are still not convinced about, despite having written it?

Gulzar: 'Main to kaare badariya se haari' (The black clouds have overwhelmed me) from *Devta*. I don't like what I have written as the antara.

 Yatindra Mishra: Which of your songs gives you joy and

creates an island of peace in the middle of all the noise and hurly-burly of life?

Gulzar: 'Dil dhoondta hai, phir wahi.' (*Mausam*)

Yatindra Mishra: Any song by another lyricist or poet which demands our salutations?

Gulzar: Sahir Ludhianvi's 'Man re tu kaahe na dheer dhare' (Ah mind, why will you not find fortitude?) (*Chitralekha*)

Yatindra Mishra: Which song of yours that made you feel contentment in the knowledge that you were writing something of great import?

Gulzar: 'Mera kuch samaan tumhare paas padaa hai' (*Ijazat*)

Yatindra Mishra: Among storytellers, whose work do you rate the highest?

Gulzar: Anton Chekhov's name comes first. A sentence in his stories can give you a lifetime's experience. You get a slice of life. You can see the same thing in Gorky's stories. Even if there is no story, no event or incident, Chekhov can create a story from a mood. That's why I find him a very great writer. In the same way there is no parallel for Maupassant's narration, for O Henry's craft, and his impeccable narrative style.

In the same way, there are incidents in Manto's stories, where the narration comes dipped in sarcasm about present circumstances. Manto is classic. His relevance will continue for a long time yet.

Yatindra Mishra: Who, among those of your time, would you name as the one whose work has influenced you the most?

Gulzar: It's difficult to take just one name.

Yatindra Mishra: As an artiste who has reached the height of his career by being awarded the Dadasaheb Phalke Award, you must have experienced many moments when life took you through slow streets and at other times through fast-moving paths. How does it feel to be where you are now?

Gulzar: *There were green leaves, on verdant and flourishing boughs*
But satisfaction arrived when a flower bloomed upon the branch.

Yatindra Mishra: Is there any regret, anything left unfinished, anything that you feel is still lacking in your creative life, which you still hold the hope of completing?

Gulzar: What a man learns in life is much lesser than what remains unlearnt, and all the wisdom he gathers is nothing compared to the huge mass of barren ignorance within him. I will emphatically admit that I learnt a lot, but there is much more that that left for me to learn and assimilate. I will be erring if I say I have become intelligent. There's is so much still left to understand and make my own.

Having borne witness to Gulzar-sahab's life, writing and his journey in cinema, I wished to capture him in the form of text. Then it occurred to me that I should ask his 'chacha' Ghalib. Thus I have taken this couplet, with due apologies to Mirza Ghalib, which completely fits his character. I invite you to read it:

These matters of philosophy
And your pronouncements, 'Ghalib'
We would consider you a man of God
Were you not a filmmaker

In giving what he wants to say the garb of the alphabet, Gulzar maintains the glory of the silence; the silence which knows how to descend from realization but knows not how to ascend to the lips and express itself. A silence which has found the alphabet but does not know how to speak...

—Amrita Pritam

I weave my life on an empty loom
Now there's no thread left to tie even a knot

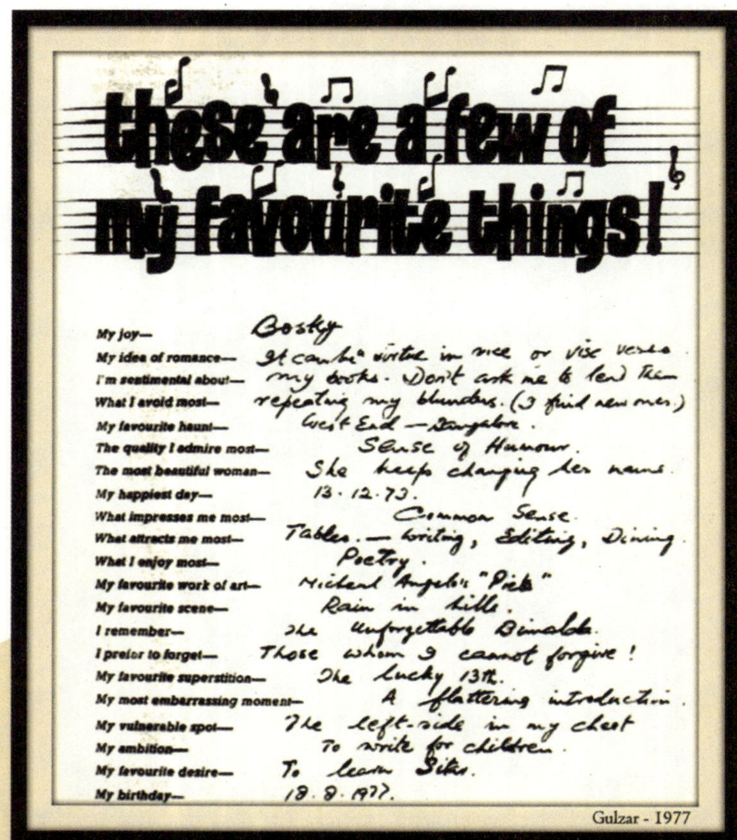

these are a few of my favourite things!

My joy— Bosky
My idea of romance— It can be virtue in vice or vise versa.
I'm sentimental about— my books. Don't ask me to lend them
What I avoid most— repeating my blunders. (I find new ones)
My favourite haunt— West End — Bangalore.
The quality I admire most— Sense of Humour.
The most beautiful woman— She keeps changing her name.
My happiest day— 13.12.73.
What impresses me most— Common Sense.
What attracts me most— Tables. — Writing, Editing, Dining.
What I enjoy most— Poetry.
My favourite work of art— Michael Angelo's "Pieta"
My favourite scene— Rain in hills.
I remember— The Unforgettable Bimalda.
I prefer to forget— Those whom I cannot forgive!
My favourite superstition— The Lucky 13th.
My most embarrassing moment— A flattering introduction.
My vulnerable spot— The left-side in my chest
My ambition— To write for children.
My favourite desire— To learn Sitar.
My birthday— 18.8.1977.

Gulzar - 1977

Mirza Ghalib

Gurudev Rabindranath Tagore

Gulzar's two gurus, from whom he learnt both culture and the craft of language

I could learn the two things from him that can be learnt: filmmaking and patience. The idea of the 'artistic concept', that cannot be learnt; it has to always be your own. I can never become Bimal-da. A saying goes: The space that a master occupies, it always remains empty.

Bimal Roy

Gulzar's guru, who ushered him into the world of cinema

My Brother
(Gulzar-sahab)

Take care that his abstracted solitude is not shattered...

He is like a soft muslin cloud
Who swallows the harsh sunlight
To provide soothing shade

Approach crouched on bended knee
So that your feet do not scatter him

Weigh the words on your lips in his presence
Measure each syllable that falls

He is a true Sufi Santa Claus garbed in white
Take care that his abstracted solitude is not shattered...

—Vishal Bhardwaj

ASHA BHOSLE • RAHUL DEV BURMAN • GULZAR
Dil Padosi Hai

रावी पार
गुलज़ार

मिर्ज़ा ग़ालिब
एक स्वानही मंज़रनामा
गुलज़ार

A
POEM
A
DAY
GULZAR

Baal-o-Par
GULZAR

GULZAR
HIS SONGS OF LOVE

The Poetry of
GULZAR
Woh Jo Shaam Tha
Sung and Composed by
BHUPINDER

GULZAR
translates
TAGORE
बाग़बान

यार जुलाहे...
गुलज़ार

कुछ संग-ए-मील...

Gulzar Sa'ab

Is Mod se Jaate Hain...

Drop not the curtain yet, stop,

Many are the stories yet to be told

Drop not the curtain yet, stop!

जाने क्या सोचकर नहीं गुज़रा
एक पल रात भर नहीं गुज़रा...

Awards and Achievements

International Awards

2008 Academy Award 'Oscar', for Best Original Song, 'Jai Ho' (*Slumdog Millionaire*) shared with composer A. R. Rahman

2010 Grammy Award for Best Song 'Jai Ho', shared with composer A. R. Rahman and singer Tanvi Shah

Awards by the Government of India

2004 Padma Bhushan

2012 Indira Gandhi Award for National Integration

2013 Dadasaheb Phalke Award

Indian Film Awards

1972 Best Screenplay, *Koshish*

1976 Best Director *Mausam*

1988 Best Lyricist for 'Mera kuch samaan' from the film *Ijaazat*

1991 Best Documentary, *Ustad Amjad Ali Khan*

1993 Best Documentary, *Pandit Bhimsen Joshi*

1996 Best Popular Film Providing Wholesome Entertainment, *Maachis*

Filmfare Awards

1971	Best Dialogue, *Anand*
1973	Best Dialogue, *Namak Haram*
1975	Critics Award for Best Feature Film, *Aandhi*
1976	Best Lyricist for 'Do deewane sheher main' from *Gharonda*
1979	Best Lyricist for 'Aane wala pal…' from *Gol Maal*
1980	Best Lyricist for 'Hazar rahein mudh ke dekhi' from *Thodi Si Bewafai*
1983	Best Lyricist for 'Tujhse naaraz nahi zindagi' from *Mausam*
1991	Best Lyricist for 'Yaara seeli seeli' from *Lekin*
1991	Best Documentary, *Ustad Amjad Ali Khan*
1996	Best Dialogue, *Maachis*
1996	Best Story, *Maachis*
1996	Best Lyricist, 'Chaiya chaiya', *Dil Se*
2002	Lifetime Achievement Award
2003	Best Lyricist, 'Saathiya', *Saathiya*
2003	Best Dialogue, *Saathiya*
2013	Best Lyricist 'Challa', *Jab Tak Hain Jaan*
2019	Best Lyricist, 'Ae watan', *Raazi*
2021	Best Lyricist, 'Chhapaak se pehchan le gaya,' *Chhapaak*

Doctorates and Other Honours

2001 Lifetime Honorary Fellowship, The Indian Institute of Advanced Studies, Shimla

2009 D.Litt., Punjab University, Patiala

2012 D.Litt, Urdu, Maulana Azad National University, Hyderabad

2013 Nominated Honourable Chancellor, Sikkim University, Sikkim

2014 D.Litt., Hyderabad University, Hyderabad

2015 D.Litt, Desikottam, awarded by the Vishwa-Bharati University, Shantiniketan, West Bengal

Special Awards and Honours

1992 Bengal Film Journalists Association Award, Best Lyricist, *Lekin*

1997 Star Screen Award, Best Story, *Maachis*

2000 Shailendra Samman, Shailendra Samman Samiti

2003 Zee Cine Award, Best Lyricist, *Saathiya*

2004 Sahir Award, Adeeb International Cultural Academy

2004 Bengal Film Journalist Association Award

2004 Satyajit Ray Lifetime Achievement Award

2006 IFFA Award Best Lyricist, *Bunty Aur Babli*

2006 Zee Cine Award, Best Lyricist, *Bunty Aur Babli*

2006 Star Screen Award, Best Lyricist, *Yahan*

2007 Star Screen Award, Best Lyricist, *Omkara*

2007 Hakim Khan Sur Award, Maharana Mewar Foundation

2008 Mumbai International Film Festival, Lifetime Achievement Award for ' Notable Contribution to Indian Film Music'.

2009 World Soundtrack Award for Best Original Film Song, 'Jai Ho' in *Slumdog Millionaire,* shared with composer A. R. Rahman

2009 Osian Lifetime Achievement Award

2011 Mirchi Music Critics Award, Best Lyricist, 'Dil to baccha hai ji', *Ishqiya*

2011 Mumbai International Film Festival Lifetime Achievement Award

2013 Apsara Film Producers Guild Award, Best Lyricist Award, 'Saans', *Jab Tak Hai Jaan*

2013 Times of India Film Award, 'Saans', *Jab Tak Hai Jaan*

2015 Global Indian Music Award (GIMA), Best Lyricist, 'Bismil', *Haider*

2019 Mirchi Music Award, Best Lyricist, 'Ae watan', *Raazi*

2019 Star Screen Award, Best Lyricist, 'Ae watan', *Raazi*
2019 Star Screen Award, Best Lyricist, 'Dilbara', *Raazi*

Films

1971 *Mere Apne*
1972 *Parichay*
1972 *Koshish*
1973 *Achanak*
1975 *Khushboo*
1975 *Aandhi*
1975 *Mausam*
1977 *Kinara*
1977 *Kitaab*
1979 *Meera*
1981 *Angoor*
1982 *Namkeen*
1984 *Suniye* (short film in Hindi)
1984 *Aieka* (short film in Marathi)
1987 Ijazat
1988 *Libaas* (screened in 2017)
1990 *Lekin*
1996 *Maachis*
1999 *Hu Tu Tu*

Television Serials and Documentaries

1980 *Sahira* (short documentary)
1985 *Ek Aakar* (documentary)
1988 *Mirza Ghalib* (TV serial and music album)
1990 *Ustaad Amjad Ali Khan* (documentary)
1991 *Potli Baba Ki* (TV serial)
1992 *Pandit Bhimsen Joshi* (documentary)
1993 *Kirdar* (TV serial)
2004 *Tahrir Munshi Premchand Ki* (TV serial)

Non Film Music Albums

1980 *Woh Jo Shayar Tha* (with Bhupinder)

1987 *Dil Padosi Hai* (with R. D. Burman and Asha Bhosle)

1992 *Main Aur Mera Saaya* (with Bhupen Hazarika)

1997 *Budhe Pahadon Par* (with Vishal and Suresh Wadkar)

1999 *Marasim* (with Jagjit Singh)

1999 *Vaada* (with Ustaad Amjad Ali Khan)

2000 *Sunset Point* (with Bhupinder, Chitra and Vishal)

2001 *Visaal* (with Ghulam Ali)

2002 *Udaas Paani* (with Abhishek Ray)

2002 *Ishqa Ishqa* (with Rekha and Vishal Bhardwaj)

2003 *Abida Sings Kabir* (with Abida Parveen)

2006 *Koi Baat Chale* (with Jagjit Singh)

2007 *Amrita Pritam* (In Memoriam to Amrita Pritam)

2008 *Chand Parosa Hai* (with Bhupinder)

2011 *Barse-Barse* (with Vishal and Suresh Wadkar)

2012 *Aksar* (with Bhupinder and Mitali)

2012 *Tera Bayan Ghalib* (with Jagjit Singh and Salim Arif)

2013 *Surmayi Raat* (with Bhupinder)

2016 *Gulzar in Conversation with Tagore* (with Shantanu Moitra, Shaan and Shreya Ghoshal)

2016 *Tapur Tupur: Tagore's Poems for Children* (with Shantanu Moitra)

2018 *Nayab Lamhe* (with Pankaj Udhas)

2018 ' Jai Hind India' (Theme song for the Hockey World Cup, music composed by A. R. Rahman)

Books

1962 *Chauras Raat* (short stories)

1963 *Jaanam* (poems)

1972 *Ek Boond Chand* (poems)

1980 *Kuch Aur Nazmen* (poems)

1989 *Dastakhat* (Urdu poems, published in Pakistan)

1994	*Pukhraj* (poems)
1994	*Mera Kuch Samaan* (collection of film songs)
1994	*Silences* (English translation of poems by Rina Singh)
1997	*Raavi Paar* (short stories, translated into English and other languages)
1999	*Autumn Moon* (English translation of poems by J. P. Das)
2000	*Kayda* (poems for children in Hindi)
2001	*Triveni* (three-line poems in Urdu and Hindi)
2001	*Ek Mein Do* (text book for children)
2002	*Raat Pashmine Ki* (Urdu poems, also in Hindi)
2002	*Michelangelo and Other Stories* (short stories in Hindi and English)
2002	*Seema and Other Stories* (short stories in Hindi and English)
2002	*Addha and Other Stories* (short stories in Hindi and English)
2002	*Raat, Chaand aur Main* (poems)
2002	*Chaiya-Chaiya* (collection of film songs)
2003	*Ek Ghar Naam Saal* (school book for children)
2004	*Parwaaz* (the Hindi translation of the autobiography of A.P.J. Abdul Kalam and audiobook)
2004	*Meera—Manzarnama* (screenplay of the film, *Meera*)
2004	*Bosky Ke Gappe* (stories for Bosky and other children)
2004	*Bosky Ke Dhanwaan* (stories for Bosky and other children)
2004	*Because He Is* (biography of Gulzar and his work by Meghna Gulzar)
2005	*Mirza Ghalib: A Biographical Scenario* (A biography of Mirza Ghalib in English)
2006	*Libaas—Manzarnama* (screenplay of *Libaas*)
2006	*Hu Tu Tu—Manzarnama* (screenplay of Hu Tu Tu)
2007	*Echoes and Eloquences: The Life and Cinema of Gulzar* by Saibal Chatterjee
2008	*Selected Poems* (poetry in Hindi, English translation by Pavan K. Varma)
2008	*Katra-Katra* (collection of songs by Gulzar and R. D. Burman, edited by Viswas Nerurkar and Vishwanath Chatterjee)
2009	*100 Lyrics* (in Hindi and English, edited by Sanjay Shekar)
2010	*Jeena Yahan* (stories)
2010	*Pandrah Paanch Pachattar* (poems)

2010 *Magical Wishes: The Adventures of Goopy and Bagha* (in Hindi and English translation)

2011 *Ijaazat: Manzarnama* (screenplay)

2012 *Neglected Poems* (in Hindi, English translation by Pavan K. Varma)

2012 *In the Company of a Poet: Gulzar in Conversation with Nasreen Munni Kabir*

2012 *Diyodi* short stories)

2013 *Pichale Panne* (collection)

2013 *Bosky Ka Panchatantra* (stories for Bosky and other children)

2013 *I Swallowed the Moon: The Poetry of Gulzar* (translation and analysis in English by Saba Mahmood Bashir)

2013 *Hindi for Heart* (poems on the Hindi alphabet with Rina Singh)

2013 *Silences* (a translation of selected poems into English by Rina Singh)

2013 *Half a Rupee* (English translation of stories by Sanjay Shekhar)

2013 *Meelon se Din* (analysis of selected film songs, edited by Yatindra Mishra)

2014 *Heads and Tails* (English versions of the screenplays of *Aandhi* and *Hu Tu Tu*)

2014 *Green Poems* (poems in Hindi translated by Pavan K. Varma)

2015 *Pluto* (poems)

2016 *Gulzar Translates Tagore: Baghbaan and Nidiya Chor*

2016 *Godaan, Nirmala and Other Stories: Screenplays by Gulzar*

2016 *Another 100 Lyrics* (a selection of lyrics translated into English

	by Sanjay Shekhar)
2016	*Munshi Premchand Godaan* (English translation of screenplay by Sabah Mahmood Bashir)
2016	*Kinara—Manzarnama* (screenplay)
2016	*Kitaab—Manzarnama* (screenplay)
2016	*Lekin—Manzarnama* (screenplay)
2017	*Footprints on Zero Line* (essays and poems on the Partition, translated by Rakshanda Jalil)
2017	*Kuch To Kahiye* (ghazal collection)
2017	*Suspected Poems* (poems in Hindi, translated in English by Pavan K. Verma)
2017	*Do Log* (Hindi novel)
2017	*Two* (English translation of *Do Log* by author)
2017	*Panta Bhate* (essay in Bengali)
2018	*Sage Saare* (a collection of poems in Hindi, Marathi and English)
2018	*A Poem a Day* (a translation of poems by leading poets writing in Indian languages)
2018	*Jiya Jale: The Stories of Songs* (conversation with Nasreen Munir Kabir on film songs)
2019	*Gulzar's Angoor* (insights into the film by Sathya Saran)
2019	*Gulzar's Aandhi* (insights into the film by Saba Mahmood Bashir)
2019	*Gulzar's Ijaazat* (insights into the film by Meera Hashmi)
2020	*Boskiyana: Baatein-Mulakaaten* (Gulzar's conversations with Yashwant Vyas)
2021	*Actually I Met Them: A Memoir* (A personal memoir, an English translation of the Bengali *Panta Bhate* by Maharagnya Chakavarty)

Contribution to Films

1960 *Shriman Satyavadi* (songs)
1961 *Kabuliwala* (songs, Chief Assistant Director)
1962 *Prem-Patra* (songs)
1963 *Bandini* (songs, Assistant Director)
1965 *Poornima* (songs)
1966 *Sannata* (songs)
1966 *Pinjre ke Panchi* (songs)
1966 *Bibi Aur Makaan* (songs)
1968 *Do Dooni Char* (script, screenplay, songs)
1968 *Aashirwad* (script, screenplay, songs)
1969 *Khamoshi* (songs)
1970 *Us Raat Ke Baad* (songs)
1970 *Anand* (dialogues and two songs)
1970 *Anubhav* (songs)
1971 *Guddi* (script, screenplay, dialogues, songs)
1971 *Seema* (songs)
1973 Namak Haraam (dialogues and songs)
1974 *Doosri Sita* (songs)
1974 *Jeevan Sangram* (songs)
1976 *Shaque* (songs)

1977 *Palkon Ki Chhaon Mein* (songs)
1977 *Khatta Meetha* (songs)
1977 *Jallian Wala Bagh* (songs)
1977 *Gharonda* (screenplay,dialogues, songs)
1978 *Devta* (songs)
1978 *Ghar* dialogues and songs)
1979 *Gol Maal* (songs)
1979 *Griha Pravesh* (dialogues and songs)
1980 *Kashish* (songs)
1980 *Gehrayee* (songs)
1980 *Swayamvar* (songs)
1980 *Khoobsurat* (dialogues and songs)
1980 *Thodisi Bewafaii* (songs)
1980 *Sitara* (screenplay, dialogues, songs)
1981 *Naram Garam* (songs)
1981 *Bharosa* (dialogues and songs)
1982 *Sitam* (songs)
1982 *Masoom* (screenplay, dialogues, songs)
1983 *Maju* (songs)
1983 *Ek Pal* (screenplay, dialogues, songs)
1983 *Sadma* (screenplay, dialogues, songs)
1984 *Hip Hip Hurray (*screenplay, dialogues, songs)
1984 *Tarang* (songs)
1986 *Musafir* (songs)
1987 *Ghulami* (songs)
1993 *Maya Memsahab* (songs)
1993 *Shikast* (TV series, songs)
1994 *Didi* (TV documentary, music composer)

1994 *Swami Vivekanand* (songs)
1995 *Rudaali* (screenplay, dialogues, songs)
1995 *Mammo* (songs)
1997 *Aastha* (songs)
1997 *Daayraa* (songs)

1997 *Chachi 420* (dialogues and songs)
1998 *Satya* (songs)
1998 *Dil Se* (songs)

1999 *Rockford* (songs)
2000 *Fiza* (songs)
2001 *Aks* (songs)
2001 *Asoka the Great* (songs)
2002 *Mitr: My Friend* (songs)
2002 *Filhaal* (songs)
2002 *Lal Salaam* (songs)
2002 *Leela* (songs)
2002 *Saathiya* (dialogues and songs)
2003 *Makdee* (songs)
2003 *Pinjar* (songs)
2004 *Maqbool* (songs)
2004 *Chupke Se* (songs)
2004 *Raincoat* (song and voice for poem)
2005 *Bunty Aur Babli* (songs)
2005 *Paheli* (songs)
2005 *Yahaan* (songs)
2005 *The Blue Umbrella* (songs)
2006 *Omkara* (songs)
2006 *Jaaneman* (songs)
2006 *Sweetheart* (songs)
2007 *Dus Kahaniyan* (songs and dialogue bubbles)
2007 *Guru* (songs)
2007 *Jhoom Barabar Jhoom* (songs)
2007 *Just Married* (songs)

2007 *Dum Kata* (songs)
2007 *Chaurahe* (songs)
2008 *Prince* (songs and special appearance)
2008 *Yuvraj* (songs)
2008 *Slumdog Millionaire* (songs)
2009 *Billu* (songs)
2009 *Firaq* (songs)
2009 *Kameeney* (songs)
2009 *Do Paise Ki Dhoop, Char Aney ki*

	Baarish (songs)
2010	*Dus Tola* (songs)
2010	*Rajneeti* (songs)
2010	*Veer* (songs)
2010	*Ishqiya* (songs)
2010	*Striker* (songs)
2010	*Raavan* (songs)
2011	*Saath Khoon Maaf* (songs)
2011	*Kashmakash* (songs)
2011	*Teen they Bhai* (songs)
2011	*Chala Murari…Office-Office* (songs)
2011	*Nauka Doobi* (songs)
2012	*Jab Tak Hain Jaan* (songs)
2013	*Matru ki Bijli ka Mandola* (songs)
2013	*Ek thi Daayan* (songs)
2014	*Kya Dilli Kya Lahore* (songs)
2014	*Dedh Ishqiya* (songs)
2014	*Haider* (songs)
2014	*Kill Dil* (songs)
2014	*Linga* (songs)
2015	*Drisyam* (songs)
2015	*Talwar* (songs)
2015	*Mohalla Assi* (songs)
2016	*Mirzya* (songs)
2017	*Ok Jaanu* (songs)
2017	*Rangoon* (songs)
2018	*Bioscopewala* (songs)
2018	*Aami* (songs)
2018	*Raazi* (songs)
2018	*Surma* (songs)
2018	*Firecracker* (songs)
2019	*The Scarf Is Pink* (songs)
2020	*Chhapaak* (songs)
2020	*Pashmina* (songs and pre-production)
2022	*Darlings* (songs)
2023	*Kutte* (songs)
2023	*Fursat* (songs)

References

The following is a list of books, writings and other material which the author referred to in his attempt to understand and form his own opinion of Hindi film history, the development of Hindi cinema, songs, musicians and its other contexts especially as it concerned Gulzar-sahab.

English

- *Encyclopaedia of Indian Cinema*, Ashish Rajadhyaksha and Paul Willemen, Oxford University Press, New Delhi, 1999
- *Mirrors of the Soul*, Kahlil Gibran, UBS Publishers and Distributors Pvt. Ltd. Noida, 1993
- *Encyclopaedia of Hindi Cinema*, Gulzar, Govind Nihalani and Saibal Chatterjee (eds.), Encyclopaedia Brittanica Private Limited, New Delhi, 2003
- *Hindi Film Song: Music Beyond Boundaries*, Ashok D. Ranade, Promilla and Company Publishers, New Delhi and Chicago, 2006
- *Romancing the Song: Hindi Cinema's Lyrical Journey*, Manek Premchand, Jharna Books, Mumbai, 2012
- *A Journey Down Melody Lane*, Raju Bharatan, Hay House India Private Ltd. New Delhi, 2010
- *Print and Pleasure: Popular Literature and Entertaining Fictions in Colonial North India*, Francesca Orsini, Permanent Black, Ranikhet, 2009

- *So Many Cinemas: The Motion Picture in India*, B. D. Garga, Eminence Designs Pvt. Ltd., Mumbai, 1996
- *Lata Mangeshkar in Her Own Voice: Conversations with Nasreen Munni Kabir*, Niyogi Books, New Delhi, 2009
- *S.D. Burman: The World of His Music*, Khagesh Dev Burman, Rupa Publication India Pvt. Ltd., New Delhi 2013
- *R. D. Burman: The Man, The Music*, Aniruddha Bhattacharjee and Balaji Vitthal, Harper Collins Publishers India, Noida, 2011
- *The World of Hrishikesh Mukherjee: The Filmmaker Everyone Loves*, Jai Arjun Singh, Penguin Random House India, Gurugram, 2015
- *And Then One Day: A Memoir,* Naseeruddin Shah, Penguin Random House India, Gurugram, 2014
- *Vasant Desai: Composer Par Excellence*, Vishwas Nerurkar and Bishwanath Chatterjee, Swaryog and Gayatri Publications, Mumbai, 2008
- *Madan Mohan: Ultimate Melodies*, Vishwas Nerurkar and Bishwanath Chatterjee, Swaryog and Gayatri Publications, Mumbai, 2008
- *Mohammed Rafi: Golden Voice of the Silver Screen*, Sujata Dev, Om Books International, New Delhi, 2015
- *Meena Kumari: The Classic Biography*, Vinod Mehta, Harper Collins India Pvt. Ltd., 2013
- *The Substance and the Shadow: An Autobiography*, Dilip Kumar, Hay House Press Pvt. Ltd, New Delhi, 2015
- *Islamicate Cultures of Bombay Cinema*, Ira Bhaskar and Richard Allen (eds.), Tulika Books, New Delhi, 2009
- *Indian Cinema in Retrospect*, R.M. Ray (ed.), Sangeet Natak Akademi, 2009
- *The Great Masters: Profiles in Hindustani Classical Vocal Music*, Mohan Nadkarni, Harper Collins India, 1999
- *Music Makers: Living Legends of Indian Classical Music*, Ashok Roy, Rupa and Company, New Delhi, 2004
- *Raga Mala: An Autobiography*, Ravi Shankar, Welcome Rain Publications, New York, 1999

- *Stages of Life: Indian Theatre Autobiographies*, Kathryn Hansen, Permanent Black, Ranikhet, 2011
- *Hindustani Music in Colonial Bombay*, Aneesh Pradhan, Three Essays Collective, New Delhi, 2014
- *Music Contexts: A Concise Dictionary of Hindustani Music*, Ashok Ranade, Promilla and Company Publishers, New Delhi, 2006
- *Narratives of Indian Cinema*, Manju Jain (ed.), Primus Books, Delhi, 2013
- *The Unsung Heroes*, Dinesh Ghate (ed.), Swar Alaap Creation, Mumbai, 2012
- *The Patels of Film India: Pioneers of Indian Film Journalism*, Sidharth Bhatia, Indus Source Books, Mumbai, 2015
- *Stardust: 100 Greatest Films of All Times*, Ashwin Varde (ed.), Magna Publication, Mumbai
- *Filmfare*, Khalid Mohamed (ed.), Bennet Coleman and Company Limited, Bombay, March 1994
- *Filmfare, Best of Filmfare*, Jitesh Pillai (ed.), Worldwide Media Pvt. Ltd., Mumbai, December 2011.
- *The Moonsmith Gulzar: Orbiting the Celebrated Words*, Shailja Chandra, Hawakal Publishers Pvt. Ltd., Kolkata, 2021
- *Because He Is*, Meghna Gulzar, Harper Collins Publishers, Noida, 2004
- *Qatrah-Qatrah: Collection of Gulzar-Pancham Songs*, Gulzar, Jeevangani and Gayatri Publications, Mumbai, 2008
- *Mirza Ghalib: A Biographical Scenario*, Gulzar, Rupa and Company, New Delhi, 2005
- *Echoes & Eloquences: The Life and Cinema of Gulzar*, Saibal Chatterjee, Rupa and Company, New Delhi, 2007
- *Gulzar's Angoor*, Sathya Saran, Harper Collins India, 2019
- *Gulzar's Aandhi*, Saba Mahmood Bashir, Harper Collins India, 2019
- *Gulzar's Ijaazat*, Mira Hashmi, Harper Collins India, 2019
- *Godaan, Nirmala and Other Stories: Screenplays by Gulzar*, Saba Mahmood Bashir (tr.), Roli Books, New Delhi, 2016

- *Silences: Selected Poems*, Gulzar, Reena Singh (tr.), Rupa & Company, New Delhi, 2013
- *Neglected Poems*, Gulzar, Pavan K. Varma (tr.), Penguin Random House India, Gurugram, 2013
- *Green Poems*, Gulzar, Pavan K. Varma (tr.) Penguin Random House India, Gurugram, 2014
- *Suspected Poems*, Gulzar, Pavan K. Varma (tr.) Penguin Random House India, Gurugram, 2017
- *Footprints on Zero Line*, Gulzar, Rashanda Jalil (tr.) Harper Collins Publishers India, 2017
- *I Swallowed the Moon: The Poetry of Gulzar*, Saba Mahmood Bashir, Harper Collins Publishers India, 2013
- *100 Lyrics*, Gulzar, Sunjoy Shekhar (tr.), Penguin Random House India, Gurugram, 2009
- *In the Company of a Poet: Gulzar in Conversation with Nasreen Munni Kabir*, Rupa & Company, New Delhi, 2012
- *Jiya Jale: The Stories of Songs: Gulzar in Conversation with Nasreen Munni Kabir*, Speaking Tiger Publishing Pvt. Ltd., New Delhi, 2018
- *Actually I Met Them: A Memcir*, Gulzar, Penguin Random House India, Gurugram, 2021
- *Two Tales of My Times: New Delhi Times and Maachis,* Gulzar, Devina Dutt (tr.), Rupa & Company, New Delhi, 2008
- *Hindi for Heart,* Gulzar with Rina Singh, Harper Collins Publishers India, 2013
-

Hindi

- *Raavi Paar Aur Anya Kahaniyan,* Gulzar, Rupa & Company, New Delhi, 1999
- *Triveni*, Gulzar, Rupa & Company, New Delhi, 2001
- *Raat Pashmina Ki,* Gulzar, Rupa & Company, New Delhi, 2002
- *Pukhraj*, Gulzar, Rupa & Company, New Delhi, 2005
- *Kusumagraj Ki Chuni Suni Nazme*, Gulzar (ed.), Vani Prakashan, New Delhi, 2007

- *Yaar Julahe...* Gulzar, Yatindra Mishra (ed.), Vani Prakashan, New Delhi, 2010
- *Milon Ke Din*, Gulzar, Yatindra Mishra (ed.), Rupa & Company, New Delhi, 2010
- *Kuch Toh Kahiye,* Gulzar, Vani Prakashan, New Delhi, 2017
- *Meera—Manzarnama*, Gulzar, Radhakrishna Prakashan Pvt Ltd, New Delhi, 2004
- *Libaas—Manzarnama*, Gulzar, Vani Prakashan, New Delhi, 2006
- *Hu Tu Tu—Manzarnama*, Gulzar, Radhakrishna Prakashan Pvt. Ltd., New Delhi, 2006
- *Kinara—Manzarnama*, Gulzar, Radhakrishna Prakashan Pvt. Ltd., New Delhi, 2016
- *Ijaazat—Manzarnama*, Gulzar, Radhakrishna Prakashan Pvt. Ltd., New Delhi, 2011
- *Kitaab*—Manzarnama, Gulzar, Radhakrishna Prakashan Pvt. Ltd., New Delhi, 2016
- *Lekin—Manzarnama*, Gulzar, Radhakrishna Prakashan Pvt. Ltd., New Delhi, 2016
- *Achanak—Manzarnama*, Gulzar, Radhakrishna Prakashan Pvt. Ltd., New Delhi,, 2016
- *Mirza Ghalib:Ek Swanahi—Manzarnama,* Gulzar, Rupa & Company, New Delhi, 2006
- *Dyodhi*, Gulzar, Vani Prakashan New Delhi, 2012
- *Pandrah Paanch Pachatar*, Gulzar, Vani Prakashan, New Delhi, 2010
- *Pluto*, Gulzar, Vani Prakashan, New Delhi, 2015
- *Do Log*, Gulzar, Harper Collins Publishers India, 2017
- *Mera Kuch Samaan,* Gulzar, Radhakrishna Prakashan Pvt. Ltd., New Delhi, 1994
- *Chaiyya Chaiyya*, Gulzar, Radhakrishna Prakashan Pvt. Ltd., New Delhi, 2002

- *Kuch Aur Nazmen,* Gulzar, Radhakrishna Prakashan Pvt. Ltd., New Delhi, 1980
- *Jeena Yahan,* Gulzar, Vani Prakashan, New Delhi, 2010
- *Pichhle Panne*, Gulzar, Bharatiya Gynapeeth, New Delhi, 2012
- *Boskiyana:* conversations-Interviews- presenting Gulzar: Yashwant Vyas, Radhakrishna Prakashan Pvt. Ltd., New Delhi, 2020
- *Paaji Nazmen*, Gulzar, Radhakrishna Prakashan Pvt. Ltd., New Delhi, 2017
- *Baghbaan: Gulzar Translates Tagore*, Harper Collins Publishers India, 2016
- *Nindiya Chor*, Gulzar, Harper Collins Publishers India, 2016
- *Samay Ka Khatola*, Gulzar, Harper Collins Publishers India, 2018
- *Bosky Ka Panchatantra,* Gulzar, Radhakrishna Prakashan Pvt. Ltd., New Delhi, 2013
- *Bosky Ki Sunali,* Gulzar, Radhakrishna Prakashan Pvt. Ltd., New Delhi, 2009
- *Bosky Ki Gappen*, Gulzar, Radhakrishna Prakashan Pvt. Ltd., New Delhi, 2004
- *Bosky Ke Dhanwaan*, Gulzar, Radhakrishna Prakashan Pvt. Ltd., New Delhi, 2004
- *Bosky ke Taal-Patal,* Gulzar, Radhakrishna Prakashan Pvt. Ltd., New Delhi, 2009
- *Hindi Film Geet Kosh,* edited by Harminder Sing 'Hamraz' Part 1 (1931-1940), Part 2 (1941-1950) , Part 3 (1951-1960) Part 4 (1961-1970) Mrs. Satinder Kaur, Kanpur
- *Hindi Chitrapat Geet Kosh*, 1981-1990, edited and compiled by Jagdish Purohit and Gulam Qureshi, Lata Dininath Mangeshkar Gramaphone Record Musuem, Indore, 2013
- *Dhunon Ki Yatra: Hindi Filmon Ke Sangeetkar*: (1931-

2005) Pankaj Raaj, Rajkamal Prakashan Pvt Ltd, New Delhi, 2006

- *Raj Kapoor*: Ritu Nanda, R K Film and Studios, Mumbai 2007
- *Jaag Uthe Khwab Kai*, Sahir Ludhianvi, Murli Manohar Prasad Singh, Kantimohan 'soz' and Rekha Avasthi (editoro, Penguin Random House, India, 2010
- *Meri Awaz Suno*: Kaifi Azmi, Rajkamal Prakashan Pvt. Ltd. New Delhi 2002
- *Cinema ke Baare Main*: Javed Akhtar se Baat cheet, Nasreen Munir Kabir, Rajkamal Prakashan Pvt. Ltd. New Delhi, 2001
- *Sadiyon mein ek Asha:* Asha Bhosle- Mimansa-Ajatashatru, Lata Dinanath Mangeshkar Gramaphone Record Museum, Indore, 2009
- *Hamsafar*: Hindi Cinema aur Sangeet, Yatindra Mishra,Penguin Randomhouse India, 2013
- Lata-Surgatha: Lata Mangeshkar ki Jeevan Yatra ka Dastavez, Yatindra Mishra, Vani Prakashan, New Delhi 2016
- Sangeet patrika: Film Sangeet Itihas Ank, edited by Dr Mukesh Garg, Sangeet Karyalay, Haatras, Jan-Feb 1998
- *Outlook*: 100 years of of Love fir Hindi Cinema, edited by Neelabh Mishra, Outlook Publishing India Pvt led, New Delhi, December 2012
- *Aha Zindagi*- Cinema Special Issue: Duniya Bah Mein Alag hai Hindi Cinema, editor Alok Srivastav, Dainik Bhaskar Corporation Ltd. Jaipur, June 2013
- *Aha Zindagi*-Music Special Issue: shastriya, lok ev film sangeet par vishist samagri (a collection of essays on classical, fork and film music) edited by Alok Srivastav, Dainik Bhaskar Corporation Ltd. Jaipur,, issue 100, December 2012
- *Tehelka*: special issue on Lata Mangeshkar, sur Avinashi, editor Sanjay Dube, Anant Media Pvt Ltd, September, 2011.

Note: Besides the above-mentioned sources, material has also been sourced from the files of old publications. These are, *Filmfare, Illustrated Weekly of India, Sarika, Madhuri, Dinmdan, Saptahik Hindustan, India Today, Outlook* and *Shama*.

Sathya Saran

Best known for her long association with Femina, which she edited for 12 years, Sathya Saran is also the author of a diverse variety of books. *The Dark Side* reflects her love of the short story, while the critically acclaimed biographies, *Ten Years with Guru Dutt Abrar Alvi's Journey; Sun Mere Bandhu Re The Musical World* of SD Burman while *Baat Niklegi toh Phir The Life Music of Jagjit Singh* and *Hariprasad Chaurasia Breath of Gold*, bear testimony to her love of cinema and music.

Sathya's books include a biography of Ritu Nanda, Tea of Life on the man and Nature relationship in India's tea gardens, an anthology on marriage titled 'Knot for Keeps', an analysis titled 'Angoor Insights into the Film'. She has also written 'How to Look Like Miss India', on the confidence building secrets known to Miss Universe and Miss World winners from India.

Venturing into translations, she has translated Caged, a book of poems by Gulzar. Her next book is on poet and lyricist, Shailendra.

Currently Consulting Editor with Penguin Random House, Sathya also teaches fashion journalism at NIFT.

Sathya has written at five serial titled Kashmakash on marital problems, 13 episodes of which were aired on DD, and 13 more on 'Star TV'.

Sathya wrote and was on the filming team of a documentary on the Computerisation of Land Records which was produced by the MP government and beamed on 'DD 1'. It had Raghuvir Yadav in the lead and was shot on location in a village.

Besides she is the India correspondent for Ms magazine, USA. And a columnist with The New Indian Express and Hindu BusinessLine.

An avid trekker and traveller, Sathya lives in Mumbai with her family and dog.

दिल अगर है तो दर्द भी होगा
इस का कोई नहीं है हल शायद...